Business
and the
Environment

The Conservation Foundation is a nonprofit research and communications organization dedicated to encouraging human conduct to sustain and enrich life on earth. Since its founding in 1948, it has attempted to provide intellectual leadership in the cause of wise management of the earth's resources.

Business
and the
Environment
Toward
Common Ground
(Second Edition)

Kent Gilbreath, Editor

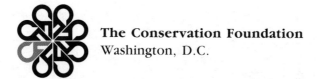

The Conservation Foundation
Washington, D.C.

**Business and the Environment: Toward Common Ground
(Second Edition)**

Cover design by Ross A. Feldner, New Age Graphics.
Typeset by Rings–Leighton, Ltd., Washington, D.C.
Printed by Braun-Brumfield, Inc., Ann Arbor, Michigan

Library of Congress Cataloging in Publication Data

Gilbreath, Kent, 1945–
   Business and the environment

   1. Environmental policy—United States—Addresses, essays, lectures.
   2. Industry—social aspects—United States—Addresses, essays, lectures.

   HC 110.E5B885   1984   363.7'0576'0973   84-5867
   ISBN 0-89164-081-9

46,342

Contents

Section Two: Defining the Issues

Section Three: Setting Policy: Closing the Gap

Section Four: The Common Ground

Foreword

The Conservation Foundation published the first edition of this book in 1977, shortly after we had begun our program in Business and the Environment. The objective was twofold: to define areas of agreement and disagreement about perceptions, values, and goals held by business leaders and environmentalists; and to provide the basis for more productive communication about some deeply divisive issues. The book sold well and has been cited frequently and used in the classroom. We thought it a timely moment to bring it up to date.

Much has happened since this book first appeared. For our part, we have initiated a dozen or so policy dialogues aimed at reaching effective agreements on critical environmental issues. Corporate executives, environmental group leaders, and other interested parties have hammered out shared positions in such areas as toxic substances control, low-level radioactive waste management, pricing of oil and natural gas, forestry management, and the siting and cleanup of hazardous waste dumps. Under the auspices of other organizations, agreements have been forged on siting of dams, urban developments, and uranium mines. As Dr. Jay D. Hair, executive vice-president of the National Wildlife Federation, makes clear in his speech, "Winning Through Negotiation," these efforts now have won a new legitimacy and we at The Conservation Foundation are proud to have contributed to their acceptance.

Environmental policies and their economic costs and impacts remain a divisive issue. This book advocates no policies and proposes no specific solutions. It illustrates the diversity of opinions held by some of the leading thinkers and actors in the field. To the extent that the book aids in understanding, it can help lay the basis for more productive communication and, possibly, for more frequent and less divisive settlements. Obviously, many differences characterize the various interests in our society and it is no service to the policy process to pretend otherwise. Conflict is not always avoidable. Nevertheless, comparing many of the statements in this edition with those in the last, makes it clear that there is a growing appreciation of shared interests, and a narrowing of the field of divisions considered inevitable. Dr. Louis Fernandez, chairman of the board of Monsanto Company and chairman of the Chemical Manufacturers Association, invites his industry and its critics as well as others to work together, stating:

> We must all pitch in—the entire business community, federal and local governments, environmental groups, and all concerned citizens. Cooperation must become the new theme of this country's new environmental efforts.

No more than Dr. Hair's would these views likely have been seriously put forward a decade ago.

In a way, then, *Business and the Environment: Toward Common Ground* is a hopeful book, for it offers evidence of a growing cooperative spirit—one that recognizes the indisputable link between economic and environmental goals. And it testifies to the increasing acceptance of a healthy environment and a productive economy as inseparable—each necessary for the other to thrive.

The Foundation is grateful to Dr. Kent Gilbreath, associate dean of the Hankamer School of Business at Baylor Univesity, who undertook the task of selecting and editing the articles, to the men and women who allowed us to reprint their work, and for the generous financial support of the publication from The General Electric Foundation, Ford Motor Company Fund, The Continental Group Foundation, Inc., The General Tire Foundation, Inc., Weyerhaeuser Company Foundation, and Getty Oil Company.

Environmentalists and business leaders, now more than ever, need to understand and communicate with each other. This anthology, and, indeed, The Conservation Foundation's entire program in Business and the Environment, attempts to help meet that need.

William K. Reilly
President
The Conservation Foundation

Acknowledgments

In preparing this book I was assisted by numerous people. In particular I thank Lea Denison who spent countless hours reading and evaluating these articles and giving me the benefit of her unique perspective. Todd Stoner provided invaluable assistance in doing the necessary research for compiling the 1,000 articles, speeches, and other pieces of literature from which the material included in this book was selected.

Both Lea and Todd were students of mine during the development of this book, but they were not the only students who assisted me in preparing the book. In 1983 and 1984, my Environmental Economics classes at Baylor University played the role of guinea pigs and read most of the articles included in this book as well as many of those excluded. Their evaluation of the material was my starting point in the final selection process. They also assisted substantially in helping prepare study questions and test questions for use with the book. I am truly grateful to all of these students for their help in making this book possible.

I also received substantial moral and editorial assistance from my wife Shirley, who read many of the articles and helped me in preparing the introductions to the sections. At The Conservation Foundation, I benefited greatly from the wisdom, sense of humor, and hard work of Yvonne Lewis. Yvonne spent countless hours helping make this an endeavor of the highest quality. Finally, J. Clarence Davies worked with me from the beginning in setting up the structure of the book and in providing administrative guidance and editorial encouragement. To all of these people, I am truly grateful.

Kent Gilbreath
April 1984

SECTION ONE
The Dimensions of Conflict

Introduction

The years have witnessed numerous clashes between business and environmental interests. Much of the underlying tension originates from philosophically different ways of viewing economic, social, and environmental systems. Sometimes these outlooks diverge so that they seem to describe separate worlds. At one extreme, society is seen primarily in economic terms, without considering the external implications of economic activity; the imposition of noneconomic concerns to accomplish social goals is said to undermine the vitality of the economy. At the other extreme are those who see society in aesthetic or ecological terms, without adequately comprehending basic industrial, economic imperatives. To them, society simply must reduce production to avoid disaster from pollution and resource exhaustion.

Such tendencies, which fail to acknowledge that modern society is far more complicated and interrelated than any single outlook indicates, erect formidable barriers to rational discussion. The resulting rhetoric and exaggeration only perpetuate the notion that opposing ideas are dangerous and must be defeated at all costs. This mentality can lead to endless misunderstanding and inhibit the reasoned evaluation of alternative positions.

In reality, few business leaders or environmentalists are fanatics. But, as groups, business persons do demonstrate a marked preference for things economic and environmentalists for things ecological. It is only natural that business leaders and environmentalists, pursuing different goals and serving disparate social functions, would look at the world through different eyes. Such pluralism is an important tenet of American society, and it is neither feasible—nor desirable—to reconcile completely the divergent outlooks of the two groups.

Nevertheless, an important difference exists between what might be called ''creative'' tension—a constructive debate from which a tenable median position emerges—and the ''zero-sum'' tension that sometimes prevails. To channel existing conflicts toward creating a better society, both business leaders and environmentalists need to look critically at their own viewpoints. In the process, it should become easier to identify areas where conflicting views might be transcended. Ultimately, much can be gained by members of business, environmental groups, and society if a positive mood of creative tension prevails.

In the seven years since the first edition of this book was published, the tone of conflict has shifted. In an era of economic and ecological crises, business leaders and environmentalists have had to accommodate dogma to political realities. The popularity of environmentalism—always ebbing and flowing—is enjoying a resurgence of power today, and environmentalists, to maintain public support, have set priorities and offered compromises. Many have discovered that for their own survival they must follow Irving Horowitz's advice and "become linked to economic problems and less to ideological posturing." Business leaders, too, have learned valuable lessons about ecological principles and environmental issues that only a few years ago seemed irrelevant to their economic world.

The task of building further consensus about economic and ecological perspectives is by no means easy. Opposing images, in spite of the progress made, continue to be firmly held and slow in dying. Today many still echo Calvin Coolidge's laissez-faire philosophy that the "business of America is business," and some environmentalists believe all corporate executives care only about raping the environment for profit. Those who cling to these extreme visions are a minority, and it is doubtful that they will guide social or economic policies in the future. However, it is folly to say that they do not exist or that they do not constitute forces with which to reckon.

Moreover, because perspectives have matured to incorporate more complicated realities does not mean that conflicts, hard feelings, and misunderstandings have ceased. Bitter controversies continue today even where world views have changed. Business groups, convinced of the need for environmental prudence, may express heated resentment over the number and complexity of environmental strictures that guide them; and environmental groups, frustrated by low public awareness of an issue and the advertising power of big business, may still opt for loud demonstrations to dramatize the issue.

The issues between business and environmental groups are vital for society and require substantive, constructive discussion. Society must replace narrow visions of the world and obsolete conceptions of the "enemy" if this discussion is to take place. Every person and institution has a stake in ecological safety and survival and economic prosperity and progress. Business and environmental interests alike must help society reconcile and integrate economics with ecology to create true quality of life.

This introduction was adapted from "INTRODUCTION: WORLD VIEWS," by H. Jeffrey Leonard, in the first edition of *Business and the Environment*.

Hooker Chemical's Michigan Mess

By Cathy Trost

What happens in a community when its largest employer is also creating pollution that poses a threat to the health of the community's citizens?

The town of Montague, Michigan, sits up against the rolling bluffs over White Lake, hundreds of miles from the industrial centers of Detroit and Chicago. Every springtime, sap from the sugar maples runs heavy and the lake is fat with perch and bass. In the springtime of 1951, however, there were also no jobs. "We were a community down at the heels," recalls seventy-nine-year-old Wendell Lipka, who lives with his wife of fifty-five years in a house over Little Buttermilk Creek.

So it was, in 1951, that the town of Montague mortgaged its best asset—the clear wilderness lake—for the promise of 125 good-paying jobs and an $11 million tax base. In time, the lake became polluted, the groundwater was destroyed, the town split apart, and a chemical company had to dig a hole as wide as thirteen football fields to accommodate the poisonous wastes those 125 jobs had created.

The spirit of expansionism has been as much a part of Montague as any other American town during the past century, and White Lake had the misfortune of always having something that somebody wanted. The loggers who founded Montague at the intersection of a river and a lake took water from it to power their saw mills. Sam McConnell, Montague's first industrialist, built his tannery on the lake's eastern shore. The tannery was enough to keep the town alive during the Depression but later, during the postwar boom years, the people of Montague became convinced that more industry was their ticket to a better life.

Copyright© 1981 by Cathy Trost. Reprinted by permission. Cathy Trost received an Alicia Patterson Foundation grant in 1981 to study toxic pollution policy in the United States.

In the winter of 1951, the Hooker Electrochemical Company was scouting Michigan for a site on which to build a chloralkali plant. Hooker was based in Niagara, New York, where it had been using an old canal bed for disposal of industrial wastes since the late 1940s. Love Canal was the name of the dump.

The people of Montague worked feverishly to induce Hooker to their town. A petition was signed by 96 percent of the local residents in support of the company's plans to build its plant on a ridge bordering White Lake. Hooker needed the vast underground reserves of salt there to make chlorine and caustic soda, and the lakewater was essential to cool its industrial processes.

At the time, White Lake was pristine. The Michigan Department of Natural Resources conducted a biological survey of the four-mile-long lake the following year and reported that its benthos, or bottom-dwelling organisms, were those of a naturally eutrophic or nutrient-rich lake. The inhabitants of a healthy aquatic environment—clams, worms, and midges—were well represented. The lake suffered only minor irritations from the refuse of the local wastewater treatment plant and the old tannery, which was still in business up at the north end.

Hooker bought 880 acres of land about a quarter mile north of the lake, ran its coolant discharge pipes from the plant down into the lake's middle basin, and went to work. No one paid much attention to what was coming out of the pipes. Pretty soon, the midge larvae started to disappear from the lake, the fingernail clams died, and the pollution-tolerant worms slowly spread across the lake floor. And thus the seeds of the conflict that would scar Montague for the next thirty years were sown. It was a war that pitted the environmentalists against the jobs in the age-old rivalry of industry versus the land.

The environmentalists fought what they considered to be the duplicity of the company, the failure of the state regulatory agencies to protect the land, and the avarice of the town politicians and businessmen. The other side argued that Hooker—with a $500,000 annual payroll in the early 1950s in a town of less than 3,000 residents—was a good provider. They argued, too, that Hooker was a good neighbor, victimized by the uncertainty of the times. Most people still thought the earth was a giant sponge, soaking up all the pollutants it was fed. The dissenting voices of scientists and hydrogeologists, raised in warning, were very small. "Hooker had been welcomed into the community because, as individuals, they were well-rounded, well-educated, well-spoken people, and nobody at that time had any idea what the attitude of industry was toward our natural environment," recalls A. Winton Dahlstrom, a local attorney. "They said they were dumping nothing but cooling water back in the lake."

In the 1950s, Michigan's Water Resources Commission was chiefly responsible for monitoring industrial discharges and enforcing the few existing laws against pollution. The commission had been formed in response to the state's Water Pollution Control Act of 1929, a broad and weakly enforced law which basically forbade the discharge of harmful things to surface and groundwater. During the past thirty years, the Water Resources Commission and its sister agency, the Department of Natural Resources, have been buffeted by the demands of industry and the weight of their own internal politics. The agencies acted more as consultants than cops and, in the end, the regulators were regulated by industry itself.

In 1952, the Water Resources Commission granted Hooker its original waste disposal permit. The decision was heavily supported by the supervisory boards of Montague and Whitehall, its twin city across the lake, despite the faint protest of a local group which raised questions about storage of the waste on company property and possible contamination of the lake and groundwater. In a moment of high drama at a public hearing on the permit, a Hooker official held up a glass of water containing what he said were all the ingredients that would be dumped into the lake. "Drink it," he urged the crowd. (There is no record to show if anyone accepted the challenge.)

That same year, the company commissioned an independent geological survey of the brine and water supply for its new plant. The survey reported that the top soils and gravels underneath the plant were "highly permeable" and warned that "with the adjacent lake, and with nearby domestic water supplies, we feel that provisions for any waste . . . should be disposed of under a procedure that will leave the company free of any possible criticism."

Hooker had built its plant on a bed of fine, porous sand eighty-feet thick. This sand contained the principal groundwater stream that supplied the major portion of the local population with drinking water, through private and public wells. The groundwater roughly followed the lay of the land, sloping down from the Hooker plant and into White Lake, which eventually discharged into Lake

Michigan through a slim channel three miles to the east.

During the next three years, the groundwater underneath the plant became contaminated with salt. For Hooker was storing its salt-laden brine wastes in sludge pits, which periodically overflowed onto the ground. Another survey commissioned by the company in 1956 could not have made the problem clearer. Any soluble contaminant placed on the surface, the report said, "will soon make its way downward and affect the quality of the groundwater."

Even though Hooker should have been aware by now that something was seriously wrong with the methods used to dispose of its relatively innocuous brine wastes, the company in 1956 went ahead with plans to begin production of an organic chemical called hexachlorocyclopentadiene, or C56.

C56 was the raw ingredient of a group of pesticides that gained wide acceptance in the early 1950s. The postwar years had brought a technological revolution in the field of synthetic chemicals used as components of pesticides, herbicides and insecticides, and as additives to fire retardants and other industrial products. The main selling point of the chlorinated hydrocarbons, a group to which DDT and the C56-based pesticides both belong, was their extreme persistence and effectiveness against a wide variety of insects. Two of the most popular C56-based pesticides were Kepone, which was used to kill cockroaches, and Mirex, which the U.S. Department of Agriculture recommended as the most effective opponent of the Southern fire ants. C56 in vapor form was particularly brutal. The U.S. Army had rejected its use as a nerve gas in World War II on grounds that it was too dangerous to be used as a defensive weapon. But, in general, the toxic effects of the chlorinated hydrocarbons were barely suspected, and the analytical tools to detect their presence in the environment had not yet been fully developed.

Start-up

Hooker started up its C56 production plant in 1956. The company told the Water Resources Commission that the maximum toxic effects of this process would be minimal levels of several chemical by-products, which could probably be treated in an oil-type residue separator before being discharged to the lake. The most critical and mysterious regulatory failure occurred shortly after Hooker began making C56. The state asked the company to supply it with more complete information about the toxicity of the five chemicals discharged in the C56 process. Hooker claims that it supplied the information in a letter. The state says it never got the letter.

A search through thirty years of Department of Natural Resources files shows a gap from the time the state asked Hooker for more information to the time the company was issued a new waste disposal permit later that year. "How did this happen?" says Dr. James Truchen of the DNR's environmental enforcement division. "I looked through the files myself and there was silence, no reply back from the company. Yet the permit was issued, without those questions being answered, with the company basically being given a pass to do anything they wanted with those materials."

During the next two decades, the Montague plant produced about 25,000 tons of C56 a year. Yet the regulatory agencies did not ask where the residues from those 25,000 tons were going. In fact, Hooker employees were quietly piling up 55-gallon drums of C56 residues in a wooded area north of the plant building. In its lawsuit filed against Hooker many years later, the state described how the drum tops were split open with an axe and then pushed off trucks onto the ground, where they began leaking into the soil. Eventually, some 20,000 barrels of C56 waste were strewn across the dumping ground, where they destroyed 2 billion gallons of groundwater, critically injured White Lake, and threatened the backyard drinking wells of nearby homeowners. The dumping began in 1957 and ended in 1972, when the wastes began to be trucked off the site to other locations in the state.

"I don't believe people realized that when it rained, water was going to run over this material and it was going to leach out," says W. Ken Hall, Hooker's current Montague plant manager. "This was a tarry substance and they took fly ash and covered up the drums with it. In their minds, if there was any possibility of any kind of leak, it would be absorbed by the fly ash."

Hooker president Donald Baeder, who was not with the company then, speculates that the barrels were stacked behind the plant as "kind of a holding action because they really didn't know quite what to do with those materials." Baeder thinks that because of the porosity of the soil, the placement of the barrels on top of the ground may actually have been better than if they had buried them in a landfill. Although Baeder is critical of the disposal methods used at Montague, he tempers his critique with the caveat that you can't judge the past by today's standards. He insists that the methods were not employed "in secret."

Yet, in a 1955 memo, another Hooker executive had written that disposal of wastes at the Montague plant "was a major problem due to local and state ordinances." For a brief time, Hooker tried a high-temperature incinerator to dispose of the Montague wastes, but it apparently did not work. The company conducted extensive research on the incineration process during the late 1950s, because it realized that the proper burial of its chlorinated wastes would be costly, according to a 1966 speech given by a Hooker executive.

However, while the contamination of ground or surface water was outlawed, the landfilling of industrial wastes on company property was not illegal, and in fact was quite common at the time. So the company turned to land disposal and the storage of waste sludges in lagoons, pits, and the ground itself.

"I think past management really cared within the limits of what they knew," adds Baeder. "I don't think they were out to foul their nests for profit at all. In hindsight, we probably put too much emphasis on operations and not enough on the environment, but it was probably universal throughout the industry at the time."

"You can't tell me," counters Stewart Freeman, the assistant state attorney general who drafted the Michigan lawsuit against Hooker, "that they didn't know that C56 was harmful. Hooker would have you believe that no one knew anything until magically one day Rachel Carson wrote a book and got everyone upset. That's just not true.

"My predecessors in Michigan were prosecuting a hell of a lot of environmental cases in the 1800s. Even Napoleon had enough sense to locate his troop latrines downstream of waters used for coffee and soaping. And engineers back in the 1920s knew that contamination of surface spreads through groundwater.

"There were very few people in Michigan in the 1950s—chemical company executives and ordinary people alike—who would have disposed of their garbage in their drinking wells." Hooker was able to get away with lax disposal methods, however, because the state looked the other way. Says John Shauver of the DNR's environmental enforcement staff, "No one ever went out Hooker's back door to look for the barrels."

The people living near Hooker's back door didn't have to look. Chemical fumes from the plant had been bothering nearby residents for decades, but no one knew quite what to do. In the early 1970s, Marion Dawson wrote the state's Air Pollution Control Commission about the strange fumes wafting from the Hooker plant. The odor was odd, like a mixture of laundry bleach and geraniums. Dawson was thirty-one years old then, a delicate-looking woman with a schoolteacher husband, an infant son, and a master's degree in biology. She surveyed residents within a two-mile radius of the plant and they told her the strongest fumes occurred between midnight and 8 A.M. People had difficulty breathing, their eyes and noses itched and watered. Sometimes, when the fumes were strong, children had to be brought in from playing outside. Six people reported the death of trees in their yards. Hooker had replaced two of them. However, Marion Dawson was told by the Hooker plant manager that she was probably smelling her "neighbor's laundry bleach."

In fact, she was smelling C56, later found in concentrations of 17 parts per billion in the air near the barrel dump. By contrast, 10 parts per billion is the established threshold limit for human exposure to C56. Moreover, the state had already found high concentrations of chlorinated hydrocarbons in Hooker's discharge to the lake and warned the company to find the source of the chemicals and eliminate or reduce it. Back came a scathing reply from Hooker: "The most that can be said is that SOME of these compounds MAY be present in the discharge. We will not embark on a corrective design for such inconclusive data."

The lake, meanwhile, was failing, Aquatic pollution is not usually a dramatic either/or proposition, with all the fish and other kinds of life killed off and the lake declared dead. It is a more steady degeneration with a concurrent rise in species that are resistant to pollution.

A biological survey of White Lake in 1975 was compared with samples taken from the same place twenty-three years earlier. In the middle basin, which received the brunt of Hooker's discharge, a grab sample showed there were zero fingernail clams where there once had been 116, and seventy-three midges instead of the original 3,298.

Nearby, perched right up against the lakeshore and just south of the Hooker plant, was a tiny subdivision of expensive, dream homes called Blueberry Ridge. Attorney A. Winton Dahlstrom was hired in 1975 to represent a family who had just moved into the neighborhood and was disturbed about the taste and odor of their drinking water, which came from a backyard well. A lab analysis identified three acutely toxic chemicals in the water, all of them by-products of Hooker's C56 operation.

However, it was not until 1976 that the state threatened to revoke Hooker's waste discharge permit because of illegal discharges of C56 into the water and air. The state charged that the company had been spewing ten pounds of C56 a day to White Lake. Hooker denied the state's calculations and said the lake was not polluted. You're asking us to play Russian Roulette, the state said. Prove that your discharges are safe or stop them. After one more year, during which the state bent its rules and allowed the company to discharge chlorinated hydrocarbons into the lake, Hooker shut down its C56 operation, unable to prove its safety.

The company claimed publicly that the cost of producing C56 had become prohibitive. Yet state officials said Hooker simply could not meet the severe and expensive pollution discharge requirements ordered by the state if production was to continue. Hooker was also in an economic bind. The domestic pesticide market was in a slump by the mid-1970s as the federal government finally began banning and limiting the use of dozens of dangerous pesticides.

Eighteen jobs were lost when the C56 operation closed, and some laid-off employees blamed the local "environmentalists" for the shutdown. A month after Hooker stopped making C56, 500 people turned out for a stormy meeting in the Montague High School gym. The town had begun to polarize along ideological lines—pro-industry versus pro-environment. It was a painful, frightening time. Almost everyone had a child, a parent or a friend who worked at Hooker. The workers closed ranks and united around their company.

There followed a sloppy, dirty-tricks campaign apparently encouraged from within the plant and carried out by some employees and their families. Pressure was put on local businessmen who advertised in the *White Laker Observer*, the small country weekly which had been closely covering the Hooker controversy. Not only was publisher Darwin Bennett's business threatened, but the plant manager called him to protest the stories about Hooker. "I told him I was just trying to do my job," Bennett recalls. "He said, 'We have ways of taking care of that, too.' "

A group of Hooker wives marched into the local supermarket one day, filled their shopping baskets with food, then abandoned them en masse at the checkout counter. The supermarket had advertised in the newspaper. The Hooker plant manager threatened to punch lawyer Winton Dahlstrom in a local restaurant, and a carload of jeering Hooker employees followed one of Dahlstrom's friends home from the high school meeting. It got so bad, remembers newspaper publisher Bennett, that he and two other friends filed a written statement with the local police department, indicating their fears that someone might try to cause them physical harm.

No one had yet learned about the barrels stacked up behind the Hooker plant. In the summer of 1977, a twenty-eight-year-old father of four who had worked for Hooker signed an affidavit describing the location of the barrels and how they had been put there. Warren Dobson, who had worked in the C56 operation, said Hooker employees had routinely dumped 55-gallon drums of C56 wastes on the ground, that some wastes had been poured from the drums directly onto the soil and killed the trees in an area called "Dead Lake," that C56 vapors and liquids were routinely allowed to escape from the plant and employees were instructed to say it was "steam."

Incredibly, the state did not bother to check the barrels until six months later. When Department of Natural Resources agents found them in March 1978, the company, according to one state official, "shrugged its shoulders. They said you people knew about this. It's been here since the 1950s."

It took several months for the full weight of the contamination to become clear. There was a 15-to-20-acre dumpsite filled with fifteen years' worth of drummed C56 waste. There was another 15-acre sludge lagoon where 3 million gallons of contaminated sediment had been dumped. More than 102 chemical compounds were eventually isolated from the waste—"a complete spectrum," said the DNR's Jim Truchan, "of all the worst chemicals we've got to deal with from the standpoint of environmental contamination." The state tests showed that the entire flume of groundwater underneath the plant was severely contaminated and moving south, through the backyards of swank Blueberry Ridge, to White Lake.

More residential water wells were found to be contaminated, and Hooker paid for bottled water to be delivered to the homes. Some $5.5 million worth of pollution-control equipment was installed, and a purge well was dropped to trap some of the groundwater and clean it before it entered the lake.

Love Canal

On August 2, 1978, a state of health emergency was declared hundreds of miles away at Love Canal. "That's when people really got concerned here," recalls Darwin Bennett. Local citizens groups were formed and angry letters fired off to Michigan's governor, the EPA, and other officials. This activity continued for the next year as Michigan's attorney general filed suit against Hooker and negotiations for settlement began. The level of fear escalated when toxicological tests on the Hooker wastepile showed that the chemical gunk was both mutagenic, or capable of causing genetic alterations, and fetotoxic, which means the chemicals were able to cross the placental barrier in rats and damage the fetus.

The report terrified Mary Mahoney, a local Brownie leader who lived less than a mile from the Hooker plant. Several years earlier, her father had died of stomach cancer, and her mother had developed cancer of the rectum six months later. Then her aunt died of breast cancer and her grandmother got spinal cancer. All four relatives lived across the street from Mahoney, who now found herself unable to sleep at night, worrying about something she could not prove.

The science of linking cause to effect in cancer is tentative at best, and Mahoney's is the sort of story that drives Hooker officials mad. "Anecdotal reporting," Hooker president Donald Baeder calls it, where the press "brings on a woman who I think honestly believes she's been hurt and you hear her screaming emotionally, 'What's going to happen to my unborn baby?' In many cases, it takes weeks and months, even a year, to find out."

The state and Hooker reached an out-of-court settlement in the fall of 1979 on a $15 million remedial cleanup program. The company installed more purge wells in an attempt to halt completely the flow of contaminants in the groundwater to White Lake. It built a completely clay-lined, 800-foot-square burial vault behind the plant to contain 1.2 million cubic yards of contaminated wastes and soils. When the top is laid across the vault, a granite marker will be erected that says: Warning—Toxic Material Burial Area—KEEP OUT.

Today the anxiety that gripped the town in the wake of Love Canal has leveled off. Most of the town's people are convinced that the burial vault will safely contain the wastes and that the groundwater cleanup program has rescued the lake. The White Lake Chamber of Commerce is launching a big publicity blitz to attract nervous tourists back to town. Warnings once placed on eating fish from the lake are now permanently lifted and the fishermen swarm across its shore. Hooker Chemical Company is still in business, down at the bottom of the hill on Old Channel Trail. "And thank God they stayed here," says seventy-nine-year-old Wendell Lipka. "I never had any trouble. I never had any odor. They've been a good neighbor."

Blueberry Ridge seems quiet now, much like Mrs. Beverly Hunt, wife of the local hardware store owner who used to raise all sorts of trouble about the chemicals trickling down from Hooker's plant into her backyard. "I've put a gag on my wife," her husband said recently. "I'd rather we not get involved in this anymore. Let's face it. I'm in business to make a dollar. And Hooker is one of my good customers."

"It's like having a retarded sister," says Darwin Bennett, the newspaper publisher who stopped writing about Hooker when people stopped wanting to hear about it. "No one wants to talk about it." Unemployment is 15.3 percent around Montague, the country's president is preaching the gospel of deregulation and free enterprise, and anti-business news is not what people want to read on the front page anymore.

There are people who are concerned for the future, but not many people are listening in Montague these days. "You can tell them: if you continue to drink that water, someday you're going to stand up and your ass is going to stay in the chair," explains Ed Volk, a local real estate man. "Maybe that would get to them. Probably not. But, you tell them, it's a mutagen. That it can cause serious damage twenty years down the road. They shrug their shoulders. They don't understand."

As for White Lake, it's healing. However, until the lake lays down enough clean sediment to cover the deeply contaminated bottom layer, and until the polluted groundwater is totally cut off, the lake will be polluted. "I would prefer to see that resource replaced in the condition it was before it was ever impacted," says John Shauver of the Department of Natural Resources. "But there are not enough dollars in the world to do that."

Middle Class, Go Home! (But Where's Home?)

By Bernard J. Frieden

Has environmentalism been perverted to protect private privilege? The author argues that it has been used to diminish the availability of housing for the poor and middle class in parts of California.

One of the big news stories of recent years has been the rising cost of home ownership. House prices, mortgage rates and operating costs all moved up so sharply that young families trying to buy suburban homes were astounded at how much they had to pay. The high housing costs that had been a problem for poor people for many years now were affecting well-off middle-income families who had to strain their budgets to pay for even modest homes.

Home ownership still is perceived as a wise investment—indeed, the escalating costs have prompted many young families to make financial sacrifices in order to buy single-family homes before they are priced totally out of reach.

But while one large group of people is beating the bushes trying to find affordable housing in the suburbs, another group, smaller but influential, is doing its best to stop suburban home building wherever possible—or at least to make sure that whatever is built is expensive. This coalition against home building consists of suburbanites opposed to growth because they fear its fiscal and social consequences, environmentalists concerned about the impact of growth on the natural landscape, and local government officials sympathetic to these views.

Very often, growth opponents exploit environmental programs mainly to block housing construction for reasons that have little or nothing to do with protecting the environment. Where barriers were once created to keep the urban poor from moving to the suburbs, the new barriers are being erected against the middle class.

The local growth controls imposed through the efforts of the "no growth" coalitions are by no means the dominant cause of the recent increase in house prices. The basic cost-push comes from factors such as high interest rates, energy prices and rising costs of building materials and labor. Those controls, however, are important contributors to the price spiral that has made inflation worse for housing than it is for most consumer items.

The growth control and environmental movements have had a very favorable press, stressing the widespread benefits they can achieve by protecting the quality of our common environment against the onslaught of the bulldozer. However, a closer look at how the growth control and environmental coalition operates in local controversies shows that its effects are far less benign. It has made a clear and substantial contribution to the escalation of new home prices—but has failed to produce important environmental benefits for the public at large. Rather, it has protected the environmental, social and economic advantages of established suburban residents who live near the land that could be used for new housing.

The reasons that lead people to oppose home building are hard to discover. By far the most frequent objections that growth opponents raise have to do with environmental impacts—harm to wildlife, destruction of natural resources, increases in air pollution. But sometimes those environmental arguments mask other motives such as keeping property taxes stable or insuring that a community remains exclusive.

By latching onto environmental issues—sometimes real, sometimes fabricated—defenders of the suburban status quo have been able to spread a cover of the public interest over what would otherwise be a narrow case of self-interest. In addition, the environmental movement has created new devices for housing opponents to use, such as time-consuming review procedures and court challenges.

It is no accident of nature that environmentalists have views similar to residents of exclusive suburbs who want to preserve their neighborhoods regardless of the detrimental effects on new housing. Often, they are the same people.

Environmental groups active in local growth politics have an upper-middle-class membership with a strong representation of professionals, executives, scientists and engineers. A recent survey of the Sierra Club membership showed that two-thirds of the primary wage earners in members' households came from the following occupational groups: doctors, dentists, lawyers, other professionals, college teachers and other teachers, managers and executives, and engineers. More than half the members had some post-graduate education.

This is not a typical cross section of people who buy homes in new tract developments. Highly educated professionals and executives can usually afford the high cost of a house in an established, desirable suburb with an attractive environment. Their opposition to home building is usually opposition to someone else's opportunity to buy a moderate-cost house, and the environment they protect is an environment they can afford to enjoy.

Why should environmentalists oppose new housing in the first place? Adverse environmental impacts, such as water pollution, are exceptional and can usually be controlled without blocking entire developments. There is almost no connection between housing and the big environmental issues of our time—use of toxic substances, nuclear radiation hazards, conservation of natural resources.

Rather than following the central concerns of the movement, the attack on home building represents a stretching of the environmental agenda to issues that are marginal. Moreover, the positions of environmental groups often are inconsistent.

For example, the San Francisco chapter of the Sierra Club opposed plans to replace an existing bridge across southern San Francisco Bay with a newer one that could handle more traffic. It argued that a new bridge would encourage more home building in East Bay communities for people who then would commute long distances to jobs on the opposite side of the bay, thus adding to air pollution and making the fuel shortage worse.

Yet earlier, when voters were asked to approve a bond issue to bring more water to southern peninsula suburbs where a large number of jobs are located, that same Sierra Club chapter came out in opposition. The club's reasoning was that the water facilities would encourage "unplanned" growth in the suburbs "at a time when San Francisco was actually losing population."

It would seem, then, that if the Sierra Club opposed building in suburbs far from jobs and also in suburbs close to jobs, then it surely must favor construction in or near the city. But when some San Francisco citizens mounted a campaign to discourage new high-density construction by limiting building heights to 160 feet in the downtown area, the San Francisco chapter supported this proposal. And when a large development was proposed on open land just south of San Francisco, the Sierra Club opposed that, too, arguing that open space should be preserved close to city dwellers.

The positions taken by another prominent California environmental group, People for Open Space, show the same pattern of argument. This group has objected to housing in the fertile valleys of northern California because it would destroy open farmland and pave over the rich black soil. Building on hillsides has been unacceptable as well—construction is more expensive, and hill developments increase the chances of landslides, floods and brushfires, according to this organization.

People for Open Space has said that it favors accommodating population growth in new towns rather than suburban tracts. But it attacked the only recent proposal for a new town in the San Francisco area on the ground that it would increase air pollution. Elsewhere, it objected to a new development because of its location in a "corridor of outstanding scenic beauty"—although very little land in the San Francisco Bay Area does not have scenic beauty.

These two groups—and environmental groups like them across the country—seem to have an endless series of objections. As a result, any proposed housing is sure to be attacked for some reason. One possible interpretation is that environmental groups are simply no-growthers who will not come out of the closet and admit that their underlying aim is to stop land development wherever it can be stopped. A more charitable interpretation is that environmental activists are not fully aware of the contradictions in their own positions and have not yet figured out how to handle growth in an environmentally sound way.

New construction will always make waves. Its local impacts always include creating *some* extra traffic and, unless it replaces existing developments, consuming *some* open land. Then again, it may have a much more significant impact such as crowding a major highway or building over a particularly outstanding landscape or causing unnecessary energy consumption. Environmental groups seem unable to distinguish between the minor environmental impacts and the major ones. It appears that, in many cases, the groups take the easy way out and simply attack all home building. The haphazard, almost incidental, origin of the environmental attack on home building, plus the elite character of its advocates, would not seem to provide a strong base for political success. Yet environmentalists and their friends have succeeded, in many parts of the country, in putting tough new growth regulations into place and in defeating home builders in political confrontations. How have they done it?

First, and most important, a large body of public opinion cares about the environment. Environmental issues do well at the polls— both the ballot boxes and the public opinion polls. In recent congressional elections, for example, most of the candidates endorsed by the League of Conservation Voters have won while most of the "dirty dozen" congressmen singled out by Environmental Action for their objectionable records have been replaced. Environmental causes have also done well in state and local bond issues and in statewide referenda such as the one that established the California Coastal Commission. The growth of environmental organizations is itself a testimony to widespread public interest. There are now about 5,000 organizations active in environmental affairs, more than half of them established after 1968.

Also contributing to a favorable political climate is the high visibility of suburban growth problems and the near invisibility of the costs of stopping growth. Everyone who enjoys a drive in the country knows of places where uninspiring new homes have replaced charming scenery. Although the new homes have helped many families improve their lives, they still clutter the view for the passer-by. The spread of ticky-tacky houses has become an acknowledged image in American folklore, and the benefits of stopping new developments are almost as visible. Fields and hillsides remain open and scenic. Nearby residents avoid the inconveniences of construction work, new neighbors crowding the roads, and new children crowding the classrooms. No one can see the families who were denied the opportunity to live there.

From Pro-Growth to No-Growth

California is the outstanding national example of opposition to home building. During most of its history, the state welcomed newcomers; as late as the mid-1960's, its local governments were making plans for more growth. California, more than any other part of the country, used to symbolize growth and the belief that growth is good. Its power to draw people from all over the world started with the gold rush and continued as the railroads reached the West and people were drawn to its farmland, natural resources, climate and economic opportunity.

Californians have thrived on the growth their state attracted. Yet in recent years, there also has been a growing undercurrent of doubt about the desirability of growth. Beginning in the late 1960's, state government and many cities began taking steps to manage growth more carefully, to control the effects it might have on the natural environment, and, in some cases, to place limits on it.

By the early 1970's, one community after another began putting up barriers to keep out new residents and electing officials who ran on no-growth platforms. Now, the politics of no-growth has reached a stage of maturity in California, particularly in the area around San Francisco, that makes it possible to see clearly who opposes home building and for what reasons. The experiences of the San Francisco area can and should be studied by those concerned about housing prices and availability in other parts of the nation.

The turnabout of attitudes has been most complete in the San Francisco Bay Area. There, a drive for increased public control over the area's future development has had exceptional success. What the advocates of growth control have done with their success, however, raises troublesome questions about how the new politics of urban development there is affecting average-income home buyers.

The Bay Area, like the rest of California, went through a binge of rapid growth between World War II and the 1960's—its population increased two and one-half times to a total of 4.6 million people. San Francisco's natural setting is remarkable for its variety, its distinctiveness and its beauty, and its natural environment deserves to be protected. As the migration to the area continued year after year, the political climate turned from pro-growth to no-growth. By the early 1970's, the no-growth movement was mature. Successful campaigns had been mounted to stop highways, protect the bay and the vineyards and preserve scenic views. Environmentalism took on the character of a political movement and each success brought new participants.

Growth restrictions and environmental controversies quickly affected a very high proportion of all the home building in the San Francisco region. Between 1972 and 1975, environmental lawsuits alone challenged developments containing 29,000 new housing units—this in an area that normally builds only 45,000 units a year.

Consumer Consequences

The cumulative effects of delays, project revisions and tight growth controls in San Francisco have reinforced the housing inflation that has afflicted the nation in general. The Federal Home Loan Bank Board, which tracked sales prices in 16 metropolitan areas from 1970 through 1977, reported that San Francisco had the highest price increase for new homes of all 16 areas. Its average sales price of $75,400 in 1977 was almost double its average price in 1970 ($39,600) and one-and-one-half times the national average for 1977 ($54,300). San Francisco's prices even outranked such traditionally high-cost places as New York ($69,300), Honolulu ($67,200) and Washington, D.C. ($66,600).

The rising prices brought about, in part, by growth restrictions have not only cut back the amount of housing available to middle-income families, but they also have reduced the number of places within the region where they can afford to live.

Large parts of the San Francisco region, such as Marin County, have had very little moderate-income housing for many years, and since 1970 other parts of the region also have closed the gates to families with average incomes.

The housing market of any large metropolitan area responds to many influences at once, and thus there is no way of knowing precisely to what extent San Francisco's housing shortages and high prices result from the impact of local growth regulations. Still, several results of these regulations are clear. Most important, the amount of housing blocked by controversies and either built after a long delay or not built at all is very large—large enough to make a difference in the price and availability of housing in the region.

Second, the cumulative effect of successful efforts to stop housing developments must be to increase prices and to restrict the number of places where middle-income families can afford to buy new homes. Third, the effect of stopping or reducing the size of developments near the built-up parts of the region must be to increase the number of home buyers who will live far from established job centers and will have to commute long distances at high personal and environmental costs. Finally, it is very likely that the pattern of growth controversies in the San Francisco area has discouraged the construction of carefully planned large developments and has encouraged in their place new home building of lower quality.

Growth restrictions also brought about unanticipated problems for already established suburban home owners. In tightly regulated communities that managed to limit new home building, increasing demand for existing homes helped drive their prices up to new levels. Many residents enjoyed the rising value of their homes until California's efficient assessors began marking up valuations to reflect the higher sales prices. Reassessment produced property-tax windfalls for local government and led to taxpayer protests that were a prelude to passage of Proposition 13 in June 1978. Proposition 13 rolled back property valuations to 1975-76 levels and set a ceiling of 1 percent on future tax rates. As a result, established residents can now continue to support restrictive growth policies, watch their own property values increase, and pay no penalty on their tax bills.

National Trends

The best evidence that California is not a national aberration is the large amount of growth-control machinery that other states have put into place in the past 10 years.

Of all the new devices for stopping home building, by far the most popular is simply to impose a temporary moratorium on requests for rezoning, building permits or water or sewer connections. The legal justification for a moratorium is to give local government time to cope with a short-term but severe problem such as a lack of sewage treatment capacity. Many communities, however, seem in no rush to solve these problems.

Although the full extent of moratoria in the country is not known, the Department of Housing and Urban Development compiled a careful tabulation of sewer moratoria from 1968 through 1976. It identified 815 communities located in 35 states—including nearly half the metropolitan areas in the country—that had sewer connection moratoria during this period.

It is difficult to measure the direct effects of the anti-growth movement on the cost of new homes, but there are signs that it has raised land costs, led to density reductions within developments, required home builders to pay a greater share of public service costs and added several months of delay to the average time for completing a construction project. All of these results raise the cost of new homes and reduce their availability to families with average incomes.

The increasingly harsh regulatory climate generates other changes in home building that are sure to raise prices. Environmental politics in California has encouraged developers to build for a luxury market. Opposition demands for low density and open space rule out moderate-cost housing and lead developers to build what they think will sell to high-income families. Besides, opponents who are concerned about protecting either their tax rates or their social prestige want their new neighbors to be wealthy—if they must have any new neighbors at all.

Environmental regulations seem to be pushing developers throughout the country to cut the number of houses they build to less than what they had originally planned. A national survey of 400 developers in 1976 asked those working in states with required environmental impact reviews what kinds of changes they made in their construction plans because of these reviews. The most common change, mentioned by 60 percent of the developers, was a reduction in housing density.

According to the environmental impact studies, the main reasons for reducing the density were to relieve traffic congestion or improve air quality. But interviews with local officials revealed a different motivation: established residents were concerned that newcomers living in higher-density housing might be socially undesirable. Beneath the environmental arguments the underlying objections were social or fiscal.

Reducing the amount of housing in a development almost always means raising the price per unit, since the developer will have to divide his land costs and other fixed expenses among fewer houses. And if the local motivation is to eliminate inexpensive housing that might attract social undesirables, political pressure will reinforce economics in persuading developers to build more expensive homes. The evidence suggests that the California tactic of whittling away at project densities, and thereby raising housing costs, is part of a national pattern.

Evidence at hand also means that the new regulation has raised housing costs without doing very much by way of improving the public environment. The major trend in project design is a reduction in housing density, which runs exactly counter to the environmentalists' rhetorical commitment to compact, efficient land development.

Finally, a predictable result of the new regulatory climate is that it encourages developers to build on the outer fringes of urban regions, where communities not yet hit by growth have not yet set up the proper machinery for harassing home builders. This result produces inconvenience and high travel costs for the home buyer, together with the environmental costs of dispersed development, extra energy use, and more air pollution from long-distance commuting.

In short, environmental opposition to home building is more easily explainable in political terms than as part of a reform agenda for improving the quality of American communities. Although it draws on several themes of current environmental thinking, its underlying rationale has little to do with mainstream environmental issues. Housing is in fact a residual item on the environmental agenda, easily neglected in the pursuit of other goals.

Opposing home building, however, serves the private interest of many environmentalists and of other defenders of the suburban status quo. It offers an attractive political position, particularly at the local level. As a result it has become an important force shaping urban development and limiting the nation's ability to supply new housing at a time when the number of families who need housing is growing faster than ever.

Free Enterprise Has Never Built a Nuclear Reactor

By Merritt Clifton

Arguing that monopoly is the antithesis of those who believe that "small is beautiful" and that government is the worst type of monopoly, the author states strongly that environmentalists would be well served by more strongly supporting the free enterprise system.

Environmentalists apparently are among the last to accept E.F. Schumacher's premise that small is beautiful, the last to understand Wendell Berry's *Unsettling of America.* "It is the overwhelming tendency of our time," Berry warned us, "to assume that a big problem calls for a big solution." But after studying how supposed big problems in agriculture are only little problems compounded by blind public policy, Berry concluded, "I do not believe in the efficacy of big solutions. I believe that they not only tend to prolong and complicate the problems they are meant to solve, but that they cause new problems." "On the other hand," Berry observed, "if the solution is small, obvious, simple and cheap," the sort farmers can develop themselves, "then it may quickly and permanently solve the immediate problem and many others as well."

Consciously or not, the small is beautiful philosophy is sweeping America. Ronald Reagan just got elected president on his pledge to decentralize government and reduce federal spending. Automobile sales figures show Americans want quality, simplicity and economy—even when choosing personal status symbols. Big is no longer better in the public imagination.

Yet environmentalists, though preaching the Schumacher/Berry gospel, continue practicing New Deal politics of scale. Barry Commoner actually wants to increase governmental power. The

From *Environmental Action*, January, 1981. Reprinted by permission of Environmental Action, Inc., 1346 Connecticut Avenue, N.W., Washington, D.C., a political lobbying group. Merritt Clifton lives in Quebec, where he is editor/publisher of *Samisdat* and writes for numerous alternative publications.

Wilderness Society virtually denies private property rights. Organized environmentalism, in short, works to deliver us further unto Big Brother, the single institution most responsible for creating our present environmental problems.

Instead of selling ecologically intelligent conduct as a route to greater personal freedom, permitting greater self reliance and more local autonomy, most environmental activists still try to impose preplanned big solutions from above. So environmentalism is unfortunately equated with the very sort of meddling interventionism Schumacher and Berry decried, while as one witness recently testified to a Senate committee investigating toxic waste disposal, "Government has not been our friend. It has been our problem." Forgotten in all this is the enduring human truth that lasting positive change comes only when diverse individuals choose it one by one. Imposition breeds resistance, and we pay the penalty in receiving a small is beautiful president who thinks smog comes from trees.

When we protest the destruction wrought by monopoly capitalism, we must realize that government is the first, most destructive monopoly of all, sanctioning and supporting the rest. We must also realize that, contrary to popular belief, capitalism is not free, individual private enterprise, that our corporate monopolies exist only through obtaining exclusive franchises from government, and that they would swiftly break up if forced to compete like small businesses in an open consumer market.

Free enterprise did not destroy mass transit in North America—government did, first by regulating the systems free enterprise built until they were no longer profitable, then by taking them over, providing such terrible noncompetitive service that they ceased attracting customers. Nor did free enterprise build the freeways encouraging our switch to automobile transport, nor the massive hydroelectric dams and transmission grids putting local energy solutions out of business. Free enterprise has never built a nuclear reactor and never will, since profit potential is nil without government subsidies. Nuclear generating continues while low head dams lie idle because of the Price-Anderson Act, which sharply limits corporate liability for nuclear accidents.

The organized ecology movement has always assumed we could somehow trade environmentally "bad" laws for "good" ones. Yet as Charles Dickens wrote, "The law is an ass," and an ass rather balkily works for whomever dangles a carrot in front of it. The Nature

Conservancy recently learned this when it donated land at Bumpus Cove, Tenn. for a state wildlife preserve. The state, presumably, has the power to maintain and protect it. But the state also has the power to lease 45 acres for use as a radioactive and toxic chemical wastes dump, and promptly did. Any time we extend any sort of regulation, we create a weapon that richer, shrewder politicians can turn against us. The Nuclear Regulatory Commission is the prime example.

The laws we need to insure environmental responsibility are the natural laws of self interested economics, backed by the criminal code. It is in our individual and corporate interest to insulate our buildings, burn less fuel, make fuller use of raw materials, recycle and replant, insuring ourselves continuing profits. It is further in our own private interest to avoid causing pollution, lest we lose the good will of aggravated customers. Government can compel patronage through taxation, but a business dependent upon consumer sales cannot and is therefore vulnerable to public opinion—with fewer resources to use trying to reshape it. Only corporations aided by government buy pronuclear advertisements, for instance; free enterprise would quickly switch to some self selling product instead.

Where a few benighted individuals and industries do abuse the environment, sacrificing the future to short term gains, we might most effectively resort to prosecution for murder, robbery, fraud and assault—amending criminal law to make corporations like the Ford Motor Co. answerable to the same statutes on the same evidence as private citizens. Plugging the legal loopholes revealed in the recent Pinto trial should become an eco movement priority, so that when damage done by a Love Canal episode surfaces, responsible officials can be promptly convicted of felonious assault on the obvious medical evidence, the sentenced to make all possible restitution. Turning such situations over to remote regulatory bureaucracies only interposes more inertia between victims and response.

Our strategy for the 80s must be the complete reversal of our 70s political directions, cognizant of past mistakes. If we diminish govenmental powers of expropriation, we may have fewer national parks—but we'll also have fewer nuclear power parks, 750 kilowatt transmission grids, weapons testing grounds and toxic waste dumps. If we reduce government regulatory power, we may replace the Nuclear Regulatory Commission and Price-Anderson with cold eyed appraisers from Lloyd's of London, willing and able to say "no nukes" and mean it. We may be unable to forbid clearcutting in private forests, but if at the same time we cease turning forests over to government, government will cease slating forests for more clear-cutting to tide the logging industry over when it fails to replant what it already owns. Corporate ecological wisdom would grow from there, from the assumption, however reluctant, of full self responsibility.

As we sow, we shall reap. Momentum is in our favor.

Reprinted by permission: Tribune Company Syndicate, Inc.

Ecologically & Socially Concerned Consumers Profiled

Are supporters of environmentalism really granola munching, backpacking, frisbee players? This profile of environmentalists sheds more light on the nature of those who are environmentally active.

Ecologically and socially concerned Americans, who comprise a significant segment of the population, not only have distinct attitudes and interests, but also distinct lifestyles and consumption patterns, according to marketing research by Michael A. Belch of San Diego State University.

Belch presented the results of his study at the AMA-sponsored Second Quadrennial Conference on Ecological Marketing held recently at the University of Texas-Austin.

Here is a profile of the typical ecologically and socially concerned consumer, according to surveys by Belch and other researchers.

"A young male or female of the higher strata in respect to income, education, and socioeconomic standing in general. Such persons are more open-minded, liberal, and secure than those demonstrating less concern, and are more likely to be rational and conservative in respect to their consuming behaviors. Both the activities and products of consumption of this segment are consistent with their attitudes regarding personal well-being, society, and the ecology."

The consumers profiled in Belch's study have strong conservationist attitudes regarding gasoline. They prefer riding a bus, are willing to pay higher taxes to improve public transportation, and say they don't drive their cars often. They believe the internal combustion gasoline engine is harmful to the environment and human health, but feel that if you must drive you should at least use a small, economical car.

This segment of the population appears to be anti-automobile.

From *Marketing News,* February, 1980. American Marketing Association. Reprinted with permission.

They're not interested in cars and know little about them mechanically. But they do feel that a car's ability to function properly, rather than its appearance, is the most important factor.

Pollution is another major concern, Belch found. This segment believes pollution is the "inevitable price of progress," and would pay "$15 more on their on their income tax for a program of federal pollution control."

Socially and ecologically concerned consumers are quite liberal when it comes to issues such as racial and sexual equality. They feel women are just as capable as men, that women should participate in family decisions, take jobs outside the home, and engage in other social activities.

In regards to race, this segment believes in equal opportunity and does not oppose integrated housing or neighborhoods. They feel progress has been made in the understanding between blacks and whites, but say more work is needed to achieve total equality.

Economically, however, this segment is conservative. They prefer to pay with cash and scorn the use of credit cards and the habit of "being in debt." They're secure now, but are pessimistic about their financial futures and feel it is a good idea to plan for a gray day.

Although they're willing to accept responsibility for their futures, they do not feel "now is the time to buy." In order to save money today they feel it is necessary to shop around for bargains.

The consumers in this segment seem to endorse the idea of participatory democracy, but do not characterize themselves as leaders in politics, professional societies, or clubs. They feel their opinions are important and that citizens should be involved in matters which affect their lives. They are also altruistic and support doing volunteer work for hospitals and service organizations.

Socially and ecologically concerned consumers do not appear to be heavy users of alcohol, tobacco or artificial stimulants. They strive to be in good physical condition and are cautious about what types of foods they eat.

They opt for health foods and home-cooked meals and dislike high-cholesterol processed or ready-to-serve foods. Although they don't feel big corporations are ruthless, they believe it is possible for unsafe foods and unreliable products to remain on the market.

Exercise, fresh air and outdoor activities are important to the consumers in this segment. They'd rather work around their homes or take long walks than stay inside and play poker or watch football on TV. They'd rather spend their summer vacations at the cabin by a lake than fly to Las Vegas. They're not lazy people. In fact, they would continue to hold down jobs even if they didn't have to work for a living.

As consumers, socially and ecologically concerned Americans are conservative, cautious, and thrifty. They believe spiritual values are more important than material possessions, and are therefore disinterested in traditional status symbols.

They dislike conspicuous displays of wealth, wouldn't hire a maid even if they could afford one and wouldn't own or fly private airplanes.

These consumers feel many products are unnecessary or frivolous (such as mouthwash), are more concerned with a product's durability than its appearance, and are not followers of the latest trends, and styles. They're loyal to their favorite stores and product brands, but remain open-minded. They feel advertising should be more factual and informative. And they put more emphasis on a products' value than its country of origin. "American made is best made" is not one of their beliefs.

"These individuals do not consider themselves to be swingers," Belch said. "They are secure and cognizant of their roles in society. But such individuals are less likely to accept the status quo and feel that the future is likely to be less than ideal.

"The luxuries of life are of little importance to them. They seek bargains and price deals and prefer products that have positive benefits. This segment is concerned with ecological problems, energy supplies, and their physical well-being.

"The implications of such findings should be evident. It is now possible to proceed beyond the previously utilized demographic and personality profiles to the point where the marketing mix strategies can be directed to a more specific target audience."

The Environmental Community: Response to the Reagan Administration Program

By Brock Evans

In the context of current struggles with the Reagan Administration, Brock Evans, a former vice president of the National Audubon Society, outlines the history of the environmental movement in America and describes the structure of the current movement.

W e all know that the debate over our public lands and what to do about them is as old as our republic itself . . . indeed, even older, because one of the first orders of business for our new nation, even before we had our Constitution, was to deal with the future of the vast lands between the Appalachians and the Mississippi River.

This history is as old as our nation, and so are the main parties to it. The names, places, and terms of reference have perhaps changed somewhat, but the concerns expressed are the same, and so basically are the participants: they were then, and are still the national government; the citizens who see the public lands as valuable for commercial use; and the citizens who see them as valuable for non-commercial uses. Each of these parties has valid and important things to say, and none of us has ever hesitated to speak out and say them!

We all even agree on one or two basic points, I think; first, that the public lands are a treasure—a priceless gift from the founders of our country to us, down through all generations. . .that is one basic agreement we all share.

Another place we agree, I think, is that we are fortunate indeed

Excerpted from *Vital Speeches of the Day*, February 1982, with permission from City News Publishing Co. Brock Evans was vice president for national issues, National Audubon Society, when this speech was delivered.

to have a system of government that permits each side, each party, to have its say, each to attempt to persuade others of the validity of its viewpoint—a system of government and interaction that is always open in the most dynamic sort of way to this ongoing discussion of just what is in the best interest of the public as we seek to work out the use of these lands.

It is no secret to any of us—and certainly it is the strong consensus of those I speak for—that there has been the most radical shift and change, both in terms of policy and emphasis, regarding the public lands and how they should be managed . . . the most radical shift in our memories. From my own reading of history, one would have to go back at least a quarter of a century, to the first two years of the Eisenhower Administration, to find anything approaching the Reagan Administration's views and philosophy on the subject . . . and in terms of sweeping across-the-board applications of this philosophy—probably one would have to go back much further than that, probably back well into the past century.

That is how we see it, at least. I think I speak for all environmentalists when I say I wish that it was not this way . . . I wish I were discussing a different set of realities, discussing ways and means to work together constructively with our government to achieve commonly agreed upon goals for management of the public lands. We environmentalists after all are only human, and contrary to what some may say, we do not relish controversy or confrontation; we seek dialogue, not conflict; we seek peace, not war. But if war is forced upon us, then so be it: we will fight back. And that I am sorry to say is where we are today.

The topic of this conference is about the Reagan Administration's program for the public lands, and the provocative subtitle is "Access to America's Natural Resources . . ." Like so many other phrases and words these days, "access" has become a buzzword too, usually meaning the presumed right of some commercial interest or other to obtain the resources of interest to them that are located on the public lands.

But I would prefer to use both the word "resource" and the phrase "access to them" in a broader sense—to make us all equal here. To me and to our community, "resources" means not just wood and minerals and oil and gas; but also means wildlife and wildlife habitat, scenic vistas, pure streams, clean air, undisturbed natural places, wild places, national parks, places which maintain the amenities of life as well as the commodities of life. And the phrase "access to them" means the right of those who treasure these resources always to be able to count upon their existence—in substantial measure—on our public lands; because we all know that it is only in the public lands, the lands that belong to the people, that these resources are largely going to be available to our growing population and to future generations. These are basic beliefs of our environmental community, and it is our concern for what is happening to these values, to these resources on public lands, that fuels so much of our alarm at the policies of the Reagan Administration.

It is certainly no secret that the environmental movement today is united as never before in its long history in its perception that the Reagan Administration has instituted changes in public lands policy of the most radical and extreme nature, breaking almost completely with the 100-year bipartisan tradition that has governed the approach of nearly every other Administration. There has never been anything quite like the approach of this Administration before— at least not for a very long time; and we do indeed have definite and very strong views about this "public lands program" of the Reagan Administration as it unfolds before us.

I want to come back in a minute to our reaction to this program as we see it. But also I feel it is important to my charge here today to not just tell you *what* we think, but *why* we think it: what is the basis for this reaction, why do we react so strongly?

To understand this, we need to understand a bit about the environmental movement itself: who we are, where we have come from— what is our history?

This is necessary I think, because to believe some of the rhetoric I sometimes listen to at public hearings, or read in trade association journals, one would think that we're just some johnny-come-latelies who just happened on the scene around Earth Day sometime . . . well meaning but confused folks whose knowledge and understanding of the environment is limited to coffee table books and cocktail parties.

We're either "rich elitists" or "long-haired hippies," depending on who is speaking—and I still can't figure out if those two are supposed to go together or not!

And then finally, there are the comments about the so-called "hired guns," the "paid people" in Washington who work for environmental organizations, and who just sit around all day dreaming up new ways to raise money or whip our members into shape . . . we don't really care about the environment, and we certainly don't speak for our members—that's at least what's been said.

It's an interesting picture indeed, and as you might imagine, it's not quite how we see ourselves.

First of all, environmentalism is a real, genuine movement; environmentalism, in the sense of commonly accepted goals, beliefs, and values, is widespread and pervasive throughout most of our society, without much distinction between ages, classes, sex, race, or geography. It is a movement of local, regional, and national organizations . . . no one knows exactly how many organizations there are, or how many members there are of these environmental groups. The EPA estimated a few years ago that there are some 12,000 environmental groups around the country, large and small . . . and that the combined membership of all of these institutions, not counting overlap, was between 6 and 10 million individuals. Although these environmental organizations work on just about every subject under the sun, from solar energy to mass transit, from wilderness to wildlife, we are all bound together by certain broad commonly held beliefs in such things as clean air, energy conservation, wildlife and wilderness and parks.

The second basic fact about the environmental movement goes beyond the membership of the many constituent organizations—right out to the American public itself. By now I think we have all read about the latest Louis Harris Poll regarding the attitudes of the public about the Clean Air Act. In this widespread sampling, Harris found out that about 75-80 percent of the American people, across-the-board: white, black, young, old, liberal, conservative, Republican, Democrat—from all sections of the country—all favored keeping the Clean Air Act as strong as it is or making it stronger.

". . . This message on the deep desire on the part of the American people to battle pollution is one of the most overwhelming and clearest we have ever recorded in our 25 years of surveying public opinion. . . ." said Harris.

Over the past 10 or 12 years there have been many, many similar polls, conducted by many different entities and interests . . . and while the polls have varied from time to time depending on the kinds of questions asked—they haven't varied very much, given the incredible fluctuations in our economic situation, energy concerns, and perceptions about national security. These polls have always shown a very high degree of support for the programs, values, and policies of environmental organizations. Sure, we can always ask the questions in different ways, and we'll get somewhat different answers—we all do that. But we cannot deny that there is a very large degree of public support out there.

To me, the hard test of whether this is so or not comes finally in those votes in the Congress, the actions of our elected representatives, politicians who must by their nature be sensitive to the feelings of their constituents. How do they believe their constituents feel about these public lands issues?

To illustrate, I could take almost any vote on issues of major importance to the environmental movement on public lands questions, whether it be the Alaska Lands bill of 1980 or the Timber Supply Act of 1970, or any of the other hundreds of votes in between.

But, let us turn to some of the most recent expressions of Congressional opinion about the actual or perceived policies of the Reagan Administration concerning our public lands.

The first example might be the vote of the House Interior Committee to withdraw the Bob Marshall Wilderness in Montana from oil and gas exploration last May—a direct reaction to the perceived intent of the Secretary of Interior to exercise his discretion to issue such leases for exploratory oil and gas drilling. This action was taken at the behest of the Congressional representative from the district affected.

The second example would be the action of the House Merchant and Fisheries Committee in adopting language sponsored by Congressman Pritchard of Washington rejecting the Administration's proposal to change the definition of the phrase "directly affecting," when referring to regulations under the Coastal Zone Management Act (CZMA) giving coastal states the rights to influence the decision of the federal government regarding outer continental shelf leasing and pre-leasing activities. The Administration wanted to prevent states from having such a say, which would mean in our view, a lot less attention to environmental impacts. It would have facilitated more off shore oil drilling without regard to state objections.

The third example might be the recent announcement by Republican Congressman Cheney of Wyoming that he was withdrawing his co-sponsorship of the so-called "Minerals Supremacy bill" due to objections from his constituents or the sponsorship by Republican Representative Lujan of New Mexico of a resolution now in House

Interior Committee to withdraw all wilderness lands in the lower
48 states from oil and gas exploration and leasing.

Each of these actions, as noted, was precipitated by a reaction to
a perceived or actual policy of the Reagan Administration, policies
which had very strong support from industry. Each of these actions
taken was initiated by representatives from essentially conservative
states, all of which went strongly for the President during the 1980
elections. These actions have to tell us something; and I think that
they tell us at the very least that there is a great deal of public support for environmental goals and values, whether the issue is the
Clean Air Act or the public lands. They tell us above all that it is
not wise policy or politics to see the environmental movement as
being a movement without large public support. I can certainly say
from my own experience that organizations such as ours which have
little financial resources simply cannot hope to prevail in the issues
we do without the kind of public support that comes from the whole
people, and not just our members.

About a year ago, in Washington, I listened to John Kyl, former
Republican Congressman from Iowa, former Undersecretary of Interior under President Nixon, and then an advisor to the Reagan Administration. He addressed a gathering of the timber industry and
he told them "many of you have come to us with proposals to change
the environmental laws . . . but only Congress can change the laws,
and Congress listens to what the people say. And the environmental
movement is a people's movement . . . that is why we have the
environmental laws in the first place. To change the laws you must
first change the people. . . ."

So yes, the environmental movement is a people's movement.

No, it does not include all the people . . . there are many valid
interests to be served in this society, we all accept that; but it is very
many people, and it is not an elitist movement at all.

I noted before that there has always been a strong bipartisan tradition in the environmental movement for the whole past century;
there are many Republicans in it from the greats like President
Theodore Roosevelt, creator of the National Forest System and Congressman John Saylor of Pennsylvania, one of the founders and main
champions of the wilderness system, to the thousands and thousands
of ordinary members who make up our rank and file, for example
the two-thirds of the membership of the National Wildlife Federation, who in a recent poll said they voted for President Reagan. If

you had been to the hundreds and hundreds of environmental meetings across the country for the past fifteen years that I have been to, you would agree with me that there is a real cross-section of individual people in our movement: young and old, both sexes, all levels of education, conservative and liberal and everything in between . . . it is a people's movement.

Finally, as to the "hired gun in Washington" statement, just a couple of quick comments will suffice.

First, those of us who are staff of membership organizations know very well that we would not last very long as that staff if our actions and statements did not have the support of the overwhelming majority of our members. Policy in our organization is always made from the bottom up, by the volunteer members, speaking through their elaborate networks of chapter presidencies, regional councils, and Board of Directors.

There is no question that Audubon's policy of strong opposition to the actions of the Reagan Administration against the public lands these days has the overwhelming support of our nearly half million members. We first found this out last May, during the time of our annual fund appeal. The appeal this year was rewritten from its normal mild form into a strongly worded call to arms, elaborating the specific policies of the Reagan Administration which we felt were very much antithetical to the cause of protection of the public lands and their wildlife. Eight times more Audubon members gave nine times as much money as ever before in any single fund appeal in response to this letter—laying themselves on the line with their dollars—a sure indication of their strength of feeling! A month later, our 36-person Board of Directors ratified all the actions of the staff vis a vis the Administration unanimously. I have been to many local chapter and regional meetings since, and I can assure you that the feelings of our membership are very strong, deep and intense . . . there is no distinction in our organization, or any of the others of our community at this time, between the feelings of the so-called "hired guns" in Washington, and the overwhelming majority of our rank and file, all of whom share a common love for the land and an alarm for its fate at the hands of this Administration.

All right. That is us, who we are, and what we are like . . . that is half of what is necessary to understand why we react the way we do. The other half is our long history and tradition as a movement . . . where have we come from, what have we been working for for so long? This is important to know, in order to understand our reaction to the present also. Environmentalism, concern for the environment, for our public lands is not a new thing—we, and our values, have been around as long as the Republic itself; we go back at least to the writing of William Bartram, who in 1775 traveled through the southern Appalachians marveling at the beauty of the forest wilderness there, lamenting its passing, and pleading for some way to protect some of it. Concern about the American wilderness in those public lands aways off to the west was a central theme of many of the writings of our early authors and poets, James Fenimore Cooper, William Cullen Bryant and many others, in the early part of the 19th century; the uniqueness of America, the things that made us different from other countries—our wild places—were extolled and glorified by painters and musicians in that first half of the 19th century as well.

This rising awareness of the vastness and beauty of the American landscape and wilderness and a concern for its rapid elimination was given a philosophical framework in the writings of Thoreau and Emerson around the mid-19th century, Thoreau specifically calling for saving the wilderness, while there was still time. This cry was taken up by others, newspapermen and writers for popular magazines, especially in New York state where the fate of the Adirondacks was being decided.

But it also reached west, into that vast public domain, and this rising chorus of concern about public lands, a feeling that they had values other than commercial values—that indeed they had spiritual values—was given its first political form and expression in 1872, when a Republican President named Ulysses Grant signed into law legislation creating Yellowstone National Park. This was a significant act indeed because Yellowstone then was a vast wilderness, far more remote to the people of the time than anything in Alaska is to us today . . . and yet it was consciously set aside by the Congress as a "permanent pleasuring ground for the people. . . ." In other words, for the first time in the history of the world we see the idea that wilderness gives pleasure just because it is—without any embellishment, any ornaments, or even any real access. That is a uniquely American idea, and has been given force and powerful expression many subsequent times in the past century.

Well, that was the beginning, and we all know what came after that in the public lands . . . the environmental movement grew up in response to the rapidly changing face of these lands, the rapid commercial exploitation of them, and the equally rapid elimination of much of our native American wildlife. The first ornithological societies, which later became the National Audubon Society, were formed in the 1880s; the Sierra Club was founded in 1892 . . . and other great organizations came along in rapid succession. The forest reserves were created in 1891, the Forest Organic Act in 1897, the Forest Service in 1905, the national parks system in 1916 . . . a host of splendid additions to the park system at that time and later . . . a whole system of bird and animal protection laws, game laws, all designed to begin to restore our wildlife . . . the beginnings of our national wildlife refuge system in the 1930s.

As we all know, after a brief hiatus during WW II and the Korean War, the wave of enthusiasm surged forward again in the 1960s and 1970s in the focus of efforts to create an effective pollution control system: the Clean Air Act, Clean Water Act, Resource Conservation and Recovery Act, Toxic Substances Control Act . . . Superfund; and it surged forward just as emphatically to bring balance, the highest quality of professionalism and orderly planning to our existing public lands systems—hence the Multiple Use Sustained Yield Act of 1960, Forest Management Act and the Federal Land Policy Management Act of 1976, among others.

And finally it created new systems to protect the fast vanishing remnants of our national heritage: Wilderness Act of 1964, Wild and Scenic River Act of 1968, Alaska Lands Act of 1980 . . . Land and Water Conservation Fund Act of 1965 . . . and millions of acres to be added to those systems in many separate laws.

To us, these were great accomplishments and we were very proud. None of these laws were perfect—either from our viewpoint or from that of industry . . . each one reflected the political balancing and tradeoffs which are such a necessary part of our system.

But from our viewpoint, the way we saw it—and that is what I am sharing with you today . . . each of these great accomplishments was the realization of a set of dreams, some of them going back decades . . . each of them representing the achievement of long-standing goals . . . and each of them, we felt, would benefit our country—would make it not only more a productive, but a more healthy country. Each would make it not only a country with a high material standard of living, but also a nation blessed by an abundance of the things that make life worthwhile.

To us, this whole great network of landmark statutes went to the very purpose of the government itself, as conceived by the founders of our nation: to protect the health and safety of the people, provide for the common welfare, to manage wisely our common resources. . . .

I have said before—and I want to emphasize again—that environmentalism, throughout its long history, has always been a bipartisan concern . . . leaders of both parties have shaped the American environmental ethic and the laws to back it up; men and women of both parties, of all persuasions, have made up the rank and file of its membership ever since its beginning over a hundred years ago.

And our bipartisan goals have been very consistent for the whole past century; they have never waivered, have not changed much; in reviewing this long tradition and history, it seems that only the place names and names of legislation have changed.

We have always sought the highest quality management of the public lands for the full spectrum of multiple uses, so that the lands will not be abused but will be passed on to the future intact and not ravaged by short term exploitation.

We have always sought special reservations of our finest scenic vistas, our superlative natural and historic wonders, the remnants of the once-vast wilderness . . . because they are part of our culture, history and traditions too.

And we have always sought the highest degree of protection for our native wildlife in parks, refuges, and wilderness areas, and through high quality management . . . so that future generations as well as our own can enjoy this abundance.

These are and always have been the goals of our movement; they have been shared by nearly every Administration, every president, every Congress, since we began this work. These are the goals largely accomplished in the landmark statutes and accompanying regulations I referred to earlier. That is where we were one year ago. . . .

But all this has changed now . . . in the space of one short year since the election, we have seen take place the most radical and extreme changes in perhaps a century, changes of approach and philosophy about the proper use and management of our public lands.

We look around us now at the whole carefully built structure of public land laws, the whole carefully thought out environmental ethic developed over a century, a philosophy of careful management and protection, of husbanding our resources, of reserving from exploitation some places which have higher values . . . and what do we see?

We see a former Secretary of Interior who preached stewardship and care for resources, but who systematically attempted to undermine, through new or "revised" regulations and budget cuts, key protective statutes such as the Surface Mine Control Act and the Endangered Species Act, the Federal Land Policy and Management Act, the Outer Continental Shelf Act and other laws too.

We see an Assistant Secretary of Agriculture in charge of our public forests who criticizes efforts of the foresters to protect wildlife—one of their statutory duties—as "just creating game farms on the national forests. . . ." We see this same official instigating efforts to rewrite regulations so as to cut citizens with no economic interest in the outcome out of the appeals process, to rewrite the regulations to weaken wildlife protection so that logging in key areas can proceed even faster . . . we see this official calling for a great increase in the cutting of the public forests at the same time that the evidence is strong that such cutting can do grave damage not only to other resources, but the forestry resource itself. We see his emphasis on getting the logs out as the only important mission of the National Forest System.

We see everywhere efforts to accelerate exploitation of the outer continental shelf, of coal lands, and of millions of acres of fragile and sensitive lands within either already protected systems or marked for further study so that they might in the future be protected, and to eliminate the necessary environmental controls on them. . . . We see efforts to open up Wilderness Areas and National Parks to incompatible, damaging uses . . . and other efforts to transfer lands out of the National Wildlife Refuge System entirely.

We see all this happening, but we see no corresponding effort to maintain already long-standing programs to acquire and protect key park and refuge areas already mandated by the Congress or state and local governments for protection; on the contrary, these programs are marked for extinction. Everywhere, making what we consider to be illegal use of the budget process, we see budget cuts in key areas of law enforcement, research and inventory—all designed to help us protect the resources we have . . . while at the same time the budget is increased or at least held the same, in the resource exploitation and development end of things.

Everywhere, throughout the whole public land sector—we see a pervasive and systematic effort to undo the work of the past 20 years, if not the whole past century.

From the Wilderness Act to the Forest Management Act, from the Land and Water Conservation Fund Act to the Surface Mine Act, from the Endangered Species Act to the Outer Continental Shelf Act—the pattern is overwhelmingly the same: cut or eliminate the budget for the protective, planning and enforcement functions of the laws—and increase the funds for the exploitive parts . . . get those logs out, and get those minerals and oil and gas out faster—and remove or weaken the laws and regulations designed to protect the environment in the process. . . .

—in a budget cutting year, increase or at least keep nearly the same the funds for big dams, nuclear power, synthetic fuels . . . but wipe them out for parks, Wildlife Refuges, energy conservation and solar power.

"We will use the budget process to accomplish policy goals," said our then Secretary of Interior . . . and that is what has been attempted.

And this shameful reversal of all past policies of all Administrations is not just confined to the public lands sector, I should add. . . .

It is the same in the pollution control sector—where the crucial regulatory functions of the EPA in administering the Clean Air Act, Clean Water Act, Toxic Substances Control Act—and other statutes . . . are also being systematically eliminated through enormous budget cuts.

No we do not, have never, sought regulation for regulation's sake—we have sought it only to protect the health and welfare of our people. . . .

No,—every regulation is not perfect—there is always room for fine tuning and improvement.

But, what is being done here is not delicate surgery, it is a radical amputation. Under the guise of "regulatory reform"—they are throwing out the baby with the bathwater. . . .

It is a sad pattern that we see, an unhappy chronicle now unfolding before us . . . and we feel we have no choice but to stand up and fight against it. . . .

That is the response of the environmental community to the public lands program of the Administration—indeed, to just about the *entire* program of the Administration . . . that is our response and that is what we are doing. . . .

We did not seek it, we would have preferred peace . . . but if war is what they want, it is war that they shall have. . . .

How are we doing it—what are we doing now?

We are resisting in many different ways, none of them secret, all of them public, all part of the dynamics of a free society . . . we are reaching out to our own membership, raising more funds from them, building up mailing lists, conducting training workshops around the country. . . .

For example my organization—the National Audubon Society has declared

—November to be Mobilization Month . . . we are holding activist workshops in 20 cities around the country to discuss ways and means of dealing with the current threats . . . we are likewise asking each of our 470 chapters to do the same . . . other organizations are doing it too . . . I am going to address an Audubon meeting in Corpus Christi tomorrow and in Long Island the next day; I expect hundreds of people to be there.

—We are reaching out far beyond our own members too, out into the community of our coworkers and neighbors . . . these are the people who say 70-80 percent in the polls that they do not want our protective laws weakened . . . we are signing them up too.

—Of course, we are fighting directly wherever there is an appropriate battlefield and if the battleground of the Administration, of its inner councils, is lost to us, is closed off as it has been for a year now—the battlegrounds of the Congress and the courts—the other 2 great branches of our government—are not . . . and that is where we are now . . . that is where you will find us.

—In short—and I say this to those of you from industry in the audience—we are exercising our rights in a free democracy to petition for redress, to try to save the things we fought for so long for. . . .

In short—we are only doing what you would do in similar circumstances—indeed what you *have* done when you perceived your protections, your goals, your values threatened. . . .

—We fought back. And we will continue to fight back until the places we love and the values we have fought for for so long, are once again safe.

I said before and I say again: we would have preferred it otherwise . . . we would prefer a constructive dialogue with this Administration and its supporters, to find the ways and means to work together in constructive harmony to achieve mutually-held goals. . . .

We would have preferred to attempt to educate this Administration to the advisability of returning to the bipartisan tradition that has always been a hallmark of American environmentalism . . . that is much the preferable course.

But sadly, this course seems not to be, for now at least . . . and so we go on, our environmental movement, and do as we must. . . .

"To fail to fight back now would be to fail to protect our history . . ." said our President of Audubon—Russell Peterson—former Republican Governor of Delaware . . . "to fail to resist these assaults on our lands and our laws would be to earn the repudiation of the countless men and women who came before us, who placed their trust and their faith in our course. . . ." That is what he said, that is how we all felt. . . .

And that is our response: we are fighting back, there is no recourse left to us . . . we will continue to fight back until at last we can have peace. . . .

The Conservatism of the Liberals

By William Tucker

William Tucker analyzes the class structure of the environmental movement and concludes that there is a certain elitism and illiberalism permeating it.

In 1965, a professor of range management and plant ecology at a California state college and senior associate of The Conservation Foundation in Washington, D.C., surveyed the growing suburbanization around him and wrote a pessimistic book called *The Destruction of California*. Newcomers were overrunning the state, he concluded, and there was little to stop them. Landscapes were being destroyed, old farms and pastures developed, water and air were being polluted, and wildlife was disappearing. In a nostalgic concluding chapter entitled "Once There Was a Place Called California," the author, Raymond Dasmann, made the following sad but revealing assessment of the possibilities of "limiting growth" in his home state.

"One of the most charming places in California is the city of Santa Barbara. It has maintained its quiet beauty by excluding the kind of industrial growth that other cities have welcomed. It has not allowed housing sprawl. It has fought the State Highway Commission and its monstrous freeway system to a halt, temporarily, at least. The continuing charm of the Carmel region, farther north, has been maintained by a firm and definite stand against 'progress' by its residents But these are small places, inhabited by the wealthy. It is most unlikely that active discouragement of population increase on a statewide scale will be tried out. It goes against the entire philosophy of the expanding economy. Too many people look forward to

Excerpted from *Progress and Privilege: America in the Age of Environmentalism,* by permission of the Conference Board and the publisher, Doubleday & Company, Inc. William Tucker is a contributing editor to *Harper's* magazine and author of the book *Progress and Privilege: America in the Age of Environmentalism.*

population growth, even while they decry its effects, for them to accept a plan for its discouragement. Such a plan would mean that all those who had a vested interest in land would find values no longer increasing. It would say to those in business and industry that they could expect no further expansion of the California market. *All of us are too used to being pushed to higher level by people crowding in from below to accept the idea that growth and expansion have ended."* (Emphasis added.)

This passage, written by a college professor and early environmentalist, expresses very nicely the mood in the mid-1960s of the slice of American society that I would like to refer to as the "upper-middle class." This sector has played an increasingly important role in our society over the past 20 years. The Age of Environmentalism has essentially been a chronicle of this educated and articulate group's initial experiences with wealth and privilege.

If we take the time to look back to 1970, at the moment when the liberal coalition of the upper-middle class and the blacks was under its severest strain—we find, not uncoincidentally, that this was almost the precise moment when environmentalism burst upon the national political agenda.

The liberal coalition of the 1960s was forged mainly by the union of interests between upper-middle-class people and the poor. But by the late 1960s, the whole situation was beginning to fray. Black rage (perhaps egged on a bit by liberal solicitation) had exploded into a series of brutal riots. Quasi-military organizations like the Black Panthers and the Puerto Rican Young Lords were spearheading a new style of political gangsterism. Moreover, the white radicals who had followed their cause into the ghettos were emerging with a strong bent toward violence themselves. Bombings and political terrorism were gaining a foothold in American society.

Into this increasingly dangerous situation, the budding environmental movement introduced a simple but powerful idea. Social conditions were certainly bad, it said. The war in Vietnam was a continuing cancer, and there was much social injustice to be set right. But far more important than that, *the earth itself was endangered.* The spread of pollution, of poisonous pesticides, and of population posed an immediate threat to human society that significantly overshadowed all these social problems. What would by the good of solving all these social difficulties, the environmental movement asked, if we destroyed the planet in the process? As Thoreau had put it,

"What is the use of a house if you haven't got a tolerable planet to put it on?" And so, in the competition of ideas which plays such a quiet but crucial role in our national life, the environmental movement was born.

I do not mean to downgrade the environmental movement by saying this. I think environmentalism was probably the best thing that happened in American politics in the early 1970s. It is fair to say, I think, that the reason the American student radicalism did not veer into violence and terrorism during the early '70s, the way it did in Europe, is probably that environmentalism absorbed so much of the energies of young people. One of the striking things about the early environmental literature was how many writers were at pains to emphasize that "you don't have to go out and throw bombs" in order to join the ecology crusade. Environmentalism was the gentle way to make a revolution:

"Students who think only of demonstrations and confrontations, who despair of finding any friends within the system, are making the same old mistake of ignoring their potential majority . . .

"The ecology movement can do much better than that. It is very different from civil rights or Vietnam, where young people on both sides of the issue already have rigid ideas and have hardened minds against each other's arguments. We can approach conservation with a new outlook."

So reads an early Friends of the Earth recruiting document. Or take this manifesto from the Sierra Club's leading publicity writer:

"Our struggle is toward what the black studies demonstrators have called 'reeducation.' Develop an island psychology in everyone on Earth, and if there are any young activist SDS hippie anarchist conspirators in the audience, I would urge you to go out and get your college to institute departments of green studies at once, and while you're at it, put away the books on traditional economics."

Once again, I do not mean to suggest in any way that early environmental activists were a bunch of dogooders, or that they were deliberately trying to undermine radical or socially oriented reform— as many leftist critics charged at the time, and still do occasionally. Environmentalism raised enormously important issues. In the process, it helped considerably to cool down the temperature of the nation. My point in reviewing these sociological origins of environmentalism is to get a clear picture of its beginnings as a way of understanding what have finally become its social limitations.

Put quite simply, the birth of environmentalism represented a withdrawing of upper-middle-class attention from the interests of the poor and a turning in another direction. The liberal agenda represented an effort by upper-middle-class people to leap over their adversary-neighbors in the lower-middle class and make friends with the poor. But by 1970 this effort was showing its limitations.

And so, many original thinkers in the upper-middle class began to realize that there was still another possible enemy-of-your-enemy alliance in the other direction. This was the *old wealth,* lying on the far side of the business elite, *above* the upper-middle class on the economic scale. Tom Wolfe probably captured this moment of realization perfectly in *Radical Chic,* when he described the bad publicity that fell upon Leonard Bernstein and other East Side literati when their efforts to entertain the Black Panthers at a fund-raising party turned sour:

"The panic turned out to be good for Friends of the Earth, somewhat the way the recession has been bad for the Four Seasons but good for Riker's. Many matrons, such as Cheray Duchin, turned their attention toward the sables, cheetahs, and leopards, once the Panthers became radioactive."

For myself, the most astute description I have ever read of the environmental movement appeared in a small article carried in a Boston counterculture newspaper in 1978 about a recent meeting of antinuclear activists. The organization, called Supporters of Silkwood, was meeting to support the court case of the family of a 26-year-old Oklahoma woman who claimed to have been exposed to plutonium at a nuclear reprocessing plant, and later died in an auto accident. The article, which was entirely sympathetic to the cause, began as follows:

"About 50 members of the Cambridge liberal establishment, including academics, attorneys, journalists, politicians, 'just plain old rich people,' and at least one Nobel laureate, attended a fundraiser at a private home in the plush Observatory Hill neighborhood last week for the benefit of the Karen Silkwood Memorial Coalition."

Without going into the merits of the particular case, the roster of guests expresses perfectly, to my mind, what environmentalism has been all about. Every survey that has ever been taken (including the Sierra Club's extensive polling of its own membership) has shown that support for environmentalism has been concentrated in the upper-middle-class, professional segment of society. Academics, attorneys, doctors, dentists, journalists, and upper-income suburbanites have been, without question, the backbone of the movement. One extensive polling showed that support for environmental causes picks up strongly when income levels reach about $30,000, and then tails off again significantly above $70,000. It is about at this level that the salaries of upper-echelon business executives usually begin. (Academics, who lead comfortably sheltered lives, are usually able to make it into the ranks of the upper-middle class without attaining quite the same salary levels.)

But the key to understanding environmentalism lies in the presence of those "just plain old rich people." Why are they so necessary to the chemistry of the environmental movement? The answer is easy, once we recognize what environmentalism represents. Environmentalism is the ideas of aristocratic conservatism translated onto a popular scale. The "plain old rich people" have brought the ideas and attitudes. (And it is important to recognize just how many "plain old rich people" there are in most of the major environmental organizations.) They have contributed those ineffable qualities of class, knowledge, and dignity necessary to such undertakings.

As Weber and Veblen both emphasized, aristocratic values do not come easily but require a great deal of training. The idea of looking on material progress and economic security as an irrelevant and vulgar nuisance cannot be picked up overnight. The old saying was that it took three generations to make a gentleman, and I have the distinct impression that it now takes at least two generations to make an environmentalist. It is usually the sons and daughters of people who have achieved complete material security who make the most strident environmentalists. In families where there is at least some memory of hard times—some generational recollection that economic security is not in the natural order of things—the impulse toward environmentalism usually does not run as strong. (Keep in mind, again, that I am not talking about specific environmental issues, but only the unmistakable loftiness which maintains that "greed," "vulgar materialism," "progress," or simply "people" themselves are the root of the problem.)

America's old wealth, its almost invisible aristocracy, then, has provided the ideas, the attitudes, and the "class" to environmentalism. What has the upper-middle class provided? They have contributed two things—the *numbers* and the *skills*.

Aristocracies are, of course, by nature, very limited in size. This has been especially true in America, where large estates never gained a foothold, and where the aristocratic ideal has always been on the defensive. We are, after all, a country whose history has been irreversibly liberal and democratic. The political parties that tried to defend the aristocratic ideal—the Federalists and the Whigs—lie in the rubble of our history. Paradoxically, it has been this very lack of aristocratic norms and institutions in our history that has made it so difficult for us to recognize it once it has resurfaced in the environmental doctrine.

As Veblen said, aristocracies are never numerous enough to rule by their size alone. They are far more likely to influence society by setting the style and tone of the public mood. With the birth of the environmental movement, America's "plain old rich people" have found a large, numerous, articulate ally in the rising ranks of the upper-middle class. Moreover, the upper-middle class, which by the late 1960s was beginning to achieve a very comfortable level of living, has been ripe for the idea that "things have gone far enough," and that it is time to start "preserving what we have," rather than "always trying to accumulate more." This has not been in any way a conspiracy between the upper-middle class and America's old wealth. It is simply a very happy and comfortable confluence of interests.

In addition to numbers and energy, the upper-middle class brought *skills* to the cause of aristocratic conservatism. Aristocracies, besides being small, also have a habit of letting their skills erode. The notion of a declining aristocracy is almost a cliche. Thus, for decades upon decades, future environmental standard-bearers—people like George Perkins Marsh, John Ruskin, Joseph Wood Krutch, and Henry Beston—were simply "lonely voices," characterized both by themselves and by others as people "out of step with the times." It was only with the rise of America's upper-middle class that fresh talent was brought into the field. Upper-middle-class people are, above all, immensely skilled at legal and bureaucratic performance. They know how to draw up laws, lobby legislators, publish newspaper stories, sway public audiences, and generally push their opinions into both the popular and legal realm. The rafts of environmental literature and the astonishingly rapid institutionalization of the environmental movement after only a few short years in the public domain are the monumental evidence of these abilities. With almost religious intensity, the upper-middle class has made environmentalism its sacred cause.

But, as I said, this wedding of attitudes between the rising upper-middle class and America's old wealth has had its restrictions and limitations, in addition to the sudden clarity of a new and useful idea. And so, what we have to examine next is just what the limitations of the environmental philosophy have been.

Environmentalism has been the mass adoption of aristocratic values by America's burgeoning upper-middle class. It is the "conservatism of the liberals." Once the liberal program of upper-middle-class people creating government programs to sponsor disadvantaged people began to exhaust itself, a very predictable turn of events occurred. Upper-middle-class people decided that *they too* were "disadvantaged" and deserved a liberal program. This accounts for one of the more annoying aspects of the environmental movement—the tendency of its exponents to borrow rhetorical terms from previous liberal programs and try to picture themselves as an "abused minority." The truth is, in fact, the very opposite. One does not become and environmentalist until one achieves some kind of privilege and feels one has something worth protecting. Environmentalists are a *privileged* minority.

In the early days of the crusade, there was a great deal of hope that environmentalism could be characterized as everybody's issue. After all, who could be in favor of pollution, or against saving the earth? The early hope was vastly encouraged by the speed with which the pro-business Nixon Administration picked up the environmental banner and made it a major issue. In his 1970 State of the Union address, President Nixon announced that the deterioration of the environment was a national crisis, and that new environmental legislation would be a major priority of his Administration. Although there has been much criticism that Nixon was only co-opting the issue and was not sincere, there is no question from the record that the Nixon Administration was remarkably sincere in its commitment to environmental legislation.

At the time of Nixon's speech, the National Environmental Policy Act of 1969 (which inaugurated the "environmental impact statement") was the only major piece of legislation that had resulted from the new movement. Over the next two years, the Clean Air Act and the Federal Water Pollution Control Act—both major departures from previous legislation—were pushed through Congress with broad bipartisan support. Memoirs from the inner circles of the Nixon Administration show clearly that the Executive branch pushed ahead on the environmental program with very few misgivings about what some of the limitations might be.

Throughout the period, environmentalism has attracted a broad variety of conservative and liberal support. On Earth Day, 1970, the inaugural moment when the academically based environmental movements "went public," the featured speaker at one very liberal Long Island university was Barry Goldwater, who reminisced about his love of Arizona's natural landscape. James Buckley, the Conservative Party Senator from New York, who was elected to his only term in 1970, was at the time, and has remained, an enthusiastic supporter of environmental causes. As late as 1979, he was still writing articles on protecting endangered species. One of the first books published on the subject, still distributed by environmental groups, was *Arthur Godfrey's Environmental Reader. Reader's Digest* also emerged as an enthusiastic and long-term supporter of environmental concerns.

The question arose, then, if Richard Nixon and Edmund Muskie, Barry Goldwater and Edward Kennedy, Arthur Godfrey and Robert Redford, Republicans and Democrats, liberals and conservatives, could all be in favor of environmentalism, who could conceivably be against it? The answer did not emerge clearly for many years, until the true implications of environmentalism began to make themselves felt.

What environmental enthusiasts unfortunately failed to recognize is that, if environmentalism was indeed everybody's issue, that only held true as long as everybody included people whose status was at least upper-middle class. What environmentalism did was to cut society *laterally*. Environmentalism, because it is oriented toward the status quo, had an inevitable appeal to people toward the top of the social ladder, and a negative appeal to those nearer the bottom. When environmentalists said "we already have enough," and "it's time to stop all this growth-for-growth's sake," they were very accurately representing their *own* position of economic security. But anyone who was further down the scale and was depending on future growth and progress to improve their lot would be instinctively opposed to the environmental doctrine. The basic flaw of environmentalism—and indeed of all the previous "environmental movements" in history—was beginning to emerge. At heart, environmentalism favors the affluent over the poor, the haves over the have-nots.

But this was not entirely obvious in 1970. What was most surprising at the point was the alacrity with which this supposedly liberal cause was adopted by "conservative" business leaders. Even environmentalists seemed somewhat surprised by this pattern, and were inevitably suspicious that the business establishment was only *pretending* to embrace environmentalism in order to subvert it. In fact, these fears were unfounded.

What emerged instead was a notable split personality among many business people—the executive who worried at the office all day about the costs of curbing pollution but found when he returned to his suburban home at night that environmentalism expressed his interests almost perfectly. Often it was the husband of the family who remained business-oriented while the wife became the strong environmentalist. Perhaps the classic example of this ambivalence is Walter Hickel, President Nixon's Secretary of the Interior and a self-made millionaire who almost wasn't confirmed by the Senate because of his views about the need to proceed with development in Alaska. After less than two years in Washington, Hickel make a complete conversion to environmentalism, and wrote a book worrying about how growth and prosperity were destroying the country. Few college radicals who had begun to swing the banner of ecology could have anticipated the tremendous fervor with which suburban America suddenly embraced environmentalism in the early 1970s. What had been assumed to be a rather radical cause suddenly had all the marking of a middle-of-the-road issue.

Who was against environmentalism then? Initially, blacks were one of the few groups heard expressing some reservations about the sudden turn in liberal thought. On Earth Day, 1970, when a group of California college students buried an automobile in order to symbolize their renunciation of materialism, the event was picketed by a group of black students, who said the resources, rather than being wasted in such a conspicuous fashion, should be put to work in improving the lot of the poor. (The event did indeed come perilously close to Veblen's description of conspicuous waste.)

This constant dissent of articulate blacks from the environmental agenda has been a running source of embarrassment to a movement that has tried desperately for over a decade to preserve the idea that it is a liberal crusade. As late as 1979, for example, Vernon Jordan, Director of the Urban League, was asked to attend a joint conference on urban and environmental affairs, intended to heal the breach in the liberal ranks. He responded with these remarks:

"Walk down Twelfth Street (in Washington, D.C.) and ask the proverbial man on the street what he thinks about the snail darter and you are likely to get the blankest look you ever experienced. Ask him what his thinks the basic urban environmental problem is, and he'll tell you jobs. I don't intend to raise the simple-minded equation of snail darters and jobs, but that does symbolize an implicit divergence of interests between some segments of the environmental movement and the bulk of black and urban people . . .

"[Environmentalists] will find in the black community absolute hostility to anything smacking of no-growth or limits-to-growth. Some people have been too cavalier in proposing policies to preserve the physical environment for themselves while other, poorer people pay the costs."

Bayard Rustin, the veteran civil-rights and labor leader has called environmentalists "self-righteous, elitist, neo-Malthusians who call for slow growth or no growth . . . (and who) would condemn the black underclass, the slum proletariat, and rural blacks, to permanent poverty." Thomas Sowell, the prominent California economist, has said: "Regulatory rules have impeded people who are climbing rather than people who are already at the top. There is a fundamental conflict between the affluent people, who can afford to engage in environmental struggles, and the poor . . . You don't see many black faces in the Sierra Club." It is probably some measure of the way in which black opinion tends to get submerged in the political arena when it does not support the liberal agenda that so little of this black opposition to environmentalism is ever visible in the press.

Labor unions have also been in the forefront of opposition to the environmental movement. By the early 70s, labor columnist Victor Reisel was repeating the joke about God telling Moses that before he parts the Red Sea He is first going to have to get permission from the Environmental Protection Agency. The bumper sticker "If You're Hungry and Out of Work, Eat an Environmentalist!" was originated by labor unions. Considering that many, many environmental campaigns have involved opposition to large-scale construction projects, power plants, highways, and factories that involve blue collar jobs, this is not surprising. Whenever enthusiastic college students go out to picket a nuclear plant they always find a group of hardhat construction workers ready to throw bricks at them. As one union official put it: "These environmentalists are a bunch of bloody elitists . . . [I]f it's 'no growth' they're advocating, then what they're really saying is: 'We've got enough for ourselves, but you stay down there.' "

The working-class, labor-union revolt against both environmentalism and the poor-oriented thrust of the Democratic liberal agenda finally made up the major factor in Ronald Reagan's 1980 Presidential majority, particularly in the Western part of the country. This revolt has often been called Populist, and I think the term is justified. Many of its roots go back to the original conservation movement of the early 1900s and the battles that were then fought about how the country's Western resources should be developed. In general, the neo-Populist revolt against environmentalism has been literally a quarrel between the haves and the have-nots, between the urban and the suburban liberal establishment intent on protecting its positions of privilege and the broad reaches of lower-middle-class and poor people, who feel that they do not yet have enough.

Nor does one have to be *absolutely* privileged in order to find environmentalism useful. It need only be a matter of relative privilege. I have often felt that the conversion to environmentalism occurs shortly after an urban, middle-class family finally purchases its first suburban home in, let us say, Maple Grove Acres. The family looks out the window at a beautiful field next door and exclaims, "At last, we're living in the country." Two months later, however, a nearly hysterical neighbor arrives with the bad news: "Do you know our beautiful field next door? Well, it's actually Maple Grove Acres II, and the builder is going before the planning board tomorrow night to get final approval on construction. We've got to go down and stop him." It is at this moment that an environmentalist is born. The problems of endangered species, overpopulation, and the deteriorating quality of life suddenly become startlingly real. It is time to stop development and start worrying about fragile ecosystems.

In 1976, Bernard Frieden, an MIT professor of urban studies, visited the San Francisco area with the intention of writing a book on how the surburbs were attempting to exclude blacks. After watching suburban environmentalism in action for two years, he came to a startling conclusion. The suburbs were no longer simply trying to exclude blacks, he said, they were trying to exclude *everybody*. Absurd environmental restrictions (such as requirements that new homes be built on stilts to protect migrating salamanders) were being written into zoning ordinances of hundreds of suburban towns. Their sole intent was to keep other people out. The old suburban game of exclusionary zoning was now being played at a much more sophisticated level. No longer were privacy and economic segregation the issue—now it was all being done under the guise of protecting nature. "The movement to stop suburban growth has done more than disrupt home building," wrote Frieden:

"In attempting to justify its position on growth, it has begun to spread a new ideology of elitism through the country's political life. This ideology has served many different uses, but with one underlying theme: it supplies a ready rationale for the defense of privilege."

The realization that affluent people can serve their own self-interest simply by preventing any more economic growth has been one of the most difficult to make. We ordinarily think of people serving their self-interest by making more money themselves, not by preventing others from doing the same. Veblen, facing the same problem in explaining the anti-industrial attitudes and opposition to progress among the wealthy plutocracy of this day, wrote: "When an explanation of this class conservatism is offered, it is commonly the invidious one that the wealthy class opposes innovation because it has a vested interest, of an unworthy sort, in maintaining the present conditions."

Instead, he argued, it was their insulation from economic stress that kept the elite from adjusting to the idea of further economic change:

"The leisure class is in great measure sheltered from the stress of those economic exigencies which prevail in any modern, highly organized industrial community. The exigencies of the struggle for the means of life are less exacting for this class than for any other; and as a consequence of this privileged position we should expect to find it one of the least responsive of the classes of society to the demands which the situation makes for a further growth of institutions and a readjustment to an altered industrial situation. The leisure class is the conservative class."

All this probably explains why, if environmentalists have been extremely efficient at turning up problems in an industrial society, they have also been ever-so-slightly inclined toward exaggerating them. Seeking to institutionalize the status quo has given upper-middle-class people a peculiar vested interest in the possibilities for impending disaster.

Writing in response to the 1973-74 Arab Oil Embargo, for example, environmentalists Paul and Anne Ehrlich told their audience:

"Unfortunately, there's very little you can do about the international situation, except to keep informed about it . . .

"[T]he obvious shakiness of the English economy might tend to stiffen your resistance to TV ads encouraging the purchase of English automobiles (where will parts come from if Great Britain's economy collapses?). Knowing that Kenyatta cannot last much longer might persuade you not to put off a long-anticipated visit to the game parks of Kenya."

And even though the Ehrlichs are talking about a complete breakdown of the world order, their tone belies any real concern:

"It would obviously be to everyone's advantage to work cooperatively in an attempt to ease the transition to a steady-state economy—especially advantageous for the middle class and the wealthy since they have much more to lose than the poor . . .

"You should . . . be taking steps to reduce your dependence on the services provided by our complex society and making arrangements to protect yourself and your family against the worst eventuality . . .

"The best choice is relatively complete independence from the system as a life-style . . . If you've had extensive camp cooking experience, you're way ahead of the game."

Perhaps the most perceptive criticism of these attitudes was written right at the dawn of the environmental era by Chicago newspaper columnist Jon Margolis. In an article entitled "Our Country 'Tis of Thee, Land of Ecology," published in *Esquire* in 1970, Margolis noted: "Searching for their hundred-fifty-year-old Vermont farmhouses, conservationists wonder how people can actually want to live in a new, $25,000 split-level in the suburbs, apparently never thinking that for most people the alternative is a three-room walk-up in the downtown smog. The suburbs are open to them, as Vermont to the more affluent, because of technology, because draining swamps and dirtying streams and damming rivers and polluting the air gave them high-paying jobs. Shouting about the environmental catastrophe, urging an end to growth, the conservationists are $20,000-a-year men telling all the $7,500-a-year men simply to stay where they are so we can all survive."

Writing in a similar vein about how prep-school boys were adjusting to the "era of limits," Nelson Aldrich, Jr., penned this prescient sentence about modern Doomsday attitudes: "Just discernible in this new Preppie idealism is a wish, barely disguised as a fear, that the era of economic growth may really be finished, and that a New Dark Age may be upon us."

It is this fervent *wish* for an environmental day of reckoning— that hope that some grand historical turning point has been reached where economic growth will be halted—that constitutes the secret of the upper-middle class's fervent embrace of the Doomsday mystique. If further progress will only lead to disaster, then perhaps the status quo will harden and remain forever.

In this kind of framework, the only disappointment occurs when Environmental Doomsday doesn't come.

Environmental Regulation: the ImMOBILization of Truth

By Gus Speth

In his defense of environmental regulations, the author rebuts many of the arguments of the opponents of current regulations. He focuses on the advertisements of the Mobil Corporation in his critique.

From an environmental perspective, the past decade reflects the American people and their system of government at their very finest. Faced with the increasingly likely prospect of leaving their children a legacy of silent springs, the American people called for action, and their government responded with imagination and creativity.

In a single sustained burst of legislation, almost without precedent in our history, machinery to reverse a century of environmental degradation was devised, perfected and set into motion. NEPA [National Environmental Policy Act], signed on the first day of the last decade, was quickly followed by important amendments to the Clean Air Act, the Occupational Safety and Health Act, the Resources Recovery Act, and establishment of EPA. Building on this foundation, Congress rapidly added the Federal Water Pollution Control Act, the Ocean Dumping Act, the Safe Drinking Water Act, a strengthened Federal Insecticide, Fungicide and Rodenticide Act, the Toxic Substances Control Act, the Resource Conservation and Recovery Act, the Noise Control Act, and the Quiet Communities Act.

I have no doubt whatsoever that future generations of Americans will look back upon this decade of environmental renaissance the way we look back upon similar creative bursts of legislation during the 1930's, for the New Deal, and 1960's for civil rights: as among democracy's finest hours.

Excerpted from "Environmental Regulation: The ImMOBILization of Truth," *Vital Speeches of the Day*, April 15, 1980, by permission of City News Publishing Co. Gus Speth was chairman of the President's Council on Environmental Quality when this speech was delivered at the Fifth National Conference of the Environmental Industry Council in Washington, D.C.

And there are other positive dimensions that must be cited.

I think it is very important that we have continued to make progress in the past few years, when energy and economic issues have competed mightily for public attention.

Despite these pressures, we have maintained the commitment to a clean, healthy environment for all of our citizens, and the [Carter] Administration's legislative program now before Congress—which includes such vital measures as the Alaska Lands Bill, the "superfund" bill to pay for the cleanup of abandoned hazardous waste sites, a new plan for nuclear waste management, proposals to increase funding for energy conservation and the development of solar and other renewable energy sources, and reform of federal water resource development—indicates a continuing environmental priority. It is important that Congress move forward with these measures.

Another positive dimension involves the actions of individuals and thousands of private groups and businesses which have contributed so greatly to protecting the environment. Much of the progress we have made so far would not have been possible without a strong pollution control industry.

But even as we rejoice in these positive dimensions, our celebration is shadowed to some degree by contrary evidence.

One of the negative dimensions we face is psychological. It stems from the fact that too often some of us exhibit a truncated attention span. Causes, ideas, attitudes have, it appears, a short half-life, with today's compelling cause tarnished into tomorrow's discarded fashion.

Those who argue against continuing the environmental momentum of the 1970's have failed to grasp the full severity and dimensions of the environmental problems that continue to face us. The issues that persist today are not just questions of esthetics, or comfort, or an idealized notion of "the good life"; they are clear threats to the health and welfare of the American people. They simply cannot be put aside until a time when it is more convenient to focus on them.

We have gained success in combating gross threats to our air and water only to discover whole new phalanxes of subtle menaces, whose danger and obstinacy often vary in inverse proportion to their ability to be quickly and easily understood. Thus, we look upon the clarifying water and purified air with satisfaction while, stealthily, four square miles of our most productive farm land are each day consumed by concrete and asphalt and lost from agriculture. Fish are returning to waters they long ago fled, but we are finding their flesh often contains significant amounts of toxic chemicals. Sulfur dioxide pollution is now a major heath problem in only a few areas, but partly because we are air-mailing sulfur oxides to places far away where it falls as acid rain.

There are a few who directly attack our environmental commitment, but a growing number have adopted the strategy of undermining that commitment indirectly. At first the strategy took the form of a refreshing concern for the working man and woman. In a kind of perversion of the Phillips curve once vainly used to explain inflation, the argument seemed to run that unemployment went up as smog and oil slicks went down. But that argument was permitted to die a quiet death when the National Academy of Sciences estimated that the nation's effort to clean up the environment actually accounted for about 680,000 jobs, 30 new jobs for every one eliminated due to decisions by manufacturing firms and others that resulted from environmental requirements. A subsequent study by Data Resources, Inc. showed that air and water pollution controls will stimulate employment during the entire 16 year period from 1970 to 1986.

The Negative strategy then moved to the issue of inflation. This has now been looked into as well, and it has been found that between 1979 and 1986, federal environmental regulations will add between one- and two-tenths of one percentage point to the annual inflation rate. For 1980, existing federal environmental regulation is predicted to add only one tenth of a percentage point to the rate at which prices increase—a rate that should continue in the period 1984 to 1986.

The first point to note is that, even by standard economic measures, the inflationary impact of environmental programs is quite minor. Moreover, any realistic modification of federal environmental regulations would produce no significant reduction in the overall Consumer Price Index. If the inflationary impact of these requirements could be reduced by a fourth—a substantial relaxation—the CPI's increase would be restrained by less than 0.05 percent: the net effect of even draconian measures could be the difference between a 7 percent and a 7.05 percent increase in the CPI. So we must look elsewhere than environmental regulations for the sources of inflation, and for the proper targets of our anti-inflation efforts.

Following the bankruptcy of these contentions, we have been told and told, and then told again, that environmental regulation is merely one aspect of an already over-regulated society, a society forced to divert increasingly scarce resources and managerial talent from productive and innovative ends. Indeed, some major corporations have undertaken rather large campaigns to convince the American people that government regulation is out of control.

In response, I would simply point out that, in light of the continuing revelations of corporate neglect or worse, much of the current protestation against government regulation rings awfully hollow. Virtually every environmental regulation, for example, has its genesis in some problem, like Love Canal or Kepone or PCB's, that threatened the public and finally brought a legitimate public demand for government action. Regulation is not going to go away until the problems do. The way we regulate can *and must* be improved, but let us face the fact that a continued high level of government regulatory activity is *essential* to national goals of paramount importance—to controlling cancer and protecting health, to preventing consumer fraud and deception, to cleaning up air and water pollution, to reducing oil imports and conserving energy, to protecting us from improperly sited or mismanaged nuclear power facilities—the list, obviously, is very long.

Some critics of government regulation do rely on factual presentations, rather than rhetorical overkill, to make their case. For example, Clifford P. Hardin, former Agriculture Secretary and now Vice Chairman of the Board of Ralston Purina Company, put it this way:

> . . .my concern, and that of most people who share my concern, is not with the idea of regulation, or even with the central purpose of most regulatory legislation. Some regulation is a must and most of us support it. Our concern is rather with such things as overlapping and duplication in requests for information often in different formats; directly conflicting rules from separate agencies; rules that are out of date, but which are not removed; and, finally and perhaps most importantly, the growing obsession with minutia—items that have little, if anything to do with protecting the consumer, environment, the safety and welfare of employees, or the growth of competitors.

I could not agree more, and this Administration could not agree more, with Mr. Hardin's sentiments. No function of government, and that definitely includes the regulatory function, should be transformed into a kind of sacred cow, immune from critical examination.

But, unlike Mr. Hardin, all critics are not responsible.

Some are merely using regulatory reform as a kind of shibboleth masking their real motivation, which is to pull the teeth from health and environmental programs. These critics hide their intentions under a flourish of slick public relations sophistries which, for lack of a better word, I might call the imMOBILization of truth.

Mobil, of course, is the company that has spent hundreds of thousands, if not millions, of dollars over the past few years on a rather strident advertising campaign on the OpEd pages of major national newspapers and magazines. Some of the ads give away their true nature by taking the form of fables; others are just as mythical and remote from reality. One such ad attacked government regulators as "new reactionaries," and accused government of trying to "turn back the clock to the detriment of today's standard of living." If I had been writing a headline for that particular ad, my first thought would have been: "Bring Back the Robber Barons."

Since the imMOBILizers are so misleading, I would like to look for a moment at a few of their favorite debating points.

The first is what I call *Zen analysis.* We all know what is purported to be the way Zen Buddhists sharpen their powers of concentration. First you think of the sound of two hands clapping and then you think of the sound of one hand clapping. It is, I imagine, a very soft sound, somewhat like the quality of reasoning employed by those who subject health, safety, and environmental regulation to a form of one-handed analysis that discovers that, lo and behold, these activities entail a cost.

Of course environmental quality costs money. The imMOBILizers want us to overlook the fact that the cost of environmental quality is invariably exceeded by the cost of environmental degradation, and that it is the general public who pays the latter, while the former involves some participation by those who would prefer to continue using America the beautiful as a kind of limitless septic field.

For those of us who would rather hear the sound of both hands clapping, I refer you to the *Tenth Annual Report of the Council on Environmental Quality,* and particularly to Chapter 12, which deals with economics.

The data in this chapter, which are objective and which look at every aspect of *both* cost and benefit, including the relevance of dollar yardsticks in assessing quality, conclude:

According to a study done for CEQ the annual benefits realized in 1978 from measured improvements in air quality since 1970 could be reasonably valued at $21.4 billion.

The *Report* also points out that

. . .the total annual benefits to be enjoyed by 1985 as a result of the nation's water pollution control legislation. . .will amount to about $12 billion per year . . .

In my estimation, those figures are worth two hands clapping any day.

The second form of sophistry employed by the factual im-MOBILizers involves careful selection of *targets of opportunity*. This involves telling us in great detail about some regulatory excess, and there are some, or about a particular form of regulation that is made to appear unnecessarily burdensome. What never gets mentioned by this form of imMOBILization is that a great deal of regulation, particularly economic regulation, has come into being because business interests of various kinds *wanted* it or found that it advanced their own goals.

Let me just quote from some remarks by Carol Foreman, Assistant Secretary of Agriculture for Food and Consumer Services. When asked about regulation, she said, "Economic regulation, as practiced by the ICC, and the CAB until recently, and certainly the Securities and Exchange Commission, tends to be heavily supported by industry. Certainly the Packer and Stockyard Administration is heavily supported by industry. Some of that economic regulation tends to raise prices and limit markets, which is exactly what it was intended to do, and the businesses that are regulated love it." And then she added, "Businessmen generally say health and safety regulations are terrible. They've opposed them. And yet my experience in meat inspection is if somebody were to propose to eliminate meat and poultry inspection, the regulated industries would be the first ones to try to prevent that because we protect them from their competitors who might cheat."

Another favorite way to imMOBILize the truth involves *Scapegoatery*. Thus, when U.S. Steel decides to close 16 plants in eight states, this action is not portrayed as what is bound to happen from time to time in a truly competitive system, or that economic history is largely the pageant of firms that decline and firms that advance, or that disinvestment in the uneconomic is just as important to healthy growth as investment in the economic. Instead, the experience of U.S. Steel is perverted into becoming a horrible example of what happens when government regulation requires environmental protection, or permits foreign competition. What is not stated is that Japanese steel, the major competitor, is produced under environmental protection restrictions that are more stringent than our own, or that trade barriers, high or low, are forms of government regulation.

If the critics really want to reduce the burden of government regulation, they must take steps to eliminate the situations that create the need for regulation. That, it seems to me, is the enlightened response to a changing society. And those companies that are increasingly taking this approach deserve our praise, support and thanks. With this approach, we will be well on our way to an age when, in the words of one editorial writer, we will fit our desires to the environment, and no longer ruin the environment to suit our desires.

The Gold in Rules

By Ruth Ruttenberg

Rather than hurting American industry, environmental regulations have provided the incentive for a profitable reevaluation of production techniques in a number of cases.

It's unpopular, if not politically suicidal nowadays, to be *in favor of* regulation. Regulation is widely blamed for reducing national productivity—putting a drain on industry resources and strangling innovation. Riding this antiregulatory tide, the Reagan administration has taken aim at dozens of environmental and health regulations, claiming that easing them will be good for business and good for the economy.

But one doesn't have to look farther than the annual reports of the *Fortune* 500 to raise serious questions about this view of regulation. There's a wealth of data in corporate annual reports and elsewhere that regulation—by spawning alternatives to business as usual—has been a major stimulus for new markets, new jobs and basic technological innovation.

Take a simple example from an industry that has historically been beset by pollution problems—the coal industry. When shipping coal by rail across the country, Conoco's trains used to leave a trail of coal dust behind them. Last year, the company began using a new spray device that keeps coal dust out of the environment. It also saves an estimated 80 tons of coal per trainload.

The chemical industry said there was no alternative to the fluorocarbon aerosol spray in the mid 1970's. Then American Cyanamid's Miss Breck company pioneered a non-fluorocarbon propellant. The day after the fluorocarbon ban went into effect, the country had a new pump spray that was free of fluorocarbons and that was also cheaper than aerosol cans.

Excerpted from article in *Environmental Action,* October 1981, by permission of Environmental Action, Inc., 1346 Connecticut Avenue, N.W., Washington, D.C., a political lobbying group. Ruth Ruttenberg is an associate in the economic consulting firm of Ruttenberg, Friedman, Kilgallon, Gutchess & Associates and an assistant professor at Howard University.

And take the electroplating industry. Less than two years ago, the Environmental Protection Agency (EPA) proposed a pollution regulation that it feared could put 20 percent of all electroplating companies out of business—the worst economic impact ever anticipated by any EPA regulation on a single industry. However, since that regulation, which limited the amount of toxic waste electroplating firms could dump into municipal waterworks, went into effect, electroplating firms that adopted pollution control technology have both met the standard and increased profits. One firm in Milwaukee found that the $30,000 capital cost of waste monitoring and recycling equipment would be paid for in two and a half years because, by eliminating the toxic waste, the company saves water and raw materials. For instance, recycling waste chrome reduced chrome purchases by 90 percent, and the company's water consumption fell from 14,000 gallons to 200 gallons per day.

Although highly visible corporate publicity bemoans the burden of environmental regulation, internal corporate literature sings the praises of new pollution control products and processes developed in response to regulation.

After all, pollution control is one of American industry's fastest growing markets. Between 1972 and 1976, sales of pollution control equipment grew 16 to 22 percent annually, while manufacturing generally grew only about nine percent, according to a study commissioned by EPA. In 1977, pollution control sales totalled $1.7 billion. Analysts now project they will reach to $3.5 billion by 1983, but the numbers may well be considerably larger. This boom has created business for a number of major corporations.

Union Carbide's 1978 annual report exclaimed proudly that "increasing application of mandatory government standards has significantly increased air pollution control markets during the last five years." By its own accounts, Union Carbide isn't a loser because of regulation; it's a winner, and it plans to increase its gains by entering the air pollution control field as well.

Stauffer Chemical, in its 1979 annual report, also looked at the problem of government regulation and found that over the long term opportunities could be more important than constraints. Stauffer cited new processes for "desulfurization of coal, sulfur dioxide abatement, extraction of metals from waste streams, fermentation technology and new methods of food preservation and production."

In its 1980 report, Stauffer discussed further ventures into such technologies as tanktruck cleaning, sulfur dioxide abatement, waste recycling and treatment, incineration and scrubbing. Recognizing the market for this technology, Stauffer said, "We hope to apply this expertise to new environmental compliance problems in the chemical, electric power, petroleum, cement and metal industries."

Despite this overwhelming evidence, popular antiregulation literature paints a grim picture of pollution control. Like the op-ed advertisements brought to you by Mobil tirading against "government red tape," this literature takes an oversimplified view of pollution control—as a kind of safety device tacked onto existing technology, increasing costs and retarding output.

Technological innovation, however, often takes on a life of its own, producing inventions that transcend the original motivations for producing cleaner or safer processes. As pollution control has become an accepted part of routine industrial design, products continue to be developed that make pollution monitoring cheaper and more efficient. Some of these cost savings may come as ideas directly from the shop floor, some from machine retooling and others from continued research and development or better planning and scheduling.

For example, Battelle Institute's Northwest Laboratories developed an entirely new process to reduce or even eliminate sulfur emissions in lead and zinc production. And American Cyanamid developed for the steel industry a new carbide-based desulfurization agent to reduce sulfur emissions in the air. Spurred by the ready market just for this product, Cyanamid has doubled its manufacturing capacity for calcium carbide.

In all these cases, new jobs have been created along with these new technologies. While the currently fashionable conservative calculations count these products and technologies as costs, it is hard to see why these are less legitimate benefits and contributors to the gross national product than, say designer jeans.

Even if some pollution control technology is good "merely" for controlling pollution, there are countless examples of other benefits. Companies often find that solutions to environmental problems lead them to develop simple and more efficient production processes. A good example is vinyl chloride production. Industry warned that proposed regulation could lead to the demise of the entire vinyl chloride industry, with losses of $65 to $90 billion to the national economy. Yet less than 18 months after the occupational safety regulations limiting worker exposure to vinyl chloride went into effect, over 90 percent of the firms had complied. Regulations led this industry to finetune a wide array of its technical processes.

Changes as simple as tightening pipe flanges and permanently welding pipes together reduced leaks and led to increased output. A newly developed, computerized polyvinyl chloride (PVC) reactor vessel increased manufacturing efficiency while at the same time reducing worker exposure.

Since environmental standards were introduced, the vinyl chloride industry has had an impressive growth record. Demand for the chemical more than doubled between 1970 and 1978, and expanded plant capacity has led to the creation of about 2,000 jobs. Growth in the vinyl chloride industry (17.5 percent) outstripped the average growth from U.S. manufacturing during the years 1975 to 1978, which was only about 7.2 percent.

Vinyl chloride companies are by no means the only ones whose compliance with environmental regulations was accompanied by growth and improvements in productivity. Greater productivity can result from such simple things as improved maintenance of equipment or from radical departures from old production procedures.

Cyprus Mines, a copper company, has developed a technique to bypass the most hazardous step in the smelting process. To eliminate pollution arising during conventional smelting operations, the subsidiary of Occidental Petroleum developed a new process to turn copper ore directly into wire bars. According to *Metals Week,* the new process cuts capital and operating costs in half.

Likewise, the steel industry developed methods to eliminate major environmental and health hazards by eliminating coke ovens in some of its production processes—and at the same time eliminated an expensive procedure.

The success that companies have had in turning their pollution problems into boons of one kind or another is the brighter side of regulating environmental hazards. There are ready markets for the new technologies like those dealing with hazardous waste disposal, and sometimes companies even sell their hazard abatement techniques to one another. In this respect, however, critics have warned about the possible growth of a "pollution-industrial complex"—a vicious cycle in which industry is seen to perpetuate the market for solutions to pollution by continuing to pollute.

This scenario may not yet be happening, but the potential does exist for such an unhealthy incentive system in which one hand washes the other. DuPont sells air pollution devices to 70 textile and nitric acid plants. General Motors sells its catalytic converters to American Motors. Alcoa is a world leader in the development, use and licensing of emission control units for aluminum plants. Exxon and Shell sell chemical products that clean up oil spills.

On the brighter side, stringent environmental restrictions have spawned a host of substitute products. The largest and fastest growing market for these could well be the market for asbestos substitutes. Like polyvinyl chloride, asbestos has numerous applications in industrial and consumer products. So when the government tried to regulate asbestos, a carcinogen, the industry reacted with loud dismay.

Yet American industrial ingenuity has risen to the occasion. A government sponsored workshop held in July 1980 on the topic had no less than 645 registrants, and the parade of new products and processes was no less impressive. Monsanto now has a new fire retardent called Phos-Chek to replace asbestos fireproofing, while Kennecott's new Fiberfrax is used for everything from protective clothing to insulation. For its part, DuPont has "Nomex" fiber and paper products. Regulation has improved the market for all.

Industry has often claimed that pollution control and hazard abatement consume not only unnecessary dollars but also extravagant amounts of energy. Not so.

Look at General Motors (GM). When the big automaker was forced to control pollution from its factories, its engineers designed powerhouse boilers that monitor emissions and set air to fuel ratios. Not only was the air workers breathed much cleaner, but the machines' fuel efficiency was improved. The company also modified filtration systems to help save money on heating bills. And currently, GM is investigating ways to use methane gas from municipal landfills to supplement natural gas.

And the large Swedish corporation Helsingborgs Atervinnings AB has developed a method to transform selected industrial waste into highly combustible pellets with the same energy value as coal. The firm claims that roughly 20 percent of the waste from Swedish industry, retail shops and households—well over a million tons a year—could be converted into these pellets, saving the country some half million tons of oil every year.

As corporations have learned to comply with regulations, health and safety considerations have become built-in criteria for judging new industrial design systems—just as energy efficiency has become a fact of life in many industries.

In light of all this, it's surprising that so many policy makers simply accept the assumption that regulation is nothing but a drag on productivity. There are certainly cases where regulation—especially in the short term—increases costs, and these must be justified in terms of the benefits to the health of the workforce and to the larger public. But there are innumerable cases in which regulation spawns far-flung benefits—and profits.

Improving workplace safety and health, for some firms, is an expensive process requiring outlays for new and improved plants and equipment. Of course, the job isn't easy to accomplish or afford. But in an increasing number of cases, regulation can force the development of new technology that simultaneously promotes the health of workers and the health of the industrial economy.

Why Alaska Is Case-in-Point of "No Growth" Federal Energy Policy

This article catalogs the frustration of Alaska's Senator Stevens with the ability of environmentalists to slow the development of his state's resources.

Spearheaded by what Senator Ted Stevens (R-Alaska) calls, "The insatiable appetite of the extreme environmentalists," Alaska is becoming classic proof that a State cannot be run intelligently by Federal regulation fulminating out of Washington, D.C.

He can recite so many examples, says Stevens. "It's hard to know where to begin."

- Item: "A guy wanted to run a packtrain north to the other side of Mt. McKinley (over Federal Park preserve.) The Park superintendent refused him a permit because "horse droppings would pollute the park's natural environment."
- Item: Alaskans wanted to rejuvenate the salmon stocks that had been depleted by foreign fishing in several streams in the Rich Kenai National Moose range. A Park superintendent there denied the permit, said it "would not be compatible with the Park's purpose."
- Item: In Kodiak, where he claims the fishery products growth potential "is tremendous," Alaskans want to build a hydroelectric project on Terror Lake. (Kodiak already is the second largest fish-handling port in the United States.) Demand for power there already is huge. The manager of the bear range there stopped the project because he found two old denning areas there. Over time, he argued, the dam would have flooded them out.(The number of lakes in that area fluctuates annually, depending on the amount of snow run-off.) Snorts Stevens, "More than 500 bears are around there. They don't mate during hibernation

Excerpted from *Government Executive,* August 1980, with permission from Executive Publications Inc.

which is when the run-off occurs. And they don't mate very well under water. And anyway, I don't think it's too much to ask that those two couples find someplace else to make love."

In sum, he says, after gaining State-hood, "Alaskans today are, as a whole, at the brink of frustration. We have conceded and conceded to get along with the Feds and still survive as a State—only to find out that despite those concessions, their demands increase with each new Congress."

A Federal State?

The latest proposal circulating Capitol Hill declares the Alaskan tundra a "wetland"—which would put land usage decisions for virtually the whole State under the jurisdiction of the Army Corps of Engineers. If that came to pass, it could be almost the final "renege" on the 1959 agreement under which the Federal Government promised to turn over to State control—within five years—105 million acres of Alaskan lands. To date, the State has been granted less than half that much. Further, more than 180 million acres, nearly 50 percent of the State's total land mass, already has been set aside as wilderness preserve and similar Federal single-use areas.

In the near term, this is coming down hardest on Alaska's ability to develop its potentially awesome oil, gas and mineral resource potential. Moreover, because of the "gerrymandered" way these Federal preserves have been set aside, they make extremely difficult if not impossible, economically, investor-developer access to what lands are still open.

"There is no question," says Stevens, "we are victims of the 'no-growth' syndrome" of people in the lower 48 who are second and third generation offspring of very rich people "who feel they have to apologize for their great wealth and the way it was acquired. They seem to believe Alaska's potential must not be realized."

Examples of the result abound. Among them:

- It takes something like 160 permits, according to Stevens, just to drill an exploratory oil well. The Alaskan oil pipeline from Prudhoe Bay—where the oil wells are on State-owned land—required 4000 permits to get built. Cost per dry well to drill: approximately $20-40 million.
- In 1960, pioneered by a group of Fairbanks Women's Garden Clubs, nine million acres of Arctic Wildlife Range (next to Prudhoe Bay) was set aside as a wilderness preserve but provid-

ing that oil and gas exploration could take place after the Federal Fish and Wildlife Service drew up a development plan that would make sure the natural environment was well protected. That plan has never been drawn up. Both the National Geological Survey people and Shell Oil Company, for one, estimate there is probably enough commercially extractable oil under the Federal lands adjoining Prudhoe Bay to replace all U.S. foreign oil imports, at current rates, for 10 years. Further, says one Atlantic Richfield executive, in all of the Alaskan land mass (about 20 percent of the U.S. total) "oil and gas development would most likely require less than one percent of the State's total land area."

- Alaska's outer continental shelf (OCS), which Stevens says is 70 percent of the Nation's total, could be producing four million more barrels of oil a day right now, "reducing our dependence on foreign oil a full 50 percent," points out one Shell executive. That is, it could if the Department of the Interior (DOI) had gone ahead with the exploration leasing schedule it announced in 1975 it was "accelerating."

Carter Lock-Up

"Over-zealous environmentalists, " growls one staffer on the Congressional Select Committee on the OCS, "already have delayed that leasing schedule by five years and cut the original plan (on what acreage would be offered for sale) by at least half. Worse than that, they've frozen out the lands where the oil companies believe there is oil and gas and are offering up those places where somebody only thinks there might be."

Adds Stevens, "We (in Alaska) have never had any problem with the conservation movement. We've worked very hard not to make these (resource and environmental abuse) mistakes. Our problem is with the extremist environmentalists."

No Public Clout

And that's why the State's small population is a liability. In the political arena, where this battle is really being fought and where emotion is more powerful than common sense, a total vote power that adds up in Washington only to that of a fair-sized city in New York or California doesn't amount to much. Says a pragmatic Ted Stevens, "Why should a Congressman (from the "lower 48," as they call the rest of the Nation in Alaska) take on a group that's only 4-5 percent of their own constituents for our benefit?"

Logic, of course, questions strongly whether any oil company really constitutes an environmental threat to Alaska. Apart from the over-regulation, notes one ARCO (Atlantic Richfield) executive, "We (the industry) have been up there for 12 years on the north slope and proven we can operate on an environmentally sound basis."

More to the point, "We've put $8-9 billion into the pipeline up there, more than $4 billion to develop the (Prudhoe Bay) reservoir. We'll spend another $14 billion before the field is fully developed. And if we're ever allowed to go after the natural gas up there, we could spend $20-plus billion for the gas pipeline plus $3-4 billion for the field conditioning plant plus the cost of drilling the wells.

"That's a huge investment. If we screw up the environment, we're out of business. If anyone thinks we're going to take (environmental) short cuts to save two bits, they're crazy. People investing those kinds of dollars just are not going to take short cuts."

Unfortunately, he also points out, "These things are decided 110 percent on emotion. It's supposed to be best use of the Public lands for the benefit of the most people. So far, it's been, instead, what's good not for the people but for the wildlife."

Adds one Alaskan State official, "So far the Feds have operated on the basis of land grants for wildlife, not people."

Environmental protection and resource development industrially are not mutually contradictory goals, notes Stevens. But in the final analysis, what may swing Alaska away from a "life by Federal permit" into controlling more of its own destiny will be citizens in "the lower 48" finding out Alaska has literally billions in energy, mineral and other resources Washington, D.C. won't let them touch.

A Simpler Path to a Cleaner Environment (Section 1*)

By Tom Alexander

The author argues that present regulatory policies are inefficient, costly, and often do not achieve their objectives.

Environmentalism emerged in the Seventies as virtually a religious movement with overwhelming political appeal. An unprecedented succession of powerful and sweeping statutes resulted. These laws produced some gratifying gains, notably a visible, measurable reduction in air pollution in many areas and the reappearance in some of our greatest rivers and lakes of fish and shellfish species that had been missing for decades.

But in the main, the most ambitious statutes have proved grandiose failures. Over half the population of the U.S. lives in areas that still violate the national air-pollution health standards, for example, and some of these regions may never comply. Some of the acts have produced environmental ills worse than the ones they addressed. The programs have been staggeringly expensive for the amount of cleanup achieved. Therein lies a special irony, for the rallying concept that produced these laws was "ecology"—the awareness of the connectedness of things. Far from perceiving any connection with economics, the prophets of ecology were virtuously disdainful of the subject.

With the Clean Air Act and portions of the Clean Water Act up for reconsideration, Congress has a ready-made opportunity for reform. It can legislate new approaches to deal with baffling pollution problems ignored or exacerbated by present statutes, and in the

* "A Simpler Path to a Cleaner Environment," Section 2, begins on page 383.
Tom Alexander is a member of the board of editors of *Fortune* magazine.

process strike a blow for economic efficiency. Lobbying groups are already weighing in with proposals. The air act, the most complex and expensive of the statutes, is the target for brigades of spokesmen from the electric utilities, trade associations, and the coal, chemical, oil, steel, automotive, and paper industries—all trying to roll back some of the act's most onerous provisions.

Opposing them are coalitions of environmentalists vowing to defend the act against being gutted, either by industry or the Reagan Administration. If anything, the environmentalists want new legislation to address pollution problems that were earlier overlooked. The chief congressional overlords flatly say they will oppose any disemboweling initiatives.

Industry for the most part denies that it has in mind anything like a gutting of the act; "fine-tuning" is the operative phrase. Corporations, after all, have a stake in bringing more constancy and predictability to the ever changing world of pollution control. So, the outlook right now is for a gradual coalescence of Washington opinion that will leave the law largely intact. If that happens, a great chance for innovative approaches to pollution control, some of which have been adopted on a limited scale in recent years, will have been missed. These approaches could deliver far more clean air per abatement dollar, even though their widespread adoption might cause some more of the temporary disruption that executives loathe.

A Spirit of Emergency

The present approaches, both for air and water pollution, virtually guarantee disappointing results and high costs. The clean air and water statutes of the Seventies, enacted in an atmosphere of emergency, were actually descendants of older federal, state, and local pollution laws. As such they inherited a local outlook and a preoccupation with a limited number of pervasive pollutants. In the case of water, interest centered on coliform bacteria and decaying organic matter that depleted the oxygen supply and thus suffocated fish life. In the air, the focus was sulfur dioxide, soot, hydrocarbons, carbon monoxide, ozone, oxides of nitrogen, and, later, lead.

The conventional toxicology of the time assumed that most pollutants had to reach a "threshold" level before adversely affecting health. The Clean Air Act, whose control stategy is based on this premise, directed the government's hapless new Environmental Protection Agency to determine quickly the common air pollutants. On the basis of these levels, the agency was further instructed to set ambient-air-quality standards that would protect human health with an adequate margin of safety and with regard for costs.

The Elusive Threshold

There were several problems with this line of logic. In the first place, no one knew—or yet knows—what the actual threshold levels for health damage from the common air pollutants really are. For some pollutants it may be considerably higher than the figure picked by the authorities, while for other pollutants or for some victims there may be no threshold at all; any concentration above zero may be hazardous.

Secondly, the act of controlling pollution concentrations in one locality has often had the effect of making them worse somewhere else. For example, the concentration of sulfur dioxide in the atmosphere of cities is about 20 percent lower than it was a decade ago. But to achieve this reduction in ground-level pollution outside the plant gate, many companies have built new plants in the countryside or have erected tall smokestacks to disperse the pollutants.

So, instead of settling out quickly, sulfur dioxide has been transported over great distances. While in transit, both sulfur dioxide and nitrogen dioxide—another common pollutant—react with moisture and other components of the atmosphere to form infinitesimal particles of sulfate or nitrate. The first indication of this was the discovery of "acid rain," which has apparently wiped out the fish life in many lakes of the northeastern U.S. and parts of Canada, and which may be damaging forests and contaminating groundwater supplies.

Most authorities now believe that sulfur dioxide is less of a health hazard than the fine particles of sulfates. So, while nearly every area of the country now meets the national ambient-air standards for sulfur dioxide, the goal of protecting human health is far from being achieved. With the national emphasis on converting oil-burning facilities to coal, predictions are that the total atmospheric burden of both sulfates and nitrates will increase by the 1990s.

The same "long-range transport" phenomenon involves several other air pollutants and seems virtually immune to present control strategies. The national standard for ozone, a byproduct of photochemical smog that is linked with respiratory ailments, is sporadically violated along the entire Eastern seaboard from Washington to Maine, and realistically there is probably little that can be done about it. Because of the ozone that drifts in from New York City, for example, portions of Connecticut would continue to be in violation of the standard even if every automobile in Connecticut were banished.

Another pollution problem that evades the conventional approach is the steady accumulation of carbon dioxide gas in the world's atmosphere, mainly as a result of burning fossil fuel. The worry is that the accumulation may cause climate changes, perhaps by the early years of the next century. A report by the Department of Energy says that carbon dioxide is "probably the most important environmental issue facing mankind." Similar global effects are predicted for emissions of chlorofluorocarbon gases such as the Freon used in aerosol cans and refrigerators. These are nontoxic, but are believed to damage the stratospheric ozone layer that filters out the sun's cancer-causing ultraviolet rays.

Another drawback of the present approach is that it fails to deal with most of the 40-odd "hazardous" air pollutants that have caused mounting concerns in recent years, most of which are not regulated at all, and some of which—arsenic and acrylonitrile, for example—are believed to be carcinogens. While the matter is still controversial, there's widespread belief that no such thing as a threshold dose exists for carcinogens: they pose some degree of risk at *any* concentration. So, to write a standard protecting human health, as the law requires, could mean a zero-emissions policy wiping out a considerable number of industries. Neither the EPA nor most of its political gadflies have yet shown themselves prepared to go that far.

Not So Swimmable

The war against water pollution has been a somewhat similar story: perfectionist standards that have proved unattainable. In the Clean Water Act, Congress set as a goal the "elimination of discharge" of all pollutants and the attainment of fishable, swimmable conditions in all the nation's waterways. The strategy required installing the "best available control technology" to prevent industrial discharges, and Washington granted large federal subsidies to municipalities to build advanced sewage-treatment plants.

By now, about 90 percent of industries and 37 percent of municipalities are in compliance, but the nation is far from its fishable, swimmable goal. While there have been notable improvements in some rivers, the President's Council on Environmental Quality notes that the "quality of the nation's surface water has not changed much in the last five years." Most of the uncontrolled pollution comes from "non-point" sources, namely, the runoff of contaminated water from fields and streets. Some comes from those fancy new municipal treatment plants, many of which aren't working very well.

The Clean Water Act has also created problems more serious than the ones it addressed. Forced to withhold pollutants from water courses, industries have impounded them in thousands of pits, ponds and lagoons. These pollutants have often percolated downward through the earth to contaminate the groundwater. Similarly, immense volumes of sewage sludge produced by those secondary municipal treatment plants—much of it containing heavy metals and other toxic ingredients—have wound up being dumped on land or in the ocean. So new laws such as the Resource Recovery and Conservation Act and the Marine Protection, Research, and Sanctuaries Act have been enacted to regulate or halt these practices.

Forever Leakproof

What the laws do not make clear, however, is what exactly is to be done with the stuff. One trouble is that no one knows how to create an impoundment that will remain leakproof through all eternity, as would be necessary with many toxic wastes. It is conceivable that the best thing would be to let some of them be carried away to sea by rivers.

While failing to deliver on their promises, the existing approaches to pollution control have also hobbled the economy. It is true that government has come a long way in the last decade from viewing economic growth as something like crabgrass—automatic and pestilential—to perceiving it as something like a fruitful but frail tomato vine. Weighing down that slender plant is a growing burden of pollution-abatement outlays. Total expenditures by industry, consumers, and government, including what companies would have spent even in the absence of regulations, amounted to about $48.5 billion in 1979, according to the Commerce Department. That represented a 29 percent increase, in constant dollars, from total outlays seven years earlier.

And there's no end in sight. The Council on Environmental Quality, using roughly comparable definitions, estimates that, assuming no new laws, cumulative costs will come to $735 billion between 1979 and 1988—again, in 1979 dollars. New laws addressing such problems as acid rain and carbon dioxide could send the bill even higher. While virtually the entire government now agonizes over how to cut federal expenditures and taxes, little attention has been paid to these expenditures, which, after all, amount to a form of taxation that hits directly at the "supply side."

There's considerable debate as to just how serious the impact is. A study by Data Resources Inc. figures that pollution-abatement regulations add about two-tenths of a percentage point to the inflation rate. They also increase unemployment by two- to four-tenths of a percentage point, the study says, and cause imports to rise somewhat.

The High Cost of Hassle

But Barry Bosworth—former director of the Council on Wage and Price Stability—contends that the inflationary effect alone is twice as high. Bosworth points out that even though people are already compensated—in the form of a cleaner environment—for the higher prices they pay because of regulations, they nevertheless demand higher wages to offset the price increases.

Hidden from these figures are the indirect costs stemming from the general bureaucratic hassle of complying with regulations. John Quarles, a former deputy administrator of EPA, argues that these costs "have a more serious effect on the economy than the direct cost burden." Quarles has now joined the National Environmental Development Association, a joint industry-labor group, and heads a task force formulating proposed changes in the Clean Air Act. He puts most of the blame for regulatory delay on Congress's flood of legislated requirements, which have swamped the EPA's ability to scrutinize applications and issue all the permits it is supposed to. Says Quarles: "People in industry say, "Look, we'll spend any amount of money to put in any degree of control, if you'll just simplify the procedures so that we can go ahead and grow."

Needed: A Booming Economy

In a new collection of studies for Resources for the Future, economist Robert Haveman of the University of Wisconsin estimates that the combined direct and indirect effect of the regulations has probably been a slowdown of between 8 percent and 12 percent in national productivity growth. Another way of looking at things is to consider that the direct 1979 outlay of $48.5 billion, mostly by business, is equal to 38 percent of manufacturers' after-tax profits. It is fair to ask how much larger the investment in productive new facilities would have been if these expenditures had been smaller.

If business had more funds to invest, the result would not only be cheaper goods but a cleaner environment. George D. Carpenter, manager of air conservation for Procter & Gamble, puts it this way: "A lot of us are becoming convinced that we've been on the totally wrong path for the last couple of years. We've put all these barriers in the way of investing in urban areas, so we have this terribly anti-quated industrial plant that needs to be replaced or modernized. The best thing that could happen would be to have an absolutely boom-ing economy in those areas that would force out of business the older plants that could no longer compete for markets or labor. When you do that, the new plants are going to emit less, because they'll have the best available technology. As you turned over the capital stock, you'd have less emissions as well as more productive, energy-efficient plants."

In the eyes of many businessmen, the greatest barrier to the intro-duction of cleaner, more productive industrial facilities is the daunt-ing set of regulations that have been issued under the Clean Air Act. Under the provisions of the act, all regions of the country are classi-fied either as "attainment" or "non-attainment" areas, depending upon whether or not they meet the national ambient-air-quality stan-dards for any given pollutant. In non-attainment areas, which contain most of the nation's industry, old plants generally are required to reduce their emissions by fixed percentages based on "reasonable available control technology." New plants must install equipment that achieves the "lowest available emission rate," regardless of how much it costs. They must also obtain "emissions offsets" by clean-ing up or shutting down existing facilities of their own or persuading other companies to do so in order to reduce emissions by an amount equal to the new plant's emissions and then some.

In attainment areas, the regulations are more onerous. Here the applicant also faces the so-called prevention of significant deteriora-tion (PSD) regulations. Attainment areas are divided into three classes, ranging from ultra-clean spaces in the vicinity of national parks to industrialized urban sections. Each class is permitted only an "in-crement" of additional new pollution before all further development is prohibited.

Doubling the Lead Times

As time goes on, both offsets and increments are becoming increasingly hard to find. In both attainment and non-attainment areas, moreover, getting a permit to build a plant means going through a gauntlet of monitoring, atmospheric modeling, "increment" bookkeeping, hearings, and other procedures so formidable as to discourage even the richest and most determined companies. Various studies carried out for government and industry indicate that it usually takes two to three years to secure all the permits to build a plant, roughly doubling the lead times for ordinary manufacturing plants. This delay is particularly serious at a time when inflation, uncertainty, and high interest costs have shortened the planning horizons of most businessmen. If new projects can't be built in a few years, there's a tendency not to build them at all.

Washington in the Grips of the Green Giant

By William Symonds

Through an examination of the collective power of the environmental lobby, the author shows the great difficulty business will have in changing present environmental laws in a direction more favorable to their interests.

Since President Reagan and the first Republican-controlled Senate in a generation took power in Washington, many of the liberal ideas and programs that flourished in the Sixties and Seventies have faltered. One that hasn't is the environmental movement, which has not only hung on to its public support but become so much stronger and more sophisticated that it deserves being ranked with the National Rifle Association and the right-to-life movement as a superlobby.

More than a dozen major environmental groups—backed up by scores of lesser ones—now roam the corridors of power in Washington. Their professional staffs number in the hundreds, and like the New Right they have become experts at using direct mail to raise money and generate grass-roots pressure on Washington from a highly motivated mass membership that exceeds five million. As a result, efforts by the Administration and business to reform environmental laws have been stopped dead in their tracks.

The environmentalists' rise to superlobby status has gone largely unnoticed; their recent achievements have been written off as a passing reaction to Reagan's controversial Secretary of the Interior, James Watt. In truth, the lobby played a big role in shaping Watt's negative image and so in generating the reaction to him that has fueled its victories in Congress, which have been little short of sensational:

- Both the House and Senate recently extended the Endangered

Species Act for three years without any significant changes. This is the law that in the late Seventies blocked completion of the Tellico Dam in Tennessee for two years to protect an obscure fish called the snail darter. It had been ridiculed as the ultimate example of environmental extremism, and even environmentalists expected it might be weakened when it came up for review this year. Then the green lobby organized a committee of several thousand scientists to educate Congress about protecting species, and a strong reauthorization sailed through both chambers on a voice vote.

- After Watt tried to permit some oil and gas leasing in wilderness areas, environmentalists stirred up such a ruckus that, as a compromise, he proposed a bill that would bar such leasing until the year 2000. In August 1982, the House instead voted by a 6-to-1 margin for an environmentalist-backed bill to prohibit oil, gas, and some mineral leasing in wilderness areas forever. The environmentalists put on such "an intensive effort in terms of personal contact and mail," says an oil industry lobbyist who opposed the House bill, that "every time we were on the Hill we would find their tracks."

- The environmentalists' National Clean Air Coalition all but dashed the hopes of the Reagan Administration and many business executives that Congress would make major changes in the Clean Air Act. The Senate Environment and Public Works Committee voted 15 to 1 to report out a tough clean air bill. John Quarles, the former EPA deputy administrator who is now head of a major industry and labor coalition working for change, characterizes the bill as "unacceptable to industry—and totally unacceptable to the auto, utility, and mining industries."

Frustration at the Roundtable

Business lobbyists concede that the environmentalists "have been very effective in promoting their cause," as Quarles puts it. But they complain that the green lobby's tactics—especially its skillful use of the press—have distracted attention from the need to devise more efficient, less costly ways of meeting environmental objectives. Businessmen's frustration was captured in a mailgram on the Clean Air Act sent to members of the Business Roundtable by U.S. Steel Chairman David Roderick, who heads the Roundtable's environment task force. "Despite past efforts, we have failed . . . to offset the work of the environmental community," Roderick wrote. He warned that if business doesn't press its views more effectively, "it is possible that the environmental community will have earned a highly publicized and stunning victory that could frustrate regulatory reform efforts for the balance of this Administration."

The emergence of an environmental lobby capable of engineering such upsets is a relatively recent development. Fifteen years ago the environmental movement consisted mainly of hunters, fishermen, bird-watchers, and other outdoor enthusiasts interested primarily in national parks, wildlife refuges, and other matters directly affecting their sporting interests.

In the late Sixties and early Seventies, this movement was transformed by the explosion of public interest in pollution and man's use and abuse of nature. A lot of new environmental groups were organized and the lobby expanded its focus to embrace "almost all of society's and nature's activities—from the fate of the desert pupfish to that of an interstate highway, from soil erosion to the sonic boom," according to Rice Odell, an editor at the Conservation Foundation.

After a period in the mid and late Seventies when the movement's growth slowed, the green lobby took off again. Except for the Izaak Walton League, the National Parks & Conservation Association, and the Wilderness Society, all of the groups that form the inner club of the environmental lobby are substantially larger now than they were in 1970. The National Audubon Society has more than doubled over this period, the Sierra Club has almost tripled, and the National Wildlife Federation has added 250,000 associate members. Many smaller groups have gone from practically zero to 30,000 to 50,000 members over this period.

Today, these groups' total membership of more than five million members, though well under the ten-million-plus members claimed by the National Right to Life Committee, makes the environmentalists an imposing force. By comparison, the National Rifle Association has 2.4 million members and the National Organization for Women a mere 214,000.

Blue-Collar Greens

The members of most of these groups tend to be better educated and more affluent than the average American. A recent survey of Sierra Club members found that they have a mean income of $38,000 and that almost 40 percent have a graduate degree. On the other hand, the more than one million affiliate members of the National Wildlife Federation are "definitely blue-collar types," according to a Federation spokesman. Though low-income and minority groups are underrepresented, the movement cuts across a fairly broad swath of American society.

The environmental lobby's resources in Washington have also grown enormously. In the late Sixties there were only two or three registered environmental lobbyists on the Hill. Today there are over 80.

As the staffs have grown, they have also become more professional. Together, the Natural Resources Defense Council, the Environmental Defense Fund, the National Wildlife Federation, and the Sierra Club Legal Defense Fund employ about 50 lawyers. Many of NRDC's lawyers went to Harvard or Yale law schools, and all of the 14 lawyers working for the Environmental Defense Fund were on law review. Most were also first in their law school classes.

Environmental groups are making increasing use of computers to quickly target those most likely to help out with a phone call or letter to a key Congressman on the eve of an important vote. The Sierra Club first started using computers in this way during the fight for the Alaska Lands Act in the late Seventies; the Audubon Society and others are more recent converts. William Butler, current director of the Audubon Society's Washington office, recalls that as recently as two years ago, "there were only four or five full-time employees in this office, and people were hand-addressing letters." Now Audubon has a Washington staff of 20, including 13 professionals, and its office boasts word processing equipment and a computer bank containing the names of more than 50,000 members who have expressed interest in getting involved.

Along with this expansion has come a sharply increased commitment to lobbying. Audubon's Brock Evans, who used to work for the Sierra Club, recalls that in the early Seventies "it was hard to get Audubon or the National Wildlife Federation actively involved" in major fights. By contrast, last year Audubon sent out a letter announcing that it was "entering a battle" with the federal government to prevent "the irrevocable destruction of much of America's natural heritage." The letter brought in almost $1 million in contributions—about ten times more than earlier fund-raising appeals had generated.

The greening of the Audubon Society and the National Wildlife Federation has been accompanied by a dramatic change in the ability of the various environmental groups to work together. In the early Seventies "there was a lot of turf fighting and some of the heads of the different groups couldn't work together," says Louise Dunlap, head of the Environmental Policy Center. But many of the groups have appointed new leadership in recent years, and since Reagan took office, Dunlap says, "the leaders have made a special effort to work together." For the past two years the heads of ten key environmental groups have been getting together about once a quarter to discuss common problems and strategies.

Killing Clinch River

This ability to cooperate is apparent in the environmentalists' extensive use of coalitions that include non-environmental groups. The most impressive example to date—and the effort that perhaps best demonstrated that the environmentalists had become a superlobby—was the campaign they waged in the late Seventies to preserve millions of acres of Alaskan wilderness. By 1980, when the effort succeeded, environmentalists had attracted more than 50 groups into the Alaska Coalition and built a network of thousands of volunteers around the country.

A similar approach is being taken by the Clean Air Coalition, which includes the American Lung Association, the League of Women Voters, the United Steelworkers of America, and the National Urban League. Meanwhile, environmental groups have been working with the conservative National Taxpayers Union and several church groups and unions to kill the Clinch River breeder reactor. That effort has been going so well that a lobbyist for the Taxpayers Union says, "We absolutely expect to defeat it this year."

The impact of the environmental lobby has been greatly magnified by the public's continued support for environmental protection. Pollster Louis Harris noted that in 1967 the public opposed—by 46 percent to 44 percent—paying just $15 more per year in federal taxes to finance efforts to fight air and water pollution. By 1971, however, "Americans listed pollution control as a national problem second only to the state of the economy." This public support hasn't faded as Americans have learned how expensive clean-up programs can be. Instead, according to a survey conducted by the Roper Organization in 1982, only 21 percent of Americans "think environmental protection laws and regulations have gone too far," while 69 percent say they are about right or haven't gone far enough.

Equally impressive is the breadth of this support. The Roper survey found that no more than 30 percent of any major group—including Republicans, conservatives, poor people, blacks, and Westerners—felt that "environmental protection laws and regulations have gone too far."

The environmental lobby has been able to capitalize on the support for environmental protection by skillfully using the press. For example, when Democratic Representative Thomas Luken of Ohio and five other House members introduced a series of industry-supported amendments to the Clean Air Act last December, they claimed their bill would reduce the cost and complexity of the act, while "maintaining a strong federal commitment to environmental protection." But these claims were quickly overwhelmed by the Clean Air Coalition's charge that the amendments were "a dirty-air Christmas present for the nation."

Blowing Smoke over CO Emissions

These tactics have distorted the public's perception of what is at stake in some of the individual amendments. One such amendment, sought by the auto industry, would have changed the standard for carbon monoxide emissions from the current 3.4 grams per mile to 7 grams per mile, which was the standard 1980-model-year cars had to meet. Such a change was recommended by the bipartisan National Commission on Air Quality—which concluded it would not hurt efforts to clean up the nation's air by 1990. General Motors calculated that it could save $60 on every car if the change were adopted; applied industry-wide, these savings would amount to hundreds of millions of dollars a year.

Days before the Senate Environment Committee was to consider this amendment, the Clean Air Coalition unveiled a study that concluded that if the CO standard were changed, "at least 16 major metropolitan areas containing over 40 million people may never meet the public health standard for CO." One of those areas was Albuquerque, New Mexico. The next morning there were banner headlines in Albuquerque warning that the city would never achieve clean air if the CO standard were lowered. The tactic worked: Republican Senator Pete Domenici of New Mexico, a key swing vote, asked that the committee postpone the vote on the standard.

The committee's staff later took a close look at the Clean Air Coalition's study and found that it had merely used more pessimistic assumptions than those used by the National Commission on Air Quality. Though this doesn't prove the coalition's study was inaccurate, it does show how much uncertainty bedevils efforts to project what a 7-gram vs. a 3.4-gram standard would mean for air quality in future years. But this uncertainty—as well as the question of whether the nation should pay hundreds of millions of dollars for the benefits, whatever they might be, of a 3.4 gram CO standard— was never really communicated to the public. Nor did the general public understand that even with a 7-gram standard, CO levels would continue to fall sharply as Americans traded in older cars that emit far more than 7 grams of CO per mile. Instead, the public was left with the impression that Detroit wanted to sacrifice the goal of clean air by "doubling" the CO standard. As an auto industry lobbyist admits, "The Clean Air Coalition has made very effective political use of these numbers."

The green lobby's clout on Capitol Hill has been so awesome that the Reagan Administration backed away from proposing bills that would make major changes in the Clean Air and Endangered Species acts. But the lobby claims to have had substantially less success persuading the Administration to adopt its agenda in other areas, especially on public-lands issues and the enforcement of environmental laws. Says Wilderness Society Chairman (and former Senator) Gaylord Nelson: "We are witnessing a wholesale dismantling of the environmental achievements and gains of the past decade and a half. It is being done by a series of executive and administrative actions, without review by Congress, and beyond the view of the American people."

"Boy, Did We Miscalculate"

That kind of rhetoric has served as a launching platform for the most agressive environmental campaign ever—the effort to get Reagan to fire Watt, which has broadened into an unprecedented across-the-board attack on the Administration as a whole. Meanwhile, environmentalists are gearing up for the largest push in their history to elect friendly candidates to Congress. The League of Conservation Voters—by far the largest of the five environmental political action committees—backed about 70 candidates in 1982 with a budget of close to $900,000, twice what it had for the 1980 elections. It also deployed hundreds of enthusiastic campaign workers. Marion Edey, League director, admits that environmental issues play a minor role in many races. But she says, "The environmental movement has only just begun to tap its political potential."

At this point, most business lobbyists are still recovering from their surprise at how well the environmentalists have been doing. "We honestly thought the debate on the Clean Air Act would be less emotional than it was," admits Albert Fry, the lead Clean Air lobbyist for the Business Roundtable. Adds Harvey Alter, a U.S. Chamber of Commerce staffer: "We were blind-sided by an emotional and dishonest attack on any proposal for change. Boy, did we miscalculate."

Some business lobbyists put part of the blame on the Administration. "There is no question that Jim Watt set back progress with some of the statements he made," says John Quarles. All agree that the environmentalists didn't help by, as Alter puts it, "viewing everything we proposed as the biggest threat since Attila the Hun."

But business lobbyists have no very clear ideas about what to do next. "We are trying to grope for a new strategy," says the Roundtable's Fry, "but we honestly don't have one now." Alter is more caustic: "I haven't heard one good idea for anything that can be done in the short term—that is, in time for the next Congress."

There is, however, a general belief that business must learn how to communicate its proposals better. That means, according to Quarles, that businessmen need a "much stronger commitment to genuine public education" regarding the problems and excesses of current environmental regulation, and how to correct them while still meeting basic environmental goals. American Mining Congress President J. Allen Overton Jr. says: "If business is to educate the public about responsible environmentalism, it has to begin with a dialogue with the media, because the media must accept blame for much of the distortion in the people's present perception."

Thus, as Quarles concludes: "Business does have a dilemma." If it fights the new green giant, it is apt not only to lose, but to harm its cause in the process. If it does nothing, it stands to gain nothing. The dilemma is made worse by the fact that the environmentalists are in no mood to be merciful. They are almost as surprised and impressed as are businessmen by the green lobby's new power.

Scuttling Environmental Progress

By Tom Turner

This article, by an editor at the Friends of the Earth organization, contains a strong critique of the Reagan Administration's environmental policies and is illustrative of one of the polar points of view in the current debate over environmental issues.

When he was a candidate, Ronald Reagan surprised reporters by saying, "80 percent of our air pollution stems from hydrocarbons released by vegetation, so let's not go overboard in setting and enforcing tough emission standards for man-made sources." When pressed later, Mr. Reagan amended his remarks: "I didn't say 80 percent, I said. . .93 percent. And I didn't say air pollution, I said oxides of nitrogen. And I am right. Growing and decaying vegetation in this land are responsible for 93 percent of the oxides of nitrogen." Looking for confirmation, reporters turned to the Environmental Protection Agency. The response: Mr. Reagan was confused. "Nitrogen dioxide comes only from man-made sources. Plants and trees produce most of the nitrous oxide in the atmosphere and that is harmless to mankind."

The air pollution remark was far from the only such gaffe: Mr. Reagan also claimed that we know all we need to know about the long-term risks of low-level radiation (we don't) and that dead trees in the forest are "harmful to wood-land ecology."

Fair enough. Politicians aren't to be expected to be environmental experts. But what alarms—not to say terrifies—environmental laymen and professionals alike is that the Reagan Administration has built an entire environmental policy based on such shallow, wrongheaded analysis. In some cases the initiatives appear to be sincere

Reprinted by permission from *Business and Society Review,* Summer 1982, Copyright © 1982, Warren, Gorham & Lamont Inc., 210 South Street, Boston, Massachusetts. All rights reserved. Tom Turner edits *Not Man Apart,* the monthly news magazine of Friends of the Earth.

if naive; in others the Administration has taken the role of point man for the most greedy and irresponsible interests in society.

It is useful to outline the strategy the President and his Administration appear to be pursuing, bearing in mind that what is being altered, dismantled, eviscerated, or only bruised is a structure whose roots go back to Abraham Lincoln and many of whose finest hours came during Republican administrations. Likewise, bear in mind that should the majority of the public not agree with the Reagan approach to environmental policy (and there's ample evidence that it does not), many of the changes wrought under the present Administration will take decades to restore.

1. Squeeze Off Access to Information: Led by the Attorney General, William French Smith, the Administration wants to severely weaken the Freedom of Information Act, one of the half dozen or so laws that are most important to environmentalists—and many others, too. Ask any European. In most European countries there is nothing resembling a Freedom of Information Act; on the contrary, in most Commonwealth countries there is an Official Secrets Act, which means in effect that the government can keep secret most anything it wants to—and jail anyone caught leaking the secret. On many occasions, officials from Commonwealth governments have visited this country to confer with U.S. officials on, say, the prospects of building nuclear power plants in New Zealand. When the New Zealand officials return home, they invoke the Official Secrets Act and refuse to divulge the content of their conversations. Environmentalists then can turn to their American friends, who ask the American officials, under the Freedom of Information Act, to make available transcripts of their meetings with the New Zealanders. Thus, the FOIA is not only an invaluable tool domestically, but also internationally. As with many of the so-called reforms the Reagan Administration is pursuing, the attack on FOIA is passed off as a money saver, a way of streamlining government and lifting burdensome regulations. It would, however, eliminate the public's access to vital information. Oddly, the dilution of the FOIA is being resisted by some large business interests—which mainly favor the rush to deregulation—because they can use the Act to steal each others' secrets.

2. Ignore Congress; Use the Budget: The most controversial member of the Reagan Cabinet was James Watt, Secretary of the Interior. Early on, Mr. Watt was quite candid about the Administration's plans to implement its policies through discretionary budget authority without bothering to let Congress have its say. The clearest example of this in Mr. Watt's empire was his attempt not to spend money Congress has told him to spend in order to acquire land for parks and reserves around the country.

3. Squeeze Off Access to People: Again in the Interior Department, Mr. Watt sought to solve his problems with environmental organizations by ignoring them. After several unsatisfactory meetings with environmental group leaders, Mr. Watt withdrew behind the barricades and proceeded to hurl insults. Furthermore, he tried to stop the senior officials in his department from talking with any environmentalists, and he even ordered his staff not to meet with staff members of congressional committees—only with the congressmen themselves. Given that congressional staff members do a large fraction of the background work on the myriad issues a congressman must vote on, this order by Watt severely stifled Congress' access to Interior Department information.

4. Pursue Supply-Side Science: George Kenworthy, Mr. Reagan's science adviser, broke the news to the American Association for the Advancement of Science: the government is dropping most of its funding of primary scientific research—except, of course, military research. Private industry, he suggested, could take up the slack.

Some have taken to calling this "supply-side science," where production is the goal and side effects are ignored. A shining example is research into what's known as the "greenhouse effect." There is a growing consensus among scientists that if the amount of carbon dioxide humans pump into the atmosphere continues to grow at the present rate, it will have serious—and probably very damaging—effects on the climate of the entire earth. Some predict the slow melting of the polar ice caps and the drowning of coastal cities. Some think the major crop-growing regions—the American plains, for example—might dry up. No one seems to think the effects will be salutary.

During the Carter presidency, the Department of Energy conducted a modest research effort into the likelihood, and the likely effects, of CO_2 loading. The Reagan approach: forget it. The budget is being cut, the man who used to run the program has been demoted, and the DOE spokesman says the problem is too far in the future to worry about. He quoted a farmer, with apparent approbation, as saying, "we'll all be dead by then anyway, so why worry."

The other reason, of course, is that most of the CO_2 overload will come from burning fossil fuels—coal, oil, and, perhaps, shale—the accelerated production of which is the cornerstone of the Reagan energy policy. But will private interests pick up the research the government is dropping? It's hard to see that happening, since those interests conduct research aimed at finding new products, new processes, and new chemicals that they can sell. What company is going to pick up CO_2 research? On another score, who now will do research into hazardous side effects of the thousands upon thousands of products, old and new, that have yet to be tested? Producers think they're already overregulated, forced to conduct too much premarketing testing. And yet nearly every week some familiar substance—be it digitalis for heart-failure patients or common table salt—is implicated as a hazard to the health of some segments of society. Figures are not available, but it's fair to say that a large fraction of the research that turns up these findings has been paid for with federal dollars.

5. Denigrate Your Opposition: Even before he was confirmed, Mr. Watt was blaming the country's problems on "environmental extremists." John Crowell, a former timber-company lawyer who now oversees the U.S. Forest Service, recently went further and said that the Sierra Club and the Audubon Society had been infiltrated by socialists and communists. Crowell's red-faced retraction did not placate Audubon's president, Russell Peterson, a former Republican Governor of Delaware. Mr. Watt tried to drive a wedge between the Washington staff of the major environmental groups and their members, calling the staff members "hired guns" who are out of touch with the grassroots. That ploy has had no apparent success.

6. Foxes for the Henhouses: Environmentalists were first amused, then astonished, finally appalled as the Reagan team began announcing its appointments to environmentally sensitive positions in the government. The aforementioned James Watt had spent the past several years as president of a Colorado law firm that spent much of its time suing the Interior Department on behalf of development interests. The head of the Department of Energy, a South Carolina dentist, thought the environmental movement was being used by subversives (he seems to mean the Russians). The list is too long to repeat here, but the policy is crystal-clear: put anti-environment ideologues at the top of each agency, then shake hard and hope any Carter leftovers fall out the bottom.

This, in fact, is what alarms many environmentalists most of all:

even if the Reagan presidency lasts only four years (or if, by some miracle, some more enlightened policy begins to emerge), there will have been damage done to agencies and bureaus that will take years if not decades to repair.

7. Go After Existing Law—Carefully: Candidate Reagan had lots of bad things to say about many laws the environmental movement holds dear, including the Clean Air Act, the Clean Water Act, the Endangered Species Act, the Freedom of Information Act, the Coastal Zone Management Act, and others. True to Mr. Reagan's word, and despite some dramatic polls that show that the public does not want these laws weakened, the Administration is pushing ahead with its assault on the laws. Pushing hard, but with one eye on the calendar.

There are dozens of examples of Administration-backed assaults on existing law. But there is some evidence that congressional support for this campaign may be waning. In February, 1982, Mr. Watt tried to fool Congress, the press, and the public into believing that he was offering a new, wilderness-saving initiative. The next day, when the fine print had been examined, it became clear that what Mr. Watt wanted was a delayed repeal of the Wilderness Act of 1964, the law that protects the nation's congressionally designated wilderness areas. Mr. Watt had great difficulty finding any sponsors for his bill.

8. Use the Free Market—Selectively: In most of his policies, Mr. Reagan has hewed to his free-market, supply-side economic theories, taking the controls off oil and natural-gas prices, for example, to stimulate producers to search for new supplies. In some areas, however, Mr. Reagan kept the subsidies flowing as if the New Deal had never ended.

The clearest case is the nuclear power program and its leading albatross, the Clinch River Breeder Reactor. CRBR has been an extremely controversial item since it was first approved by Congress in the early 1970s. The breeder project promised to be exceedingly expensive, partly because the technology was inherently more dangerous than conventional nuclear power plants. Jimmy Carter tried to scuttle CRBR, but Ronald Reagan attempted to resurrect it partly to please the majority leader of the Senate, Howard Baker of Tennessee. Guess where Clinch River is. Interestingly, when he was a member of the House, David Stockman wrote an impassioned essay about how support for Clinch River was bad conservative economics.

The Stockman argument held that if a breeder reactor is a good economic investment than private industry will find funds to conduct research and development itself. This was the Reagan approach to most other enterprises, but not this one: here, Howard Baker was more important than theory.

Likewise with dams. Here again, Jimmy Carter tried to eliminate public funding of what environmental activists like to call porkbarrel water projects. Carter lost—at least on some of the battles—so when Mr. Reagan came to town the anti-dam people hoped that the budget cutters would take their knives to these unnecessary, expensive, environmentally destructive projects. No such luck. Pork is powerful.

Countermeasures

What are environmental organizations doing in response? Growing! If the Administration thinks, and it claims to, that the American public agrees with its initiatives, it hasn't paid much attention to what's been happening to the established environmental groups. Nearly all are enjoying unprecedented surges in membership and support. Friends of the Earth, for example, has seen its membership grow by more than 50 percent since Reagan's inauguration, and other groups have experienced similar growth. A Sierra Club/FOE petition calling on the Congress to force Mr. Watt from office garnered well over a million signatures in a matter of months, the biggest such petition ever submitted to Congress.

With the Reagan forces calling the shots in Washington, many environmental groups are concentrating more of their efforts elsewhere. They are concentrating on organizing the grassroots to turn up the heat on Congress and the Administration from all over the country and, no less important, to ensure enlightened environmental decisions by state governments, county governments, city councils, zoning boards, and all the other organs of government that affect land, water, and air, profoundly, every day.

When Friends of the Earth held its maiden press conference in the fall of 1969, a part of its statement announced that, among other projects, it would establish a "League of Conservation Voters," which would endorse and support candidates for office. The League, which split off from FOE early owing to a legal problem, has been active and influential in the intervening dozen years, but the major environmental groups didn't begin to get involved in politics themselves until very recently. The main reason for this was that until 1974 or so it was illegal for corporations to endorse candidates for public office. But in the post-Watergate reforms, Congress passed a law that permits the creation of political action committees, PACs, that can raise money and spend it to support or oppose the candidacy of people running for office. The unions were the first to take advantage of the new law; then came industry. Then, in the last couple of years, environmental group PACs have begun to crop up. The Sierra Club's was first, then FOE's and Environmental Action's. These subgroups can accept donations only from members of the parent organization, so they can't and don't hope to match the overwhelming contributions given by some PACs to certain candidates.

Environmental PACs hope to match the influence of the better-heeled PACs by providing workers for the campaigns of their favorite candidates. It is too early to tell how well this will work, but early experience has made the PAC-tivists hopeful. The first major test of the strength of organized environmental voters came in the congressional election of 1980. FOE, without a formal PAC for a few more months, endorsed four candidates. It recruited volunteers who walked precincts, passed out literature, stuffed envelopes— and all because they were enthusiastic about their candidate's environmental record. What's more, they stressed the environmental issues as those on which people ought to put considerable weight as they were making up their minds. In the end, three of the candidates won—and they were tough, hard-fought elections, with the Reagan tide to overcome.

So this is the strategy of environmental organizations in the Reagan years. Since the Government is largely hostile, these groups are taking their case to the public. If the environmentalists' policies are right, if they make sense, and if the public supports them, then one way or another the word will get back to Washington, even if it means sending some politicians to an early retirement. And, after all, in a democracy, that's how it should be.

Environmental Bankruptcy

By Jay D. Hair

Mr. Hair, the executive vice president of the National Wildlife Federation, argues that the Reagan Administration's environmental policies are based on bad science, bad management, and too much reliance on the marketplace for solutions to problems.

The National Wildlife Federation, the world's largest private conservation organization, is dedicated to the wise use of the living resources of this planet. That casts our lot with Ansel Adams, who believes that the Reagan Administration knows "the price of everything and the value of nothing and would casually encourage transfer of priceless public possessions to private wealth." The Federation is also an organization whose membership voted two to one for Ronald Reagan over Jimmy Carter. That would appear to put us on the side of the Reagan Administration, which hired an Interior Secretary who feared "our states may be ravaged as a result of the actions of the environmentalists—the gravest threat to the ecology of the West." In theory, we should be undergoing institutional schizophrenia. We are not. We want President Reagan to end the disastrous budget cuts and reorganizations that are destroying the U.S. Environmental Protection Agency and other federal environmental programs.

The National Wildlife Federation is an educational organization—our ability to affect public policy is based on the quality of our research. In the past, our research has focused on particular problems resulting from mankind's manipulation of the environment. We expected that a serious problem, once identified, would become the subject of public debate and action. We have studied the decimation of our nation's raptors (birds of prey), the poisoning of millions of ducks by lead shot, the destruction of hundreds of lakes by acid rain, and the accelerating sacrifice of our wetlands—the breeding grounds of waterfowl—to agricultural development. In each case,

Reprinted from a 1982 article by permission of the author. Jay D. Hair is executive vice president of the National Wildlife Federation.

once we identified and documented a problem, the public agreed that something had to be done. Laws were enacted, programs were begun, and honest efforts were made to deal with the problems.

Times have changed. The Reagan Administration has quickly and drastically cut the research programs that help us document these problems. Without information on rates of soil erosion, rangeland deterioration, atmospheric carbon dioxide build-up, we cannot respond to national and global environmental danger signals. President Reagan appears to have adopted the theory that what we don't know won't hurt us. The Administration is unable or unwilling to ask Congress to rescind the Clean Air Act, the Clean Water Act, the Toxic Substances Control Act, or any of the other environmental laws enacted over the last twenty years, but it is systematically killing these programs through budget cuts, reorganization, and deregulation—a buzzword for eliminating the rules that safeguard public health and welfare.

In response, the National Wildlife Federation has continued to report to the American public. Instead of analyzing problems and recommending solutions, however, we now find we must report on federal agencies' performances of statutory duties. Reports on the Department of Interior and the EPA are already out, and a balance sheet on the entire Administration is under consideration. On the basis of the record to date, the bottom line is environmental bankruptcy.

The basic problem arises from the Administration's superficially attractive and probably well-meaning attempt to base the management of natural resources on cost-benefit analysis. Following the cost-benefit approach, the formation of public policy with respect to natural-resource management theoretically involves three tasks: defining costs, assigning costs to each resource, deciding whether we as a society are willing to pay the assigned cost for each resource. If so, use it. If not, conserve it for future use.

The approach is an impossible one. "When we try to pick out something by itself," John Muir wrote in 1869, "we find it is hitched to everything else in the Universe." We can't look at a bald eagle, a prairie pothole wetland, or even a strip mine in economic isolation.

How, then do we set priorities when the calculation of costs and benefits is impossible? Until Ronald Reagan's inauguration, there was general agreement that we must balance the long-term health of our natural resources with immediate needs. This principle guided Teddy

Roosevelt when he established our system of national forests and wildlife refuges and expanded our national parks. It was the basis upon which later Republican administrations sponsored and enacted a variety of environmental laws. And it is the approach of the National Wildlife Federation. Develop, yes, but keep the important pieces hitched to the universe.

The Reagan Administration, in contrast, has launched an unprecedented attack on the natural resources of this nation. In so doing, it has outraged conservationists, frustrated professional managers, and politicized resource conservation to the point where the environment apparently ranks second only to the economy as the issue of greatest concern to the American public. The Administration's attack is based on bad science, bad management, and an almost religious belief in the ability of the invisible hand of the marketplace to allocate the uses of public resources. Relying on the market to justify exploitation of our mineral resources makes economic exploitation the dominant purpose of public-land management. This principle of management, if pursued to its logical conclusions, will destroy our natural heritage; it will mortgage the health of our children for present private gain.

The Administration's bad science is most blatant in the two agencies—the Department of the Interior and the Environmental Protection Agency—that have the greatest stake in the protection of the environment. Interior Secretary Watt, while professing to restore balance to the agency, has actually systematically cut funding for programs that would allow him to make informed, balanced decisions. He cut or eliminated the following projects: inventories of rangeland vegetation; studies to determine the minimum stream flows necessary to protect fish and wildlife; evaluations of the habitats destroyed by federal water projects; comprehensive conservation planning that is required by law for the management of wildlife refuges; studies to determine the effects on the marine environment of leasing rights to offshore oil and gas; studies to determine the effect of acidic mine drainage on trout streams and other bodies of water. In fiscal year 1982, 276 full-time personnel and $42 million were cut from the resource management programs of the U.S. Fish and Wildlife Service alone. A further $6 million cut was proposed for fiscal year 1983. Meanwhile, Secretary Watt accelerated oil and gas leasing and resumed coal leasing on federal lands. He proposed a revision of rangeland policy that would allow more intense grazing on public rangeland, over half of which is seriously overgrazed. His actions make it impossible to evaluate the effects of immediate exploitation on the long-term health of resources.

The same bad science is evident at EPA. Upon her arrival, Administrator Anne Gorsuch accused the agency of issuing regulations without sufficient scientific justification. Nevertheless, in her budget submission for fiscal year 1983, she proposed dramatic decreases in the research budgets of the programs for air (down $15 million or 23 percent), water (down $20 million or 42 percent), and hazardous-waste cleanup (down $8 million or 53 percent). The toxics program, which was cut 30 percent in fiscal year 1982, will be cut further in fiscal year 1983—although approximately 800 new chemicals come on the market each year and 55,000 existing chemicals remain to be tested. Agency-wide, the proposed fiscal year 1983 R & D budget is cut 27 percent—hardly the action of an Administration that seeks to base regulation on "good science."

Interior and EPA are also good examples of bad management. Over the past twenty years, Congress has passed a number of acts that direct the Interior Department to plan for the multiple use of our public lands. These uses include extracting oil and gas, coal mining, timbering, grazing, uranium mining, developing water resources, and—yes—conserving fish and wildlife. These laws made it possible for more oil wells to be drilled in 1980 than ever before, and for coal production to jump from 638 million tons in 1975 to 876 million tons in 1981. The five-year Outer Continental Shelf (OCS) leasing plan, published in 1980, proposed to double the area already under lease.

Interior's new leadership reversed this multiple-use policy and, relying solely on economic considerations, made development of oil and gas and extraction of minerals the dominant uses of our public lands. In contrast to President Reagan's statement that Congress, not the Executive Branch, should establish national policy, Mr. Watt categorically stated that he would "use the budget process to be the excuse to make major policy decisions." And what about the laws that require planning for multiple use? "Paralysis by analysis" was Mr. Watt's response. Yet, with mineral extraction booming under these very laws, the claim that planning prevents mining rings hollow.

Secretary Watt made economic exploitation of our public lands his dominant objective. He proposed a rangeland policy that concentrates money and personnel in those areas that provide maximum economic return, and he wrote off those damaged areas most desperately in need of funds for recovery. He proposed a revised coal policy that allowed the coal industry to identify areas to be leased, including sites in wetlands or floodplains. He asked the oil and gas industries to identify areas within wildlife refuges in Alaska they would like to lease before he prepared the comprehensive conservation plans required by law. Likewise, in revising the five-year OCS leasing plan, he ignored the fact that some of the areas of interest to industry are prime commercial fishing areas, are near fragile coastal habitats, or contain significant noncommercial marine resources. These actions reflected an assumption that the public interest is best served through single-purpose management. This assumption is flatly unjustified without some understanding of how each of these resources is "hitched to the universe."

Low morale is causing career staffers to leave EPA at a record rate. Since January 1981, seventy-eight regulatory proceedings have been delayed more than two months and forty have been cancelled, withdrawn, or postponed indefinitely. Nine are still on schedule, and only one—a minor amendment to an existing monitoring rule—has been completed. Enforcement actions against polluters have been cut more than 50 percent. The Office of Public Awareness has been eliminated. The EPA operating budget has shrunk from $1.35 billion in fiscal year 1981 to a proposed fiscal year 1983 level of $961 million, which, when adjusted for inflation, represents a 40 percent cut in purchasing power. The Office of Management and Budget estimates that an agency essentially ceases to function when its operating budget is cut more than 20 percent in any one year. The recent managerial, regulatory, and budgetary decisions made with respect to EPA therefore appear to be a deliberate attempt to terminate federal participation in the air, water, hazardous-waste, and toxic-control programs duly enacted by Congress. As is the case at the Department of Interior, no attempt has been made to assess the long-term effects of these actions on public health. In fact, studies undertaken by the Carter Administration to evaluate the long-term health effects of pollution were cancelled by the Reagan Administration. The question of whether we can afford to control pollutants and toxic chemicals has not been squarely put before the public.

Another line of attack against our natural resources is implicitly to challenge the notion that resources can become scarce. Here, perhaps, lies the explanation of this Administration's belief that "the invisible hand of the marketplace'' will manage both our economic and our non-economic resources. Reliance on the market to dictate the rate of mineral extraction, they say, actually makes our natural resources less scarce, not more so.

The proposition that natural resources are becoming less scarce is vigorously asserted by University of Illinois economist Julian Simon. Mr. Simon asserts in his book *The Ultimate Resource* that the only measure of scarcity is price, and then he demonstrates that, over the course of the century, the real price of virtually all renewable and nonrenewable resources has declined. This decline has been achieved through the miracles of technology. Through reliance on human ingenuity—the ultimate resource—we can look forward to ever-decreasing scarcity for the indefinite future.

Simon ignores the earth's biological limits. Due to the wonder of modern agricultural techniques that allow us to harvest from fencerow to fencerow, we are dumping fifteen tons of precious midwestern topsoil into the Gulf of Mexico every *second*. Wetlands, which are natural soil conservers, water purifiers, flood buffers, and breeding areas for waterfowl, are being destroyed at the rate of 600,000 acres per year. We are spewing carbon monoxide into the air at a rate that is warming the upper atmosphere, which in turn threatens to make deserts of our prime farmland. We are exterminating species at a worldwide rate of one species per day. Man's over-stepping of this planet's biological limits is nowhere calculated in Simon's price theory of scarcity, yet we will pay for this trespass— or, worse, our children will pay for our arrogant disregard of the living resources that share this small planet with us. Life is not simple. It cannot be understood through cost-benefit analysis. This is both a blessing and a burden: a blessing because it guarantees for the inquiring mind an everchanging subject for research through which we can learn more about this world and our place within it; a burden because it vastly complicates human behavior. We cannot continue to manage our public lands, our air, and our water for single dominant use by man and expect to long survive.

Environmental Trade-offs: A Need for Balance

By Robert O. Anderson

Robert O. Anderson, chairman of the board of ARCO, appeals for a balance between economic concerns and environmental concerns and calls for a greater recognition of the opportunity costs of environmental programs.

We are ten years into the environmental era in this country—the first major legislation was passed in 1970—and ten years is not a bad interval for an overview.

I have followed the environmental movement with considerable concern and enthusiasm. In 1968 I spoke at a UNESCO meeting in San Francisco. The subject of my speech was the blue planet. I was prompted to speak on the subject by several articles written by Garrett Hardin and by the comments of the earliest astronauts who, upon returning to earth, universally marvelled at the beauty of our planet. Hence the title "The Blue Planet."

But the astronauts also commented on the fact that as one looked to the east and the setting sun, a dirty haze could be seen across the horizon, going around the world with the sunlight. The fact that this haze could be seen from space—and observed to extend from the United States halfway across the Atlantic Ocean—convinced me that we are living in an era when people can and do affect life on earth in a significant manner.

The Need for Global Balance

Overall the problem is basically one of providing on a global basis the proper balance among human needs, social needs, and environmental needs. To date we really have not addressed ourselves to this broad issue. Instead we have been attempting to cure what

Excerpted from "Environmental Trade-offs: A Need for Balance," *Corporations and the Environment,* 1981, Graduate School of Business, Stanford University. Reprinted by permission. Robert O. Anderson is chairman of the board of Atlantic Richfield Company.

seemed to be the most obvious and immediate environmental problems. But I think we would all have to agree that the problems of the human condition and social needs must be addressed at the same time that we attempt to deal with the environment. Hundreds of millions throughout the world are structurally unemployed. They will never have a job. They will never be able to raise a family in anything but abject poverty. Their social needs are clearly very pressing. We have a major global problem: providing a living and some hope for people who have had very little of either. A job, together with basic food, shelter, and clothing, are the minimum ingredients for self-respect. Whatever we do in the environmental era must recognize this need. With a projected world population of five and a half to six billion people by the end of this century, the next twenty years appear to be a formidable undertaking.

Three Major Areas of Concern

There are three major areas of concern in which I feel we must make improvement, or the world we would like to see, the world any of us would care to live in, is simply not going to materialize.

First there is the question of air quality, where conditions unfortunately continue to deteriorate. We have run into a phenomenon, industrial dust, in which tiny particulate matter goes up in the air but never comes down. Each year the dust level of the planet rises. The last I heard, it was going up about a thousand feet a year. It is now at the 11,000- to 12,000-foot level, where it remains airborne for a matter of years, not months or days.

The industrial-dust phenomenon, together with the carbon dioxide buildup and climatic side effects of pollution, are the subject of continuous examination. The National Center for Atmospheric Research, for example, is currently working on a major study. Those working on it are unanimous—or as close to unanimous as scientists ever get—in their evaluation that we are moving toward a cycle of industrial dust, airborne particulates, and carbon dioxide that will create a major warming in the next forty to fifty years. If their projections are correct, it will be the largest temperature shift in the history of the planet within a short period of time. If they're right, it would mean warmer and significantly dryer interiors. These include the grain belt in our country, the Russian Ukraine, and China, the three principal cereal- and feed-grain-producing areas of the world.

Rather cynically, those studying the problem say that probably little can be done to prevent the warming trend because we must continue a certain level of human activity, including agricultural and industrial production. As a result, we are almost irrevocably locked into a cycle of building up air pollution in the upper atmosphere. Even if this is true, however, it does not mean that we should fail to make an all-out effort to at least start correcting the erosion the scientists feel will occur.

Our second major concern after air quality is fresh water, another diminishing resource. The quality and quantity of ground water under our major cities decline every year. Anyone who has lived in California knows what fresh water means in terms of irrigation, crop production, and the whole lifestyle enjoyed in this state. Sea water is somewhat lower on the scale of priority, with the exception of areas like the Mediterranean, where lack of circulation and discharge have created essentially dead bodies of water.

The ocean is an enormous sink. Everything that leaves the land masses goes into the oceans. Over the years hundreds of billions of barrels of oil have gone into the ocean as large oil-bearing structures throughout the world have eroded away. The resulting oil seeps have permitted tremendous amounts of hydrocarbon materials to escape to the oceans. Fortunately crude oil is biodegradable. It is dirty, it is nasty, no one wants it around, but it does oxidize and biodegrade and, presumably, enter back into the global cycle.

The third major category of environmental problems that I see—and the most recent—is that of soil and groundcover. Humans probably did their first environmental damage to soil. Certainly their first visible impact on the globe was the result of overgrazing sheep and goats in the Middle East. The Middle East was at one time a forested region. Today, North Africa and the Middle East stand as a man-made desert, primarily through overgrazing.

In light of these three principal problem areas, it becomes clear that we must produce a major effort to conserve our air, our water, and our soil because they are essentially irreplaceable. The air cycle is estimated to be in the hundreds of thousands of years, lost soil is not replaceable except on a geologic basis over the long term, and the renewal of fresh water is also a long-term process.

The Need for Self-Discipline and Cooperation

As mentioned above, these issues can only be dealt with, in the final analysis, on a global basis. This effort will require self-discipline. We in the United States live in a nation that governs itself. We view government as subservient to people. That's the way we want it, and that's the way it should be, but we have never really learned to discipline ourselves in our role as self-rulers. We can discipline ourselves in war. We can take all kinds of measures to ensure and protect our national security. But when things are going well we are not particularly inclined to discipline ourselves. Our leaders have discovered that it is not a popular issue at the ballot box, so they really don't press us much. And yet, if we are going to meet the environmental challenges I have been outlining today, it is going to take a lot of self-discipline. It is going to take commitment and cooperation.

As we move through the second decade of the environmental age, I think we have to recognize that we need a degree of unity, information sharing, and cooperation that we did not have during the first ten years. The first ten years, as I said earlier, were constructive. A great deal was achieved. But we have to figure out a way of doing it without continual confrontation, without the adversary approach. Fighting has always been a favorite occupation in this country. Until recently we've had the time and money to do it, and we could always stand the excitement.

But times have changed. We are no longer as wealthy a country. And, given the speed with which our problems are accumulating, we no longer have the time to kick them around at our leisure. In short, we have to learn to work together to an extent unknown in the past. We also have to recognize the difference between improvement and perfection. Most of us want perfection, nothing short of it. But we have to recognize that there are first steps and that improvement is the key.

The Need for Assessment Capabilities

We have to figure out some way to *assess* the environmental problem. I happen to be paranoid about anyone cutting down a tree without some obvious necessity. Yet I have lived long enough to discover that trees grow. I didn't know that when I was younger, and it seemed to me then that it took forever for a tree to grow. As I got older I discovered that they grew faster than I thought.

In fact, the regenerative capacity of our natural system is amazing. Trees, ground cover, and almost everything else will grow back, if we give them a chance. Now that I know the things that can be corrected as opposed to those that cannot, it is our failure to give our growing things a chance that is, in some ways, more distressing to me than any other environmental violation. On the other hand, the loss of topsoil through erosion cannot be corrected, as I said, except in geological terms. So we have to pick our priorities. We can't do it all. We don't have the means to finance it. We couldn't stand the social disruption that would occur if we moved into the remedial process abruptly. We still need social improvement, in this country and in the rest of the world, and we can't get there by cutting people off. If we in this country were willing to opt arbitrarily for a declining standard of living to achieve an environmental goal, the rest of the world would never go along with it. There are people out there who insist that they are entitled to as much as we are, and they are going to spend their lives and their children's lives trying to get it.

So as we look at all these problems, we must devise a way to assess them. Which are the critical problems? For which is it most desirable that we discover a solution? They're all important, of course. We'd like to solve them all, but we do have to *concentrate* on the really key ones. After all, we only have twenty years left in this century. That isn't much time, as you will discover twenty years from now. We have to make those years count. If the predictions of the climatic changes are true, the changes will be very evident in a twenty-year period. If so, we will have our hands full simply feeding and meeting the social needs of a growing world population.

The Next Environmental Decades

For my part, I would like to propose—or at least hope—that the second and third decades of the environmental age will find a public and private sector working together. We have a nation that is full of single-purpose interest groups. They are great. They are what made America great. But, as John Gardner said, when somebody leans over and puts his finger on one checker and says, "That's my checker, you can't move it," pretty soon somebody has a finger on every checker on the board. Nothing moves.

The moral is simple: we cannot become a nation deadlocked into inaction and inactivity because each of us has personal interests that are focused on one checker. We have to recognize that *all* the checkers have to move, and occasionally in a direction that we don't like. Building that base of understanding and cooperation is essential to this nation's hope of progress in the 1980s, in environmental matters and much more besides.

It has taken ten years to drive home the fact that we do have an environmental problem. It's a very real problem. We've got to go at it in a better way. We can't afford to go at it in the time-consuming way we have in the past. The future is going to require a good deal of ingenuity and, as I said, self-discipline on the part of the American public. At root, however, I am an optimist. I think the American people will put their minds to it.

Environmental Protection and Resource Use from a Business Viewpoint

By Harvey Alter

A business point of view stressing the importance of balance between multiple use resource management and conservation is presented in this article published by the national Chamber of Commerce.

Introduction

Public discussions of environmental protection and natural resources policies are unfortunately confused by confrontation and polarization of viewpoints between business and environmentalist groups. It would help if the discussions could be put in the perspective of an historical view of policy development over the past 100 years, so that the tenor might become positive and environmental protection achieved at a reasonable cost to the country. If not, then as Santayana taught, those who forget the lessons of history are doomed to repeat them.

Under the American system of government and economy it is the role of the private sector to develop, extract, beneficiate, fabricate, and distribute the products derived from natural resources to meet the food, clothing, shelter, health, security, and amenities needs of the country. With this task comes a responsibility to help formulate national policies and priorities in the inseparable concerns of wise use of resources and environmental protection.

Governmental natural resource policies probably began, if only indirectly, in the earliest days of the Republic with the decision to open the Northwest Territories. The policies were codified in laws such as the Homestead Act of 1862, the Mining Laws of 1872, the Rivers and Harbors Act of 1899 (the first "water pollution control"

Reprinted by permission of the author. Harvey Alter is manager of the Resources Policy Department, Chamber of Commerce of the United States.

law), the Reclamation Act of 1902, and a score of other legislation through the Alaska Lands Act and "Superfund" in 1980. In addition, many environmental laws are re-authorized by Congress at approximately four year intervals, thus re-opening debates over their contents.

Natural resource management and environmental policies are discussed here together. As will be seen, the two subjects are really one. Perhaps surprisingly, there is a connection say between wilderness preservation and hazardous waste management, at least in philosophical approach.

History of National Policies

Near the turn of the century, the arguments over policy direction were elegant, when advocates such as John Muir and Gifford Pinchot debated preservation versus conservation. It is important to understand a bit of that argument, and how it has evolved and continues today, in order to understand why the private sector is so involved in the current debates over some the the same issues and "-isms."

Four major philosophies of American natural resource management can be distinguished: utilitarianism, progressive conservationism, romantic preservationism, and environmentalism. Each consists of beliefs about natural resource management goals and associated ecological conditions and each is related to an underlying political philosophy.

Utilitarianism is related to the growth of the country and the cornucopianism that persisted into the 1960's. This view teaches that natural resources were inexhaustible and should be used to raise individual and national (even international) standards of living. Whether there is an intellectual or factual basis for this philosphy, it nonetheless was practiced in varying degrees and provided a strawman for critics in both the nineteenth and twentieth centuries. Utilitarianism was also the basis for nineteenth century *laissez-faire* development and was used to justify the gold and silver rushes and the opening of the West. It became untenable and gave rise to the counterview of progressive conservationism.

The progressive conservationist movement came at the turn of the century. Its greatest advocate was Theodore Roosevelt, aided by his natural resource advisor and friend, Gifford Pinchot. Their philosophy was based on opposition to the domination of economic affairs by narrow special interests (such as the cattle and railroad barons) and a fundamental belief in science and rationality. One of Pinchot's principles of conservation was that natural resources must be developed and preserved for the benefit of the many, and not merely the profit of the few. The basic tenet was "wise use," not locking-up of resources, still elements of the national debate.

Thoughtful people will agree that conservation is a good idea but there are still wide differences as to how best, and how much, to protect future claimants. Should resources be used to provide the needs of this and the next generation or should some of their wants be denied so as to provide for far future generations? The dilemma was approached in a definition of conservation given by the Paley Commission in their 1952 report to President Truman:

> . . . It may not be wise to refrain from using zinc today if our grandchildren will not know what to do with it tomorrow. But following a course of conservation which, as here suggested, weights economic factors carefully, is very different from the eat, drink, and be merry philosophy which sees no point in judicious self-restraint and no cause to worry over posterity's welfare.

Countering any such view of conservation is the preservationist doctrine, articulated early in this century by people such as Henry Thoreau and John Muir, that nature is a retreat from the artificiality and cacophony of the cities and technology. This philosophy continues today with the setting aside of large tracts of public land as parks, refuges and wilderness preserves.

The various views of an interaction with nature evolved into what is currently called environmentalism, a belief that mankind is interrelated with nature and neither superior to it nor apart from it. One of the early philosophers of the current environmental movement, Barry Commoner, emphasized that the stability of the biosphere depends on the maintenance and renewal of resources in a way that all species, including man, take from the biosphere and return what is consumed in an altered form, with no net change in the system. This is what Commoner referred to as "The Closing Circle."

Nature comes first for both the environmentalists and the preservationists in any conflict between human use and nature's requirements. This statement is the foundation of the debates over natural resource and environmental protection policies more than any other. It has led to confusion, mistrusts, and misuse of a host of labels: preserve vs. protect, explore vs. exploit, develop vs. despoil, conserve vs. consume, latitude vs. lock-up, egalitarian vs. elite.

In the 1960's and 1970's, the debates led to the passage of landmark legislation to preserve wilderness and other public lands by adding greatly to the National Park system, and legislation such as the Wilderness Act, the Roadless Area Review and Evaluation Act, and the Alaska Lands Act. Either lands were locked up or a process was established by which they could be locked up, i.e., withdrawn from most uses, which *de facto* is all uses except wilderness. This means there is no exploration or extraction of fuel or non-fuel minerals or other resource utilization which added to other restrictions on the one million acres or so of federal lands in the continental forty-eight states.

During the 1970's, a variety of Administration decisions, or in some cases indecision, reinforced preservationism in the name of environmentalism. During this same period, the United States became involved in what has been termed a "Resource War." The first loud shot was the OPEC oil embargo of 1973-74, followed by the Iranian oil cut-off in 1979. Added was the attempted embargo by some bauxite producing states and the general political instability and Soviet adventurism in central African countries which supply this country with several strategic and critical minerals. This vulnerability is not new. It was recognized by the National Conservation Commission, convened by President Theodore Roosevelt (which in 1909 predicted that domestic resources of petroleum and high grade iron ore would be depleted by mid-century), and described eloquently by the Paley Commission and by many, many other "blue ribbon panel" reports since then. All came to similar conclusions: the United States is heavily dependent on other nations for strategic fuel and non-fuel minerals and steps must be taken to strengthen domestic sources of supply. Business and industry conflict with the preservationists and environmentalists on how to strengthen these sources. Without these minerals, neither the private nor the public sectors could provide basic societal needs, public health or national security.

As an important aside, there is a school of thought that the United States should become self-sufficient in strategic and critical minerals. This is impossible because this country is not blessed with sufficient appropriate deposits of minerals such as cobalt, chromium, platinum, and manganese. Thus, we must trade with friendly nations and exercise a foreign policy that permits access to needed materials. However, the lessons of oil embargoes must not go unheeded and the greatest insurance policy against losing strategic supplies (including oil) is development, or at least inventorying, of domestic resources.

The history of environmental protection laws is not as long. Except possibly for the water pollution control law passed in 1948, modern environmental protection laws came about rapidly, starting in the 1960's. They were the congressional response to a truly grassroots movement and belief that, in the concepts used here, utilitarianism was overcoming conservationism. Cornucopianism had to be tempered by effluent controls.

Conservation vs. Preservation in Law

In natural resource policy formulation, the debate centers on what is wise use and multiple use. Environmentalism and preservationism are antithetical to multiple use, for example as defined in the Multiple Use-Sustained Yield Act of 1960. This key law states the policy of the Congress is that the national forests are established and shall be administered for outdoor recreation, range, timber, watershed, and wildlife and fish purposes. "Multiple use" means the management of all of the various renewable surface resources so that they are utilized in the combination that will best meet the needs of the American people; making the most judicious use of the land for some or all of these resources over areas large enough to provide sufficient latitude for periodic adjustments to conform to changing needs and conditions. It is a codification of the historic conservation mission to promote, in Pinchot's terms, "the greatest good of the greatest number over the long run" and is a defense against extreme resource demands.

Multiple use is mentioned in several other acts, including the Wilderness Act of 1964, which permits mining, but controls access. The Act provides for withdrawal of lands of

> . . . primeval character and influence, without permanent improvements of human habitation . . . which (1) generally appears to have been affected primarily by forces of nature, with the imprint of man's work substantially unnoticeable; (2) has outstanding opportunities for solitude or a primitive and unconfined type of recreation.

These are areas of 5,000 acres or more where no motorized vehicles are permitted and "man himself is a visitor." Access can be denied by administrative restraints, for example by requiring helicopters or pack animals, and thus be so costly as to preclude permitted multiple uses. Further, the Wilderness Act had a deadline of December 31, 1983, when all mining exploration in designated areas had to be completed. This was not accomplished, indeed hardly even started over the twenty year life of the Act.

Thus, there is a conflict between congressional intent of multiple use and the preservationist and environmentalist view of keeping man out of the wilderness area. (Advocates of wilderness areas like them for backpacking, which is judged by some to be an elitist sport for the hardy. Likely, most people displaying a "Preserve the Wilderness" bumper sticker are not familiar with the narrow definitions in the Act and do not realize they cannot take a vehicle into a wilderness area.) Industry has long argued that the multiple use concept be exercised and that artificial barriers, such as restrained access and political deadlines, be removed. Without access to the resources and extraction—for which a royalty is paid to the treasury—industry does not have the domestic raw materials to supply consumer demands.

The situation with environmental law is different. Most environmental protection laws are neither conservationist nor preservationist in the same sense. Rather, they impose both quality and technology standards to meet public health goals. This is true of the Clean Air Act, the Clean Water Act, the Resource Conservation and Recovery Act governing solid waste management, and so forth. A difficulty is that this is complex legislation, not well understood by most people in the country, including many members of Congress.

No thoughtful person is likely to oppose the structure of the laws or, more important, the goals. The public arguments are over the strategies for achieving the goals and the necessity for new regulations independent of achieving the health goals. Again, any proposal to simplify the strategies is mistakenly opposed as an attempt to weaken the laws. Further, preservationists and environmentalists (in the sense used here) generally support environmental protection strategies that hinder growth.

Environmental Protection and Resource Development

Environmental protection and natural resource management laws come together when a resource tract is to be developed. The connection is best illustrated in the context of leasing of federal lands or outer continental tracts (federal lands from three to 200 miles offshore).

The federal government will run a bid sale, which means an action for a lease, and the winner pays the treasury for the right to enter the game. The leasee, by winning, pays for the right to submit an Environmental Impact Statement, development plans and environmental management schemes in accord with a dozen or more laws. The land, water, air, antiquities, vistas, wildlife, and other values must be protected and the leasee must indicate, in detail, how this will be done. The plans must be approved before the land can be disturbed or a drilling rig moved onto the tract—before the player can enter the game.

A lease in itself does not permit use.

Balancing Environmental Protection with Economic Growth

Needless to say, it is the goal of business and industry to balance economic growth with environmental protection. Both are necessary.

The United Nations Environment Programme (UNEP), established after the landmark 1972 Stockholm Conference and subsequent international agreement to protect the world environment, and probably the main protector of the environment in developing countries, has addressed the balance. In a recent paper, UNEP stated:

> Long-term economic growth is essential for meeting the aspirations of people in most countries. Wise use of resources and enlightened conservation strategies are consistent with the growth imperative and must be considered prerequisites if this growth is to be sustainable over the long run.

The United States, too, has a growth imperative because environmental protection can be afforded only by wealthy nations or wealthy companies. At the same time, it must be recognized that Americans are environmentalists, meaning that as a nation we cherish and wish to preserve environmental values as a societal ethic. "Environment" extends beyond the physical and biological *milieu* to include human health and well-being. The ethic is valued independent of political persuasion, state of residence, profession, or other demography. It does not have to be justified or excused, but practiced and taught to our progeny.

The evidence frequently cited for this ethic is the result of opinion polls. This is somewhat backward logic, however. A poll may find, for example, that 92 percent of the public wants clean air or water, but who has ever met the other eight percent? The response to the polls has to do solely with the ethic, not with the understanding of the relevant laws and national policies. Further, the polls cannot easily, if at all, define the locus of the needs balance.

The balance between environmental protection and economic growth, and the balance among the needs of nature, the preservation of the environment and the needs of people are the key issues. Perhaps one of the most famous debates over balance concerned the snail darter versus a dam for flood control. Should the darter be preserved and the dam abandoned? Extending this argument illustrates the conflict of -isms because it can always be maintained that a dam isn't needed when people can move elsewhere—a rather patronizing view. When carried to the extreme, the primary issue of societal needs versus other habitat for the darter was overlooked.

The arguments over how to protect the environment are too often polarized and not as a result of the issue content. The polarization results from where on the spectrum of -isms the participants' philosophies lie. As mentioned, preservationists believe in withdrawal and non-use. Progressive conservationists believe in multiple use. Preservationism is a "don't" or inaction; conservation is a "do" to achieve the growth imperative. Somewhere, somehow, business and industry must still provide the food, clothing, shelter, jobs and physical and intellectual amenities for our society.

With polarization, any concept of balance is lost. The polarization exacerbates the argument at the extreme with emphasis on a few environmental horror stories or speculation, not necessarily by experts, enhanced by stereotypical images that all environmental proponents are good, that none work for the private sector, and all large companies are uncaring, if not evil.

This is not to say that some combination of conservation and growth, with elements of preservation, are useful. Prudent public policy includes some land withdrawals and preservation for future generations. Again, at issue is the locus of the balance.

A Potential Solution

Growth can be achieved with environmental management, a systems approach to protect the environment from damage and to mitigate the effects on nature that began eons ago when *homo sapiens* stood erect.

Environmental and public health protection are paramount and are achieved in several ways. First is management of effects on man, animals and biota which means setting emission and performance standards, so-called end-of-pipe requirements. Second is avoidance of effects which relate to design and health standards, and process and practice changes, to avoid end-of-pipe discharges. Third is the selection of strategies to achieve the standards consistent with other societal goals and the growth imperative.

All of these functions must be supported by a research function to elaborate causes, effects and extent, as well as to provide a scientific and engineering basis for change and regulation. Not all effects are an insult to the environment, hence need not be regulated or controlled. This concept, in this context, must be understood or the country will be spending human and financial resources needlessly.

Research need not be a hunt for yet undiscovered effects of unknown origin or unknown relation to environmental and public health protection. Unfortunately, there are some who want to find more and more obscure environmental effects and seemingly want to frighten the public so as to generate a perception and fear of environmental degradation. Such tactics are out of place in our society; they serve well a no-growth preservationists view and are contrary to all established trends that environmental quality is constantly improving.

Succinctly stated, the business viewpoint is multiple use resource management and environmental protection through environmental management, using strategies and methods that are simple enough to protect human health and the environment. Complex strategies and excessive regulations do neither, but provide fodder for the public debate.

Industry's Environmental Challenge: Prevention

By J. T. Ling

Dr. Ling, vice president of environmental engineering with the 3M Company, outlines the evolution of how society views environmental problems and stresses the importance of "prevention" rather than "clean up."

The decade of the 1970s is almost universally known as the Environmental Decade. It was a time when the environment became one of the most important national and international issues. As a result, a Conference on the Human Environment was held in Stockholm, and it was a landmark in the development of global environmental consciousness among all nations.

Since then, many activities have been undertaken in both the developed and developing countries. The United Nations Environment Programme was established in 1973. Meanwhile about 100 developing countries have established governmental agencies and adopted means of regulation to protect and improve the environment.

During the 1970s, some steps were taken that permitted control of immediate dangers to the environment, but they were not necessarily steps in the direction in which the world ought to be going in the future.

To help plan our future activities, I would like to mention the wisdom of an ancient Chinese philosopher. He who handles gunpowder has two options to consider. One, either take precautions so the gunpowder does not explode. Or two, keep a broom handy for your survivors to sweep up afterward.

In a manner of speaking, he who deals with the environment has a similar option: One, either prevent pollution at its source, or two,

---

Excerpted from speech delivered at the International Conference on the Environment, Stockholm, Sweden, April, 1982. Reprinted by permission. Dr. J. T. Ling is vice president of environmental engineering and pollution control at 3M Company.

clean up the problem after it has been created.

With gunpowder or the environment, prevention is the obvious first choice of how to handle the situation. In both instances, this wisdom has been achieved through a combination of experience and hindsight. As history teaches us, human beings are not always right the first time.

In terms of gunpowder, the need for prevention became immediately obvious to those surprised survivors of accidental explosions. Most people came to understand the prevention concept very easily. For some, unfortunately, the lesson was "here today, gone tomorrow." However, applied to the environment, the concept of prevention means "here today, still here tomorrow."

Prevention is a relatively new concept of pollution abatement, but one which is especially pertinent in a world that has just begun to understand the limits of its resources and their use, and what all this means for our future lifestyle—and even our lives.

In the United States, the environmental explosion was ignited by a very short fuse that was lit on one eventful day in 1970, Earth Day. This was an occasion when the country's entire attention was focused on evironmental problems that had existed for many years. In other words this one event raised the consciousness of an entire country. And in the United States, when you raise the consciousness of the whole country, you can be certain of a political response. It's inevitable.

This response, similar to activities in other countries at the time, was to establish a body of environmental laws and a consolidated federal Environmental Protection Agency (EPA) to administer those laws. This federal function was duplicated on the regional and state level, and, in some instances, even on the local level. Thousands of people have been involved as well as many billion dollars.

At the present time, the U.S. has at least nine major environmental laws which are enforced by the federal Environmental Protection Agency. This federal agency doubled in size and spending in a decade. It began with 7,100 employees in 1971 and grew to more than 15,000 employees in 1980. The spending of this agency alone jumped from 2.3-billion-dollars in 1971 to 5.6-billion-dollars in 1980, or a total of about 40-billion-dollars for the decade.

The objective of all these actions was to produce environmental benefits, but our experience tells us that the efforts to do so were not well coordinated, nor were the costs carefully considered.

Unfortunately much early legislation was conceived theoretically and was brought forth through regulations with an emphasis on the specifics of control technology. Confusion and contradiction occurred as the environmental problems were dealt with not as a system but as several, individual segments, such as water or air. That was understandable, however, considering the tempo of the time. At the time, business and industry were considered part of the overall environmental problem, and they were not consulted about how to solve it. The perceptions were different then, and the political decisions made on this emotional issue probably foreclosed on any industry contributions at that time.

The very important fact that an emotional environmental issue was followed by a political response failed to consider a third reality: any environmental solution is basically a technical matter. Water-pollution-control laws and regulations, for example, were enacted without considering the impact of their actions on air pollution, and vice versa, or the impact of air—and water—pollution controls on waste disposal. Nobody thought about the Immutable Law of Conservation. You can change the form of matter, but matter does not disappear. Purifying wastewater creates sludge. Burning chemical wastes creates gases and particulate matter. Both of these residues constitute pollution and disposal problems of their own. And regulations make residue disposal a very complicated and expensive endeavor.

To meet the requirements of these laws, the immediate response in the United States was to clean up pollution that already had been created. This generally was accomplished by providing a pollution-removal facility at the end of a production line. I refer to this costly pollution-control facility as a "black box."

Natural resources, energy, manpower and money were consumed to build a "black box," and more resources were consumed to operate the "black box" throughout its life span. At its very best, the "black box," according to the Law of Conservation, only temporarily contained the problem; it did not eliminate the problem. By using the "black box" we also created what I call off-site pollution—waste generated by those who supply the materials and energy consumed in the pollution-removal process itself. In addition, resources consumed and residue produced for pollution control rise exponentially when removal percentages increase to the last few points. Most laws demand higher removal efficiency as time goes by.

When all these factors are considered, it's apparent that the "black box" approach, which is needed at first to clean up the pollution, at some point creates more pollution than it removes, and consumes valuable resources out of proportion to the benefit derived.

Author Joseph Heller wrote in a way that has certain relevance to pollution control by the "black box" approach, because Heller deals with paradox and irony, and so do environmental professionals on many occasions. The book's title refers to rule 22 which battle-fatigued pilots call "Catch-22." Regulations allow a pilot to remove himself from flight status to recuperate from mental disturbance created by battle fatigue. According to "Catch 22," however, if a pilot can recognize that he has become mentally disturbed, he is, by definition, capable of rational thought. Therefore, he is not mentally disturbed and must continue to fly, at hazard to himself and his comrades.

By stressing conventional "black box" pollution controls, as most laws require, we also have created a "Catch 22" situation. It takes resources to remove pollution. Pollution removal generates residue. It takes more resources to dispose of this residue. And, disposal of residue also produces pollution.

In addition, conventional control technologies work best with ordinary organic matter—suspended solids—and other basic pollutants that are present in relatively large quantities. However, modern manufacturing processes have produced many new pollutants such as benzene, vinyl chloride, and tetrachloroethylene which are toxic and which exist only in very tiny quantities, measured in parts per billion or trillion. In many cases, there are no effective technologies to remove these pollutants in their trace concentration at reasonable cost.

When all these factors are considered, it's apparent why it's no longer possible to rely merely on conventional pollution-removal technology to resolve increasingly complicated environmental problems. Pollution is a form of waste, and controlling pollution diverts resources from other productive activity. This also is a form of waste of valuable resources. Neither can be tolerated in a world which is painfully coming to realize the finite limits of its available resources.

Toward the mid 1970s, it began to appear as if environmental professionals had become the spiritual descendants of the 13th century Italian poet, Dante, who wrote his immortal "Inferno" about a journey through hell with the ghost of Virgil, representing human reason, as his guide. Like Dante through the "Inferno," many environmental professionals were looking for a Virgil of their own. . . that is, a source of human reason to help them find their way through an infernal tangle of conflicting demands and unreasonable, and sometimes even irrational, laws and regulations.

Consider these statistics:

In the period from 1970 to 1978, more than 400-billion-dollars was spent in the United States to control air pollution only. From 1978 through 1987, the rate of expenditure for air pollution control was forecast to increase by 125 percent annually in real terms. And these figures do not include total potential cost to society, including losses to foreign competition for our industries because of higher product costs, construction delays and uncertainties, and inability to locate production facilities in optimal areas. These secondary costs can become greater than the total of direct costs.

According to the U.S. Council for Environmental Quality, in the decade 1979 through 1988 the United States is expected to spend 518-billion-dollars merely to meet federal environmental requirements. This figure jumps to 735-billion-dollars when you include a response to state and local regulations and voluntary pollution-control efforts.

Dr. John Hernandez, former deputy administer of the E.P.A., estimated that from 1973 through 1981 the United States spent about 63-billion-dollars on water-pollution-control alone. This amounted to about 3-thousand-dollars per capita. In testimony prepared for a U.S. Senate committee, Dr. Hernandez said the 63-billion-dollars included local and state-government spending of 11-billion, federal grants of 33-billion, and industry spending of as much as 18-billion-dollars.

Any way you add up the numbers, they come out too large to ignore. No business or country can afford spending of this size endlessly, without some kind of cost/benefit evaluation. In a very broad context, cost and benefit are point and counterpoint which must be offset to determine net social gain from environmental activities. The problem is that net social gain is a moving target as society's priorities change. Therefore, net social gain is difficult to define, let alone measure. Thus, the promotion of energy-saving measures, reduction of unemployment, control of inflation and many other concerns may have an impact on just how social gain is defined and acted upon.

What we need is a means for evaluating environmental activities in context with the total demands of an economy or industry for manpower, energy, materials and money. The base level should be protection of public health, about which there should be no compromise. However, definite cost/benefit criteria should be established for benefits that go beyond health protection.

In 1981, the National Economic Research Associates of Boston, Massachusetts, conducted an analysis of air-quality regulations that approached the subject from a different perspective—direct evaluation of cost versus benefit—instead of the impact on productivity. The NERA study adjusted its figures for what it said were four sources of error in evaluating benefits in past studies. These include:

- Over-estimation of air-quality improvement likely to result from specific regulations.
- Failure to consider other influences in assessing the effects of air pollution on health.
- Over-estimation of the exposed population when calculating health effects.
- And over-estimation of the willingness to pay for reduction in health risks.

With these areas factored out of the equation, NERA found that measured benefits were about half the overall cost of air pollution abatement in 1978 and that projections to 1987 produced only marginal improvement. Mobile source benefits were said to lie somewhere between one-tenth and one-fourth of control costs, and stationary source control benefits were said to be about 10 percent less than control costs.

Two conclusions emerged from the study. One, mobile sources are overcontrolled, and two, stationary source cost/benefit ratios are certainly not high enough for the time being to justify additional regulations without further evaluation.

These figures are not the most interesting part of the report, for the cost figures always have been large and alarming. The most intriguing portion is a claim that the cost of these limits could be reduced by 35 percent if only the law provided for gains to be achieved in the most cost-effective way. I am not saying that NERA's study is entirely accurate and all-inclusive. However, it does point out how a favorable benefit to cost balance can be eroded by unnecessarily increasing regulatory stringency and imposing economically inefficient regulatory constraints.

That's where environmental professionals should remember Virgil's advice to Dante. . . "he must go by another way who would escape this wilderness." The other way is the preventive approach, which is the third and most current phase of our response to the environmental explosion.

The first phase in the United States was Earth Day. The second phase was the legislative response to this phenomenon. Phase three is now the realization that all parts of our environment are linked together and the impact on one segment is felt by all the others. It appears that the prevention measure is the most logical approach to solve our increasingly complicated environmental problems wherever and whenever possible.

At my company, 3M, we have established a special program to encourage technical employees to develop preventive technologies for environmental problems. We call it Pollution Prevention Pays, or the 3P Program for short. This effort has been in effect since 1975 and centers around four areas of activities: product reformulation, process modification, equipment redesign, and recovery of waste for reuse.

The 3P Program was established to achieve:
- An improved environment.
- Reduced capital and operating costs for pollution control facilities.
- Reduced material and energy costs.
- Increased sales of products with reduced pollution potential.
- The spin-off of technologies, perhaps leading to commercial development of new products.

The name Pollution Prevention Pays was selected after considerable debate over whether the word "pays" should be associated with pollution prevention. Since the program strives for environmental and cost-control payoffs, it was decided that payoff not only should be equated with the effort but was an essential motivating factor.

From 1975 through year-end 1981, the program has produced total savings of 97-million-dollars. This includes 76-million from U.S. Operation and 21-million from International. In the U. S., 3P savings include 19-million-dollars for pollution-control equipment and facilities; 42-million for operating costs; 4.2-million for energy savings not included in operating costs and 11-million for sales retained for products that might have been taken off the market as environmentally unacceptable. About 60 to 70 percent of total cost savings are repeated annually but are not included in the totals.

Each year, the program has eliminated environmental discharges that average 130,000 tons of air pollution, 4,500 tons of water pollutants, over a billion gallons of waste water and 13,500 tons of sludge and solid waste. In addition, the program's annual energy savings are estimated at 1.2 trillion BTUs, the equivalent of 228,000 barrels of oil. These results have accrued from 545 projects in 20 countries, where the program has been put into use by various subsidiary companies.

Contributors to the program have proven to be among 3M's most creative technical employees, and this recognition serves to reinforce their reputations and contribute to career growth.

It has been comparatively easy for companies that are oriented toward developing new products and processes to incorporate the pollution-prevention concept into their technical activity. In some industries, however, processes cannot be changed, or at least not easily, without disrupting or halting total production. Changeover may be too costly, or there may be no resource-conservation technology to eliminate the pollution sources.

Our recommendation is to use resource-conservation technology wherever and whenever possible and practical. Overall, success in this type of endeavor depends upon individual companies or industries developing their own technologies to prevent pollution, as they adopt their own techniques to produce their own products and services.

A person might ask "what does this all really mean?" My answer would be this. It means, we have come a long way since the environmental explosion of the early 1970s brought pollution to the forefront as a public issue. It means that we took some steps to control pollution, but these were not necessarily steps in the right direction for the future. It means that we began getting on course by adopting a prevention approach to pollution abatement. But we still have a ways to go.

First of all, some important environmental issues will have to be addressed at the international level. These include carbon, sulfur, and nitrogen cycles, potential changes of stratosphere ozone, long-distance transport of pollutants, resilience of the aquatic ecosystem to long-term and low-concentration of pollutants, and a host of energy-development-related environmental problems. While it may take years to solve these problems, there are several immediate issues that deserve our consideration.

First, pollution-control efforts should be continued. However, prevention technology must be adopted more thoroughly . . . to the best of our technical capability. Second, better approaches are needed for determining and utilizing cost versus benefit concepts. There can be no compromise on human health, but direction is needed on how far to go beyond that necessary baseline. Third, it must be understood that there is no such thing as zero risk or zero discharge and establish our priorities on the basis of this verity. Fourth, the environment must be managed as opposed to protected. Protection implies non-use of a resource. We protect money by burying it in the backyard, but we lose the use of this money. Likewise, society cannot survive on any level by not intelligently utilizing the environment, which is an integral part of our life support systems. We must manage the environment so that we can intelligently use the environment for ourselves and sustain it for our children and their children. Fifth, industry must adopt policies and procedures for environmental self control. In the legal system of a country, if we don't do what's right by ourselves we will be locked into unnecessarily strict laws and regulations that can be counterproductive. Finally, governmental bodies should establish laws and regulations to encourage the development of innovative, resource-conservation-oriented technologies that can help to solve our increasingly complicated environmental problems.

Benjamin Franklin said that "We hang together, or we hang separately." He spoke about the American Revolution, but we can apply these words to the turbulent times in which we live and the need for all countries to contribute as appropriate to the common good. Franklin also noted that "An ounce of prevention is worth a pound of cure." What more could anyone say, even today.

A Call for Tougher— Not Weaker— Antipollution Laws

The American public's support for a clean environment continues to grow as shown in this Harris poll concerning the Clean Air and Clean Water acts.

1 983 is the year that the Reagan Administration targeted for legislative overhaul of the major environmental statutes—overhaul in the direction of less stringent regulation of polluting industries. Unfortunately for the deregulators' plans, 1983 also appears to be the year when the American public is dramatically renewing its commitment to keeping antipollution laws intact—and even to strengthening them.

That is the principal finding of a public opinion poll commissioned by *Business Week* and conducted by Louis Harris & Associates Inc. early in January. From the first days of the Reagan Administration, when support for the environmental movement and the laws it promoted was at a historic low ebb, public backing for even tougher environmental laws has skyrocketed.

Perceived hostility. Support for a stricter Clean Air Act has risen from 29% to 47% and for more stringent provisions in the companion clean-water legislation from 52% to 61%. Pollster Lou Harris also points out that sentiment opposing any rollback has risen from 80% to 86%, while the proportion favoring less stringent clean-air laws has dwindled from a respectable 17% in 1981 to only 7% in the *Business Week* survey.

What caused the dramatic shift of opinion? Harris says it was "the intervention of a political event," namely Americans' dismay over what they perceive as the hostility of [former] Interior Secretary James G. Watt and [former] Environmental Protection Agency Administrator Anne M. Gorsuch to the laws they are charged with enforcing.

What is significant in respect to Administration policy, of course,

---

Reprinted from January 24, 1983, issue of *Business Week* by special permission. ©1983 by McGraw-Hill, Inc.

is that the hardening of the public's mood is broad-based and seemingly impervious to the economic arguments advanced by proponents of revisions in the Clean Air Act. For example, Harris interviewers asked people whether a factory whose air pollution level is dangerous to human health should be granted relief from environmental standards for any reason.

Among the mitigating reasons suggested: that jobs would be saved and that a factory that otherwise would shut down might remain open. By an overwhelming 78% to 17%, the verdict was that no reason is sufficient to grant an exception. And among the most uncompromising were people who identified themselves (or their families) as skilled laborers and union members.

Despite the problems of the automobile industry and the obvious effect of those problems on the U.S. economy, support for relaxation of current auto-pollution standards has dwindled since 1981 from 38% to 26%. Similarly, support for easing air standards so that power plants would be able to burn coal and high-sulfur oil declined from 29% to 19%.

Americans are particularly adamant when it comes to federal standards on hazardous-waste disposal and toxic substances in lakes and rivers. Opposition to easier regulation is virtually unanimous in both cases—on the order of 86% and 88%, respectively.

"A Fraud." The *Business Week*/Harris survey presents another striking finding: The so-called "Sagebrush Rebellion" appears to have less reality than had been thought. Harris, in fact, labels it "a fraud." In the late 1970s, Western politicians, including Watt, declared that the Western states and their citizens demanded an end to federal regulation of land use and federal control of environmental quality in the region.

If Westerners have been clamoring for a return of local control, it is not apparent from the current survey. In fact, comments Harris, "the West wants more and tougher federal regulation than any other part of the country." For example, while 17% of the national sample believed that a polluting factory deserved exemption from the clean-air regulations under some circumstances, only 8% of Westerners shared that view.

Westerners consistently are less sympathetic than other Americans to proposed relaxation of various environmental statutes: nine percentage points on auto pollution, five points on air pollution in parks and wilderness, and nearly nine points on power-plant air pollution.

Less Than zealous. Politically, the hardening of American opinion on environmental issues has the potential, at least, to become dangerous for the Reagan Administration. For one thing, the Administration is widely perceived to be less than zealous in enforcing the law: Only 25% of Americans believe that the Administration is doing a good or excellent job in enforcing air- and water-pollution standards. By contrast, more than a third of Americans credited previous Administrations with a good or excellent record. Significantly, U.S. industry fares no better than the Reagan Administration on this issue. Environmental organizations score well: 55% believe they do a good job in working to enforce standards.

When it comes to membership in, or support for, environmental organizations, the survey is a good reminder that the environmental movement has deep historical roots in the Republican Party, beginning with Theodore Roosevelt and Gifford Pinchot. A slightly larger proportion of Republicans (13%) than Democrats (10%) claim membership in one or another environmental group. And the pattern holds for financial support.

SECTION TWO
Defining the Issues

Introduction

A s the tone and rhetoric of the debate between the business and environmental communities have shifted in the last 10 years, so, too, have the environmental issues upon which national attention is focused. While no threat to the environment ever totally disappears from public discussion, one threat is often superseded by another in its perceived importance. The issues of population growth and hazardous waste disposal, for example, have attained urgency in the last few years relative to such issues as energy scarcity and the debate over continued economic growth.

New environmental problems—more complex, less reducible to simple solutions—are "discovered" almost daily. And, as John H. Sheridan predicts in the first article in this section, the year 2000 will find people still at the task of discovering and solving yet more problems.

What are the issues being debated today? Which issues should take precedence for national attention? There are voices on the fringe that urge, at one extreme, removal of environmental laws and, at the other extreme, a radical restructuring of society in order to avoid an environmental Armegeddon. But confronted with the practicalities of protecting the environment, these voices are fading, and the debate over the environment—of necessity—has matured, shifting the focus away from broader philosophical questions to specific issues and techniques. Indeed, half a dozen studies have been conducted recently in an effort to delineate, and, to some extent, rank the major environmental issues on the national and international agendas. Approximately 50 issues are identified in these studies, beginning with war and nuclear accidents and ending with wilderness and river degradation. Fifty issues make for a rather lengthy, complicated agenda for an overburdened public to tackle—in some cases, immediately.

In this section only a few topics could be selected for examination. They include population growth, energy development, acid rain, toxic waste disposal, and the wilderness system. While the primary focus is on national issues, the final few articles examine several international pollution problems as well.

Pollutants do not recognize international boundaries, and nowhere is the interdependence of humankind more apparent than in the area of environmental protection. Whether it is acid rain, oil spills in the ocean, or export of polluting industries from developed to less-developed countries, pollution issues are moving to the forefront of international affairs. Dealing with global pollution problems may prove even more difficult than dealing with domestic or national pollution problems, but they must be dealt with if this delicate planet is to be adequately protected.

Will Industry Come to Terms with Mother Earth?

By John H. Sheridan

In this article, we see industry's view of what it believes the environmental issues will be in the year 2000.

Excerpt from a news broadcast in the year 2000:

A joint committee of Congress today completed work on a comprehensive bill that will postpone the final target date for meeting national clean air standards until 2010. A spokesman for the U.S. Environmental Protection Agency explained that the extension will allow several stalled energy development projects to go forward and will give state officials additional time to adopt new strategies to curb automobile pollution in urban areas. . . .

Meanwhile, at the United Nations, the debate over allocation of carbon dioxide permits remained snarled as the world's emerging industrial nations protested that they cannot meet their economic development goals unless they are permitted to burn more coal and other fossil fuels. . . .

The U.S. Congress has shown a penchant for setting five-year deadlines for accomplishing major environmental objectives, then granting extensions when the deadlines aren't met. At the turn of the century, this country will still be struggling with the remnants of today's pollution problems—and also with new challenges that have yet to be documented. In the meantime, the doomsday prophets, like inebriated guests at a cocktail party, will continue to startle us with unsettling predictions.

Over the next 20 years, we'll continue to worry about nuclear wastes, fret about possible alterations in the earth's climate, debate the connection between chemicals and cancer, and grope for something resembling a consensus on socially acceptable risks.

While we do all that, we will continue to breathe air that won't

Excerpted from article in *Industry Week*, February 5, 1979. Reprinted with permission. Copyright 1979 by Penton/IPC Inc. John H. Sheridan is feature editor of *Industry Week* magazine.

be quite as clean as the Sierra Club would like. By 2000, international air pollution issues—including trans-boundary disputes—will command greater attention than today. And scientific pronouncements in the next 20 years may stir global controversy about the dangers associated with rising levels of carbon dioxide in the atmosphere.

In the U.S., despite measurable progress in controlling traditional air pollutants like sulfur dioxide and particulates, the return to air of pristine quality will remain an elusive goal. Over the next two decades, laws and regulations that were adopted with unrealistic expectations will undergo new compromises to accommodate economic and political realities.

"Off the road." William Ruckelshaus is well acquainted with political reality; his past encounters with unreconcilable demands provide some perspective on what lies in store. Until recently a senior vice president at Weyerhaeuser Co., Mr. Ruckelshaus served as the first administrator of the Environmental Protection Agency (EPA), and has been called back to that position by President Reagan. He understands that public support for environmental policies has a breaking point; a motorist, for example, draws the line when he is told he must give up his automobile.

In 1973, Mr. Ruckelshaus told motorists in the Los Angeles area to do just that. Realizing it wasn't going to improve his popularity one iota, he flew to California and ordered 90 percent of the automobiles in the Los Angeles basin off the road. "I did that," he explains, "recognizing full well it was never going to happen."

At the time he had no choice but to issue the futile decree. The law was the law and the courts insisted that the law be enforced. The 1970 Clean Air Act demanded that all areas of the country be brought up to national air quality standards for six pollutants—including photochemical oxidants (smog)—by 1975. And the law dictated that if stationary source controls didn't accomplish that objective, then transportation controls were to be employed.

A California environmental group sued the EPA and Mr. Ruckelshaus to force the agency to impose transportation controls. But it was clear, given the meteorological conditions in the Los Angeles area, that the oxidant standard could not be met without near-total abandonment of the highways. "In the court suit I was threatened with contempt," the present EPA chief recalls. "So I went out there and made that order. It was the only way we could figure to achieve the standard."

Subsequently, EPA beat a hasty retreat on the transportation control issue—though it remains a thorny question as states amend their clean air plans in an attempt to meet the 1977 clean air amendments' 1982 and 1987 target dates.

The agency has retrenched on other issues as well, and backtracking—buying time until legislative deficiencies can be corrected—will continue to play a role in environmental policy-making.

Meanwhile, however, the public may become disillusioned about the failure of government programs to accomplish stated environmental goals. And that disillusionment could hamper efforts to make the laws more rational, Mr. Ruckelshaus fears. The public, largely because of the way the news media treats environmental issues, tends to view antipollution standards as "strong" or "weak," he observes. "But the question of strong or weak is usually irrelevant in looking at an environmental standard or law. The only relevant question is whether it is wise. . . . The Los Angeles basin is appreciably cleaner today than when we started. But the problem in Los Angeles isn't a five-year problem, it is a 50-year problem."

An international scientific panel today released a report calling for further cutbacks on coal combustion to reverse a detectable warming trend in the Earth's atmosphere. . . .

Such a message might be delivered sooner than century's end—or perhaps not at all. But the specter of a continuing accumulation of carbon dioxide (CO_2)—and the present meager understanding of what it will mean to the inhabitants of this planet—could typify the kind of concerns that will become paramount in future years. Issues of worldwide significance—climate changes, protection of the ozone layer, loss of arable land to encroaching deserts—will force world leaders to focus increasing attention on the global aspects of ecological imbalances.

For the rest of the 20th century, the dominant issues will continue to be those related to environmental quality, such as air and water pollution abatement, predicts Dr. Mihajlo Mesarovic, director of the Systems Research Center at Case Western Reserve University (CWRU) in Cleveland and a coauthor of the second Club of Rome report, *Mankind at the Turning Point.* Beyond 2000, the more critical concerns will be with the "environmental limits" on future development and growth. One of those limits might be the CO_2 problem.

Dr. Mesarovic notes that measurements taken since 1958 show an "unmistakable trend": an average annual 4 percent increase in the amount of carbon dioxide in the atmosphere, which scientists correlate with the increased use of fossil fuels, primarily coal. "If that continues," he says, "it would mean that the CO_2 in the atmosphere will double in the next 30 years. It will have a dramatic impact on global climate patterns and the distribution of weather conditions." The resulting implications for agriculture would be far-reaching. And scientists have speculated that a global warming trend, some time in the next century, might cause the polar icecaps to begin melting.

Theories have been mixed regarding the likelihood of a warming trend, Dr. Mesarovic observes. Some have speculated that the CO_2-related "greenhouse effect" may be offset by increased cloud cover that would shield out more sunlight. But more recent thinking, the CWRU scientist points out, is that "a warming trend is really in the cards."

The big melt. A Worldwatch Institute report to the U.S. Council on Environmental Quality last year noted that, rather than melting the icecaps, higher temperatures in the polar regions might result in increased snowfall, causing the icecaps to "thicken." This could produce physical stresses that might trigger "rapid slippage of huge ice masses into the oceans and thus raise sea levels—potentially by several meters, enough to swamp coastal settlements."

It may turn out, as one industry source suggests, that the CO_2 problem will come to be regarded as "one of the superstitions of the 1970s." The jury is still out, but it will become clearer in the next few years just how serious the problem is. If CO_2 does, indeed, pose a threat of potentially calamitous proportions, it will add a new element of crisis to the energy picture. If international limitations on coal usage are found to be necessary, the U.S. and other industrialized nations may become entangled in an intense debate with less-developed countries over who should burn coal—and how much.

Dr. Mesarovic thinks the industrialized world is likely to come under increased pressure to turn more to nuclear energy sources.

The Nuclear Regulatory Commission today approved placing nuclear wastes stored in Idaho since the 1960s into concrete blocks for final underground disposal. . . .

A major stumbling block to nuclear power development in the U.S. is the fear associated with disposing of radioactive waste materials.

Arguments raised in the waste disposal controversy have been misleading, contends Dr. Walter Meyer, chairman of the Nuclear Engineering Dept., University of Missouri, Columbia. The question is not whether present technology is adequate to provide reasonably safe long-term disposal, he says. The question is how far to go in reducing any risk of public exposure—and whether the necessary regulatory mechanisms will be put into place.

Nuclear power opponents have found the waste disposal issue a successful tactic because of limited public understanding of present state-of-the-art technology and because of past "blunders." One such blunder was the leakage of high-level radioactive wastes at the Hanford (Wash.) Reservation in which 105,000 gallons of materials leaked out over a 14-day period in 1973. Yet even that incident did not result in a serious public dose exposure, a National Academy of Sciences study panel concluded last year.

"This begins to put the problem into context," Dr. Meyer emphasizes. "We have been handling nuclear wastes—and not in a state-of-the-art manner—and yet the result has not been severe in terms of the impact on the public." Much better engineering techniques are now available than those used at the Hanford Reservation. Solidification of nuclear waste materials can eliminate any danger of radioactive materials migrating through the soil and into groundwater supplies. A solidification plant in Idaho has been converting nuclear wastes from Navy reactors since 1963.

Advanced solidification techniques can encase the wastes in glass or ceramic material. "The question is—is it worth going to that extreme? Should we construct a Cadillac to dispose of nuclear materials when a Volkswagen would be adequate?" Dr. Meyer asks.

Cooling off. Antinuclear groups have emphasized that nuclear wastes remain radioactive for tens of thousands of years—and they raise a moral issue with their assertion that we are endangering future generations. But Dr. Meyer points out that the level of radioactivity—and the heat intensity—decreases with time. By about the year 2010, the heat level from the wastes at the Idaho site will have fallen to the point that they can be cast into concrete blocks for ultimate disposal. And after 1,000 years, the wastes will be "about as toxic as natural uranium ores. That is the period you have to isolate for.

And man has built structures that have lasted several thousands of years, using primitive technology."

The Missouri professor expects that the nuclear waste controversy will be resolved long before the year 2000—perhaps early in the 1980s. What is needed now, he stresses, is an approved "institutional mechanism" to adequately regulate site selection and disposal. "We know what to do. We just need to be allowed to do it."

The U.S. Senate today approved a scaled-down version of the President's Economic Development Bill, which establishes procedures for waiving clean air restrictions when they conflict with economic priorities. . . .

In the first decade of experience with the Clean Air Act, the most vociferous complaints addressed potential or actual forced closings of existing plants and the diversion of substantial amounts of capital into "non-producing" facilities. But in the years ahead, attention will be increasingly directed to the antigrowth implications of the rules now being drafted and implemented by EPA.

A scenario that seems plausible to some industry observers unfolds like this: By the middle or late 1980s, most of the allowable "increments"—increases in pollution levels in PSD (prevention of significant deterioration) areas—will have been consumed by new development. Existing sources of emissions will have gone as far as they can in installing control equipment. And most of the practical emissions "offsets," or compensating emissions reductions, in non-attainment (dirty) areas will have been accounted for. Thus a delicate balance will have been reached. And whatever margin for growth now exists under the complex air regulations will have disappeared, at least in areas attractive to industry. The price for building a new plant will be the closing of an existing one. And the U.S. will enter a period of economic stagnation.

Stifling progress. It is an unsettling prospect. Yet the blueprint, in EPA's PSD rules and nonattainment policy, has already been drafted. And, ironically, if the envisioned growth crunch occurs, it would significantly retard progress in achieving air quality goals. When planning for new facilities becomes an exercise in futility or companies are discouraged by the prospect of interminable delay, the inclination will be to patch up marginal plants and keep them in operation long beyond their normal life expectancy.

Douglas Costle, the former EPA administrator, agrees that that would not be a happy turn of events. "A lot of industry sectors are looking at a substantial turnover of plant and equipment in the next 20 to 30 years," he observes. And the nation's ex-chief cleanup official sees that transition period as an opportunity to eliminate a good many environmental sore spots with plants better engineered for pollution control. "It would be tragic," he emphasizes, "if in the pursuit of legitimate concerns over environment, safety, and health . . . we somehow stifle that transition."

Analysts differ on whether the U.S. is truly being thrust toward a no-growth society. Among those who tend toward pessimism is Dr. J. William Haun, vice president-engineering at General Mills Inc., Minneapolis, and chairman of the National Assn. of Manufacturers' Environmental Quality Committee. He describes the effects of the clean air regulations metaphorically: "For about ten years now, we have been slowly swimming through a congealing mass. And as the mass continues to congeal, we flounder harder and work at it harder and we keep making progress. The question is: will that mass ever overpower our ability to make progress? We don't really know."

Dr. Richard D. Siegel, supervisor-air quality at Stone & Webster Engineering Corp., Boston, and chairman of the air section, American Institute of Chemical Engineers, New York, observes that the states will ultimately bear the burden of reconciling economic development needs with federal air quality restrictions. In revising their clean air plans to meet the 1982 and 1987 cleanup deadlines, state officials will be exploring further measures to reduce pollution in nonattainment areas while at the same time trying to accommodate new sources of pollution. And they will be wrestling with questions on how to allocate increments for growth in PSD areas: Should permits be issued on first-come, first-served basis?; should they be issued selectively, based on state development priorities?; or should air rights be auctioned off to the highest bidder?

Frustration. John Quarles, former deputy EPA administrator and now an attorney with a Washington law firm doesn't foresee the nation's economic development grinding to a standstill—although he expects that industry and government agencies will experience "a helluva lot of frustration." Many proposals will bog down in the PSD review process, which may take up to three years. "As the regulations come to full flower and are applied by individuals reluctant to make bold decisions, a lot of cases are going to require a full three years," Mr. Quarles thinks. But although cumbersome, the regulatory machinery will continue to issue permits for new facilities, he argues.

Plant siting, Dr. Siegel stresses, "is no longer a decision-making function handled in the corporate boardroom—but a case of 'What will the air quality analysis allow us to fit in?' The basic problem is not whether control technology exists, but [with] procedural requirements—implementing all the analyses needed to obtain a permit." Even when the chances of winning approval are good, built-in delays may convince companies to look overseas for plant sites. To prevent that, "mid-course corrections" in the Clean Air Act will be needed in the early 1980s, he is convinced. "But unless industry establishes its case and shows how it tried to work with the regulations, and identifies the problems, then I'm afraid the problems will continue."

Imagination. The growth issue will become more apparent as time passes, suggests William Sullivan, president of the Western Reserve Economic Development Assn. (WREDA), which has been fighting to preserve steel industry jobs in Ohio's Mahoning Valley. The project which may crystallize the consequences of present policies, he says, is U.S. Steel Corp.'s proposed greenfield steel complex near Conneaut, Ohio. "It may be the first real test of whether we can build a major new industrial plant," he notes. "There will be a lot of skirmishes involving minor players. But when you're talking about U.S. Steel, which has the resources to be very tenacious, and about a project that commands national attention, then you're talking about playing for very large stakes."

The final decision on Conneaut will set a strong precedent, Mr. Sullivan believes. "If the project squeaks by on technicalities, everyone will know it. It will be a clear message to everybody to look for technical ways to avoid the regulations." The tendency of environmental regulators in the past has been to "use their imagination" to extend the application and severity of regulations, he observes. The Conneaut project, he adds, offers an opportunity to use imagination to "limit" the severity of regulations.

After an unsuccessful court attempt to block construction of a coal liquefaction plant, an environmental group today petitioned the EPA administrator to reverse the agency's decision to grant a permit. . . .

When controversial projects are involved, long delays are now inevitable because the U.S. legal process permits an "endless" series of reviews, observes Mr. Ruckelshaus, the present EPA administrator. "Our whole legal system just plain lacks finality. In some ways, the Congress and the other branches of government are confusing the public's right to be heard, or desire to be heard, with the right to be heeded." When an environmental group isn't successful in one forum, it repudiates the decision made and "just goes on to the next forum."

Legislative efforts to correct that flaw in the decision-making process will succeed before the end of the century, the ex-Weyerhaeuser executive believes. "There are existing laws which do provide for finality—and work," he notes. "It simply takes a Congress willing to say, 'We've got to bring some end to this round of disputes going from Congress to the Administrative branch to the courts and back to Congress again.' "

One solution may be to give the EPA administrator greater flexibility and "the right to be final" in resolving disputes. It would mean giving the administrator additional power, which might be abused, Mr. Ruckelshaus points out. "But that is true of locating power anywhere. When you locate power, you locate the possibility of its abuse."

"If you don't trust anybody to exercise power responsibly, then you just diffuse it all around so that it never gets exercised. Which is what we've done up to a point. You can read the Clean Air Act as an expression of the mistrust of the Executive Branch by the Congress."

A truce? Whatever success is achieved in curbing the forum-hopping referred to by Mr. Ruckelshaus, adversary relationships will not disappear by the year 2000. While industry and environmentalists may manage to forge an occasional truce, attitudes will remain polarized on some issues.

The scorn with which many businessmen now regard the regulatory bureaucracy surfaced one morning last summer when an Ohio manufacturing executive addressed a small gathering at the dedication ceremonies for his firm's new water pollution control plant. Complaining about regulatory overkill, the executive declared: "We should start electing politicians who will promise to eat a bureaucrat for breakfast!"

No one expects the environmental bureaucracy to disappear—either by decree or at the breakfast table—in the foreseeable future.

But in the next two decades the hostile attitudes it now tends to provoke in some quarters will be less evident as industry comes to regard environmental control as a routine business cost. The metamorphosis can be hastened by a serious effort to balance costs with benefits and to prescribe "least-cost" control strategies. Many of the adjustments will occur, however, as a result of legal confrontations.

More industry-initiated court suits are in the cards—including challenges to air standards that aren't supported by health data and efforts to block implementation of unreasonable regulations. A successful chemical industry suit last year established a pattern for future actions. In that case, a federal judge invalidated EPA's hazardous pollutant spill rules. Rather than watch his program wither away, the agency's chief water pollution official helped forge a compromise: a legislative "quick fix" that was agreeable to industry, environmental groups, and the court. Congress passed the needed amendment on the final day before adjournment.

Gary Knight, director for environment and land policy at the U.S. Chamber of Commerce, thinks the trend will be to continue litigating compromises. "Industry has finally discovered that the courts work for us, too," he stresses. And the courts will have to keep stepping in "because Congress often ducks the tough ones."

Simplification of environmental laws and procedures—with, perhaps, less emphasis on rigid numerical standards—could reduce adversary tensions in the future, some analysts say. But for now, the U.S. is still on "a rising trend of complexity and cost" in environmental regulations, notes Jerome T. Coe, corporate staff executive for environmental quality and safety at General Electric Co.

Priorities. An overriding problem today, Mr. Coe stresses, is the difficulty in "sorting out our priorities" in the absence of firm data on health effects and the expected benefits of meeting standards. However, in the next 20 years, "vastly improved perspectives on environmental issues will be available to industry and to environmental groups. We should have a much better mutual understanding of which problems are of greatest importance"—and what can be achieved for a given cost.

Robert W. Crandall, a senior fellow at the Brookings Institution in Washington, contends that environmental activists have "obfuscated" the true costs of environmental policies, but are now beginning to "realize that they have to take economics into account."

In 1975, the combined impact of EPA and workplace safety regulation reduced "real" economic growth by 17 percent to 20 percent, a Brookings study estimates, and, it adds, by the middle 1980s, annual business spending for environmental projects alone will be pushing into the $40 billion range (in 1975 dollars).

By 1990, most of the retrofit work to install antipollution gear on existing plants will be complete, but industry will continue to face heavy costs to maintain and operate the facilities. By the turn of the century, industry will regard environmental compliance costs in much the same light that building and zoning codes are seen today. Three things will cause greater acceptance of cleanup standards, WREDA's Mr. Sullivan predicts: "We will lower our goals to something achievable. We will solve many of the technological problems in achieving them. And we will have phased out the oldest industrial plants." Coke batteries, for example, represent the most antiquated segment of steel manufacturing. "By the year 2000," Mr. Sullivan says, "most of the coke oven batteries in the U.S. will have come to the end of their useful lives—and their replacements will be much cleaner."

The Environmental Protection Agency added two new pollutants to its list of airborne carcinogens and will begin work to develop emissions standards to control them. . . .

In the year 2000, the U.S. will not only still be trying to attain the air quality standards now on the books, but many new ones as well. The chamber's Mr. Knight expects there will be more air standards for hazardous or carcinogenic pollutants "than you can shake a stick at." Among the earliest additions to the list could be cadmium, arsenic, radioactive materials, and polycyclic organic matter.

With the evidence that will be accumulated in testing required under the Toxic Substances Control Act (TSCA), new cancer scares will surface, prompting a steady flow of new regulations. In time, Mr. Knight believes, the federal government's cancer policy will come to rival the energy issue in importance.

Trade war? Meanwhile, the toxic substances law will not only impede the introduction of new chemicals in the domestic marketplace, but will also trigger international trade problems. When the TSCA was adopted in the U.S., some observers viewed it as an "invitation to a trade war." It threatens to erect nontariff trade barriers—prohibiting overseas chemical firms from exporting to the U.S. unless they meet TSCA's testing and procedural requirements.

That would invite retaliatory actions which might cost American firms overseas markets.

To ward off that possibility, efforts are underway under the auspices of the Organization for Economic Cooperation & Development (OECD) to "harmonize" international toxic substances regulations to avoid duplication in testing requirements and other difficulties. At present, notes General Mills' Dr. Haun, there is a "gulf" between the U.S. and European approach to toxics regulation. Further, passage of TSCA in this country may have violated an OECD treaty which requires consultations when the actions of one country impact international trade.

While TSCA is designed to control toxic chemicals before they reach the marketplace, two other U.S. laws which will create pressing problems address the ultimate release of toxics into the environment. Effluent standards for toxic water pollutants, which EPA is drafting for an initial group of 21 industry categories, will challenge the ingenuity of the engineering community. And regulations due this year on the disposal of "hazardous" industrial wastes will require industries to rethink their waste generation and disposal practices.

Landfill crunch. EPA surveys indicate that, at present, 80 percent to 90 percent of all industrial hazardous wastes are landfilled. But by the end of the century, land disposal will account for only 10 percent to 15 percent of the total, predicts Steve Siegel, vice president, SCA Services Co., Boston, which operates both landfill and chemical waste treatment facilities. In the future, he says, most hazardous wastes will be handled by incineration or recovery and neutralization.

When EPA's rules take effect, many industries will find that their present on-site disposal practices have been outlawed, adding to the growing demand for off-site disposal. "There will be a lot of growing pains" as industry adjusts, Mr. Siegel insists. In time, chemical recovery and treatment complexes will spring up to meet the demand for disposal capacity.

As disposal costs soar, manufacturers may find that certain product lines—those entailing large volumes of waste byproducts—are no longer competitive.

Some firms will scrutinize existing processes, looking for ways to reduce waste volumes or even to change raw material formulations if that will keep disposal costs down. In some cases, believes Richard

Sobel, director of environmental services at Allied Chemical Corp., Morristown, N.J., companies may discover that by switching to more expensive raw materials they will improve the overall process economics. "There is a real opportunity here for creative process engineering, " he insists.

Up-front answers. Process changes will also play a bigger role in enhancing the economics of complying with air and water pollution standards. For example, a continuing shift to electric furnaces may occur in the steel industry, says WREDA's Mr. Sullivan. But there is a limit—subject to wide fluctuations—on the availability of the scrap which electric furnaces require. Direct-reduction technology, which converts iron ore into "sponge iron" that can be used interchangeably with scrap, could expand the potential for electric steelmaking, which minimizes air pollution control costs. But at present, the only commercial direct-reduction processes are gas-fired. What is needed, Mr. Sullivan adds, is development of coal-fired direct-reduction, which is now in the experimental stage.

To date, process change hasn't often been a cost-effective solution. Dr. Siegel at Stone & Webster observes, "So far it has been the add-on approach. But as new-source standards are set, they will be an inducement to looking at process changes."

Con Edison announced today it has reached a consent agreement with the Environmental Protection Agency that will permit construction of its new coal-fired generating plant. The company has agreed to enclose the plant in a huge plastic dome. . . .

Farfetched? Perhaps. But John Taulman, president of Taulman Co., an Atlanta-based manufacturer of filtration equipment and computerized controls for treatment plants, thinks that technology for controlling air emissions will have advanced greatly by the end of the century. "By then, the stacks will be as clean as it is possible to get them," he says. Most of the technology will be developed by the late 1980s and installed by the year 2000, he believes.

Among the immediate prospects are fluid-bed combustion techniques, which capture sulfur during combustion, and dry SO_2 removal with baghouses—two approaches that minimize the sticky sludge disposal problem which currently plagues scrubber systems.

Many of today's abatement practices won't be radically different in 20 years, however. In wastewater treatment, Mr. Taulman observes, "We've been filtering the same way since Pompeii. You pull the water through some sand, and if what comes out looks clean, you drink it." But many currently available technologies will find wider applications in the years ahead—including ozonation as a substitute for chlorination (which is suspected of causing a chemical reaction that produces carcinogens in drinking water).

Closing the loop. Most observers predict a significant increase in water recycling by 2000. In some areas, tertiary treatment will permit the effluent from public treatment plants to be used for irrigation, water cooling, and perhaps even as a supplement to drinking water supplies. Mr. Taulman believes that utility planners will seek powerplant sites that are near wastewater treatment facilities in order to use the treated effluent as a source of cooling water.

Industrial firms have discovered that meeting EPA effluent standards can produce water of such quality that "there is no point in discharging it to a stream," points out John Sproule, president of the Water Quality Control Div. of Rexnord Inc.'s Envirex subsidiary. But that is only one of the incentives for recycling water. Robert Agnew, manager of the Envirex Environmental Sciences Div., adds that firms see a further advantage in closed-looped systems which eliminate discharges: "you immediately remove the EPA from your neck."

Among the technical advances expected in the water pollution field are further improvements in the analytical capability to measure the components of water discharges. But that may give rise to new abatement challenges. "One of the problems now is that we don't measure wastewater by constituents," notes Mr. Agnew. "We merely say it is BOD or COD—which are measures of the organic strength of the waste. We never measure that the effluent contains 3 parts per million of carbon tetrachloride. . . . As the technology of measurement improves—and we are making great strides—we may find we are putting things in the water which we don't want."

For the U.S. and the rest of the world, the biggest challenge for the remainder of this century will be to unravel the mysteries of what is "really happening" in the environment and whether the standards that are being set are too tight—or not tight enough.

"I don't know if we'll ever have the answers," Mr. Agnew laments. "The cost of finding the answers might be more than the cost of abating the pollutant."

The Economic Impact of a Clean Environment

By Charles Doherty

The impact of environmental regulations on employment, inflation, and output is the subject of this article written under the auspices of the AFL-CIO.

Invariably, U.S. labor weighs government actions in terms of impact on workers, jobs and the economy—whether the legislative action is on job creation, tax cuts, the federal budget or any similar topic. The same is true of action on environmental legislation, where labor couples its longstanding commitment to a clean environment with judgments in terms of employment and economic impact.

Sometimes, the economic effects of environmental measures are direct and broad scale. At other times, the impact is sizable—but no less real—only for a particular region of the country or for a particular industry or community. Labor continues to assure itself that environmental laws will not disrupt the nation's goals of full employment and economic growth, while consistently supporting the nation's environmental goals to clean up U.S. air, water, soil and workplaces.

In the pursuit of such goals, many questions arise. Do environmental regulations affect the nation's economic parameters—inflation, unemployment, productivity and the gross national product (GNP)? How many jobs have been lost as a result of company shutdowns stemming from government anti-pollution programs? How many jobs are created as a result of such programs?

One of the arguments frequently raised against environmental legislation is that it disrupts the economy and raises unemployment. But a recent comprehensive study analyzes the economic effects of federal air and water pollution control programs on a wide range

Excerpted from article appearing in *AFL-CIO American Federationist*, October 1979. Reprinted with permission. Charles Doherty was the 1978–79 intern in the AFL-CIO Department of Occupational Safety and Health.

of variables such as inflation, unemployment, productivity and the GNP. The study, by Data Resources, Inc. (DRI), covers the period 1970-1986 and had these findings:

- The rate of inflation would be raised less than one-half a percentage point (0.5 percent) by pollution control expenditures.
- The increase in consumer prices from investment, operating and maintenance costs would average 0.3 percentage points, so if the inflation rate would be 7.3 percent with the program, it would be 7.0 percent without.

The result then for the 14 years, including projections, is for an 0.3 percent increase each year for 14 years, or a 4.2 percent higher cumulative consumer price index than it would have been otherwise. Wholesale prices, increasing at an average of 0.4 percentage points a year, would be slightly greater at 6.2 percent in 1986. However, DRI estimates that these figures are slightly higher as a result of the inflationary pressures during the years 1973 and 1974. The maximum impact on the inflation rate during the 1970-1986 period occurred during the early 1970s. And for 1979, the CPI will grow only 0.1 percent faster with the program than without it. An overall 0.1 to 0.2 percent increase in the inflation rate is predicted from the present through 1986.

Throughout the period of analysis, the unemployment rate is lower with pollution control expenditures than without. In the early part of the period, the pollution control investments cause the GNP to be higher as a result of the increased employment. In the later part of the period, the operation and maintenance of the pollution control equipment results in increased employment. The average annual decrease in unemployment overall is 0.2 percent in 1986, with a range from 0.1 to 0.4 percentage points.

The rate of productivity is lowered by 0.1 percentage points with the pollution control programs. Businesses are using more capital equipment and more labor to meet the pollution control requirements, while producing a given amount of marketed output. But, at the same time, they are producing cleaner air and water which cannot be measured by dollar values of productivity. However, these latter goods are not included in normal measures. The range of decreases in annual productivity is estimated at 0.5 percent lower in 1978 to 1.4 percent lower in 1986.

The impact of pollution control programs on GNP differs according to point in time. Early in the period (1970–1978), the GNP is estimated to have increased, due to additional investments stimulating the economy. In 1979–1981, the GNP is forecast to be almost the same with or without the programs. By 1982, the presence of environmental programs will cause the level of GNP to fall below the level without them. In 1986, the difference between the "with or without" in the programs will be 1.0 percent. Again, computation of the dollar benefits of pollution control are not included in these projections of the GNP.

The Environmental Protection Agency (EPA), which commissioned the DRI study, summarized the findings this way: "The study confirms previous findings that environmental regulations have some positive effects on employment. Even without taking into account the benefits of regulation, the study shows inflationary impacts that are relatively small. We must continue to be vigilant in reducing the costs of individual regulations, but this study indicates that the total impacts are within reason."

Perhaps an examination of micro-economic principles will indicate otherwise.

On the other hand, industry believes pollution control programs to comply with clean water or air standards and abatement orders are an intolerable burden. Often, the deadline for abatement is not met and such industries as steel, coal, chemicals and petroleum claim the only alternative is to lay off workers, shut down plants, or move away to regions or countries that aren't so concerned with environmental quality.

The threat of job loss by employers which has come to be known as "environmental blackmail" has often been used as a convenient method to disguise declining profitability, costs of modernization and shifts in demand. But it is very much a live question whether closing a plant is usually due to environmental factors or is just an excuse concocted by business.

It would appear plausible that expensive pollution control equipment would increase the costs of the product and thus create a fall in demand, with resulting layoffs and plant closings and relocations. But the evidence for this entire scenario is weak because environmental measures have contributed to the creation of jobs in a number that far outweighs those lost through plant closings. The issue of environmental job loss requires a closer analysis.

The EPA, in its "Economic Dislocation Early Warning System," has collected data on the number of jobs lost in industries and utilities due to environmental regulations. Since the record-keeping began in January 1971, 136 firms have been listed on the threatened list—but today only 26 remain on the list. Of the 111 firms that have been removed from the list, 77 (or 55 percent) resolved their compliance problem, 21 (or 15 percent) closed for environmental reasons and 13 (or 9 percent) closed for other reasons. Primary metals, chemicals, food and pulp and paper industries were the major industry groups affected by the closings. Altogether, almost 23,800 workers lost their jobs.

However, it isn't known how many of these plant closings were due to the environmental regulations or how many could have been avoided if the true basis of the company's decision were known. A classic example of a firm's playing an environmental shell game with a community to escape proper regulations took place in Ketchikan, Alaska.

The Ketchikan Pulp Co. (KPC), a bleached sulfite dissolving pulp mill, was owned jointly by Louisiana-Pacific Corp. (L-P) and the Food Machinery Corp. (FMC). In 1974, Ketchikan Pulp was found in violation of EPA water pollution standards for dissolved pulp emissions. Compliance with the EPA requirements would necessitate installation of secondary treatment facilities at a cost of $32 million, which the firm said it could not afford. It alleged that such a costly outlay would effectively eliminate the mill from maintaining competitive pulp prices, so the firm announced it had no other choice but to close the mill. A company official announced three unfavorable cost factors unique to the Ketchikan location: 1) lack of suitable land at the mill site; 2) the need for a high-cost activated sludge treatment system; 3) construction and operating costs higher than those for the competing mills in the lower 48 states. The shutdown would end the jobs of 600 workers at the site, along with 400 to 500 loggers.

Charges of environmental blackmail were made by local community and union officials in March 1974. The charge was denied and the controversy came to include not only the company and the union, but also citizens fearing disruption of the community and loggers in outlying areas. The suspicion was that the shutdown was an L-P ploy to transfer operations to a new mill in South Korea. The loggers went on strike in sympathy of the KPC employees, and the true financial status of L-P came to be known.

Stockholders' reports for 1974 revealed quite healthy operations at KPC. Profits from the KPC facility had nearly doubled—from $12 million in 1973 to $21 million in 1974. Even if the funds were tight, low-interest, long-term state-backed bonds were available to KPC to meet the $34 million compliance costs. Ketchikan Pulp's attempt to blame a shutdown on environmental regulations was finished. In the end, L-P was able not only to buy out FMC for $46 million, but also could afford the $43 million investment in the pulp mill. Because many structural modifications in the production line were long overdue, only $6 million of the $43 million was used strictly for pollution control. The improvements in production greatly reduced the amount of water requiring secondary treatment. Louisiana-Pacific, which had the money all along, tripled the investment in Ketchikan and obeyed the environmental regulation.

Legislation to curtail such environmental blackmail was written into the 1977 amendments to the 1972 Clean Water Act. Under this provision, allegations of environmental blackmail can be brought to EPA. EPA will then hold a hearing to determine if a decision to close down an operation was really a result of environmental regulations enacted by EPA under the Clean Water Act. If the hearings should reveal that the threatened shutdown was due to reasons other than environmental regulations, the results of the hearing would be made public by EPA. Unfortunately, the proposed punishment of $10,000 or one year in jail in this amendment was deleted by Congress before passage, and as a result, this hearing process has yet to be used. Stiffer penalties for violations of environmental blackmail provisions would help all federal environmental statutes.

Several economic studies over the past decade demonstrate the link between environmental control programs and the creation of new jobs—quite the opposite of the many corporate contentions about the abolition of jobs. These studies have mainly countered business claims that massive unemployment stems from fighting pollution.

One of these early studies, "The Economic Impact of Pollution Control" conducted by Chase Econometrics in 1972, predicted that employment would increase from 1975–77 or 1978 with the installation of pollution control equipment. This equipment covered not only the air and water pollution, but also noise and radiation control, solid-waste disposal and recovery and the reclamation of strip-mined lands. The study predicted a slight rise in employment as investments in environmental controls were made, followed by a slight dip of less than 1 percent after installation, and then a leveling off of the employment rate by 1982. This same study predicted that environmental regulations would produce an estimated 50,000 to 125,000 layoffs by 1976. However, this number was far less than the number claimed in the business community and far less than the 500,000 lost jobs that resulted from multinational corporations exporting their capital investments to foreign nations during the 1960s and 1970s.

Several sectors of the economy have been the beneficiaries of environmental laws. The pollution control industry (PCI) which manufactures the equipment and instrumentation systems for monitoring the environment is a large source of jobs. In September 1978, Arthur D. Little, Inc., released a report on the pollution control industry which stated that the PCI sector has had an above average growth rate—16 to 22 percent per year for the period 1972–1976—as compared to a 9 percent rate for all U.S. manufacturing. The market for these pollution control products totaled $1.8 billion in 1977 with a projected growth to $3.5 billion by 1983. Assuming a 5 to 7 percent inflation rate, this means a rate of growth in the PCI to 11 to 12 percent per year.

Contingent upon refinement of resource recovery technologies in the next few years, this market has a potential average growth of 15 to 20 percent by 1988. In recent years, this sector reported sales in the $50 to $100 million range.

These figures serve as a backdrop to the favorable employment estimates given in the Arthur D. Little study. The 1977 level of demand is estimated at a rate of 35,850 jobs annually. By 1983, employment is projected to grow to 43,900, or an increase of 3.5 percent per year. Two factors are considered in calculating this projection: an overall growth rate in PCI demand of 11.5 percent per year and an 8.0 percent per year increase in the sales-per-employee ratio. This increase assumes that inflation and other business factors will continue to affect the ratio in proportionally the same manner as they did in 1972–77. This employment demand is somewhat under-estimated. Jobs associated with the design and construction of pollution control facilities are not included in the study. Similar analysis extended to the consulting, engineering, fabrication and construction business would certainly increase the estimated job creation.

The labor movement has maintained and strengthened its long-standing commitment to a clean environment for America. It has broadened to areas of agreement and often joint action in cooperation with responsible environmental organizations.

The AFL-CIO retains its concern, however, over the vexing issue of the offset between quantity of jobs stimulated by investments in the control of environmental hazards, as against the quality of jobs that may be lost in the process. Moreover, labor continues to watch for the effects of layoffs or of closures of small plants on workers in small communities where the economic mainstay of the community dies a slow death attributable to source regulation of the environment.

The rule making role of federal agencies with workplace and general environment regulatory responsibilities inevitably becomes a concern of organized labor as the public debates whether there should be more or less regulation of private business in the public interest.

The issue of cost-benefit analysis is a favorite topic of discussion for players of the regulation game. In controlling toxic substances, for instance, the calculated costs of control technology are quite easily derived while placing a monetary value on the many benefits—like the value of a human life—is virtually impossible.

There are similar unrecognized intangibles in a clean and healthy workplace—e.g., lower rates of absenteeism, greater productivity, less job stress leading to an increased sense of job worth and better family relations. Many of these same benefits, in addition to lower morbidity and mortality rates, result from a clean environment.

The rewards of a clean environment can mean much to countless individuals downstream and downwind and add to the definition of the greatest good for the most people.

A New Look at the Population Problem

By Jean van der Tak, Carl Haub,
and Elaine Murphy

Population growth is considered by many to be the main source of most environmental problems facing the world. This article outlines the history of population growth and details the nature and scope of the problem.

The human population of the earth probably passed the 4.3 billion point in 1979, increasing by some 74 million each year. We say "probably" because population data are still scanty and unreliable for parts of Asia and Africa although demographers are becoming adept at making plausible estimates from deficient data. At its current 1.7 percent rate of increase, every three years the world population grows by nearly as many people as the 220 million living in the U.S. in 1979. Every five days we add another million people to our human population.

This population explosion seems all the more awesome when seen in the perspective of humanity's development as a species. During the hundreds of thousands of years of the Old Stone Age when *Homo sapiens* was a hunter and food gatherer, for example, the world population probably never exceeded 10 million.

The world reached its first *billion* around 1800—some two to five million years after the appearance of the first humanlike creatures. Adding the second billion took about 130 years to 1930. The third billion was reached after only 30 years, in 1960, and the fourth after 15 years, in 1975. About 1965, the world's rate of population growth climbed to 2 percent—a rate at which numbers double in 35 years.

The explosive buildup of world population is putting tremendous

Excerpted from article in *The Futurist,* April 1980, with permission from the World Future Society. Jean van der Tak is director of publications, Carl Haub is staff demographer, and Elaine Murphy is director of population education at the Population Reference Bureau in Washington, D.C.

pressures on the earth's resources, environment, and social fabric. The pressures are currently felt most acutely in less developed countries (LDCs) where hundreds of millions already live in abject poverty and hunger. But the pressures are compounded by the developed countries' high per capita consumption of resources and output of pollution. The population predicament is shared by all humanity.

Historical Population Changes

A look at the changes in birth and death rates in developed countries over the last two centuries, in fact, gives a partial indication of how the population explosion came about. We use Sweden as an example, but the historical pattern of Sweden's birth and death rates is typical of other Western European countries. Until the late eighteenth century, both rates fluctuated at a relatively high level. Then as the Industrial Revolution accelerated in the early nineteenth century, the death rate began to fall gradually, followed some 50 to 70 years later by the birthrate. By the 1930s both were at low levels. Today, following a brief post-World War II rise in the birthrate, Sweden's annual births and deaths are in balance and the population has stopped growing from natural increase. This pattern applies generally to the now developed countries, although there are exceptions.

Since the 1930s, demographers have sought to explain how and why this evolution from high to low birth and death rates came about in today's developed countries. The best known explanation, based mainly on what was thought to be the experience in Western Europe, is known as the demographic transition theory. In its "classic" form, this theory describes three stages:

- The initial stage of potentially high population growth evolves from a backdrop of high death rates reflecting harsh living conditions and high birthrates needed to compensate for high infant mortality. With improved living conditions and control over disease brought about by "modernization," death rates begin to fall. At first, birthrates remain high, causing a rise in population growth.
- During the subsequent transitional stage, the rate of population growth is still relatively high, but a decline in birthrates becomes well established. The small-family ideal arises first among "upwardly mobile" couples, particularly in cities, who come to see too many children as a hindrance to taking advantage of the

opportunities offered by the expanding industrial economy. The preference for few children gradually diffuses throughout the country, aided by declining rates of infant mortality.

• The stage of very low or zero population growth is reached when mortality is low and fertility hovers around replacement level. Fertility could stabilize below replacement level, leading, in the absence of net immigration, to an eventual decline in the absolute size of a country's population.

Birth and Death Rates in Transition

Most of today's growth is taking place among the some three-quarters of the world's population living in the less developed regions—Latin America, Africa, and Asia (minus Japan). Here, previously high death rates fell rapidly after World War II and by about 1977 were at the comparatively low level of 12 deaths per 1,000 population per year. Birthrates are still at an average 33 per 1,000 population annually. As a result, the developing regions are growing at a rapid 2.1 percent each year. By contrast, among the other quarter of the globe's population in developed regions (the U.S. and Canada, Europe, the U.S.S.R., Japan, Australia, and New Zealand), the annual rate of growth now stands at a much lower 0.7 percent—reflecting an average birthrate of 16 per 1,000 and a death rate of 9.

Although reliable data to verify trends are lacking for many less developed countries, most demographers are now convinced that fertility has begun to decline in developing countries as a whole, and in some LDCs the decline is much more rapid than it was in Europe. At the same time, the precipitous decline in LDC death rates that marked the 1950s and early 1960s appears to have slowed.

Parker Mauldin and the late Bernard Berelson, former Population Council researchers, estimated that in the decade from 1965 to 1975 the birthrate of 94 LDCs with 98 percent of the developing world's population declined on average about 13 percent, from about 41 to 35.5 births per 1,000 population. In 28 developing countries containing over two-thirds of the world's population, the decline ranged from 10 to 40 percent. The decline was most marked in Asia and Latin America. Sub-Saharan Africa showed virtually no fertility decline and, with death rates continuing to fall, population growth in Africa had climbed to 2.9 percent about 1977, the highest of any region.

The slowdown in declining death rates, which economist Davidson

Gwatkin calls "the end of an era," seems related to the rise of dysentery, diarrhea, and pneumonia as leading causes of death, particularly among infants and children. These diseases, often precipitated by malnutrition, are harder to control with modern medicine and physician- and clinic-based health services. Eradicating them takes improved living conditions, especially more and better food and education. For most developing countries, rapid population growth has frustrated this possibility.

The beginnings of fertility decline in many LDCs and the slowdown in mortality decline have combined to stop the steady rise in the world's rate of population growth. The peak was probably passed somewhere in the mid-1960s—a time that some experts have called a "demographic watershed." The world's birthrate fell below 30 for the first time on record around 1975 and by 1977 was at an unprecedented 28 per 1,000 population.

Though encouraging, these trends still add up to huge numbers. The current 1.7 percent world growth rate is adding some 74 million a year to today's global total of about 4.3 billion. By 2000, the United Nations projects a total world population of 6.2 billion, with the lowered growth rate of 1.5 percent translating into an annual net increase of about 93 million people. Some 90 percent of the 2 billion increase in the next two decades will take place in the developing world.

Consequences of Rapid Population Growth

The consequences of rapid population growth are evident across the spectrum of human, animal, and plant life. In the less developed world, despite the recent slight slowdown, population is still growing in some countries at rates that could double the numbers of people in just over 20 years. These countries are already hard pressed to supply their current populations with decent living conditions.

Economic Development

Besides exporting the medical and public health revolution to the rest of the world, the Western industrialized nations have also tried, since World War II, to speed economic development and hence raise levels of living in the developing world. Improving living conditions requires that economic growth significantly outpace population growth. From 1960 to 1976, overall economic growth in low-income developing countries nearly matched that of the industrialized countries, and economic growth in middle-income LDCs was spectacular. But because of much more rapid population growth, the developing world's gain in income *per capita,* and thus levels of living, was much less. Rapid population growth diverts resources that might otherwise be available for investment in development.

Unemployment and Urbanization

In the two remaining decades of this century, the disheartening effects of past and future population growth in developing countries may be most evident in their exploding labor forces and cities.

The International Labour Office (ILO) estimates that in 1975 there were around 283 million people unemployed or underemployed in the non-Communist developing world—40 percent of the workforce.

According to the ILO, the high and in some cases rising population growth rates of the 1960s and early 1970s will translate into an increase in the developing world's labor force from 1.13 billion in 1975 to 1.91 billion in 2000. With these 780 million new workers added to the 283 million currently unemployed or underemployed (outside China), this quarter century will see the need for more than a billion new jobs in the developing world, where job-creating development is proceeding all too slowly. Particularly worrisome is the high projected labor force growth—and hence probably also unemployment—among urban youth aged 15 to 24, politically and socially the most volatile of all age groups.

To make matters worse, by the year 2000, over half the world's population is likely to be living in towns and cities, up from 39 percent in 1975.

Enormous numbers of people are involved. Between 1950 and 1975, the urban population of developing countries grew by some 400 million people. Between 1975 and 2000, the increase will be close to one billion.

The problem is aggravated by the concentration of urban dwellers in very large cities. In 1950, only one city of the developing world (Greater Buenos Aires) had a population over 5 million, compared to five such cities in the industrialized countries. By the year 2000, according to World Bank projections, the developing world will have about 40 cities this size and the developed world 12. Eighteen cities in developing countries are expected to have more than 10 million inhabitants, and one at least—Mexico City—may well have three times that number.

Housing, both urban and rural, is another critical problem. In Asia, the backlog of needed housing units in urban areas increased from 22 million dwellings in 1960 to 72 million in 1975; in Asia's rural areas, the need for housing units went from 125 to 219 million in the same 15 years.

Health facilities are on a similar treadmill. Inability to keep up with the demand from growing populations is part of the explanation for the recent slowdown in mortality declines in less developed countries. The World Health Organization estimates that 80 to 90 percent of rural populations in developing countries have no access to health care. The urban poor are scarcely better off. In Sao Paulo, for example, infant mortality has recently risen, malaria and bubonic plague have reappeared.

Food

Since World War II, food production worldwide has increased at a slightly faster rate than population. But most of the improvement in food supply *per person* has been in the already well-fed industrialized countries.

From 1961 through 1976, developing countries as a whole improved food production at a faster rate than developed countries, but because of rampant population growth, their per capita food output grew at a much slower pace. The gain in per capita food production averaged a steady 1.4 percent in industrialized countries during this period. In developing countries by contrast, annual per capita gains were already below 1 percent in the 1960s and nearly vanished in the early 1970s when droughts slashed yields across Asia and Africa. With better weather, expanded irrigation, and other investments, argicultural production has since improved in the developing world, particularly in Asia, but the situation remains precarious.

Environment

A last critical issue for future generations is the growing pressure of population on the global environment.

In recent decades, the earth's vegetation cover (croplands, forests, and grasslands), fisheries, water sources, and atmosphere have undergone a sharply increased rate of depletion and pollution.

A large part of this is again due to high production and consumption life-styles, coupled with still-growing populations, in industrialized countries. Environmental degradation has also resulted from the desperate efforts of rapidly growing impoverished populations in developing nations to survive. Vast areas of Africa, South and Southeast Asia, the Middle East, and Latin America have been crippled by slash-and-burn agriculture, overcropping, overgrazing, and consequent wind and water erosion.

This environmental loss and damage is occurring in a world of 4 billion people. In 20 years, the number of human consumers and polluters is expected to be around 6 billion and still growing.

World Response to the Problem

Over the past 10 to 15 years, there has been an encouraging increase in world awareness of population problems. Many developing countries have seen the need for urgent action to reduce rapid population growth if their development efforts are not to be greatly impaired or totally frustrated. In 1960, of *all* countries in the world, only India and Pakistan supported organized family planning programs, both for the avowed purpose of reducing birthrates. By 1978, 35 less developed countries—with 77 percent of the developing world's population—had offical policies to reduce population growth. Another 30, with 15 percent of LDC population, supported family planning programs for other than demographic reasons. Only 7 percent of the developing world's people lived in the 66 nations that have no family planning activities.

The Outlook

What lies ahead? All are agreed that the world's present growth rate of 1.7 percent, which would double human numbers in just 41 years, cannot continue indefinitely. It is also clear, however, that— barring a nuclear holocaust or massive famine—a much larger population lies ahead for the developing countries and the world as a whole. With close to half of the developing world's population now under age 15, the relentless arithmetic of population momentum will carry waves of population growth into the twenty-first century even if replacement-level fertility—essentially, an average family of two children—were miraculously to be achieved everywhere tomorrow. Just when the earth's population will stop growing and how large it then will be depends crucially on when that worldwide replacement-level fertility is reached.

Current "medium" projections for world population in the year 2000, just around the corner, range from a low of 5.9 billion to a high of 6.4 billion—a difference of "only" half a billion. For further into the future, demographers' opinions vary much more widely. Demographers Donald J. Bogue and Amy Ong Tsui predict a rapid slowdown to zero growth and a peak global total population of about 8.1 billion by 2050, provided that family planning programs are pursued vigorously in the developing world and steady gains in social and economic development continue. The most recently published long-range projections of the United Nations put the peak at about 11 billion about a century and a half from now. World Bank estimates fall in between. "If current trends continue," the Bank projects replacement-level fertility for the world as a whole about 2020 and a stabilized population of 9.8 billion some 70 years later.

Worldwatch Institute President Lester Brown doubts that global population as high as 12 billion (an earlier projection of the United Nations) will ever be reached. He sees crucial biological systems— fisheries, forests, grasslands, and croplands—and oil resources already showing unsupportable strains at the current 4.3 billion. He predicts that further mounting pressures on vital resources, translated into unemployment, lowered per capita income, and inflation, will force restricted childbearing on individual couples and stablilized population policies on governments that do not now have them. To ward off collapse of the earth's major biological systems, Brown urges a "concerted global effort to slam on the demographic brakes" with the aim of halting population growth just short of 6 billion about 2015.

Brown admits that this "exceedingly ambitious" target would be extremely difficult for African countries in particular, where birthrates are now between 40 and 50. But the alternative could be the return of the famines that claimed hundreds of thousands of lives across the southern fringe of the Sahara in the early 1970s. And in achieving the target, Brown observes that "no country would have to reduce its birthrate any more rapidly than Barbados, China, Costa Rica, Indonesia, and Singapore already have."

To Speed Fertility Decline

Efforts heroic enough to meet Brown's timetable are probably unimaginable in the two decades remaining to the twentieth century. But clearly birthrate declines must be accelerated now in most LDCs if the world is to avoid an eventual population so massive that the future of humanity and its ecological support system would be jeopardized. The approaches currently being pursued or proposed to speed these declines include both efforts to improve family planning services and "beyond family planning" measures to enhance motivation for smaller families. They can be summed up as follows:

- More and improved family planning services.
- Information and education.
- Restructured development.
- Incentives/disincentives.
- Pressures and sanctions.

Although the emphasis may vary with individual country situations, all of these approaches are and will doubtless be necessary if fertility is to decline rapidly to replacement level in the coming two or three decades. The only other alternative to staving off an intolerable ultimate global population size is higher death rates and that choice is unacceptable. Migration to industrial countries has eased population pressure for some small and medium-size developing countries—Algeria, Mexico, Morocco, Tunisia, and Turkey, for example. But international migration on the scale that would be required to make a significant difference for countries the size of India and Pakistan is now impossible. India alone adds 13 million to the world's population every year—the same number currently estimated for the refugees that are now straining the entire free world's absorptive capacities.

The world is already over-crowded at 4.3 billion—in both developed and developing countries—and is destined to become much more crowded. We can no longer avoid a world of at least 6 billion and then, probably, some decades later, 8 billion. But the actions we take now could—and must—avert the even greater stresses, poverty, and hunger that would prevail in a world of 10, 11, or more billions.

The Case for More People

By Julian L. Simon

Taking an unusual point of view, Julian Simon argues that there may be an actual population shortage and that neither logic nor statistical evidence supports the view that resources are finite.

Much of technological advance comes from people who are neither well-educated nor well-paid—the dispatcher who develops a slightly better way of deploying taxis in his ten-taxi fleet, the shipper who discovers that garbage cans make excellent cheap containers for many items, the retailer who develops a faster way to stock merchandise on shelves, the check out clerk who works up a method of bagging groceries faster, and so on.

Even in science one need not be a genius to make a valuable contribution. There have been many more discoveries and a faster rate of growth of productivity in the past century than in previous centuries, when there were fewer people alive. Whereas we develop new materials almost every day, it was centuries between the discovery and use of, say, copper and iron. If there had been a larger population, the pace of increase in technological practice might have been faster, even accounting for the growth of knowledge to work from.

Since the first edition of Malthus, however, classical economic theory has concluded that population growth must reduce the standard of living: The more people, the lower the per capita income, all else being equal. This proposition derives from the concept of diminishing returns: Two men cannot use the same tool at the same time, or farm the same piece of land, without reducing the output per worker.

Many statistical studies conclude that population growth does not have an observed negative effect upon economic growth. Among these is a long-run historical analysis by one of the most respected

From *American Demographics*, November/December 1979. Reprinted with permission. Julian Simon is a professor of economics and business administration at the University of Illinois at Urbana-Champaign.

economic-demographic statisticians of recent decades, Nobel prize winner Simon Kuznets, whose results are shown on this page. You may verify for yourself that neither a positive nor a negative relationship is shown by the data.*

These studies do not show that fast population growth increases per capita income. But they certainly imply that one should not confidently assert that population growth decreases economic growth.

More People, More Knowledge

These data, which conflict so sharply with the received theory, have naturally provoked explanations such as the advantages of youthfulness in the labor force, the increased opportunities and consequent flexibility in a growing economy, and the greater mobility of the labor force in a growing economy. But the most plausible explanation almost surely is the positive effect of additional people on productivity by creating and applying new knowledge.

Population Growth and Economic Growth: No Clear Relationship

		population growth rate per decade	output per capita growth rate per decade
France	1896–1966	3.5	18.6
U.K.	1920–1967	4.8	16.9
Belgium	1900–1967	5.3	14.3
Italy	1890–1967	6.9	22.9
Switzerland	1910–1967	8.8	16.1
Germany	1910–1967	10.4	20.5
Netherlands	1900–1967	14.2	15.1
U.S.	1910–1967	14.2	18.4
Australia	1900–1967	18.8	13.1
Canada	1920–1967	19.4	20.9

Source: Kuznets

---

* There are obvious differences between the more-developed and the less-developed countries. This article looks at developed economies such as the United States, although similar conclusions can be reached for less-developed economies, but for different reasons.

Why is the standard of living so much higher in the United States or Sweden than in India or Mali? And why is our standard of living so much higher now than it was 200 years ago? The all-important difference is that there is a much greater stock of technological know-how available, and people are educated to learn and use that knowledge. The knowledge and the schooling are intertwined; in India today, unlike the United States 200 years ago, the knowledge is available in books in the library, but without schooling and productive social organization the knowledge cannot be adapted to local needs and put to work.

The stock of industrial capital is also intertwined with the stock of knowledge and education; the value of much of our capital such as computers and jet airplanes consists largely of the new knowledge that is built into them. And without educated workers these chunks of capital could not be operated and would be worthless.

Because improvements—their invention and their adoption—come from people, it seems reasonable to assume that the amount of improvement depends in large measure on the number of people available.

But is it certain that the recent productivity increases in the United States would not have occurred anyway, even if population had been smaller? The connections between numbers of scientists, inventors, ideas, adoption and use of new discoveries are difficult to delineate clearly. But the crucial links needed to confirm this effect seem obvious and strong. For example, data show clearly for developed countries that the bigger the population of a country, the greater the number of scientists and the larger the amount of scientific knowledge produced.

Science is not the same as applied knowledge put into operation, but there is other evidence of the relationship between population increase and long-term economic growth: An industry, or the economy of an entire country, can grow because population is growing or because per capita income is growing, or both. Some industries in some countries grow faster than the same industry in other countries, or than other industries in the same country. Comparisons of faster- and slower-growing industries show that in the former the rate of increase of productivity and technological practice is higher. This argues that faster population growth—which causes faster-growing industries—leads to faster growth of productivity.

Newborns don't come up with new productive ideas while still in diapers, of course. And though the parents pay most of children's expenses, society also shells out to finance children's intellectual development into productive maturity. This means that if your time horizon is very short—extending only, say, 25 years into the future—the gains in productivity due to someone else's newborn child won't impress you, and you will feel that your taxes are ill-invested in the child. But if you take a longer perspective, perhaps because you realize that you, yourself, are now the beneficiary of social investments of children of past decades, then you will consider as a great social benefit the knowledge that the newborns of today will create in the future.

A Bigger Market

The phenomenon economists call "economies of scale"—greater efficiency of larger-scale production where the market is larger—is inextricably intertwined with the creation of knowledge and technological change, along with the ability to use larger and more efficient machinery and greater division of labor.

A larger population implies a bigger market. A bigger market is likely to bring bigger manufacturing plants that may be more efficient than smaller ones, as well as longer production runs and hence lower set-up costs per unit of output. It also makes possible greater division of labor and hence an increase in the skill with which goods and services are made.

If the market for its goods is small, a firm will buy a machine that can be used in the production of several kinds of products. If the market is larger, the firm can afford to buy a separate, more specialized machine for each operation. Larger markets also support a wider variety of services. If population is too small, there may be too few people to constitute a profitable market for a given product or service. In such a case there will be no seller, and people who need the product or service will suffer from not being able to obtain it.

Economies of scale also stem from learning. The more television sets or bridges or airplanes that a group of people produce, the more chance they have to improve their skills with "learning by doing," a very important factor in increasing productivity. The increased efficiency of production within firms and industries as experience accumulates has been well documented in many industries starting with the air-frame industry in the 1930s.

A bigger population also makes profitable many major social invest-ments that would not otherwise be profitable—railroads, irrigation systems and ports. The amount of such construction often depends upon the population density per given land area. For example, if an Australian farmer were to clear a piece of land very far from the nearest neighboring farm, he might have no way to ship his pro-duce to market, as well as have difficulty in obtaining labor and sup-plies. But when more farms are established nearby, roads will be built which will link him with markets in which to buy and sell. Of course, there may also be diseconomies of increased scale, for example congestion and pollution.

A Richer Computer Model

Population size and growth have a variety of economic effects, some negative and others positive. If economists are to be worth their keep, they must take account of the size and importance of the various effects, and calculate the net effect. One can only ob-tain a satisfactory overall assessment by constructing an integrated model of the economy, and then comparing the incomes produced by the economy under various conditions of population growth.

If one adds to the standard Malthusian model another fundamen-tal fact of the economic growth of nations—the increase in produc-tivity due to additional people's inventive and adaptive capacities—one arrives at a very different result.

I studied the effects of five different rates of population growth in a computer simulation of output per worker. The first, ZPG, has zero population growth; BASE has 1 percent population growth per year; PLUS-HALF has a 50 percent jump in the birth rate above BASE in year zero and subsequent years; TWO has 2 percent population growth per year; TEMP has a one-year temporary increase in the birth rate.

The most important outcome of comparing these five demographic structures is that under every set of conditions simulated by the com-puter, those demographic structures with the more rapid popula-tion growth come to have higher per-worker income than structure BASE in less than 80 years, even with technology assumed to in-crease as low as one percent per year. In many runs the higher fer-tility structures overtake the BASE structure's per-worker output after only 30 years—that is, only about 10 years after the entrance of the first additional children into the labor force. Furthermore, the short-run economic differences between the various demographic structures are small by any absolute measure, though the long-run differences are large.

The time horizon is sufficiently short so that any possible major changes in the natural resources situation may be disregarded. But it is sufficiently long so that the delayed effects of knowledge increase can come to play their role. And though the models refer to the United States, it would be more appropriate to think of this analysis as applying to the developed world as a whole, because of scientific and technological interdependence.

Models such as these would have had no chance of being accepted 15 or 30 years ago because of the preeminence of physical capital in the thinking of economists. But with the recognition in recent years of the fundamental importance of knowledge, education and the quality of the labor force in the productive process, these demographic models and their economic implications should enjoy a more welcome reception.

What About the "Limits to Growth"?

Often one hears the objection that even if additional people really will have a positive effect upon per capita output and income, this positive effect would be offset by such negative impacts as pollution of the environment, shortage of agricultural land due to paving it over for cities and highways, increased scarcity of energy and other natural resources, and increased chances of world starvation and famine. The main basis for this objection is the assertion that these trends are for the worse. The simple truth, however, is that these trends are for the better.

Hard as it may be to swallow the fact, fewer farmers are producing much more food and feeding more people than in the past, despite population increase. If the decline in the U.S. farm population is carried to its logical absurdity, one farmer eventually will feed everyone else, a far cry from the spectre of starvation from the skyrocketing population portrayed in equally absurd doomsday forecasts. And urban areas and highways consume only about 3 percent of the United States' land area.

Despite gasoline lines and the frantic attention devoted to the energy crisis in recent years, even growing long-run energy scarcity is a myth. The only meaningful measure of scarcity, barring emergency or wartime needs, is the economic cost of the good. The economic cost of almost every natural resource—including the proportion of our incomes spent for energy—has declined throughout human history. Although OPEC can control prices, the cost of production of a barrel of oil has not risen, but rather has declined over the last century since the introduction of petroleum.

Conventional wisdom has it that resources are finite. But there is support for this view neither in logic nor in statistical evidence. There is no support in the long-term data to doubt that we will continue to find new lodes, invent better production methods and discover new substitutes, bounded only by our imagination and the exercise of educated skills. The only constraint upon our capacity to enjoy unlimited raw materials at acceptable prices is knowledge.

Space Age Cargo Cult

By Paul and Anne Ehrlich

This article, a rebuttal to Julian Simon's population ideas, illustrates the intensity of the emotions and rhetoric that often characterizes the debate over environmental issues.

When we two were born almost 50 years ago, there were 2 billion people in the world. Today there are 4.5 billion. Within our short lifetimes the human population has grown more than it did in the several million years between the time the first people walked Earth and our births. And growth continues at a frightening pace. Some 75 million people are added to the population annually—the equivalent of a new United States every three years.

By almost any standard, Earth is already grossly overpopulated. Virtually every nation on the planet is straining its resources and its environment in order to support its citizens. Human numbers everywhere are pressing on values—freedom, equality, safety, employment, prosperity, leisure, and so on. Even with a large proportion of people living in misery, the current population can only be supported by using up its resource capital. Humanity is rapidly consuming resources that cannot be renewed on a time scale of interest to society. Prime examples are petroleum, soils, and "fossil" freshwater.

Perhaps the most crucial nonrenewable resource being depleted is the diversity of life forms with which *Homo sapiens* shares Earth. Species and genetically distinct populations of plants, animals, and microorganisms are working parts of ecological systems. And those systems provide us with a wide variety of free public services that are essential to industrial society. Those vital functions include: controlling the quality of the atmosphere; ameliorating climate; providing fresh water; producing, replenishing, and protecting soils; disposing of wastes; recycling nutrients essential to agriculture; controlling the

---

Excerpted by permission from an article in *Defenders*, February 1982. Copyright 1982 by Defenders of Wildlife. Paul and Anne Ehrlich are members of the Department of Biological Sciences at Stanford University.

vast majority of potential pests of crops and carriers of diseases; and maintaining a vast genetic library from which humanity could withdraw everything from cancer cures to crops from which gasoline can be extracted. These largely unappreciated functions underlie society's elaborate economic structure; they are a vital part of our life-support system.

Yet those services most involved in supplying humanity with nourishment—providing food from the sea and supporting agriculture—are already faltering. World per-capita food reserves have dropped back to their record lows of the mid-1970's, and options for dealing with future production shortfalls are becoming fewer while the probability of such shortfalls occurring is rapidly increasing.

In spite of the problems, recent prominence has been given to the population ideas of the economist, Julian Simon. Simon's view of the way the world works would not deserve a moment's consideration were it not for the people who have seen fit to disseminate it. Let's take a look at some of his "ideas."

In *Science* magazine in June 1980, Simon wrote that "the quantity of copper that can be made available to humanity cannot be calculated even in principle" because "copper can be made from other metals," and the theoretical limit on the amount of copper thus obtained would be "the total weight of the universe." It is probably not necessary to point out that large-scale alchemy is impossible. Indeed, producing even a flyspeck of copper by bombarding other elements with subatomic particles in an accelerator would be a gargantuan enterprise. And the laws of physics make quite clear that no technological breakthrough in the future is going to change that fact.

Simon, however, does permit us an amusing vision. Everything in the universe—except a gigantic copper converter, itself made from copper (lighted and powered by an extra-universal force), and Simon (representing humanity)—has been converted to copper. All other people have already been changed into guess what? Simon then leaps in front of the machine and his vision is fullfilled: "the total weight of the universe" would be copper—a most unexpected version of the heat death, to say the least!

Simon's weird ideas are not, by any means, restricted to physics. He treats us to mathematical amusements as well. For example, in a 1981 book, *The Ultimate Resource,* he has managed to return to ancient Greece to resurrect Zeno's paradox for a "proof" that the amount of various resources is infinite. He says, for instance, ". . . the length of a one-inch line is finite in the sense that it is bounded at both ends. But the line within the end-points contains an infinite number of points: these points cannot be counted because they have no defined size. Therefore the number of points in that one-inch segment is not finite. Similarly, the quantity of copper that will ever be available to us is not finite."

Zeno's paradox is usually exemplified by a race between a hare and a tortoise which has a head start. The hare never catches the tortoise, because the tortoise has always left each point before the hare arrives. Unfortunately for the tortoise and for Simon's argument (and as all modern students of mathematics know), there is no relationship between the number of points in a line and its length, which is the crucial measure in races. In traveling a finite distance in a finite time, the hare passes an infinite number of points, including those occupied by the tortoise. By Simon's reasoning, the amount of copper on Earth would be counted as infinite even if the actual total quantity were only an ounce. Simon, in short, has confused infinite subdivisibility with infinite quantity.

In fact, his proposition is doubly incorrect: while every line, regardless of length, can indeed be subdivided into an infinite number of parts, a resource cannot. After a finite number of subdivisions, one is left with groups of molecules (for instance coal), single molecules (methane), or atoms (copper), which cannot be further subdivided without destroying the properties of the resource.

Simon's recent ventures into other areas are marked with the same sophistication. On agriculture he has declared that "food has no long-run physical limit"—on the basis of a series of logical errors similar in style to his copper fiascos. He has announced that pollution is decreasing rather than increasing by, among other grotesque mistakes, using *life expectancy* as a measure of pollution. (This, of course, would be a simplistic measure, even if one were considering only direct health effects of pollution, since public health measures might easily be increasing life expectancy more rapidly than the effects of pollution were lowering it.) Simon naturally ignores other pollution problems, such as the steady increase of acid rains that today is one of the most potent threats to those crucial ecosystem services.

In areas such as fisheries statistics and land use, Simon shows the same kind of marvelous insights. For instance, he has concluded that "the combined increases of income and population do *not* increase 'pressure' on the land," because "the absolute number of acres per farmer rises when income becomes high, *despite* increases in population.'' In support of this astonishing conclusion, he cites data from overdeveloped countries showing a decrease in the absolute number of farm workers accompanied (curiously enough!) by an increase in the absolute amount of land per worker.

Strangely, Simon's discussion does not include any mention of the well-known cause of this trend, the mechanization and energy-intensification of agriculture. That change has contributed not only to the deterioration of farmland itself, but also to environmental deterioration elsewhere as pesticides disperse, fertilizers run off, and soils are converted to dust and silt. More damage is done far from farm fields by mining, drilling, damming, logging, smelting, and the like as energy and materials are mobilized to support the agricultural enterprises.

Naturally, Simon also expresses no concern about the annual loss of some 1,500 square miles of prime United States farmland to urbanization. After all, shopping malls and high-rise buildings are considered more valuable today than corn fields. If the value of corn should rise enough to change all that in ten or a hundred years, Simon presumably believes that then an economical way would be invented by scientists to peel cities off the land. Sadly, however, if that *were* possible, the bared land would not be prime farmland but wasteland, since the process of first disturbing and then covering it would destroy the physical and biological characteristics that make the soil productive. Furthermore, in the even more overpopulated world that Simon (as the leading advocate of the benefits of human population growth) envisages, one must wonder how easy it would be to tear down homes and other structures on land desperately needed for reconversion to agriculture.

Needless to say, the ignorance of the laws of thermodynamics that Simon's writings display is not limited to confusions about resource availability. There is no hint of recognition that (as the second law dictates) environmental insults inevitably accompany human activities, or that *the limited capacity of environmental systems to absorb such insults and still supply the services society requires places fundamental limits on growth of the physical economy.* In short, even if alchemy were possible and available energy were infinite, all of Simon's fundamental theses would still be dead wrong.

As might be expected, in this and all other discussions Simon consistently ignores, from both compassionate and practical viewpoints, the fate of humanity's co-inhabitants of Earth. As thoughtful humans realize, an attempt to follow Simon's recommendation to expand human population and activities to infinity would spell doom for most wildlife, as well as for civilization.

One might be tempted simply to write off Simon's views as being unworthy of consideration by any educated person. After all, there have always been flatworlders, and there probably always will be. But taking such a position would be a mistake. The most prominent space-age cargo cult is supported by powerful people who are much too clever to be taken in by voodoo or witchcraft.

Consider, for example, that Simon's remarkable analysis of copper appeared in *Science,* the most prestigious North American scientific publication. All papers submitted to *Science* are supposed to be reviewed by scientists. Are we to assume that Simon's manuscript (which is dense with other nonsense as well) somehow was sent to a scientist who had never had any contact with junior high school physics? Is it likely that the editors of *The Atlantic Monthly,* which published two of Simon's articles, are unable to see through his arguments? His book was issued by the press at Princeton University, home of some of the world's best physicists and population biologists. Could the editors have found someone to review Simon's manuscript who had to take off his shoes to count to 20? Could laudatory reviewers of the book for the *New York Times* and *Washington Post* really have been incapable of detecting that the volume was simple-minded from cover to cover?

We think not. We think that there are many people who rarely, if ever, consider the long-run persistence of either humanity or other organisms. Their focus is on the "bottom line" today and tomorrow; future generations will have to fend for themselves. These people don't care to analyze Simon's arguments; Simon is attacking the environmentalists—that's all that matters. Simon says that by simply turning the old crank faster, the human condition will continually improve: "The natural world allows, and the developed world promotes through the marketplace, responses to human needs and shortages in such a manner [as to] keep us headed in a life-sustaining direction."

This is music to the ears of those who find the basic message of environmentalists—that humanity in general and the rich nations in particular must change their ways—offensive or subversive. It is pleasing to establishment scientists who believe with religious fervor that science will solve all human problems. So what, they think, if Simon and his ilk don't understand how the world works; *they still draw the right conclusions.*

There is now a national administration struggling to turn back the environmental clock, and it has the Western equivalent of Melanesian cargo-cultists providing an intellectual justification for its behavior. Those of us who are interested in the survival of all of Earth's living beings, both because it is morally right *and* because it is the only route to the survival of our society, must redouble our educational efforts. These must not be in the direction of "believe what we tell you" but in the direction of "think for yourself." When every high school student can figure out what is wrong with the creed of the cargo cult, the future will be considerably brighter.

Supply-Side Ideas Challenge Old Population Theory

By Rice Odell

This article offers a further examination of the idea that population growth has a positive impact on national welfare. It argues that the long-term adjustments and potentialities of a growing population may be overwhelmed by short-run adjustment problems.

One of society's most critical and difficult questions still nags us: What is the optimum level of population?

It is a question that applies to individual countries, including the United States, and to the world as a whole. It is a question that many people feel has been answered adequately in the past decade. A seemingly critical mass of expert and public opinion—shaped to a significant degree by environmental and ecological concepts—accepted the view that population growth should more or less be halted, so as to avoid inevitable conflict and suffering due to resource scarcities, ecosystem impoverishment, excessive crowding, and a deteriorating quality of life.

In 1972, the President's Commission on Population and the American Future said in its final report that "after two years of concentrated effort, we have concluded that no substantial benefits would result from continued growth of the nation's population."

Now, however, there is a fervent backlash against neo-Malthusian views. A basic challenge has been mounted, principally by economists who espouse a kind of supply-side theory of reproduction. They contend that more is better.

The current charge of the economics brigade is based principally on two theories: (1) population pressure on resources is not a problem in the long term because human ingenuity and technology can be expected to continue increasing resource extractions, food production, and so forth, as it has in the past, and (2) economic growth is not jeopardized but enhanced by population growth because more people generate more production.

In other words, the idea of limits to growth is bunkum. Julian L. Simon, professor of economics at the University of Illinois, has summed it up a different way: "Life can't be good unless you're alive."[1]

The challenge to population theories that are endorsed by most environmentalists is important because so much is at stake—hunger and poverty, the pace of economic development, the quality of life, even the future course of civilization. Population policy (or lack thereof) is important to Americans because the U.S. supplies enormous amounts of food to other countries and because it receives large numbers of immigrants and refugees. (The U.S. also is a fount of research and technology and the only strong citadel of democracy, both factors related to the capacity of society to deal with population and resource problems.)

A number of measures that will affect population growth are under scrutiny in Washington. They involve: curtailing the flow of illegal immigrants; reducing quotas for legal immigrants; changing policies and appropriations for population assistance under foreign aid programs; altering laws dealing with abortion; changing appropriations for domestic family planning assistance; and formulating an overall national population policy.

State and local governments also deal with most of these issues. They are most directly affected by the abrupt changes that often accompany illegal immigration, an influx of refugees, and internal migration within the country, including that accompanying new energy development. They also are affected by any metamorphosis in the population's age structure, such as that caused by the "baby boom" bulge.

Gross, long-range projections gloss over such short-term surges, yet they can cause problems more serious than long-term change whose impacts can be smoothed out over time with appropriate social and economic adjustments.

Oddly, the debate—much of which has lately centered on the pronouncements of professor Simon—is a born-again version of one that took place more than a century ago. It is reminiscent both in the absolute polarity of dearly held viewpoints and in the poverty of supporting evidence on both sides.

In response to Malthus, essayist and social critic William Godwin said, "Man is to a considerable degree the artificer of his own fortune. We can apply our reflections and our ingenuity to whatever we regret." And American economist Henry George wrote, in 1880:

"I assert that in any given state of civilization a greater number of people can collectively be better provided for than a smaller. I assert that the injustice of society, not the niggardliness of nature, is the cause of want and misery which the current theory attributes to overpopulation. . . . I assert that, other things being equal, the greater the population, the greater the comfort. . . ."

Meanwhile, in 1848, economist John Stuart Mill had written of the law of diminishing returns as applied to agriculture: "It is vain to say, that all mouths which the increase of mankind calls into existence, bring with them hands. The new mouths require as much food as the old ones, and the hands do not produce as much."[2]

But, says Simon—to bring the debate abruptly into the present—"it is your mind that matters economically, as much or more than your mouth or hands."[3] Babies don't come into a Malthusian world of hands and mouths; they come with heads, and "it's from heads that all our resources come eventually."[1]

These heads have a sense of will and a capacity for innovation. They can cope with society's problems. The more heads, the greater the stock of human knowledge and solutions to these problems. "And this contribution is large enough in the long run to overcome all the costs of population growth,"[3] according to Simon.

Erik Eckholm, a visiting fellow at the International Institute for Environment and Development, has replied that, under current circumstances, the fact that babies have minds and hands as well as mouths to feed is of "very dubious relevance" because newcomers will have "no education, no land to farm, and no access to productive jobs."[1]

Taking another tack, Simon also argues that a larger population also achieves economies of scale. "It implies a larger total demand for goods; with larger demand and higher production come division of labor and specialization, larger plants, larger industries, more learning by doing, and other related economies of scale."[3]

Garrett Hardin, head of the Environmental Fund, says that "economies of scale don't go on forever," and he notes, for example, that there are no economies of scale in teaching: When classes grow up to 1,000 students, there is less chance of passing on the excitement and creativity that produces useful knowledge and ideas.[1]

From another perspective, that of Ben Wattenberg, editor of *Public Opinion,* the United States should increase its population so it will not decline relative to the rest of the world. "Population is still a critical factor in the power equation," says Wattenberg. He adds that there are populous nations that are not powerful but no powerful nations that are not populous.[1] Others have replied that at some point, any population-power correlation must break down, with increasing population then a liability.

Those espousing the value of an increasing population also welcome substantial immigration. As Simon puts it, reflecting the considerable evidence that immigrants are a positive factor economically, "Immigrants are a better deal than native births. They bring a remarkably high rate of return."[1] It also is argued that their diversity and ambition help energize American society. There are, of course, serious short-term problems of adjustment, but Emery N. Castle, president of Resources for the Future, says, "Our history strongly suggests that over the long run the economic and social fabric of the country is strengthened by immigrants."[1]

However, with the recent disputes about immigration focusing on socioeconomic factors, there is a tendency to overlook the possible serious consequences for the environment and natural resources. The focus also tends to devaluate humanitarian and foreign policy considerations.

Simon's overall thesis relies heavily on an historical trend data which in his opinion shows that, for most resources, relative prices have been stable or have declined, thereby revealing an absence of scarcity. "There is no persuasive reason to believe that these trends will not continue indefinitely," Simon says. "The limits of the physical world are becoming more relaxing."

In some cases, Simon's data or use of them are disputed, and in other cases critics question the relevance of long-term historical trends when it comes to questions of finite resources and exponential change.[4] "The more recent past is a better guide to the future than the distant past, " says Hardin. "It's like buying a stock."[1]

Simon notes that "the overall trend in recent decades has been an increase in food produced per person."[3] There has indeed been an increase, though obviously not enough to prevent widespread distress. Also, more conservative observers point out that the *rate* of increase is in decline. They see this—along with indications that yields per acre cannot rise indefinitely—as cause for pessimism. For example, in rough terms, world per capita food production rose 15% in the decade from 1950-1960, 7% in the decade 1960-1970, and then only 4% in the decade 1970-1980.[5]

Even if these figures are a bit skewed because they use fixed points rather than trend analysis, trend lines appear to show similar results. For example, Katherine Gillman, formerly a senior staff member of the Council on Environmental Quality, says, "A trend line based on the years 1950-1960 points to growth of nearly 30% in the 1970-2000 period. But a trend line based on the 1967-1977 figures indicates growth of less than 18% for 1970-2000."[6]

A similar point of contention arose as a result of Simon's enthusiasm for the fact that the number of trips to parks has risen "phenomenally." In response, Hardin asked, "What was a visit like 25 years ago, and what is it like now?. . .There is no way to increase the number of quality parks. People go to the parks for quiet, solitude, and the feeling of space."[1]

It is worth repeating that aggregate figures on such resources as land and food sidesteps the obvious problems of environmental damage and scarcity in the present and in particular locations. These may involve air pollution, deforestation and firewood shortages, filling of wetlands, and excessive urbanization.[7]

Curtis Farrar, a deputy assistant administrator at the Agency for International Development, said he thinks of the poor in Bangladesh "sitting on the shore watching for new islands to rise from the waves, so they can rush out and farm it." It was in a similar vein that Hardin said, "The larger the population, the smaller the fraction that can enjoy wilderness."[1]

In the debate between the so-called doomsayers and the Pollyannas, theoretical observations about resources and human ingenuity in the future obscure not only the present empirical evidence of inadequate resources but also humankind's inability to manage them. Can ingenuity in the future devise political institutions, economic systems, and social cultures that are adequate to utilize and properly distribute available resources? It could be said that one prerequisite to this condition is the cessation of warfare. Anyone who wishes can form his or her own opinion on the likely degree of success in this area, as no appreciable evidence is available—none that is, except history itself.

William W. Murdoch, of the University of California at Santa

Barbara, says that the notion of population in balance with a fixed carrying capacity of resources is "simply not appropriate" to issues of development in poorer countries because these countries are not close to the limit of their biological and physical resources. "Constraints are set by political and economic, not ecological or physical, factors," he says.[1]

In the absence of a clearer picture of the future, one can examine the present situation, as Nick Eberstadt, a visiting fellow at Harvard University's Center for Population Studies, has done: "The numbers of people malnourished and starving are statistics which nutritionists hotly contest. It can be said with some certainty, however, that over 400 million people live in nations where conditions are so harsh that the average citizen will die more than a quarter of a century sooner than his American counterpart."[8]

(Those who seek to derive optimism from current figures can turn to Jacqueline R. Kasun, a professor of economics at Humboldt State University, who says that "only" about 2% of the world's population suffers from "serious hunger."[8] Of course, others put the figure considerably higher.)

A good deal of the disagreement over population policy involves the time period under consideration. In fact, Simon seems to agree with his opponents that current and short-term population-resource problems can be serious; he allows that his approach does not promise an altogether rosy path to the future. Simon's "short-run" period runs up to some 60 years. It is around the end of that period, he insists that a larger population will begin to result in higher per capita income.[9] His theory chiefly applies to a "long-run" that is up to 120-180 years away.

"These debates provide no consensus on the proper directions of public policy in the near-term," says an Agency for International Development internal report. "A more significant question for LDC's [less developed countries] and for the U.S. government is how population growth affects the development process in the *shorter-term,* that is, within the time-frame of five to 20 years that is appropriate for government decisions regarding assistance . . . Within the next two decades, smaller families can mean better health care, better education, better housing, and more job opportunities for present populations, thus helping to meet basic development objectives in many LDC's."[10]

Similarly, Lawrence R. Kegan, senior consultant with the Popula-

Shifting Population Dialectics

Family planning assistance in the U.S. and abroad always has had its opponents, and it now appears to face strong new challenges by those who oppose abortion, by those who simply see population programs as appropriate targets for budget cutting, and by those who would let free-market forces determine family and population size.

Foreign aid law already prohibits the Agency for International Development from funding abortion *services* as part of family planning assistance programs and also from funding biomedical *research* on abortion as a family-planning technique. Therefore, says Peters D. Willson, of the Alan Guttmacher Institute, critics of population programs are forced to develop an economic argument against them. "The debate has shifted so there is a greater challenge to the programs' effectiveness."

"There already is a small but growing body of new literature, from both pro- and anti-choice advocates, challenging the idea that rapid population growth is detrimental to the economic development of developing nations, and opponents of international family planning efforts already are putting it to use," says Willson.[17]

Nick Eberstadt, a visiting fellow at the Harvard Center for Population Studies, is among those who does not see population as an economic evil. For example, he says, "There is no evidence that population growth in the poor nations is causally connected to hunger."

However, Eberstadt recommends repeal of the congressional taboo against foreign aid funds being used to serve the purposes of abortion—and he does so on health grounds. "This law is hypocritical," he says. "To the extent that it is effective, it imposes needless suffering on poor women in poor countries. Somewhere between 40 and 60 million abortions are performed in the world each year, and most of these are performed in the poor countires." Most of them also involve unsanitary conditions and unqualified personnel, often resulting in death, says Eberstadt.[8]

tion Crisis Committee, says that Simon fails to appreciate many of the short-run consequences of population growth: For example, "to meet the food needs and eliminate malnutrition would call for an increase of food output of at least 4 percent a year, a rate not reached in the last 20 years." In addition, "about 1 billion new jobs may be needed in the developing world, mostly by young people between the ages of 15 and 24, the group most volatile politically and socially."[11]

It is true that the annual population *growth rate* for the less-developed countries as a whole has declined by more than 12 percent since 1970—from 2.35 to 2.06 percent. But the rate is still high and the *absolute increase* per year is large and growing; the total population of the LDC's increased 62.2 million in 1970 and 68 million in 1980.[10]

Philip M. Hauser, director emeritus of the Population Research Center at the University of Chicago, also has elaborated on the differences between LDC's and developed countries: "Rapid population increase in a traditional agricultural economy with little change in technology and productivity tends to be accompanied by diminishing returns rather than economies of scale. Moreover, the rapid population growth that characterizes the LDC's is occurring at a time when the population is already large in relation to resources, and before critical cultural changes of the type experienced in the Western more-developed countries, such as the Renaissance, the Reformation, and the emergence of science and advanced technology. Furthermore, population growth in the LDC's . . . is occurring while the great masses of population remain illiterate, unskilled, bogged down in poverty and, often, in despair."[12]

Still another factor is that the LDC's have a younger age structure and therefore large population increases are in the cards before any braking can take place.

The 1980 population census figure of 226.5 million represents a gain of 11.4 percent over 1970—the second smallest increase ever recorded. (The smallest, during the Depression of the 1930's, was 7.2 percent.) Still, population grew by 23 million, the third largest increase in the nation's history.

The total fertility rate for American women in 1980 was down to 1.8—meaning that, on average, they were having 1.8 children during their reproductive years. This was a notable decrease from the 2.1 rate for 1970, and the 3.4 rate for 1960. (Over time, a fer-

tility rate of 2.1 will result in zero population growth—not counting immigration.)

In rough terms, the U.S. population may be increasing now at a
rate of 1.2 percent—or 2.7 million people—per year. An estimated
40 percent is due to immigration (including legal immigrants,
refugees, and illegal immigrants who remain in the United States).
If the fertility rate remains low enough to suppress natural population growth a continued high level of immigration will play an increasingly important role in population size.

The population growth estimate is comprised of a series of other
rough estimates as follows:

Annual increases (current)

Natural growth (births minus deaths)	1,600,000
Net legal immigration	600,000
Net illegal immigration	500,000
	2,700,000

The last two figures are somewhat arbitrary, though they generally
fall around the middle of various estimates.[13]

The question is, what do these figures portend for U.S. population growth and its impacts on American society and the environment? Future scenarios present problems because of the continuing
variables (such as economic conditions in Mexico and elsewhere,
U.S. couples' decisions on having children, immigration policy, abortion policy, and the like) and the difficulties in linking population
factors to other factors such as economic growth and quality of life.

Concerning the immigration issue, various types of reform legislation are being supported in Congress and the Administration. For
example, one bill sets a strict cap of 350,000 on the number of immigrants and refugees who can be admitted by the U.S. each year.[14]
"Our current quota can be stretched like a rubber band," said the
bill's sponsor, Senator Lawton Chiles of Florida. The bill also would
make it a crime for firms in the U.S. to hire illegal aliens and would
increase border patrols.

Unfortunately, any more restrictive policies would have to buck
the strong headwinds of demographic change in poorer countries.
Michael S. Teitelbaum, program officer at the Ford Foundation, has
pointed out that in the next two decades alone, the total population of the 21 countries currently sending the most immigrants

to the U.S. will increase by more than 600 million: "Of course," he adds, "other countries may join the ranks of these 21 nations as their populations grow rapidly."[15]

It is worth noting that, contrary to widespread belief, by no means do all illegal immigrants come from Mexico; experts generally believe that no more than 50-60% are Mexicans.

The immigration dilemma has produced what Teitelbaum calls "bizarre coalitions that defy all normal political logic."[16]

A "conservative" businessperson might be in favor of a liberal immigration policy that makes it possible to hire cheap migrant labor. This might put that person in the same camp as a "liberal" union leader seeking new members or a religious leader with a humanitarian concern for the poor of other countries. Yet a "liberal" labor leader might favor a restrictive immigration policy that protects union jobs. This might put the labor leader in the same camp as someone seeking exclusion for racist reasons. Or an environmentalist worried about resource scarcities and ecosystem damage.

The fact that the "liberal-conservative continuum is utterly meaningless" contributes to the confusion of the debate, says Teitelbaum. It also helps explain why so many people prefer to avoid the issues entirely.

Perhaps the essential question—after sifting the evidence and the guesswork alike—is this: Does it seem safest to err on the side of increasing population size or on the side of stabilizing population growth?

Footnotes

[1] Annual meeting, American Association for the Advancement of Science, Washington, D.C., January 3-8, 1982.

[2] The quotations, and full discussion of the debate, can be found in *Malthus: An Essay on the Principle of Population*, edited by Philip Appleman, W.W. Norton & Co., 1976.

[3] *The Ultimate Resource*, by Julian L. Simon, Princeton University Press, 1981.

[4] Simon's views are elaborated in his recent book (see footnote 3) and in two issues of *The Public Interest*, Winter 1981 and Fall 1981.

Highly critical rebuttals have been numerous: memorandum of Population Crisis Committee, November 1981 (by Lawrence R. Kegan); memorandum of Alan Guttmacher Institute, January 12, 1982 (by Sharon Meluso); *The Public Interest*, Fall 1981 (by Katherine Gillman); *Bulletin of the Atomic Scientists*,

January 1982 (by Herman E. Daly); *New Republic*, October 28, 1981 (by Garrett Hardin); *Audubon*, November/December 1981 (by Robert Cahn); *Interaction* (Global Tomorrow Coalition), November/December 1981 (by Thomas B. Stoel, Jr.); and memorandum of Alan Guttmacher Institute, undated (by Peters D. Willson).

Among reviews of Simon's book *The Ultimate Resource* have been those in the *New York Times*, September 13, 1981; the *Washington Post*, September 20, 1981; and the *Wall Street Journal*, October 23, 1981.

[5] Derived from statistics of the Food and Agriculture Organization and the Department of Agriculture.

[6] *The Public Interest*, Fall 1981.

[7] Among the publications dealing with population pressures on the environment and natural resources are *Building a Sustainable Society*, by Lester R. Brown, W.W. Norton, 1981; "U.S. Carrying Capacity: Sketching the Bounds," by Maryla B. Webb and Judith E. Jacobsen, *Carrying Capacity*, forthcoming; *Population Bulletin*, August 1979; and *Worldwatch Paper 5*, March 1976. Also see *Overshoot*, by William R. Catton, Jr., University of Illinois Press, 1980.

[8] Policy paper on population assistance prepared for State Department.

[9] "Domestic Consequences of United States Population Change," report of House Select Committee on Population, December 1978. Also see footnote 3.

[10] "Rationale for AID Support of Population Programs," January 1982.

[11] See footnote 4.

[12] *World Population and Development,* by Phillip M. Hauser, Syracuse University Press, 1979.

[13] To arrive at the 600,000 figure for net legal immigration it was estimated that 675,000 per year enter the U.S. legally. In recent years the figure has been calculated at about 600,000 but in 1980 there was a jump to around 800,000 due to a surge from 200,000 to almost 400,000 refugees, primarily Cubans, Vietnamese, and Haitians. The 675,000 figure is chosen to represent a substantial but not total falling off from the high 1980 figure. Subtracted from it is 75,000, an estimate of the number of Americans who emigrate overseas per year.

As to the figure for net, or permanent, illegal immigrants, some estimates are lower, some much higher, such as those of the Environmental Fund, for example. ("Projecting the U.S. Population to the Year 2000," May 1978.) As noted, the difficulty here is that no one can measure either the inflow or the extent to which the illegal entrants return home after a short time. As one report says, "There is considerable evidence of two-way movement across the U.S.-Mexican border, reflecting a pattern of periodic, temporary migration." (Final report, House Select Committee on Population, December 1978.)

[14] S. 776, *Congressional Record*, February 2, 1982, p. S323.

[15] *Family Planning Perspectives*, March/April 1980.

[16] *Foreign Affairs*, Fall 1980.

[17] *Washington Memo*, January 22, 1982.

Energy: Audubon's Answer

The National Audubon Society's plan for overcoming America's energy problems is summarized in this extract from their 100-page technical report.

The energy crisis boils down to three questions: How much energy do we need? Where are we going to get it? How much are we willing—or able—to pay?

Our government and the energy industry keep coming up with the same answers: we need an ever-increasing amount of energy; we should get it by developing domestic energy supplies to the fullest; and we should pay whatever it costs, both economically and environmentally. These conclusions are based on the assumption that continued growth in America's economy is essential, and that such growth and a rising standard of living are inextricably linked to growth in energy consumption. Ergo, unless we are willing to tolerate very high levels of expensive oil imports—levels which may make our political and economic independence hostage to the whims and ambitions of a few oil-rich countries and draw us into military and diplomatic quagmires—we have no choice but to follow the road of full-scale development of domestic energy sources.

According to this logic, we must search desperately for more domestic oil and gas; we must proceed headlong with nuclear power development; we must strip-mine more coal; we must produce synthetic fuels from coal and wring the oil out of shale and tar sands. Never mind how much these undertakings will cost; how much damage they will do to human health and to the environment upon which our health, wealth, and happiness ultimately depend. We have, according to the government and the energy industries, no realistic alternatives.

The Audubon Energy Plan is one such alternative. It is a practical proposal for assuring ourselves of sufficient energy in the future to produce more goods and services than we do today, providing a higher standard of living for a larger population. And it demonstrates that economic growth need not be linked to energy growth and its resulting environmental degradation.

Unlike virtually all government and industry forecasts, the Audubon Plan proposes to hold total energy demand constant by increasing our energy efficiency, using existing and incipient technology to get more work out of the familiar fuels we are using now. In addition, the Audubon Plan relies on the inexhaustible energy of the sun, tapped by available or emergent technologies, to supplement and eventually supplant 25 percent of our traditional energy by the year 2000.

The Audubon Plan is the work of National Audubon Society scientists, using the best and most current data from academic experts, government agencies, and energy companies. In its present form, the plan has been strengthened by suggestions from many of the country's foremost energy experts. As better, newer data become available, the plan will be revised. Meanwhile, the plan will be improved by public discussion at all levels of our society, until the issues it raises are addressed in a national energy policy that can command the support of American citizens and their elected leaders.

The energy problem—a short course: There is no disagreement between the Audubon Plan and other energy proposals on the nature and source of our present predicament. When energy— especially oil—was plentiful and easy to get, therefore cheap, we quite naturally got into the habit of using a lot of it; more than we needed to, and more than some other countries use to support similar, even superior, standards of living. We abandoned fuels that were harder to get at and messier to burn in favor of oil, which we now use not only for transportation, for which it is uniquely useful, but also for generating heat and electricity, for which it is not.

With the depletion of our easily recoverable domestic oil reserves, we have turned increasingly to imported oil, placing our economic and military survival in jeopardy. We are not alone: most of the industrialized countries, and a growing number of the developing countries as well, are hooked to the same international oil pipeline. It was inevitable that the oil exporting countries would sooner or later form a cartel to exploit the situation by controlling oil supplies and multiplying prices, putting the rest of us over a barrel.

The results of our folly are now manifest. We pour tens of billions of dollars annually into purchases of foreign oil, with no hope of

relief, while we live in constant fear of shortages dictated by decisions and events in far-off lands. Our diplomacy, foreign policy, and
military strategy are distorted by petro-political considerations. At
home, we are tempted by ill-considered, extravagantly expensive
energy-development schemes, without rational regard for their
economic, social, and environmental side-effects. The Audubon Plan
proposes to eliminate the effects of the energy crisis by dealing
directly with its causes: our failure on the one hand to moderate
our demand for, and waste of, energy, and on the other hand to
develop energy supplies from renewable sources that are not subject to interdiction or exhaustion.

The demand side of the equation: On the demand side, the
plan's point of departure is a calculation of the total amount of energy
in various forms needed in the United States by the year 2000 to
provide a generous, modern standard of living. Recent studies by
energy companies, private-sector research organizations, and federal
agencies arrive at widely divergent projections of total United States
energy demand 20 years hence. In terms of quads—the quad is a
standard measure of energy equal to one quadrillion (10^{15}) British
thermal units, the equivalent of 500,000 barrels of oil per day for
one year—the projections for the year 2000 range from 57 quads
all the way to 122, or from 25 percent less energy than we use today to 50 percent more. The divergence of these projections reflects
both future technical uncertainties and the influence on energy demand that different government energy policies can have. Audubon's
figures for future energy demand are conservative, based on work
by individuals and organizations with no clear "environmentalist"af-
filiation. The demand figures have been chosen to allow for a substantial margin of error, and to allow for unanticipated shortages on the
supply side. With all these caveats, Audubon scientists have pegged
80 quads as a reasonable target for the total United States energy demand in the year 2000—about the same as our energy demand in 1981.

The plan's central premise is that the same amount of energy can
be used more efficiently and productively to provide a more abundant, healthier, and happier life than we enjoy today. The idea that
a constantly rising standard of living can only be sustained by ever-
increasing energy consumption has been preached as gospel by the
energy establishment for so long that it has become part of the common wisdom. The example of other Western, industrialized coun-

tries demonstrates, however, that it is possible to provide standards of living equal or even superior to our own with far lower per-capita rates of energy consumption. The enviable, high-quality technological comforts enjoyed by our European cousins testify that a moderation in our own energy demand need not entail a return to the simple life.

Rather than a renunciation of the high standard of living enjoyed by most Americans today, the Audubon Plan calls for renunciation of profligate energy use. If we replace and retune our technology— our cars and houses, our machines and factories, and everything else that uses energy—we can get more work out of every barrel of oil and ton of coal that we use. As a result of such an increase in our energy efficiency, according to Audubon calculations, by the year 2000 we can produce as much as 50 percent more goods and services than we do today without using any more energy. With 80 quads of energy, we can have as many goods and services as would require 122 quads today, and a healthy economic growth rate of 2 to 3 percent per year for the next 20 years. At the same time, per-capita energy consumption will decrease by about 25 percent, balancing the anticipated 25 percent growth in the United States population. In short, by increasing our energy efficiency, we can get more for less. The Audubon Plan calls not for doing without, but for doing it better.

The energy efficiency required by the Audubon Plan will come about through a combination of factors. What's needed is the working of natural market forces *plus* regulations, incentives, and education to encourage energy-efficient appliances, higher auto-mileage standards, energy-saving standards for new buildings and the required retrofitting of old ones before resale. About half of the targeted 40 quads of energy savings from improved efficiency will come about without any regulatory interference in the marketplace, prompted by the increasing cost of energy. In particular, the industrial sector of the economy, which accounts for fully 50 percent of the nation's energy demand in the Audubon Plan for the year 2000, as compared to 37 percent today, already is acutely sensitive to the effect of energy prices. Virtually ignored as insignificant for decades, energy now is recognized along with labor as a major factor in the cost of production. There is no industry that is not already committed to major investments in energy-conserving technology.

Demand-suppressing effects of higher energy prices also are visible in transportation, which today accounts for most of our oil consumption. Gasoline consumption has fallen 13 percent in only two years, back to the level of 10 years ago. Nevertheless, the Audubon Plan requires supplementing effects of higher prices in the transportation sector, which is projected to represent 25 percent of the total energy demand in the year 2000, with mileage standards that are more strict than present ones. An increase in the fuel efficiency of our automobiles from an average of 15 miles per gallon to 30 miles per gallon, along with a similar improvement in our fleet of light trucks, would bring us well along the way to reducing the flood of foreign oil to a trickle. Audubon scientists estimate that an increase in mileage standards to an EPA rating of 37.5 miles per gallon will be necessary to reach this goal. Many of the latest automobiles, domestic as well as imported, already approach the 37.5 mile-per-gallon EPA rating and can easily exceed it long before the turn of the century.

Reductions in demand also can be foreseen in the buildings sector, due to improvements in insulation, heating systems, air conditioning, and domestic appliances. The Audubon Plan projects a 25 percent increase in the number of buildings by the year 2000, but a decline in building energy demand. The projected decrease in energy consumption in buildings will come about as a result of higher prices, supplemented by a small number of specific regulatory changes—including the requirement of appliance and building energy standards—and novel methods of providing credit for the financing of major efficiency improvements.

A 30 percent growth in the demand for electricity by the year 2000 will be met by an increase of just 10 percent in centralized electricity production. This seeming paradox is the result of increases in on-site generation, particularly in industry.

The supply side: To supply the nation's demand for 80 quads of energy in the year 2000, the Audubon Plan relies on 20 quads of renewable solar energy in various forms. Some 9 quads of energy—almost half of the solar energy in the plan—will be derived from biomass: wastes from plant and tree crops, crops grown especially for sustained energy production, and garbage and other organic wastes.

Biomass can be burned to provide energy, or it can be turned into methanol and ethanol fuels. With its tremendous agricultural and forest production and its staggering production of organic wastes, the United States has a very large potential for biomass energy production. In the nation's commercial forests alone, for example, the annual growth of tree biomass has an estimated energy value of 15 quads. Only one-third of that is harvested today, but under proper land and forest management the yield could be increased substantially without impinging on wilderness areas or other noncommercial woodlands, and without diverting timber from the forest products industry.

Supply Side of Year 2000

Energy Supply	Percent of 80-Quad Energy Supply	
	1980	2000
Nonrenewables		
Coal	20%	28%
Domestic Oil	26	16
Imported Oil	18	4
Natural Gas	25	19
Nuclear	4	8
Solar Renewables		
Biomass	3	11
Low-Temperature Collectors	—	3
Medium-Temperature Collectors	—	2
Hydropower	4	5
Windpower	—	3
Photovoltaics	—	1
Total	100%	100%

There is sufficient evidence from the United States and Europe that forests can be managed to produce a sustained annual yield without suffering significant damage. No such evidence exists for other ecosystems, such as wetlands, that have great potential as sources of biomass energy. The Audubon Plan, therefore, does not include energy from these areas. Also, to avoid potential competition with food demand, the plan does not contemplate significant use of food-quality biomass to produce alcohol fuels.

Wind energy, primarily from 50,000 large, utility-owned turbines, will contribute 2.4 quads to the nation's energy supply by the year 2000. To get this much energy from the wind, we will have to tap only about 3 percent of North America's high-wind potential. We can increase our existing hydropower by almost 1 quad, according to the plan, simply by installing turbine generators in existing single-purpose dams, without building any new dams or flooding any additional land, using only half the existing dams. More than 4 quads of the solar energy in the Audubon Plan will come from low- and medium-temperature solar heat collectors used to heat space and water. Less than 1 quad will come from photovoltaic cells, which produce electricity directly from sunlight.

The Audubon Plan has little or no need for the exotic, costly, and dangerous energy schemes that are advanced as technological miracle cures for the energy crisis by some members of the energy establishment. The plan includes only 25 percent as much energy derived from synthetic fuels as is forecast by the U.S. Department of Energy. Oil from shales and tar sands, despite the hopeful forecasts of the government and the oil industry, does not figure at all in the Audubon equation because of the unacceptable economic and environmental costs associated with these still-unproven technologies. The conversion of coal to liquid and gaseous fuels, another major contributor in many energy forecasts, figures in the plan only in relatively small plants which can produce low-Btu gas from coal to generate heat and electricity for their own consumption. No geothermal energy is included in the plan, pending a careful review of its environmental effects.

With various forms of solar energy supplying about 20 quads in the Audubon energy budget, the remaining 60 quads—75 percent of the total—remain to be derived from traditional, nonrenewable sources. Oil will provide about 20 percent—16 quads—of our total energy, compared to 44 percent today. Oil imports will be only one-quarter of their present level. Most of this imported oil will come from the Western Hemisphere, posing a tolerable security risk.

Reluctantly, but realistically, the Audubon Plan projects significant increases by the year 2000 in the use of coal and nuclear fuels. The increases foreseen by Audubon, however, are modest compared to those urged by government and industry. The Audubon Plan assumes that no new nuclear plants will be licensed and begin construction, only two-thirds of those currently under construction will actually come on-line, and several existing plants will be shut down because of accidents or public opposition. Nevertheless, Audubon concludes that nuclear power production will virtually double to 6.6 quads by 2000. Thereafter, nuclear energy's share gradually will decrease as old plants are decommissioned.

Coal combustion contributes fully 28 percent of the Audubon Plan's total energy supply, a 40 percent increase over its present share. The plan provides, however, that coal mining and combustion include the best available land reclamation and pollution controls. Even so, the plan embraces coal only as a transitional fuel until sometime in the next century, when renewable energy sources (including photovoltaic conversion) will be sufficiently developed to supplant coal to an increasing extent. Meanwhile, the current Audubon Plan assumes conservatively that only 15 quads of natural gas will be available in the year 2000. Any available gas in excess of this estimate will replace coal, avoiding some of the human and environmental costs associated with coal mining and combustion.

Conservation costs and benefits: The introduction of energy-efficient technologies throughout the American economy to limit total energy demand to 80 quads while producing more goods and services will require a capital investment of some $700 billion over the next 20 years. The average annual investment of $35 billion is only 10 percent of our total annual expenditure for energy of $350 billion; and it appears is much less than the cost of increasing our energy supplies to support a continued growth in demand, as urged by government and industry. The Audubon Plan's proposals for saving energy by increasing efficiency will cost less than developing new oil and gas supplies; less than producing synthetic fuels; and less than building coal-burning and nuclear powerplants to produce electricity.

The only other alternative, increasing our oil imports as domestic production declines and demand increases, would of course require no new capital investment. In the long run, however, it would prove the most expensive course of all. By the year 2000, assuming that the price of a barrel of oil rises to $50 in 1980 dollars (it has already reached $40 on occasion in some markets) we would be paying $350 billion per year to purchase 40 quads of imported oil. The total cost of improving our technology to eliminate forever the need for those

40 quads is only $700 billion, or twice the annual cost of importing it. Moreover, all of the money we spend to increase our energy efficiency will stay at home creating jobs and domestic capital, instead of swelling the already burgeoning treasuries of the OPEC countries.

Synthetic fuels derived from coal are expected to cost as much as oil. At $50 per barrel, using either of these liquid fuels to supply 40 quads of energy would cost about $3.5 trillion by the year 2000—five times the cost of energy conservation. The Audubon approach also is cheaper than relying on electricity generated by coal or nuclear fuel. The coal or nuclear fuel would have to be used in 700 additional 1,000-megawatt powerplants built during the next 20 years at a cost of about $1 trillion—$300 billion more than the cost of conserving energy in the Audubon proposal.

Despite rhetoric to the contrary, we do not have the option of replacing imported oil with increased domestic production from new or existing fields. Petroleum production in the 48 contiguous states and offshore peaked in the early 1970s. Even with the subsequent increase in exploration and drilling and the improvement of recovery techniques stimulated by rising oil prices, most experts expect domestic production to continue its gradual decline. The addition of oil from Alaskan fields can only delay the inevitable. The various schemes proposed for increasing domestic production through so-called tertiary recovery are so costly—and risky—that they can be justified only by pricing the new energy at the exorbitant levels set by the OPEC cartel. Even if these schemes were successful, therefore, domestic oil would cost as much as imported oil, and far more than improving our technology to use less energy in the first place.

In addition to the capital investment in energy-efficient machines, buildings, and industrial processes, the Audubon Plan requires the investment of some $570 billion over the next 20 years—$130 per person each year—in solar energy. This investment would be cheaper than relying on oil, nuclear power, or gas. Solar collectors to provide heat and hot water for homes and other buildings make up almost half of the total investment in solar energy in the plan. The capital cost of such installations, like the cost of many other conservation measures, such as insulation, can be provided by a lending institution as part of the building's mortgage financing, or by a local utility, which would add monthly principal and interest payments to the customer's bill in the same way that the costs of fuel and generating facilities are added to electric bills today. Utilities in

California are already pioneering as lenders for solar energy and energy conservation projects. The availability of credit to finance energy-efficient technology and solar energy systems is an essential element of the Audubon Plan. It is the only way that these technologies can be made financially attractive enough to appeal to all income groups in American society—the only way that these technologies can be expected to reach most American households in the next two decades.

According to strict cost-versus-benefit calculations, we will save money in the long run by investing in energy efficiency and solar-energy technology, instead of endlessly increasing our supplies of traditional, nonrenewable energy. The Audubon Plan has more than its purely economic virtues to recommend it, however. All energy programs entail environmental costs which are not taken into economic account: strip-mining, especially in the ecologically fragile western coalfields; air and water pollution resulting from the production and use of virtually all nonrenewable fuels; acid rain from fossil-fuel combustion; and nuclear wastes, not to mention the uniquely frightening potential of lethal pollution from nuclear accidents. The Audubon Plan reduces the need for such unwise, costly, and unnecessary energy developments. Moreover, the more modest new energy developments called for in the Audubon Plan, such as biomass combustion, will include the most effective pollution controls and other environmental protection measures from their inception.

Toward transformation: Economic and environmental considerations coincide in favor of the Audubon Plan. The promoters of expensive energy-supply schemes such as synthetic-fuel and nuclear power development have no justification for claiming that their projects merit public support and huge subsidies simply because we have no alternative for avoiding energy starvation. In fact, their schemes divert the very human and financial resources required to renovate our energy economy toward efficiency and solar energy.

Nevertheless, the technological and economic transformations called for by the Audubon Energy Plan are profound and extensive. But Americans are used to change; we thrive on it. By the year 2000, in the ordinary course of things, we will have replaced most of our consumer goods, automobiles, household appliances, and other machines. Much of our housing stock and industrial plant will have been renovated or rebuilt. As we shop for a new generation of capital and consumer goods, the increasing cost of energy will influence our choices toward technologies that are more energy efficient and that use solar energy. The marketplace will respond by making things like improved insulation materials and solar collectors as common in stores and catalogs as refrigerators and electric water heaters are today. And as we invest in goods that have lower energy costs, we will also be providing a healthy stimulus to the American economy.

Regulations, laws, and public education all have supplementary roles to play in encouraging the conservation and solar-energy development necessary for meeting the Audubon Plan's goal of 80 quads. Perhaps equally important will be the influence of individual American citizens. As individuals, we can do our utmost to conserve energy and reduce waste and look for solar-energy opportunities in our personal lives. As citizens, we can encourage the political choices that must be made at the local, state, and federal levels to turn our society away from its tradition of endlessly increasing energy supply and consumption toward the policies suggested by the Audubon Plan.

We can, for example, audit the energy policies of our own states to make sure that they include heavy doses of conservation and solar energy, that they encourage state-chartered banks and utilities to finance energy improvements by their customers, that they require state agencies to set minimum standards for energy efficiency and require energy information on all appliances. We can press the leaders who court our support to stop spending our tax dollars on subsidies for misconceived and wasteful synthetic-fuel programs and nuclear power projects. We can encourage them to support practical mileage standards and speed limits for automobiles.

Through such efforts, we have the opportunity to choose the energy program for our next crucial decade.

Note: The National Audubon Society is in the process of revising its energy statement. It will be issued during 1984.

Tilting at Windmills

By C.C. Garvin, Jr.

In a speech to the Environmental Defense Fund, the chairman of the board of Exxon Corporation gives his views on the trade-off between energy development and environmental protection, arguing that it is unrealistic to expect renewable sources of energy to supply the bulk of our growing energy needs this century.

The title of my remarks, Tilting at Windmills, is meant to imply neither that environmentalists are fighting lost causes nor that oil companies are taking up arms against an ancient form of soft energy. Neither is true. That the two groups sometimes take pleasure in having at one another, however, is well known. My judgment is that we shall have fewer broken lances and perhaps a quicker solution to the energy problem if we aim instead at greater mutual understanding.

That we have much in common would seem apparent from your [the Environmental Defense Fund] literature. You say that you intend to expand your work in the field of energy, and I have hopes of doing the same. You describe yourselves as being neither anti-growth nor anti-progress which I find reassuring because neither am I. To resolve the energy problem, you would rely substantially on energy conservation, as would I.

That we have important differences, however, is also clear. We see our missions differently and we tend to set different priorities. Occasionally, differences may be so deep that we simply have to

Adapted from remarks made before the Environmental Defense Fund, New York, April 30, 1981. C. C. Garvin, Jr., is chairman of the board of Exxon Corporation.

Author's Note: Between the delivery of this speech and the publication of this book oil demand and prices weakened; public opposition to nuclear energy intensified; apprehension about acid rain grew; and prospects for near-term development of synthetic fuels and renewable forms of energy receded. All these ongoing changes make for greater uncertainty than either environmentalists or producers of conventional energy would like. But it reaffirms the need for open-mindedness which is the principal thesis of the speech.

accept the fact and accomplish what we can with goodwill and compromise. But when the views that separate us can significantly affect the future of our country, as our divergent attitudes toward energy may, then we must do what we can to resolve them.

The Environmental Defense Fund, for instance—as I understand its position—endorses economic growth but expresses serious reservations about nuclear energy, the increased use of coal and the development of synthetic fuels to support that growth. Exxon Corporation looks to these same options as the principal hopes for a transition to an era of clean, renewable energy sometime in the next century. If we are to escape the indecision and confusion that arise from such differences, all of us are going to have to think hard, and dispassionately, about why we feel as we do. I hope, in these remarks, to explain how we at Exxon have arrived at the views that we hold.

The assumption from which we start is that Exxon's primary role is to contribute to society's legitimate needs for energy—and in the process to earn a reasonable return for its shareholders. We are fully aware that this must be done in a socially acceptable manner. But our starting point, our bias if you will, is to find and produce energy, and there is little doubt in our minds that the need is going to be for more rather than less in the years ahead.

This is true even if, as we expect, future economic growth is much slower than in the pre-energy-crisis era and there are major improvements in the efficiency with which energy is used. For both the world as a whole, and for the United States, we foresee real economic growth, between now and the turn of the century, at average annual rates only about two-thirds as great as in the years preceding 1973—or about the same as we have known in the past eight years of intermittent energy crisis and erratic economic performance.

Some would urge that we provide the energy for such reduced growth largely through conservation, especially in the United States. There is no question that, compared with other parts of the world, the U.S. has been generous in its use of energy and that, despite the substantial conservation already achieved, a potential for much more remains. Precisely how much, however, is difficult to pin down. Our own judgment is that a realistic policy of pricing energy at its replacement cost will in time achieve *most* of the conservation that is socially desirable and economically feasible.

The real challenge before the nation, it seems to me, is to conserve in a way that permits economic growth to continue. The emphasis should be not so much on doing without as on getting a greater result per unit of energy consumed. With a dynamic economy, and a speed-up of the rate at which capital stock is turned over, there will be all sorts of opportunities to replace energy inefficiencies with energy economies. To go beyond this by subsidizing conservation on a broad scale is something that we must be very careful about. On the other hand, I am not so doctrinaire as to rule out every nudge to the system. I am on record as favoring the 55-mile speed limit and as having speculated that if higher gasoline prices do not satisfactorily restrain gasoline consumption, it might at some time be necessary to impose a higher excise tax. But, in general, I incline to the view that conservation is desirable primarily for the economic sense it makes and that the best overall guide to what is sensible is to be found in the marketplace.

That the marketplace works, even when under partial wraps, seems clear from recent history. In the years since 1973, when the first major oil price increases hit us, the rate of growth in total U.S. energy demand was less than a tenth as rapid as in the preceding seven years and oil consumption was virtually level. Part of this reflected slower general economic growth, but there would seem no doubt that response to price was also a significant factor.

And there is more to come in the future. We are assuming in our outlook that by the year 2000, gross national product in the United States will be roughly 50 percent greater, per unit of energy consumed, than it was in 1973. We see the same trend in Japan with somewhat less improvement in Europe. These gains are not as great as some advocates of extreme conservation urge, but by historical standards they are impressive indeed. It may turn out that more can be done, but to assert that it *must be done,* no matter the possible consequence for economic growth, raises difficult questions.

Factoring in our projections of both economic growth and energy conservation, we arrive at an end-of-century requirement for world energy some two-thirds greater than is currently consumed. Most of this growth is in the underdeveloped part of the world and in the centrally planned economies. In the United States, where economic growth is expected to be somewhat slower than elsewhere and opportunities for conservation greater, our forecast is for an approximate 20 percent growth in energy demand over the 1980-2000 period. This compares with an expected 65 percent expansion in real GNP. Other forecasts with which I am familiar yield a variety of results, but almost all point in the same general direction—toward increased use of energy in the future.

In a world long accustomed to growth, this comes as no surprise. What is new and different is the uncertainty we now have about meeting projected needs. There is uncertainty about the willingness of major suppliers to produce oil in the quantities that we would like and uncertainty about how rapidly technology will allow us to bring on alternative sources of supply. And, of course, it is on the supply side of the equation that many of the issues arise that particularly concern environmentalists.

The most striking feature of the outlook for energy supplies is the shrinking share of conventionally produced oil. Although some students of energy hold the view that the oil industry, suitably freed from restraints, could find all the oil we will need for many years into the future, the fact is that since about 1970, the world, and particularly the United States, has been consuming more oil than it has been finding. To a growing extent, we have been living off our accumulated savings. Our guess is that this trend will continue despite intensified oil exploration. If so, the consequence is obvious—oil consumption is approaching a limit. Indeed, we believe that in the United States oil use reached its peak several years ago and is now on the way down. We project a year 2000 consumption about 10 percent less than today.

What, then, picks up the load? Two near-term candidates are nuclear and coal. Both have potential for major expansion at competitive costs. If there were no disputes about the health and safety consequences of these fuels, I suspect that we would all agree that they constitute our best bet over the next decade or two. But there *are* such questions—to many of you overwhelming, to me serious but manageable. In our outlook, we have concluded that nuclear and conventionally burned coal will provide the bulk of increased U.S. energy needs between now and the end of the century, but I know this is not a certain thing. What worries me, and I hope occupies you from time to time, is what the nation will do if it does not go this route. What are the feasible alternatives?

Even with a substantial expansion of nuclear and coal, there are other things that we shall have to do. Useful as these fuels are as providers of Btu's, they are not geared to our needs for energy in liquid or gaseous forms. For many transportation purposes and certain chemical uses, petroleum continues to be the ideal raw material. I said earlier that we expect oil consumption to decline in our country. But since we expect conventionally produced oil from domestic sources to decline even more rapidly, and since growing reliance on imports is questionable policy, we must look elsewhere. Synthetics made from coal or shale offer one possibility. Our nation has vast reserves of the necessary raw materials, and the technology to get started is available now. Fully developed, a synthetics industry could, by sometime early in the next century, be providing about 15 million barrels per day of oil and gas to the U.S. economy. That would be in the neighborhood of a quarter to a third of all the energy that we would then be consuming.

In our judgment, it is an alternative that the nation cannot afford to ignore. My company has been a leading advocate of synthetic fuels, not as the exclusive or lasting solution to the energy problem but as one important bridge to the future. We have been doing research in the field for a number of years and more recently have begun to invest in the early stages of commercial development.

From the beginning we have been concerned about the environmental problems that could arise. Creating new towns in sparsely populated areas, finding the large volumes of water necessary to convert coal and shale into usable products, disposing of waste materials and managing effluents acceptably will require the best efforts of many people. Industry will be held primarily responsible for solving these problems, but governments at the federal, state and local levels will all be involved—as well, I am sure, as such interested groups as your own. No one should minimize the problems that lie ahead. We certainly do not. But we have thought about them enough to believe that they are manageable.

Among the things we have done, and which other large oil companies are also doing, is to intensify our efforts in health research. Exxon recently dedicated a $22 million environmental health sciences laboratory employing 55 toxicologists, epidemiologists, industrial hygienists and other health professionals. We have for many years had such professionals on our staff, but not at this level and not engaged in such a formal effort. There is a new sense of urgency, and I believe that it will help build a sound environmental basis for a synthetics industry. There are no guarantees, of course. In an undertaking of this magnitude there are always risks. But with the security of the nation and the economic well-being of its citizens at stake, can we afford not to take them? As with nuclear and coal, I ask myself—if not this, then what?

Well, and I am sure that you have been eager to get to this point, we can turn to the wind, the waves, the sun and other renewable energy sources, perhaps augmented in due course by nuclear fusion as well. We at Exxon share the view that in the long run, renewables *must* play an important role in meeting energy needs—in all probability the *major* role. We do not believe, however, that they will make a quantitatively significant contribution over the rest of this century. Our assessment is for a 6 percent to 8 percent share of total U.S. energy supply by the year 2000, as compared with perhaps 10 percent to 12 percent from synthetics and more than 40 percent from nuclear and coal. And of this 6-8 percent roughly half would be hydropower.

As with our other forecasts, this one, too, may be wrong. But we do not think it so wrong that the need for nuclear, coal and synthetics that we have forecast can be wiped out or seriously reduced. Even if the necessary technology were available right now, it would take many years and great sums of money before renewables could be substantially incorporated into our economy. Let me give you an example from a non-Exxon source. The National Audubon Society has recently estimated that if all new houses built in the U.S. over the next 20 years were to have solar collectors, and if all existing houses were to be retrofitted by the year 2000, the total contribution to our energy balance by then would be 5.3 percent. Assuming $5,000 per house to do the job, we estimate the total cost of 60 million homes would come to $300 billion. It is not impossible that this will be done, but neither is it likely.

Our view at Exxon, therefore, is not that renewables be regarded with less enthusiasm—only that they not be counted on for too much too soon. Progress needs to be made on all energy fronts—conservation, solar, biomass, synfuels, coal, nuclear—as well as our old friends, oil and gas. No one solution will produce the desired result. But what we and others are doing is—and should be—constrained by economics. In an economy that already has ample problems, we should avoid solutions that are unacceptably expensive, however attractive they may be on other grounds.

So where does all this leave us? I am firmly convinced that most people want the energy that will make further economic growth possible. Environmentalists are equally convinced that they want clean air and water. Public opinion polls support us both. I doubt if there is one among us who does not aspire to these twin goals. As we struggle to reach them, I believe that our choices will be made less difficult if we can avoid the automatic, and all too human, assumption that it is we who are always right and the other fellow who is wrong. The problems before us are hard enough without that. It might be a useful exercise for environmentalists to keep posing to themselves the question—what if conservation and soft energy can accomplish less over the next quarter of a century than they hope, what would they do then? And for us energy producers to have always in mind—what if the environmental consequences of our proposed actions are as severe as some environmentalists fear— what then would we do?

From our perspective, we cannot procrastinate in developing new supplies of energy. The public holds the energy industry accountable. This has been made completely clear to us each time lines have formed at service stations or prices have risen precipitously. But we also hear what you are hearing. When there is a tanker accident or a well blow-out, we hear it loud and clear. So where I come out is that Exxon *must* continue its efforts to supply the energy that people want, and it *must* do this with close attention to environmental consequences. We believe we are doing this, and we are sure the environmental community will let us know if it thinks otherwise. I hope and trust that we in the environmental and the business communities will be successful in arriving at a meeting of minds.

Nuclear Energy Facts: Questions and Answers

Some of the most-asked questions about nuclear energy are discussed briefly by members of the American Nuclear Society.

Do we really need nuclear power?

Yes. A look at our fossil fuel resources and our increasing dependence on foreign supplies will explain why. Oil and natural gas supplies are running out and becoming increasingly costly. Because of the long time it takes to build a new plant (about 12-14 years) and the even longer time it takes to develop new technologies, we have to start making some hard decisions right now. Unlike oil and gas, our coal supply is relatively abundant, and also unlike oil and gas, the generation of electricity is its major use. With world energy use growing as the populations expand and economies develop only coal and nuclear energy are now available in large supply. Coal has its own problems in terms of air pollution. However, coal will be needed in the future as a substitute for oil and natural gas. There are few uses for the uranium other than for the production of nuclear energy; the quantities necessary are much smaller; and nuclear power plants are cleaner. Thus, nuclear energy is needed to take over an increasing share of electrical production if we are to become less dependent on foreign oil.

Won't conservation of fossil fuel resources and generated electricity make nuclear power unnecessary? Why do we need nuclear?

Conservation is important and must be encouraged. However, conservation alone will not solve the energy problem. We are unlikely to want zero economic growth, if for no other reason because our population growth will not achieve equilibrium until the 21st century, even with continuation of low birth rates. Even moderate population and economic growth will require increased production of energy.

Nuclear is important because the recoverable energy released from the nuclear reaction for the generation of electricity is about 68,400 times greater than the energy recoverable from burning an equivalent weight of coal in a fossil fuel plant. Ton for ton, uranium ore yields over 50 times the energy of coal. The amount of uranium required each year for a nuclear plant is extremely small (about 30 tons) compared with the amounts of fossil fuels required for the same size plant (2.3 million tons of coal, or 10 million barrels of oil, or 64 billion cubic feet of gas). In addition, 97 percent of the 30 tons of uranium fuel is reusable. It's cheaper than any way you can think of.

How about the costs of power? Isn't nuclear power more expensive than the other sources?

No. Actually it's less expensive. The 1978 average total cost of producing electricity was: Nuclear—1.5 cents per kilowatt hour; Coal—2.3¢/kwh; Oil—4.0¢/kwh. Nuclear power saved nearly $3.6 billion in 1978 over the weighted average cost of all coal or oil-fired generation. This saved the equivalent of more than 130 million tons of coal or nearly 470 million barrels of oil. Costs for building nuclear plants have greatly increased due to regulations and court delays; many of these delays have done nothing to improve reactor safety or reliability. Coal-fired plants are also facing increasing costs due to regulations, so nuclear plants will remain cost effective. Over the long term, nuclear generation of electricity can produce large savings over coal generation because of the difference in fuel costs and transportation expense.

Why should we depend on nuclear power when some critics say the reactors are unreliable and uneconomic?

The reliability of nuclear plants, on the average, is as good as, or better than, coal plants of the same age and size—within 1 or 2 percentage points of each other. This is true both for number of hours the plants are available each month and for the percentage of generating capacity actually achieved. A few nuclear plants, especially some older ones, have had operating problems that delayed their startups or reduced their operating times. Generally, the problems (in both coal-burning and nuclear plants) are with conventional steam equipment and are unrelated to the nuclear reactor.

A lot of people are worried about radiation from nuclear power plants. How much radiation do I get from the generation of nuclear powered electricity?

Very little. As a gauge, a person in the U.S. receives on an average 180 millirem (mrem) per year from all sources. A millirem is a measurement of the effect of radiation on living tissue. Most is natural: from soil, water, rocks, building materials, food. Since 1970 radiation from all commercial nuclear energy averaged 0.01 millirem for each person in the U.S. In the year 2000, assuming nuclear energy becomes a dominant source of electricity, the average citizen will receive an estimated yearly dose of less than 1 mrem from commercial nuclear energy. Those living near nuclear power plants will receive less than 5 mrem per year.

Why is any release of radioactivity permitted?

It is as impossible to have zero releases from nuclear plants as it is to have zero releases of pollutants from any industrial process. What is done is to assure that any releases are well below the levels of significant environmental or human health effects; these limits are set by national and international groups and are based on vast quantities of data collected for over 50 years. This attention to releases has been observed in the nuclear power industry from its inception. In contrast, most other technologies were fully developed and in use before pollution control was required or achieved. Radioactive materials are routinely released, with no controls, from coal-burning power plants; this radioactivity comes from minerals that are a natural part of the coal.

What kinds of accidents can occur with nuclear power plants? How likely are they to occur?

First of all, nuclear power plants cannot explode like an atomic bomb because they do not contain the necessary concentration of fissionable material. Reactors are designed and constructed to withstand the kinds of accidents that could occur. Most often mentioned is an accident that could cause loss of the coolant water as the result of a rupture of a large pipe. This has **never** happened in a commercial reactor. Despite the damage to the core and the small releases of radiation at Three Mile Island, the defense-in-depth design philosophy prevented any serious damage to the rest of the plant or to the health and safety of the public. According to a comprehensive study of the probabilities of various kinds of nuclear accidents, the "Rasmussen Report," an accident that might kill as many as 10 people could occur about once every 30,000 years with 100 reactors in operation.

Doesn't the 1979 accident at Three Mile Island prove that nuclear power is too dangerous?

No. The accident at Three Mile Island (TMI) had a traumatic effect on some of the people in the vicinity of the plant because of a fear of a meltdown of the nuclear fuel. Several expert studies, including the Kemeny Report commissioned by President Carter, agree that a meltdown would not happen and that the defense-in-depth safety design worked to protect the public health and safety. They also agree that the effects on the population in the vicinity of Three Mile Island from radioactive releases during the accident, if any, will certainly be nonmeasureable and nondetectable. The accident was serious, but no lives were lost, no one was physically harmed or is likely to suffer future ill effects. The industry and government are diligently searching for and applying "lessons learned" from the accident at TMI to plant and reactor design, operator training, communication, and regulation.

How good is the nuclear power plant safety record?

In over 20 years of nuclear reactor operation by electic utilities in the U.S., no property damage or injury to the public or operating personnel has ever been caused by radiation from these facilities. U.S. naval vessels have a similar accident-free record for an even larger number of nuclear plants. Studies show that public risks of adverse health effects from nuclear plants are less than from power plants using other kinds of fuel. This remains true even after the accident at Three Mile Island, Pennsylvania, in 1979. The greatest injury resulting from that accident was mental anguish caused by fear.

Why is there a "nuclear exclusion" clause in homeowner's property loss insurance?

Most homeowner's policies have clauses excluding coverage for nuclear damage as well as for various natural disasters. Nuclear exclusion clauses exist because such coverage is channeled into nuclear insurance pools. Groups of private insurance companies, together with Federal Indemnity and the nuclear utilities, supply the legally required liability coverage for all nuclear facilities that could cause damage to the public, to a maximum of $560 million. The nuclear utilities pay appropriate premiums for both the private insurance pool coverage and the Federal Indemnity. The private insurers have committed $160 million for damage to the public, plus $30 million of secondary liability coverage, and $300 million of property coverage, thus making a current commitment of $490 million for home-owner's property insurance from the insurance industry.

Isn't the Price-Anderson Act a subsidy to the nuclear industry? Without it, wouldn't the industry cease operation?

No. First, there is nothing new about Federal Indemnity programs. They already include crop insurance, national flood insurance, medicare, and other large-scale programs. Second, the nuclear utilities have and are paying premiums to the Federal Government for the indemnity (the government has never had to pay a claim under the coverage). Since the indemnity portion of the Price-Anderson Act is being phased out as a responsibility of the government and is being assumed by the nuclear utilities, it is apparent that the loss of this indemnity is not causing the industry to cease operations. Three Mile Island demonstrated the need to cover the cost of power purchased to replace the power lost as a result of the accident; industry has now established Nuclear Energy Insurance Limited (NEIL) to help pay for replacement power in future accidents that result in loss of power production.

Why hasn't the waste disposal problem been resolved?

The high-level radioactive waste disposal problem has not been resolved because it has neither been politically expedient nor physically necessary to do so. Several plans for handling these wastes have been worked out. Scientists, through many years of research, have developed alternate ways to contain and store radioactive waste safely. The need for permanent waste disposal exists even if commercial nuclear power is not continued. Wastes from defense programs at Hanford, Washington, Savannah River, South Carolina, and Idaho National Engineering Laboratory, Idaho, already far exceed the quantities that will be produced by the year 2000 from commercial nuclear power plants.

The volume of wastes is readily manageable. If the liquid wastes from fuel reprocessing are "cooled," converted to stable solid form, and permanently stored at a federal repository, all the nuclear waste—including the low-level waste—from the entire U.S. nuclear power industry until the year 2000 would fit into a cube 250 feet on a side. The high-level portion of the radioactive wastes would take up a cube 50 feet on a side within the 250-foot block.

The National Academy of Science and other noted scientific organizations have stated clearly that the technology exists now for safe disposal of radioactive waste. The problem, then, is a political one, centering around federal licensing of facilities, states' rights in siting, and the need of fuel reprocessing to concentrate the wastes. A demonstration of the feasibility of safe waste storage requires action by Congress to mandate immediate construction of such facilities.

Is it right for us to leave a "legacy" of radioactive wastes as a hazard for future generations?

The consequences of alternatives to nuclear power should be pondered in determining if we consider it morally acceptable to establish carefully guarded and monitored repositories for the high-level radioactive wastes. We may burn up all the fossil fuels that ever existed on earth in only a few hundred years just to sustain industry, to feed current world populations, and to satisfy the growing demand around the world for an adequate standard of living with hope of improvement. Should we leave our descendants without fossil materials (coal, oil, gas) from which to extract fertilizers, medicines, and plastics because we elected to burn these fossil materials instead of using nuclear power? Is it fair to leave them without adequate energy to provide employment and the chance to choose their own lifestyles? In a democratic society, a public consensus based on informed opinion must answer these questions.

The nuclear industry says we need breeder reactors. Why?

Only an estimated 30 or 40 years' worth of uranium remains that can be readily and economically extracted from the ground for use in nuclear reactors. If we are not to use up this resource—the way we are using up our fossil fuel resources—we need to make more efficient use of our nuclear fuels. Worldwide, there is a strong agreement on developing the "breeder" reactor. Breeder reactors can turn the vast majority of uranium atoms (which are not fissionable) into fissionable fuel that can be recycled to produce more energy. Because they produce more fuel than they burn, such reactors are said to breed fuel. The breeder could increase the usable amount of uranium by more than 70 times, stretching 40 years' worth of uranium into many centuries worth of fuel. In the U.S.A., non-fissionable uranium sitting in drums at government sites is equivalent to all of the estimated oil resources of the entire world if we utilize it in breeder reactors.

This source alone, worth more than $60 trillion dollars at today's oil prices, could provide our total electrical energy needs for several centuries.

How do the risks from nuclear power compare with other everyday risks?

Nuclear power offers less risk. This sort of comparison was examined in the many safety studies, most notably the Rasmussen Report. Events such as air crashes and explosions have more than 100,000 times the chance of killing 10 people than 100 nuclear plants, the study concluded. It also found that a dam failure has 10,000 times the chance of killing 1,000 people than 100 nuclear plants. Far greater consequences are calculated for natural disasters— earthquakes are 2,000 times more likely to kill 10 people than 100 nuclear plants. Hurricanes are 60,000 times as likely to kill 1,000 people as 100 nuclear plants.

What is our responsibility?

Some affluent people contend that there is too much technology today; that it is the basis for many of society's ills, and that we must, therefore, put a stop to further development. Exaggerated are the problems caused by technology while forgotten are the truly large societal problems that technology has helped solve. For example, as we condemn Detroit and auto emissions, let us not forget New York early in this century with 150,000 horses in the street and their emissions.

Throughout history, mankind has had two basic choices when confronted with a problem that technology could solve. The first choice has been to ignore the promise of technology and endure the problem—a choice which has invariably led to reduced comfort.

well-being, and security. The second choice has been to put technology to work to solve the problem—a choice which has assured increasing prosperity, opportunity, and hope for all mankind.

It is essential that any decision be based on scientific facts and not on dreams. It is the responsibility of the scientific community with expertise on energy technologies to inform the public on the facts. It is your responsibility to become informed and to choose on that basis.

The Case of the Nuclear Turkeys

By Fred J. Cook

While others have pointed out nuclear power's environmental problems and its potential for nuclear weapons proliferation, this author argues that the end of nuclear power will come because it is not economically feasible.

When a Miami music teacher named Mark P. Oncavage picked a legal fight with Florida Power & Light (F.P.&L.), he hurled a stone at the nuclear Goliath. His suit before the Nuclear Regulatory Commission's Atomic Safety and Licensing Board revealed the nuclear power industry's financial vulnerability by publicizing the fact that many reactors presently in use, which were built in the 1970's for a few hundred million dollars, have deteriorated because of corrosion, metal embrittlement and other problems. As a result, they have become dangerous and must be completely rebuilt at several times the original cost.

Florida Power & Light has two such cripples—its Turkey Point Units 3 and 4, which are located on the shores of Biscayne Bay. The company estimates that dismantling and rebuilding the two plants, which were constructed for $120 million each, will cost $468 million. (This figure is disputed by outside experts, who put the cost at closer to $730 million.) F.P.&L. is not the only power company experiencing such problems; at least twenty-five other plants elsewhere in the nation are deteriorating much as the Turkey Point units are, and it will cost billions of dollars to repair them. Moreover, retrofitting these plants will produce tons of radioactive nuclear waste in the form of discarded reactors, pipes, tubing and other equipment. Disposal of this contaminated equipment will be a major problem.

Although the highly publicized accident at Three Mile Island in March 1979 jolted the nuclear power industry, most people saw it

The Nation, Nation Associates Inc., 1982. Reprinted by permission. Fred J. Cook writes frequently for *The Nation* on energy issues.

as an isolated incident. There is little public awareness of the chronic technical problems afflicting many plants. Oncavage's suit focused attention on these problems. A music teacher for ten years, Oncavage became concerned about environmental issues after taking some college courses in his spare time. And when F.P.&L.'s troubles at Turkey Point made news, he decided to act.

"I saw a lot of problems that no one was paying any attention to," he told me. "Not the power company, not the government, not the Nuclear Regulatory Commission." With Miami attorney Neil Chonin representing him, he filed an action to intervene in the hearings on F.P.&L.'s application for an amendment to its original license, which would permit it to tear apart and rebuild Turkey Point 3 and 4.

The arguments before the Atomic Safety and Licensing Board and the board's decision of May 29, 1981, reveal a chronicle of nuclear misadventure. Turkey Point 3 went into operation on December 14, 1972; Turkey Point 4 came on line September 3, 1973. By 1974 F.P.&L. admitted, "the sodium phosphate secondary water chemistry treatment for the steam generators was converted to an all-volatile chemistry treatment. Following the conversion, in 1975, certain corrosion-related problems such as denting of steam generator tubes began to occur." And by December 13, 1977, the problem had become so serious that F.P.&L. notified the Nuclear Regulatory Commission and requested permission to rebuild.

In its decision on F.P.&L.'s application, the licensing board summed up the difficulties at Turkey Point:

> The wastage and denting phenomena have led to . . . several instances of coolant leakage through cracked tubes. As of November 1980, tube plugging for various reasons has resulted in removing about 20 percent of the steam generator tubes in Unit 3 and about 24 percent of the tubes in Unit 4 from continuing service. . . .

Denting occurs when a buildup of rust pinches the tubing at its support plates inside the generator; wastage refers to the destruction of the tubes' inner walls by rust. The tubes carry hot, radioactive coolant water from the reactor's uranium core and discharge it in an adjacent stream or body of water. There are 3,200 tubes in each generator, so defective ones can be sealed without a loss of power—up to a point. Plugging at the Turkey Point plants was so extensive that generators were operating at only 65 percent of capacity.

The Turkey Point units were designed by Westinghouse and equipped with machinery built by the company. So were twenty other nuclear generators in the United States. All have experienced similar tubing and cracking problems—as have some generators built by another firm, Combustion Engineering. Virginia Electric Power's Surrey plant, which was designed by Westinghouse, has already been rebuilt, and three other applications for retrofitting operations are pending before the N.R.C.

"Back when the first nuclear plants were built, " Oncavage said, "everybody considered nuclear power a terrific idea. They didn't see the problems. They didn't understand the hazards of working in a plant that was gradually becoming completely contaminated. Now it's extremely dangerous to workers who have to go in and try to take it apart."

Oncavage and Chonin, joined by Joel V. Lumer, a Miami attorney representing Floridians United for Safe Energy, argued before the N.R.C.'s licensing board that F.P.&L.'s application to rebuild the Turkey Point units should be held up for at least a year until it could be determined that repairs had corrected the flaws at the Surrey plant. "There is no proof that Westinghouse has solved the problem," Lumer said. "Westinghouse thinks it has, but is it just guessing? There is no guarantee that the plants, once repaired, won't break down again."

Oncavage added: "The nuclear industry has changed designs for various plants, but the problems are generic. Between Combustion Engineering and Westinghouse, there are twenty-five of these plants in the nation that are suffering from the same kind of corrosion, and they haven't been able to solve the problem. Florida Power & Light has added insult to injury by ordering new Westinghouse generators." He laughed ironically. "It will get the usual one-year Westinghouse guarantee."

In permitting F.P.&L. to go ahead with its rebuilding plan, the licensing board cited a staff report that concluded: "A number of changes have been made in the materials, the design, and the operating procedure for the replacement steam generators to assure that the corrosion and denting problems will not recur." The new steam generator design, the report said, "incorporates features that will eliminate the potential for the various forms of tube degradation observed to date." It added: "[It] is *assumed* that the life of the repair is the remainder of the plant life, or about thirty years.

There is no guarantee of this plant life; however, the Staff safety review found no reason to doubt that steam generators would last the life of the plant." (Emphasis added.)

One accepts this *assumption* with some hesitancy; in the brave new world of nuclear energy, things have rarely gone as planned. Certainly the Turkey Point repairs have not gone as planned. The licensing board described the power company's proposed course of action:

> FPL plans to repair all six generators in Turkey Point Units 3 and 4. The Unit 4 steam generators have the most tubes plugged and, therefore, would be repaired first. The repair of Turkey Point 3 generators is expected to begin about one year later. Since FPL experiences operating peaks of longer duration in the summer, and the repair is expected to take from six to nine months per unit, the repair should be started in the fall to be completed before the next summer peak demand.

But it didn't happen that way once work began. F.P.&L., in a footnote to its final brief, explained: "However, because of an unplanned repair outage at Turkey Point Unit No. 3, the repairs were, in fact, commenced on Unit 3 immediately following the authorization of the operation license amendments on June 24, 1981."

Oncavage, who has monitored the repair work closely, contended that Number 4 was the newer plant—and the worse plant—and should have been dismantled first. But in May a steam generator in Number 3 blew, which meant that the plant would have had to be closed down anyhow. F.P.&L. decided to repair that plant right away and to struggle along with Number 4. But now there is another problem. One of the reactors in Number 4 is suffering from embrittlement. This is in the actual core, and it results from the fact that the metal has changed its characteristics. The great fear now is thermal shock from a sudden gush of cool water if something gives way, Oncavage said. "If this should happen and the core should blow, you can evacuate all of southern Florida. And the thing is, nobody knows what to do about it."

The embrittlement Oncavage spoke of has occurred in the eight-inch-thick steel shield that surrounds the radioactive core. The N.R.C. has admitted that the constant bombardment of this shield by neutrons from the reactor has altered the metal, making it brittle and weak. This has happened not just at Turkey Point but at seven other nuclear plants around the nation. "The pressure vessel of any reactor has to be considered inviolate," said Karl Kniel, a branch chief in the N.R.C.'s division of safety technology. "If it were breached, there would be no assurance that we could keep the reactor in a condition that would not lead to a fuel meltdown."

The "thermal shock" Oncavage mentioned actually happened in 1978 at the Rancho Seco nuclear power plant in California. A sudden infusion of cool water caused the temperature inside the pressure vessel to drop 300 degrees in an hour. Fortunately, this plant had been in operation for only three years, and the protective shield had not become brittle.

If the entire pressure vessel at Turkey Point 4 should have to be replaced, it would represent a mammoth task, far beyond the one currently under way at Turkey Point 3. And the costs would be even more astronomical.

Oncavage argued that energy conservation measures along with solar energy would save more megawatts in sunny Florida than the Turkey Point plants could produce. The hundreds of millions of dollars being spent to recondition the plants was "money thrown away," he said. His argument, though not heeded by the N.R.C., seemed especially relevant after F.P.&L. had to shut down Turkey Point 3 during the mid-summer peak usage period instead of in the fall and winter as had been originally planned.

The additional electricity the company needed for its 2.2 million customers had to be purchased from plants in southern Georgia at a cost that F.P.&L. estimated at $756,000 a day. Repairs will take 270 days, and when work is started on Turkey Point 4, power-replacement costs will soar to $809,000 a day. Two-thirds of consumers' bills go to pay for this imported electricity, Lumer has said. As a result, bills of $200 to $300 a month are not uncommon.

The saga of F.P.&L.'s two Turkeys raises other issues. Oncavage argued in his intervention briefs that the availability of alternative sources of energy should be weighed by the N.R.C. before granting F.P.&L.'s request to rebuild its nuclear plants. The environmental impact of dismantlement should be considered, he contended. But the licensing board rejected these arguments, claiming that the issues had been settled when the original licenses for the plants were granted.

Oncavage demonstrated that the only alternatives considered in the original licensing procedure were different sites for the plants and whether their wastes should be discharged into Biscayne Bay or Cord Sound. Conservation measures that might eliminate the need for nuclear power weren't considered, nor was the increased use of solar power, a potentially important energy source in Florida. Forty years ago, before electricity became so "cheap," the use of the sun's rays to heat water was widespread in the state.

The narrow interpretation that enabled the licensing board to dismiss Oncavage's environmental-impact arguments becomes especially significant in view of the hazards posed by radioactive fixtures in the dismantled plants. The initial danger is to the workers. In the course of dismantling the Surrey Plant in Virginia, workers who entered the reactor to cut apart pipes and tubing were exposed to almost double the safe level of radiation. As a result, F.P.&L. has adopted a method of removal that would subject workers to less exposure to contaminated materials.

A far more serious problem is disposing of the radioactive equipment from the two plants, including three steam generators in each, weighing 200 tons apiece. "They are completely contaminated and radioactive to the core," Oncavage pointed out. "The power company was going to store them in a building with a dirt floor only 1,300 feet from Biscayne Bay. We fought so hard that we won at least one victory. The power company built a hill with the building on top into which the generators will be placed on a six-inch concrete floor. [The "hill" is actually a mound seventeen and a half feet high.] Then they added 180 feet of buffer to protect the hill from waves in Biscayne Bay in case of a hurricane or storm.

"So the steam generators will be sealed up in this building, but other radioactive wastes are being stored in drums outside the plant. The N.R.C. let me go in and study the situation—the only time, I think, that an outsider has been granted such permission—but then they gagged me. They said I couldn't disclose any of the data I had gathered to anyone."

In one of his last briefs, however, Oncavage entered into the record the fact that 1,312 fifty-five-gallon drums containing wastes produced in generating electricity are already stored at the site. In addition, he argued, even the N.R.C.'s own studies showed that "between 1,100 cubic meters and 2,300 cubic meters of low level waste, per unit, will be generated by these repairs. This is in addition to the lower assemblies of the steam generators."

How does F.P.&L. plan to dispose of this deadly stuff? In the past, nuclear wastes have been stored at the Federal government's Barnwell, South Carolina, nuclear-waste storage facility. But Barnwell has become so overloaded that it has cut back on the quantity of wastes it will accept. Oncavage has estimated that the enormous amount of radioactive debris from the dismantling of the two Turkeys will have to be stored in an additional 10,000 drums. Turkey Point could become a permanent dumping ground, and the wastes there might leak into Biscayne Bay, contaminating fish and entering the food chain.

"Anyone who knows Miami weather," Oncavage said, "realizes that there is a lot of heat and humidity here. Drums rust and corrode rather rapidly. Yet pipes, tubing and other radioactive wastes torn out of the plant are being stored on the ground in these drums and boxes. The amount of waste indicates the hazard. At a minimum, there will be 70,000 cubic feet of wastes from the two plants, and the total could rise to 180,000 cubic feet. There are many different estimates on the amount of the wastes and the degree of toxicity." *

Whatever figure one accepts, the situation at Turkey Point is scary. But Turkey Point is more than a local issue; it is indicative of a national problem. As Oncavage said in one of his briefs, citing government studies:

> Fifteen Westinghouse nuclear power units have had adverse experience with their steam generators. . . . Three licensees with Westinghouse units have already filed Steam Generator Repair Reports seeking license amendments to make repairs. . . . There is a good probability that twelve more applications will be filed. Each of these repair projects will cost hundreds of millions of dollars. In total, the decisions on how to remedy the problem caused by a combination of the need for energy and tube degradation in Westinghouse nuclear power units will involve the commitment of billions of dollars.

The Turkey Point experience, which opens up a whole new chapter in the growing account of the potential hazard of nuclear power, comes at a time when the nuclear industry faces a host of problems. Design changes mandated after the near-meltdown at

---

* The Atomic Safety and Licensing Appeal Board rejected Oncavage's appeal in a decision in early December [1981]. In doing so, it ruled it did not have to consider the environmental issue. About the same time, F.P.&L. announced that it had removed all the drums and boxes Oncavage had found at Turkey Point, sending what Barnwell could not take to a storage facility at Hanford, Washington. It is not clear what will be done with the *new* radioactive material accumulated from the dismantling of the two plants.

Three Mile Island, escalating construction costs, high interest rates and technical uncertainties have combined to give many utilities second thoughts about nuclear power.

- Boston Edison has canceled plans to build a nuclear reactor at Plymouth, Massachusetts. Construction and financing costs, estimated at $400 million when the plan was first proposed in 1971, had soared to $4 billion.
- The Washington Public Power Supply System in Seattle has decided to spend $150 million to mothball two partially completed nuclear plants until at least July 1983 because $2.5 billion raised by a bond issue to finance them has been exhausted.
- Errors in engineering calculations have been found in California's controversial Diablo Canyon nuclear plant located by the Pacific Gas & Electric Company only three miles from the Hosgri Fault, a part of the San Andreas system. The N.R.C., which has admitted that it "knew the location was wrong," is now re-evaluating the entire project.
- In New York State, Consolidated Edison is encountering leakage problems at its Indian Point Number 2 and Number 3 plants that are similar to those at Turkey Point. Like F.P.&L., it has had to plug some defective tubing, and it fears that the eight-year-old Indian Point 2 (which was supposed to last for forty years) may have to be shut down completely for a year in order to make repairs tentatively estimated to cost $100 million.
- In Georgia, Texas and Indiana, work is behind schedule, and some companies are trying to shed commitments to build nuclear plants costing from $4 billion to $5 billion. To make matters worse, all of the nation's seventy-two operating plants must now install new and safer electrical equipment to insure that reactor cores will remain cool in the event of an accident. In May 1980, the N.R.C. set June 30 of [1982] as the deadline for the completion of this work, but few, if any, of the plants are likely to be ready by that time.

Even if complaisant public-service commissions pass on the costs of industry's mistakes to helpless consumers, the problems are still too immense for the utilities to handle. An article in the August/ September [1981] issue of *Technology Review* reported: "There is a de facto moratorium on reactor orders in the United States and ten other countries, nuclear energy has been abandoned in at least seven countries, and one country, Sweden, recently voted to phase out nuclear power permanently within 25 years."

As Mark Oncavage says, "Nuclear power is just not economically feasible." And that, more than anything else, is likely to spell the end of our flirtation with the nuclear millenium.

Public Opinion and Nuclear Power Before and After Three Mile Island

By Robert Cameron Mitchell

While it increased public awareness about nuclear power, the Three Mile Island accident, as revealed in this opinion poll, did not cause a radical change in attitudes toward nuclear power.

Several years ago Alvin Weinberg went so far as to call public acceptance "the most serious question now facing nuclear energy." At the time of Weinberg's statement, however, the Harris poll showed supporters of nuclear power outnumbering those who opposed it by three to one. In the next years, however, the ratio of support declined somewhat, although it still stood at two to one in an October 1978 Harris poll. Then, in March 1979, came the accident at Three Mile Island. Among the important questions raised by this highly publicized occurrence was whether its apparent confirmation of some of the critics' accusations would lead to a wholesale rejection of nuclear technology by the public.

A careful review of the many relevant national and state polls after the accident reveals that, although the accident heightened public opposition to nuclear power, those who support nuclear power continue to outnumber those who oppose it. Six months after the accident a majority of Americans were still willing to believe that nuclear power can be made safe enough to warrant its further use. The level of uncertainty about this technology is high, however, and, if given a choice, large majorities would prefer the use of coal and, especially, solar energy.

Between April and January 1980 more than forty publicly available polls were conducted by the leading pollsters, asking national and

From *Resources,* January/April 1980. Reprinted with permission. Robert Cameron Mitchell is a senior fellow in the Quality of the Environment Division at Resources for the Future.

state samples their opinions about the accident and about nuclear power more generally. Although singly many of these polls have weaknesses, taken together they can be cross-checked against each other and evaluated in the context of earlier preaccident polls. What emerges is a reasonably clear picture of the public's reaction to the accident.

Reaction to the accident. Only the polls taken in the first weeks after the accident probed the public's views about the accident itself. These early surveys showed an almost universal awareness of the accident and a very high level of public concern about it. For example, 66 percent of Washington, D.C., area residents regarded the accident as "very serious"; 41 percent nationally in an ABC-Harris poll were "deeply disturbed" about it; and 12 percent nationally and 22 percent in the East said they were "extremely worried about self or family's safety." Unfortunately, we do not know whether people changed their views about the accident's seriousness once the news coverage died down because none of the later polls chose to probe this issue.

An important finding in the early polls was that relatively few people were inclined to write the accident off as an aberration. Depending on the working of the question, from 50 to 75 percent of those queried in three of the early national polls rejected the view that the Three Mile Island accident was a freak occurrence. Moreover, when asked about the likelihood of a "much worse" accident occurring, 20 percent in a Washington, D.C., area poll said it was "very likely," and a further 32 percent judged this possibility to be "somewhat likely."

The handling of the accident by the press, by the federal government or Nuclear Regulatory Commission, and, especially, by the Metropolitan Edison Company was criticized by fairly sizable segments of the public. In one poll, only 47 percent said the government handled the situation as well as possible. In another poll, the performance of the Nuclear Regulatory Commission received a positive rating from 44 percent and a negative rating from 41 percent of a national sample. Consistent majorities accused Metropolitan Edison of concealing the danger from the public. The press, on the other hand, was accused by one person out of four in a national poll of "greatly exaggerating" the danger, and the Rocky Mountain Poll reported that about as many people believed the press, radio, and television coverage of the accident to be "basically opinionated and emotional" (40 percent) as believed it to be "basically factual and objective" (38 percent). Furthermore, in spite of the massive press coverage, 21 percent of the people interviewed in the Rocky Mountain states by this poll, a week after the accident, claimed to be "basically uninformed" about it. Only 23 percent said that they considered themselves "well informed," while 50 percent felt "somewhat informed."

Its impact on public acceptance. The two major trend lines on nuclear power in the 1970s, compiled by Harris and Cambridge reports, provide the best glimpse of public support for nuclear power following the accident. Although the Harris and Cambridge trends differ somewhat, both reveal moderate gains in opposition. The Harris trend for 1975 to January 1980 is shown in figure 1. Shortly after the accident the previous 26 percent gap between those who favor and those who oppose building more nuclear power plants narrowed to a 1 percent difference. As the accident, with no apparent damage to human health, receded from the headlines, support for building more plants gradually recovered. This recovery peaked in August when the gap widened to 19 percentage points and then dipped again when the Kemeny Commission Report was

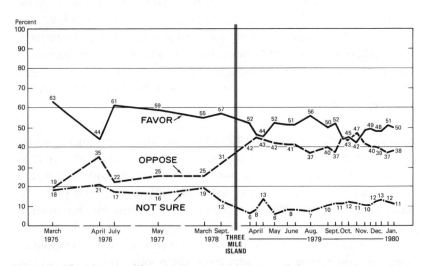

Figure 1. The Harris poll trend line on building nuclear power plants. Each poll is based on a national sample. Some were telephone but most were personal interview surveys. The question asked was, "In general, do you favor or oppose the building of more nuclear power plants in the United States?" Harris Poll data made available by the Edison Electric Institute.

released in late October. Twice in the October-November period pluralities opposed to building more plants were registered. Support recovered again, and by January 1980, nine months after the accident, the gap in favor stood at 12 percent, half of what it was before the accident, signifying a net gain of 7 percentage points in the number who oppose building more plants. The Cambridge Report's trend line for a very similar question also shows a continued plurality in favor of building more nuclear power plants by a narrower margin than before the accident.

Two reasons may lie behind this relatively mild longer-term reaction to the accident. First, the nature of the accident was itself contradictory, leading to different interpretations according to one's prior disposition toward nuclear power. To some people, the accident provided sufficient cause for optimism because no one was hurt and the emergency systems worked; to others, the accident was sufficient cause for pessimism because they believed only luck had prevented a catastrophe from occurring.

The other reason which may partially explain the mild reaction to the Three Mile Island accident is that a shift in opinion against nuclear power had already occurred *before* the accident. Both the Harris and Cambridge trend lines showed increased opposition to nuclear power in the months preceding it and, in an October 1978 poll, Harris for the first time found strong majorities opposed to having a nuclear plant in their community (56 percent to 35 percent). This represented a sharp reversal of Harris's findings on this question in previous years. That this prior shift may have mitigated the impact of Three Mile Island to some extent is suggested by the fact that when the local nuclear plant question was repeated, by the CBS News-*New York Times* survey, shortly after the accident, there was virtually no shift of opinion on this issue from the Harris survey of six months before.

Contrary to the expectations of the antinuclear movement, polls taken before and after the accident show only a slight increase in those who sympathize with the movement. Furthermore, the polls also show a corresponding increase in the percentage of those who express a lack of sympathy toward the movement, suggesting an increased polarization of views. In 1978, 21 percent were unsympathetic and 44 percent expressed neutrality. When this question was repeated a year later, three months after the accident, the number declaring neutrality was down by 9 percent, while 4 percent more were favorably inclined toward the antinuclear movement and 5 percent more expressed opposition to it.

While the bottom has not dropped out of the support for nuclear power, and while only 15 to 20 percent in any postaccident poll approve the antinuclear militants' demand that all nuclear power plants be shut down permanently and no more be built, a close reading of the polls shows that a large percentage of the population have a distinct lack of enthusiasm for or ambivalence about the nuclear option. If there are 15 to 20 percent hard-core shut-them-down-now opponents, those strongly in support of nuclear power are hardly greater in number. For example, only 25 percent in a CBS News-*New York Times* poll chose nuclear power over burning coal, or, in answer to another question, chose nuclear power over "cutting back" on their "own use of energy." Given the opportunity to say that they "haven't made up their mind yet" on the issue, approximately one out of three persons chose that option, a high figure. Moreover, when given the choice, most do not prefer nuclear to other forms of energy unless the alternative involves paying higher prices for imported oil.

Why then does nuclear power continue to show pluralities on general questions such as the Harris trend item? The answer is simple: despite Three Mile Island, many people believe nuclear power is needed and are still willing to believe that nuclear power can be made safe. Astonishingly, none of the postaccident national polls asked a direct question about this latter topic, but the Rocky Mountain regional poll did, and 70 percent of its respondents said they thought "the safety systems for nuclear power plants can be perfected enough to prevent accidents such as the one that occurred in Pennsylvania from happening again."

What the national polls do show on this topic is that the level of support or opposition to nuclear power is highly dependent on the degree of assurance about safety contained in the wording of the question. Analysis of the twelve questions which link building more plants with a statement about safety shows that the level of opposition can be made to shift by 40 percentage points, just by varying the assurance of safety. At one extreme, 67 to 75 percent approve of a temporary moratorium on new plants until safety questions are answered. At the other extreme, only 21 to 26 percent would disapprove of the federal government issuing more licenses for nuclear plants if it insisted on better safety standards.

The national polls also show that the accident apparently had very little effect on people's views about the safety of nuclear power plants. One of the most revealing of all the postaccident poll findings was the Harris poll trend for the question, "From what you have heard or read, how safe are nuclear power plants that produce electrical power—very safe, somewhat safe, or not so safe?" Harris asked this question in a telephone poll the week after the accident and compared it with the results from three previous polls, including one conducted in October 1978. Right after Three Mile Island, 21 percent said nuclear power plants are "very safe," 46 percent said "somewhat safe," for a total of 67 percent, while 30 percent said they are "not so safe." Comparing these data with those from the October 1978 survey, the April data show only a 2 percent increase in those who said the plants are "not so safe." Although there is a 5 point decline from October to April in the percentage of those who regarded the plants as "very safe," the total for the "very" and "somewhat safe" categories actually increased by 3 percent over that time period, from 64 percent in October to April's 67 percent.

Three Mile Island has occasioned a national seminar of sorts on the nuclear option. As a result, public awareness of nuclear power is now far greater than it was before the accident when many people were unaware of even the simplest facts about producing electricity by nuclear fission. Thus far, the polls show this more knowledgeable public is still willing to accept the Faustian bargain offered them by this technology, albeit by a narrower margin than before.

Acid Precipitation: Causes, Consequences, Controls

By Eugene M. Trisko

In this overview of the acid rain issue, the author cautions against hasty, ill-conceived legislation designed to deal with a problem that is not thoroughly understood.

Acid precipitation is one of the critical environmental policy issues of the 1980s. Proposals for controlling it usually focus on the electric utility industry as a major source of acid precursor emissions: sulfur dioxide (SO_2) and nitrogen oxides (NO_x). What is known about the causes of acid precipitation? How does it affect the environment? Can it be reduced or eliminated? Are immediate further controls on SO_2 or NO_x warranted? If they are, which controls would yield the most cost- and environmentally effective results? What are the long-term industrial and energy development implications of a major emission reduction program?

These basic questions now confront the United States Congress. In August, 1982, the Senate Environment and Public Works Committee approved a proposal (S 3041) to reduce SO_2 emissions in a 31-state eastern area by 8 million tons by 1995. The total required reduction would be about 10 million tons in order to offset emissions from new sources coming on line before 1995. Emissions in this area are now some 19 million tons of SO_2 per year. The cost of the Senate proposal is conservatively estimated at $3 billion annually by 1995 (in 1982 prices), mainly for flue gas scrubbers at some existing generating units and for the substitution of more than 100 million annual tons of costly low-sulfur coal for high-sulfur coal now burned at many eastern generating units.[1]

Despite considerable scientific uncertainties about the causes and

Excerpted from article in *Public Utilities Fortnightly,* February 1983, with permission from Public Utilities Report, Inc. Eugene M. Trisko is an attorney in Washington, D.C., an adjunct professor of law at West Virginia University, and an advisor to Stern Bros., Inc.

effects of acid precipitation, the new 98th Congress will face a powerful lobbying effort in favor of emission reductions like those proposed by the Senate Environment Committee. Aided by the popular media, a coalition of national environmental organizations and representatives from the Northeast and Canada will press Congress for a quick solution to this extremely complex environmental problem. A vigorous rebuttal from the utility and other industries can be anticipated. Historically, however, environmental causes have fared extremely well in Congress. In this instance, the simple—but demonstrably wrong—solution may prevail unless reasonable alternatives can be advanced.

This article examines the bases for concern about acid precipitation, the state of scientific knowledge about its formation, and the implications of proposed control actions. Finally two alternative control approaches are suggested: a standards-based demonstration project focusing on ecologically sensitive areas of the Northeast, and a voluntary industry and state government program of emission reductions.

An Overview of Acid Precipitation

Nature and Sources

"Acid rain" is a misnomer for the wet and dry deposition of acidic substances from natural and man-made emission sources. In wet forms such as rain, snow, and fog, precipitation is considered acidic if its pH is less than 5.6 on the logarithmic pH scale of zero to 14. The pH of "natural" rainfall is disputed and may be as low as five.[2] Precipitation in the eastern U.S. typically has a pH of 4.2 to 4.6.[3] There is no credible support for claims that rainfall acidity in the East has increased markedly in the recent past.[4]

The principal acids in precipitation are sulfuric acid (H_2SO_4), nitric acid (HNO_3), ammonium bisulfate (NH_4SO_4), and hydrochloric acid (HCl).[5] Man-made emissions of sulfur and nitrogen oxides are the dominant sources of acid precipitation in the eastern U.S.[6] In southern California, NO_x emissions are responsible for extremely acid precipitation.[7]

In 1980, 27 million tons of SO_2 were emitted by man-made sources in the U.S., including 18 million tons from electric utilities.[8] Natural sources of SO_2 in this country are negligible in comparison. The transportation sector accounted for 9 million tons of the total 21 million tons of NO_x emitted by man-made sources in the U.S. in 1980, with utilities responsible for 6 million tons. Estimates of total

NOx emissions are imprecise due to uncertainty about natural and man-made source contributions. Unlike sulfur, an inherent element of most fossil fuels, nitrogen emissions are influenced by combustion chamber operating characteristics.

The two major components of acid precipitation, sulfuric and nitric acids, are derived in the atmosphere from the interactions of SO_2 and NOx with sunlight, water vapor, hydrocarbons, hydrogen peroxide, metal catalysts, and other chemical species. Sulfuric acid also is emitted in "primary" form directly from fossil fuel combustion. Gaseous SO_2 is converted in the atmosphere to fine particulate sulfates (SO_4) which are deposited in dry form and as liquid sulfuric acid. Emissions of NOx undergo complex chemical transformations to nitrates and nitric acid, which also are deposited in dry and wet forms.

An estimated 50 percent of NOx emissions are converted to nitric acid in the atmosphere and are deposited as such.[9] There is no scientific agreement about SO_2 conversion and deposition rates.

Emissions of SO_2 and NOx account for roughly equivalent amounts of acidity in the U.S.[10] On a seasonal basis, most wet and dry deposition of sulfur compounds is thought to occur during the warmer months of the year, while wintertime acid deposition is dominated by nitrate and nitric acid.[11]

Local versus Long-Range Sources

The use of extremely tall stacks at utility power plants gained momentum with the promulgation of national ambient air-quality standards for SO_2, NOx, and other pollutants in 1971. Tall stacks aid in the dispersion of pollutants, but their role in the formation of acid precipitation has been overrated. Recent scientific analyses indicate that local sources, particularly oil-fired sources in the Northeast, are responsible for a large share of the excess acidity in precipitation in that region.[12]

Long-range atmospheric transport modeling is at the frontiers of science. Available models indicate, however, that depositions decline at an exponential rate at distances greater than 60 miles from particular sources. Breaking eastern North America into quadrants shows that each region is its own largest source of deposited sulfate. Only a small fraction of sulfate is deposited at distances beyond 300 miles from individual sources.

Comparable data for regional NOx depositions are not available.

However, NOx depositions tend to be more localized than sulfur patterns since large amounts of NOx are emitted at ground level by transport sources.

Environmental Impacts

The major categories of suspected environmental damage from acid precipitation are the acidification of lakes and streams with consequential damage to aquatic fish and plant life; depletion of soil nutrients and diminished forest productivity; impairment of crops; accelerated deterioration of metals, stone, and other materials; toxic metal contamination of edible fish and drinking water; and certain human health effects. Of these, good evidence exists for aquatic acidification, fish mortality, and some soil effects. Documentation of adverse crop and forest impacts is limited but warrants much concern. Allegations of adverse human health effects depend upon extremely controversial statistical measurements. Materials damage from a variety of local and long-range sources has been incorrectly attributed to acid precipitation.

High levels of sulfate and nitrate deposition in watersheds with inadequate neutralizing capacity contribute to the acidification of lakes and streams. Extensive aquatic effects research in the Northeast and in Scandinavia has linked acidic precipitation to increased lake and stream acidity and resulting fish mortality.[13] Spring fish kills in Adirondack lakes result from the release of large amounts of acidity and toxic aluminum from watersheds during spring snowpack melt. Dry nitrate deposition in the wintertime appears to be the primary cause of this phenomenon.[14]

Forest, crop, and soil effects are receiving much research attention. Red spruce and other trees in New England are dying or growing abnormally, and acid precipitation is suspected as a contributing factor.[15] Swedish studies suggest that sulfur and nitrogen inputs from acid deposition have a beneficial short-term impact on forest growth, but imply that addition of nitrogen to nitrogen-deficient soils eventually may lead to deficiencies in other nutrients, with long-term detrimental consequences.[16]

Acid precipitation has adversely affected some crops in laboratory and simulated field experiments.[17] Other crops, however, seem to benefit from acidic precipitation. Atmospheric ozone probably is a greater source of crop injury than acid precipitation.

There is little evidence that acid precipitation is a major cause of materials damage. Claims about accelerated weathering of stone and statuary and metal corrosion are not well substantiated due to failure to isolate the effects of acid precipitation from other weather- and pollution-related factors.[18] Local sources of pollution appear to be responsible for most of the materials damage alleged to result from acid precipitation.

The inhalation of fine particulate sulfates has been cited as a cause of adverse human health effects. One recent study estimated that tens of thousands of premature deaths may result each year from sulfate concentrations in the U.S. and Canada.[19] This is a severely disputed allegation without broad support in the scientific community.[20] If such a claim were supportable, however, it would indicate a need to revise the Clean Air Act's national ambient air-quality standards for the protection of public health. Health effects from sulfate are not directly regulated now by the national ambient air-quality standards.

The Senate Proposal

The Clean Air Act reauthorization bill (S 3041) approved last year by the Senate Environment and Public Works Committee provides for additional acid precipitation research and for a major emission reduction program.[21] It would require an 8 million ton reduction from 1980 SO_2 emissions in a 31-state eastern area, to be accomplished by 1995 or 1993 depending upon emission reduction strategies.[22] Sulfur dioxide emission increases from existing or new stationary sources coming on line in the 31-state area before 1995 must be offset by equivalent emission reductions at existing sources. Emission offsets also would be required for increased NOx emissions at existing sources.

An Emissions Freeze?

S 3041 omitted a feature common to earlier versions of the Mitchell bill: an emissions freeze to take effect once the initial emission rollback had been accomplished.[23] The proposals would have imposed a ceiling on SO_2 emissions at 9 to 12 million tons per year, to be maintained by an offset requirement for all new source SO_2 emissions. Due to political pressure within the Environment Committee, the final bill eliminated offset requirements after 1995 for new sources equipped with best available control technology which achieve "the most stringent emission limitation" attained by similar sources in the 31-state area.[24]

EPA data suggest that in the absence of an emission offset require-ment after 1995, eastern utility SO_2 emissions eventually would ap-proach pre-rollback levels due to new source growth.[25]

Thus, S 3041 engineers a 30-year roller coaster dip in eastern utility SO_2 emissions. Any environmental benefits resulting from the initial rollback would be short-lived with this approach. Recognizing this, proponents of permanent emission reductions may seek to restore an emission ceiling to the Senate bill, to include one in other bills, or to impose one if and when an emission rollback has been ac-complished under enacted law.

The emission freeze issue highlights a poorly understood aspect of the acid precipitation debate: A major, permanent reduction in eastern SO_2 emissions would entail far more than controls at some existing power plants. It is a *new source* control issue as well. Long-term maintenance of an emission ceiling implies the need for new source emission controls more stringent than EPA's 1979 perfor-mance standards.

A new source offset requirement following an 8 million ton or larger SO_2 rollback would cost $2,000 or more per annual ton of SO_2 to be offset.[26] Each million tons of new source emissions thus would raise the price tag of an emission freeze by $2 billion annual-ly (in 1983 prices). With the cost of the proposed 8 million ton rollback (without any freeze) pegged conservatively at $3 billion an-nually by 1995, the addition of a freeze would sharply increase total program costs. To date, there has been no systematic evaluation of the long-term cost or industrial development implications of an emis-sions freeze policy.[27]

In sum, the plan approved by the Environment Committee is lit-tle more than a costly, temporarily effective rollback of one acid precursor, sulfur dioxide. It is exceedingly unlikely that implemen-tation of this proposal would generate environmental benefits com-mensurate with its costs.

Uncertain Benefits

In its report in S 3041, the Environment Committee spoke to the question of the benefits and costs of its emission reduction proposal:

> The committee concluded that strategies now exist which are economi-cally feasible for the control of acid rain precursors. This is not to say that all controls are inexpensive, although some are. Control costs do,

however, compare quite favorably to estimates of damage as calculated by Dr. Thomas D. Crocker of the University of Wyoming who estimated that annual losses due to acid deposition amount to $5 billion per year in 1978 dollars.[28]

Dr. Crocker's $5 billion damage estimate is an attempt to measure, within the constraints of available economic methodologies, the resource damages due to acid deposition. In order to use this estimate as a proxy for the benefits of a given control program—i.e., a measure of damages avoided by controls—the control program would have to remedy fully all of the damages included in Dr. Crocker's estimate.[29]

Materials damages—$2 billion
Forest ecosystem damages—$1.75 billion
Direct agricultural damages—$1 billion
Aquatic ecosystem damages—$250 million
Other damages—$100 million

The Senate proposal would not remedy all or even most of these damages; no control program has been proposed which would eliminate all acid deposition. It thus is misleading at best to suggest that the costs of the Senate proposal "compare quite favorably" with Dr. Crocker's damage estimate.

The benefits of a particular emission control program can only be estimated through measurement of its physical resource impacts. Incomplete scientific understanding of atmospheric chemistry and ecosystem responses to acid deposition precludes such measurement for S 3041 or other proposals. The "roller coaster" emission trend allowed by S 3041, and its modest emission reduction requirements for the Northeast, suggest that it would not generate meaningful long-term environmental benefits in ecologically sensitive areas like the Adirondacks. Moreover, the bill's basic neglect of NO_x emissions means that it may have no mitigative impact whatsoever on spring fish kills, or on other environmental effects of nitrate and nitric acid deposition.

Traditional benefit-cost analysis will not provide a complete picture of the benefits that may result from a reduction of acid depositions.[30] Some environmental impacts such as the loss of diversity of plant and fish species cannot be quantified by available methods. But even if better yardsticks for benefit measurement were available, insistence upon a favorable benefit-cost relationship as a condition precedent for emission controls would be politically ineffective; in essence, the acid precipitation controversy is a challenge to the Clean Air Act's lack of effective mechanisms for resolving interstate pollution disputes. Costs and benefits are not as much at issue as is the "right" of one state or group of states to "dump its garbage" in other states.

Alternative Control Approaches

The Reagan administration and most industry groups oppose enactment of acid precipitation control legislation until additional research has been completed. Control proponents argue that enough already is known to warrant an emission reduction program. Congress is uncomfortably interposed between the factions. At no time in recent history has Congress rejected a major environmental initiative once it had been approved by one of the two committees of primary jurisdiction. The Senate Environment Committee approved S 3041 by a 15-1 vote. Recent changes to that committee's membership will strengthen its resolve to push control legislation through the 98th Congress.[31]

When Congress considers acid precipitation legislation in 1983 or 1984, advocates of near-term emission reductions will try to posture the issue as a vote "for or against acid rain." If such a strategy were pursued successfully—and the sheer technical complexity of the subject matter enhances this possibility—representatives of any but the largest emitting states would be hard pressed to resist pro-rollback votes. If environmental groups marshal their grass-roots lobbying forces behind this issue, an emission rollback bill might be approved overwhelmingly.

There is a clear and pressing need for reasonable alternatives to S 3041. One alternative recently suggested by some industry groups is lake liming in the Northeast. A liming program to mitigate obvious aquatic damage should be authorized. However, a liming program alone would be attacked by environmentalists and northeastern Congressmen as a Band-Aid remedy for a cancerous disease. From a political standpoint, some type of emission reduction program is a foreseeable response to the acid precipitation controversy. Nonetheless, considerable latitude remains for creative solutions to it.

A Demonstration Project for the Control of Acid Deposition in the Northeast

Given the substantial scientific uncertainties about the effectiveness of the controls proposed in S 3041, a strong case can be made for an acid deposition control demonstration project focused on the Northeast.

A demonstration project for the control of northeastern acid deposition might have four major elements:

- Congressional designation of the Adirondacks and portions of New England as "vulnerable receptor" areas requiring immediate protection from acid deposition;
- Determination by EPA or the National Academy of Sciences of current rates of acid deposition in these areas, and target deposition standards to protect them from further damage;
- A phased program of source controls, starting with nearby— e.g., 200 miles or less—sources, and expanding later to more distant—e.g., 200 to 300 miles—sources as necessary, with intervals for monitoring the effects of each round of controls; and
- A modest tax on coal- and oil-fired electric generation in the 31-state eastern United States to finance emission control costs, mitigation measures such as liming, and additional acid precipitation research. (A tax of one mill per kilowatt-hour in the 31-state East would generate revenues of roughly $1 billion annually.)

This approach has several features which might attract widespread political support.

First, it reduces the risk of a high-cost regional emission rollback with little measurable benefits. Controls are imposed gradually, starting with the sources most proximate to—and most directly responsible for acid deposition in—the areas of the country evidencing current harm from acid precipitation. If further research justifies acid deposition controls for other areas of the country, experience developed in the Northeast demonstration project could be applied to control programs for these areas.

Second, a standards-based approach to acid deposition is consistent with other Clean Air Act programs. Defining a particular area for protection from acid deposition also has a precedent in the act's designation of national parks and wilderness areas as "Class I" areas requiring strict air-quality and visibility protection. In contrast, the arbitrary rollback formula employed in S 3041 makes utter nonsense of several Clean Air Act programs.[32]

Third, a demonstration project in the Northeast could provide the framework for a solution to the difficult diplomatic problem that acid precipitation poses for U.S.-Canadian relations. The two countries could initiate joint control programs once the U.S. had signaled an intent to protect sensitive areas of New England and the Adirondacks. A counterpart electric generation tax could be levied by Ontario or other provinces to finance Canadian controls, mitigation measures, and research.

Fourth, the generation tax for financing a demonstration project would eliminate the threat of pockets of severe economic hardship for some utilities and their ratepayers.[33]

Self-Help Options

Short of enactment of control legislation by both houses of Congress, a number of voluntary actions could be pursued by industry and state government to obviate the need for congressional intercession.

Faced with a commitment to voluntary controls at the state level, Congress would be reluctant to interpose its judgement on control requirements. Indeed, it is difficult to imagine a more effective means of defusing the congressional politics on this issue than voluntary state-industry cooperation.

But the prospects for interstate cooperation are bleak at this time. The key interest groups potentially involved in the development of an interstate agreement—governors, state agencies, utilities, and utility fuel suppliers—lack a common perception of the probability of federal emission rollback legislation. And without the perception of a common advantage to be gained through compromise, little incentive exists to forge an agreement. If the sponsors of S 3041 and similar legislation have their way, the cost of this misjudgement will be measured in millions of tons of additional emission reduction requirements and billions of dollars of annual control costs.

References

1. ICF, Inc., "Preliminary Forecasts Evaluating the Impacts of the Senate Bill for a 1995 Reduction in Sulfur Dioxide Emissions Assuming Intrastate Trading" (memorandum to the Environmental Protection Agency staff, September 16, 1982). The ICF estimate is based on a least-cost optimization linear programming model. Other estimates of the cost of the Senate bill are as high as $8 billion. See John M. Wootten, Peabody Coal Company, "Acid Rain Control: Impact on the High-sulfur Coal Industry" (presented at the Second National Symposium on Acid Rain, Pittsburgh, October 6, 7, 1982).

2. "An Updated Perspective on Acid Rain," Edison Electric Institute, November, 1981, pp. 13, 14.

3. National Academy of Sciences, "Atmosphere-biosphere Interactions: Toward a Better Understanding of the Ecological Consequences of Fossil Fuel Combustion," National Academy Press, 1981, Figures 5-8.

4. Comptroller General of the U.S., "The Debate over Acid Precipitation: Opposing Views, Status of Research," EMD-81-131, September, 1981, pp. 19-21.

5. "Effectiveness of Control Strategies for Reducing Acidification of Rain," by W. Wilson, J. Homolya, R. Husar, and A. Lazrus (presented at the 74th annual meeting of the Air Pollution Control Association, Philadelphia, June 21-26, 1981), p. 1.

6. National Academy of Sciences, op. cit., pp. 140-147.

7. See "Chemical Composition of Acid Fog," by J. Waldman et al. *Science,* Vol. 218, pp. 677-680, November 12, 1982.

8. All emission data cited in this paragraph are from U.S.-Canada Memorandum of Intent Working Group IIIB Report, 1982.

9. See footnote 5, op. cit., p. 10.

10. Ibid., p. 13.

11. Ibid., Figures 3 and 4.

12. Ibid., pp. 4-7.

13. National Academy of Sciences, op. cit., pp. 149-167; Comptroller General, op. cit., pp. 4, 5; U.S. Office of Technology Assessment, "The Regional Implications of Transported Air Pollutants: An Assessment of Acidic Deposition and Ozone," interim draft report to Congress, July, 1982, pp. H-1-5; U.S.-Canada Memorandum of Intent Impact Assessment Working Group I, "Phase II Interim Working Paper," October, 1981, pp. 3-107-109.

14. "Measurement of Anions in the Snow Cover of the Adirondack Mountains," by P. Galvin and J. Cline, *Atmospheric Environment,* Vol. 12, p. 1163 (1978); U.S.-Canada "Phase II Interim Working Paper," op. cit., pp. 3-3, 6.

15. U.S. Office of Technology Assessment, op. cit., pp. F7-10; "Catastrophe on Camel's Hump," by H. Vogelmann, *Natural History,* Vol. 91, No. 11, November, 1982. EPA's Draft Acid Precipitation Critical Assessment Document (1982) notes that "The decline is widespread, easily discerned, dramatic, and of unknown origin. . . . Acid deposition could be a contributing or controlling stress, but it is not known at which point in the decline it may act, or the pathway(s) by which it may act."

16. National Academy of Sciences, op. cit., pp. 167-173; U.S.-Canada Memorandum of Intent "Phase II Interim Working Paper," op. cit., pp. 4-15-28.

17. National Academy of Sciences, op. cit., pp. 167-170; U.S. Office of Technology Assessment, op. cit., pp. F5-7; U.S.-Canada Memorandum of Intent "Phase II Interim Working Paper," op. cit., pp. 4-2-11.

18. Comptroller General, op. cit., pp. 10, 11; U.S.-Canada Memorandum of Intent "Phase II Interim Working Paper," op. cit., pp. 6-4-7.

19. U.S. Office of Technology Assessment, op. cit., pp. J-3-8.

20. Comptroller General, op. cit., pp. 11, 12; U.S.-Canada Memorandum of Intent "Phase II Interim Working Paper," op. cit., pp. 5-1, 5-12.

21. S 3041, "Clean Air Act Amendments of 1982," 97th Cong., 2d Sess., 1982.

22. Emission reductions must be accomplished by January 1, 1993, if conventional emission reduction techniques are employed—e.g., fuel switching or scrubber retrofitting—or by January 1, 1995, if innovative technologies are used or existing facilities are replaced by new ones.

23. Whether S 1706 contained an emission freeze is a matter of interpretation; it proposed a 10 million ton reduction from 1980 SO_2 emissions in the 31-state East (19 million tons) and prohibited "significant" increases in SO_2 and NO_x emissions from stationary sources in this region unless such increases were offset by emission reductions in excess of the proposed increase in emissions. This can be construed as an emission freeze at 9 million tons per year of SO_2, plus adjustments for any NO_x:SO_2 trading. The acid rain proposal put forward on June 29, 1982, by Senators Mitchell, Stafford, Moynihan, and Chafee also required a 10 million ton rollback and stated that "emissions for out-years are capped at 10 million tons below 1980 levels." This proposal was the basis for the 8 million ton rollback plan subsequently adopted by the Environment Committee, without any freeze on future SO_2 emissions.

24. EPA has indicated that it would interpret this requirement as equivalent to new source performance standards. See, Comptroller General of the United States, "Analysis of the Acid Rain Proposal Approved by the U.S. Senate Committee on Environment and Public Works on July 22, 1982," September 24, 1982, p. 16.

25. Data are from ICF, Inc., memorandum to EPA staff, op. cit., Table 4.

26. Current costs of scrubbing low-sulfur coal are $1,000 to $3,000 per ton of SO_2 removed. ICF, Inc., "Effect of Acid Rain Proposals on Emissions, Costs, and Coal Production," by C. Hoff Stauffer, Jr., presented at the Second National Symposium on Acid Rain, Pittsburgh, October 6, 7, 1982.

27. The $3 to $5 billion annualized cost estimates often cited for S 3041, and similar estimates of the cost of the original Mitchell bill, are based on the life cycle costs of the initial emission reductions (fuel switching and scrubber retrofitting). The cost of maintaining an emission freeze through new source offset requirements or technological improvements to emission controls has never been estimated.

28. Senate Report No. 97-666, 97th Cong., 2nd Sess., 1982, p. 61.

29. "Methods Development for Environmental Control Benefit Assessment—Methods Development for Assessing Acid Precipitation Control Benefits," by T. Crocker et al. prepared for U.S. EPA Office of Research and Development, 1980, p. II-51.

30. See "Conventional Benefit-cost Analyses of Acid Deposition Control Are Likely to Be Misleading," by T. Crocker, presented at the Conference on Acid Rain, SUNY at Buffalo, May 1, 2, 1981.

31. Senators David Durenberger (Republican, Minnesota) and Gordon Humphrey (Republican, New Hampshire) will replace Slade Gorton (Republican, Washington) and Frank Murkowski (Republican, Arkansas). Senator Durenberger was a cosponsor of the initial Mitchell bill, and Senator Humphrey is strongly sympathetic to control legislation.

32. The act's program to prevent significant deterioration of air quality in areas attaining the national ambient air-quality standards (NAAQS) would

become largely irrelevant for the control of new source SO_2 emissions in the 31-state East since a rollback would guarantee a significant *decrease* in SO_2 emissions. Similarly, a rollback would affect emission control requirements in nonattainment areas, potentially requiring more stringent controls on sources in these areas than the act requires to protect human health through the primary NAAQS. With rollback requirements determined by average emission rates, it is conceivable that some sources now causing exceedances of the health-related NAAQS may escape control requirements altogether under S 3041, while other sources in full compliance with the NAAQS would be faced with substantial emission reductions.

33. Individual utility systems have estimated the rate impacts of SO_2 rollback proposals, and results vary widely: Tennessee Valley Authority, 7 percent; American Electric Power Company, 63 percent; Southern Company Service, Inc., 20 to 30 percent; Union Electric Company, 20 to 25 percent; and Public Service Company of Indiana, 50 percent. See Senate Report No. 97-666, 97th Cong., 2d Sess., pp. 70-72.

"I find this acid rain gives a nice little fillip to it."

Drawing by Joe Mirachi; ©1981, *The New Yorker Magazine, Inc.*

Investigate, Educate, *Then* Regulate: An Agenda for Dealing with Acid Rain

By Alvin W. Vogtle, Jr.

Arguing that there is much left to learn about the problem, the president of The Southern Company presents a businessman's view about acid rain regulation.

It's an unhappy fact that not all who express a concern for the environment have chosen the road of reason. When the Environmental Protection Agency resisted rash and hasty rule-making on acid rain, a dissatisfied spokesman for one advocacy group said the EPA is—and I quote—". . . virtually alone in believing that we don't know enough to act." This opinion came, I should note, from an attorney—not a scientist. But regardless of who said it, the statement is untrue . . . unfair . . . and unfortunate.

It's untrue because the roster of respected scientists who've pointed out how much we don't know about acid deposition would fill at least a page of fine print. Even a laymen like myself must give great weight to the questions raised by authorities like Dr. Volk of Florida, Dr. Rahn of Rhode Island, Dr. Semonin of Illinois, and Dr. Wetzel of Michigan, to name but a few.

The statement was also unfair. It takes advantage of the total freedom from responsibility that the critic enjoys. He will never have to answer for the action he urges if it should misfire.

And the statement was unfortunate because it tends to divide and polarize those who should be working together.

We believe in the process of working together—and we don't believe in polarization. I cannot imagine why anyone would think that we who provide electric power must be antagonists to the ef-

---

Excerpted from *Vital Speeches of the Day*, August 15, 1982, with permission of City News Publishing Co. Alvin W. Vogtle, Jr., is president of The Southern Company.

fort to protect the environment. We, too, live and walk and work in this air and on this land. Our children play here. We do not dwell in walled-off enclaves, with our own private air supply.

I'm not going to assume a defensive posture, nor will I argue about pH factors. I'm not going to discuss Antarctic ice cores or Adirondack lakes. And I'm certainly not going to deny the acid rain question—nor am I going to set the limits or define the terms of the acid rain debate. I'm not going to do these things for one reason—I lack the qualifications to do so.

But I will do what I am qualified for, and that is to speak for The Southern Company and the Southern electric system. In that role, I will make this clear and simple statement. We are not in the business of endangering human health or of creating an unfit environment.

And we never will be.

In fact, I'll go further. We of the Southern electric system will continue to cooperate in every way possible to determine whether there is a health or environmental hazard directly related to emissions from our power plants. And if there should prove to be such a hazard, we will bend every effort to find an effective remedy and put it to work.

We have a common concern, a shared commitment, and a joint task. But the task we face is not simple. And it would be a disservice to the people we all serve if we pretend that the task is simple.

I emphasize this because I've seen articles which treat environmental issues as if they were simple. The public, we are told, wants clean air and water.

Well, of course the public wants clean air and water. But the public also wants lower taxes, more industry and new job opportunities, less inflation, and lower electric bills. And, as you and I know, we cannot have more stringent controls on power plants without the cost showing up in higher electric bills. That's why we—together— must accept three difficult tasks. We must learn more about acid deposition. We must define for the public the choices and costs indicated by what we learn. And we must recommend—to both the public and the government—policies that will achieve the best balance between goals and costs.

I suggest that we undertake this threefold responsibility in the form of an agenda on which we all can agree—a program which can assure a positive outcome. And this is how I would express that agenda in three clear and direct words: investigate—educate—regulate.

As I've said, I do not hold the credentials to lecture on the scientific findings about acid rain. As Will Rogers said, "I only know what I read in the papers." Among the reports I have read, however, there is the testimony given last month before the Environment and Public Works Committee of the United States Senate.

At this hearing, Dr. Volker Mohnen, director of the Atmospheric Sciences Research Center, said that a reduction in sulfur dioxide emissions would not yield an equal reduction—and might not yield any reduction—in acid rain in the eastern United States. Then a spokesman for the Environmental Defense Fund said reductions in sulfur emissions will lead to nearly comparable reductions in acid deposition in the Northeast.

Now, we all know enough to realize that this disagreement does not reflect to the discredit of science, nor to the discredit of these capable men. From the days of the ancient Greeks, controversy has marked the progress of science. Indeed, controversy shapes the very path on which science advances. But even to a layman like myself, the differing views expressed by these two scientists make one thing clear—we do not know enough about the relationship between sulfur emissions and acid rain.

When Ph.D.s disagree, what's a poor layman to do? There's a commonsense answer that every layman will understand. Be patient—but be persistent. Wait for clear answers—but keep watch to ensure that the search is diligently pursued.

But how long should we wait? That's the troubled question raised by those sincerely concerned—those who believe that grave harm may be continuing while researchers pursue their investigations. And I'll not deny it's a valid question. We cannot wait forever. Our natural inclination to avoid choice amid such a cloud of uncertainty must not become an excuse for indefinite delay. Would it seem unreasonable, then, to limit the delay to five years?

I didn't pick that five-year figure at random. As you know, the Congress established a 10-year study program in 1980. And there's a proposal going through the committee process right now to speed up that study program, to cut it to five years, and to focus on the issues most crucial to formulating policy. We in the Southern electric system fully support this move to accelerate both the funding and the work of that study program. And I believe this support is widespread throughout the electric utility industry.

The agenda I proposed a moment ago had three elements—

investigate, educate, regulate. We in the electric utility industry give our full support to speeding up the "investigate" phase. Now, why did I propose education as a second phase?

Let me begin by repeating a simple fact of economic life. The public pays for everything it gets. Not only is there no such thing as a free lunch—there's no such thing as free environmental quality, either. Clean air and clean water have a price.

By saying this, I do not mean that price alone should be our guide. If clean air and clean water have a price, it is true also that they have a value. One of the triumphs of the environmental movement is that, in the short span of about 20 years, virtually every American has come to accept the value of environmental quality as a goal.

But, there's another simple principle of economic life that every American understands and accepts. The price paid should bear some reasonable relation to the value received. Let us assume that after this period of investigation—and let's put that at five years—we'll have some clear-cut proposals to bring before the public and their elected representatives. We'll need wholehearted support to get those proposals accepted enthusiastically by all segments of the public— by young voters, by retired folks, by industry, by everyone who will have to pay part of the price. To get that broad support, we must be able to explain exactly what the nature of the problem is and exactly what people can expect in return for paying the price.

In truth, we cannot give such an explanation today. That's why any present proposal to rush into regulation is unacceptable. Research people in our company have studied carefully one of the proposals now before the Congress—Senate bill 1706, or "the Mitchell bill," as it is called. As nearly as we can estimate now, the cost of complying with this bill's provisions would add at least 20 to 25 percent to the average residential customer's electric bill.

Our company has had some experience with this sort of thing. So, I'll tell you what we've learned about going to the public and telling them to expect higher electric bills.

They don't like it.

And I don't blame them one bit. Nobody enjoys paying bigger bills—even when the reasons can be clearly explained.

So imagine how much greater the public outcry would be under the impact of premature legislation like the Mitchell bill—especially when we couldn't say clearly what people would get in return for paying more.

We are dealing with a complex issue. And we're dealing with a political issue—political in the sense that it involves large-scale public policy. The success enjoyed thus far by the environmental movement has been made possible by its efforts to educate the people. Public support has rested directly on our ability to explain the issues, the hazards, the remedies, and the costs.

Do we hope to get similar public support for an effective program to deal with acid rain? Then we'll have to offer similar education on the issues, the hazards, the remedies, and the costs that will be involved. But, until we gather the facts through investigation, we cannot succeed with the work of education.

Investigation.

Education.

And then we'll be ready to develop the necessary regulation. That's the third phase of my proposed agenda.

Believe me, this subject of regulation is one I can discuss with confidence. I wouldn't recognize a hydrogen ion if it came up and bit me. But I've been working in and with America's most regulated industry.

Some people are quick to assume that we in the utility industry have one and only one attitude about regulation—that we are just plain "agin it." That's not quite true. We deliberately chose—perhaps for reasons only a psychiatrist would understand—to make our careers in a highly regulated business. We're quite used to living with regulation. In fact, we're the first to acknowledge a need for well-conceived controls.

However, we've also become very sensitive to poorly conceived regulation. Living with regulation as intimately as we do, we can spot a bad regulation before it leaves the banks of the Potomac.

Two of the surest hallmarks of bad regulation are that you can't tell in advance whether it will achieve its proposed objective and you can't predict with reasonable accuracy its ultimate cost. Both of those characteristics apply to the Mitchell bill and several other legislative proposals under discussion.

I've already noted that reputable scientific authorities disagree as to whether reducing sulfur emissions will bring comparable reductions in acid rain. Every person in this room probably has an opinion on one side or the other of that disagreement. Speaking for myself, my industry, and our shareholders—we have a great interest in the outcome of this debate. And we feel a great obligation to work for legislation that is based on fact—and regulation that is cost effective. Meanwhile, the very fact that there is such debate argues persuasively that we are not yet ready to regulate.

The other mark of poor regulation—the inability to predict ultimate cost—adds further reason to avoid hasty regulation. As I've said, we estimate the Mitchell bill would cost the Southern electric system at least $845 million per year. This would add at least 20 percent to the average residential customer's electric bill. I assure you, that estimate was not cooked up casually. It was calculated carefully—because we need estimates that cover every contingency as accurately as possible for our own advance planning.

Even so, our research people found it necessary to qualify their estimate by saying that ". . . many factors which could cause these costs to increase by a factor of two or more have not been included in these considerations."

Rushing to regulate now—before we investigate and educate—would be the same as asking the public to sign a blank check, with no assurance of what they'll get in return. And speaking for myself and our companies, we will stand beside you all through the battles for environmental quality—but we will not ask our customers to sign a blank check in return for a question mark.

In the context of the money and effort that our companies already have committed to environmental quality, I don't believe our position can be characterized as negative. We have demonstrated our concern for the quality of life in the region we serve. And for the three-year period running from 1982 through 1984, we have placed more than $428 million in our construction budget for environmental controls. That's an investment of almost half a billion dollars in the interest of clean air and clean water.

But we're always sensitive to the fact that, ultimately, it is our customers' money we're dealing with. And that is why I come with a positive program for approaching the many questions about acid rain.

Investigate. Educate. Then regulate. And accelerate the first phase—the investigation—from a 10-year to a five-year program, with full funding.

How to Stop Talking About Industrial Wastes and Do Something About Them

By Jackson B. Browning

Hazardous waste disposal is the subject of this article in which the author appeals for a more sophisticated discussion of the issue and offers some suggestions for dealing with the problem.

There is probably no issue in the media and in public policy debate about which more is said and less understood than the issue of hazardous waste disposal. The problem is usually discussed in the context of a life-or-property-threatening accident or event. The fact that actual harm is minimal or nonexistent gets lost in tomorrow's headlines.

This creates some very real problems for public officials who carry the responsibility for legislating effective procedures for the siting and handling of industrial wastes.

And it creates some equally stressful problems for people like me who are responsible for seeing to it that the wastes from Union Carbide plants are handled so that neither our employees nor the environment are put at risk.

It means that important work must be done and vital public interests protected in an atmosphere that is highly charged with the rhetoric and manipulation of interest groups that are sometimes well-meaning, and sometimes not.

The most insidious manipulation of issues is the linking and equating of today's disposal problems with those which society has inherited in the form of failing, abandoned dumps.

A Sense of Proportion

I do not want to suggest for a moment that industrial wastes are

---

Reprinted by permission of the Union Carbide Corporation, New York, New York. Jackson B. Browning is corporate director of health, safety and environmental affairs for Union Carbide.

not a problem and a serious one, nor that some of these wastes do not pose real hazards. But I want to emphasize that that problem, like many others in our complex society, is and has been demonstrated to be solvable. What is most pressingly needed to deal with this problem, however, is a sense of proportion.

In the first place, the term hazardous waste as it is used generically is a pejorative term. The hazard posed by any chemical waste, for example, is rarely intrinsic to the material. There are more than 20,000 different chemical compounds produced in this country, and only a handful pose any intrinsic risks. The hazard, if any, is almost always a relative or quantitative measure, and it is often highly specific to a particular location or environment. In other words, a substance may be generally harmless in small quantities or in a disposal site in the desert, but a real problem in large concentrations or in an underground aquifer that serves a town water supply.

So, the message is that wastes in general do not constitute a specific category of chemical materials that are intrinsically harmful at all times and in every place. On the contrary, wastes generally become hazardous because of their quantity or concentration or because of the specific location in which they are found.

Second, let me assure you that hazardous wastes are not something new that have suddenly burst on the environment. Nor is the United States inundated in a flood of hazardous wastes that we cannot control.

Potentially hazardous wastes have been produced in this country for centuries. The first tannery that opened in colonial America to make leather produced potentially hazardous wastes. So did the first textile dyeing mill. So did the first mint. So did agriculture.

Yesterday's Concerns, Today's Technology

Why, then, are public officials and industry plagued with the waste disposal problem of today? First, three-plus decades of extraordinary economic growth and industrial expansion have resulted in an explosion of products, by-products and wastes which must be accommodated. Second, the explosion of knowledge in chemistry and in the related environmental and health sciences has resulted in the identification of problems not previously suspected.

Forty years ago a much smaller United States economy produced far fewer materials. And it disposed of them many times in locations that were then isolated, but are today known as suburbs.

Until very recently, we simply did not have either the scientific competence or diagnostic tools to really know when a waste disposal system was presenting real or potential threats to human health or the integrity of the environment. The Chemical Manufacturers Association has identified 500-to-600 potentially hazardous existing waste sites in the United States—sites which need expensive engineering treatments to be neutralized. Yet in almost every one of these cases, there is no "criminal" or "culprit" to be held responsible. These sites were generally opened and operated by manufacturing companies, federal government agencies, or municipalities according to the prevailing wisdom and scientific understanding of the time. What is important is not finding somebody to blame. The point is to get these sites cleaned up.

Finally, there is a growing public concern and apprehension. At issue is not whether the public has been badly used and misinformed by some journalists and some political activists; the issue is that opinion polls tell us that the public considers chemical wastes a major concern, and they feel that too little is being done to reduce the hazards.

People have been alarmed by phenomena like Love Canal. The word "phenomena" is used advisedly, because Love Canal was above all else a media event. Unfortunately, when the Environmental Protection Agency finally got around to admitting that its initial report linking Love Canal to chromosome damage was scientifically unsound, it got far less press coverage than the earlier scare stories. When a respected panel of scientific inquiry headed by the eminent Dr. Lewis Thomas reported that no significant health effects could be attributed to Love Canal and that the EPA report "damaged the credibility of science," it was a small story. When the State of New York released data showing that the incidence of cancer among Love Canal residents was no greater than that of people anywhere else in the state, it didn't make many headlines.

Ultimately, the State of New York was forced to underwrite the relocation of Love Canal residents, not because real health hazards had been sustained, but because of the very real psychological harm experienced by residents in the process of becoming media celebrities.

I don't blame anyone subjected to the confusing claims of public and industrial spokesmen for becoming alarmed about Love Canal. The process of understanding the issue of hazardous waste is a difficult one, and it is unreasonable for us in industry to expect to gain people's confidence in our mastery of safe waste disposal systems overnight.

But the task of creating mechanisms that assure the public that hazardous waste treatment facilities can be sited, designed and operated in a manner that will properly protect public health and the environment rests in large part not with industry but with state officials. We in industry have the technology to insure safe waste treatment and disposal systems. But the public looks to their elected representatives—and quite rightly, I think—to provide mechanisms that guarantee that these systems are properly deployed, operated and monitored.

Gaining Confidence

Waste management is an enormous responsibility, and it is an undertaking that demands confidence. Nobody in this country has any business doing anything that poses unacceptable risks to public health or the environment.

Let me give you one example of the kind of capability that has been available for a number of years. At Goff Mountain in West Virginia, Union Carbide operates a waste disposal facility that has been judged a model of its type. Goff Mountain is a facility in which chemical wastes that have first been treated are mixed and churned with soil to facilitate breakdown of materials—in other words, to make them biodegradable.

Goff Mountain handles the wastes from three major chemical plants we operate in West Virginia, as well as those from our research and development center in Charleston. As a consequence, it is a huge operation that extends over a hundred acres. In order to make sure that no waste substance deposited in the Goff Mountain site ever leaches into the ground to pollute the water table, the base of the site is sealed with a packed clay liner that is up to 42 feet thick.

We have been operating this waste disposal site for 15 years, and we have accumulated abundant evidence that it is environmentally safe and poses no risk to health. It was by no means inexpensive to build or operate, but we have never questioned that it represents an excellent value.

In the planning stages, our engineers and scientists had to convince our management and public officials that this costly undertaking would, in fact, perform as they promised, and prove effective in disposing of wastes without undue risk to employees or the environment.

While we have provided our own solution to some of our own problems with the Goff Mountain facility, the inescapable fact is that the United States urgently needs to provide more industrial waste disposal sites—sites that are properly located, designed, operated and monitored. The high standard of living we all know and love is the fruit of industries that of necessity produce wastes. We cannot realistically expect to have one without the other.

Towards Effective, Practical Legislation

It is not terribly difficult to elicit a political consensus in support of the need for siting sound hazardous waste treatment facilities. The majority of voters will readily agree that such sites are necessary, and that you should move with all deliberate speed to locate them—at the other end of the state.

I think it is reasonable to infer that such sentiments are often rooted not only in apprehensions about the safety of such sites, but in concerns about issues like property values.

Effective legislation in the face of local opposition is an arduous proposition. And notwithstanding hazardous waste siting laws that are already on the books, I think it is useful to explore which elements are necessary to insure that siting legislation is in fact effective—and not a token gesture doomed to be stalemated in implementation.

The Chemical Manufacturers Association has drafted a model statute for the siting, construction and financing of facilities for treatment, storage and disposal of hazardous wastes. I've compared this with other statutes. And I've found a small number of key elements in common that I would recommend for your consideration.

First, I think it is essential to establish clear and straightforward criteria establishing what constitutes an acceptable site for treatment and disposal of hazardous wastes. By using objective environmental impact standards, the public perception that such sites are located by political decision or "clout" is undermined.

Second, I think it is important to communicate these criteria to the public. When the point is explicitly made that hazardous waste facilities are to be sited in those locations best suited to insuring proper protection of health or the environment, the process can be appreciated as deliberate and not arbitrary.

What should some of the objective criteria for siting be? Not to belabor the obvious, I think we would all agree on these guidelines at a minimum:

- Hazardous waste sites should be located away from densely populated areas, and away from heavily travelled thoroughfares.
- They should not present any potential hazard to underground aquifers.
- They should present no potentially adverse effects on prized natural scenery or recreational and wildlife areas, nor to the economies of communities dependent upon such attractions.

That still leaves plenty of room for potential waste treatment sites. Nonetheless, any potential site is bound to be proximate to some community. And this brings us to a third and critical point: the involvement of local communities in the siting of waste disposal sites.

I would ask you to consider the merits of legislation that empowers an appointed hazardous waste siting council to identify and catalogue all the locations in a state that meet the criteria for safe and effective waste treatment sites.

Such a procedure might then involve participation in the actual siting process by temporary commission members drawn from each locality identified. And it might profitably involve consideration of tax or other financial benefits for the local governments in which waste treatment sites are planned and constructed.

Fourth, I think there is no practical alternative to legislation that ultimately reserves to the state the right to preempt local zoning and land-use ordinances in order to locate waste treatment sites that meet the criteria of the statewide plan. Our legal system simply affords so many ready opportunities for individuals and local special interest groups to pursue their own interests that the vital interests of the commonwealth are paralyzed in the courts.

Finally, I would suggest that some provision is needed as a last resort to empower the state itself to acquire waste sites and either finance, construct, and operate a waste treatment facility, or lease it to a private operator.

If this sounds like a formidable task, it is one that has been successfully undertaken by some states. I think it is a responsibility that can be made easier by a concerted effort to help people understand that government and industry do have the tools to handle the industrial waste problem safely, without undue risk to people or the environment—and that we have been doing precisely that for some time in both the private and the public sector.

Starting Over, Again: Rethinking U.S. Water Quality Programs

By Jackson B. Browning

Industry's criticisms of the Clean Water Act and some proposed solutions are discussed in this article by an officer of the Union Carbide Corporation.

By now we are all in the process of learning that one piece of campaign rhetoric that seems to have some real meaning and force in the Reagan Administration is the question, "Are you better off today than you were four years ago?" A host of federal programs appear to be coming under surgical scrutiny and are being assayed against the hard measure "Are things better because of this program?"

It is admittedly difficult to judge critically the value and cost-effectiveness of a federal program if you are a supplier to that program. It can be equally difficult if you are a complier with said program. As a result, we in these United States find ourselves supporting a number of government programs whose goals have never been adequately thought through or certainly have not been reexamined recently. These programs are sometimes designed to solve problems that have never been defined, and in some cases problems that have never really been shown to exist.

We are not, as Americans, unusual in this predicament. It is in the nature of elected governments to respond to the concerns of their constituents, and to be instinctively guided toward action rather than sober reflection. The tendency of elected officials when confronted by public insistence that something is wrong is not to analyze what it is that is wrong, but to set out to fix it.

In 1972, the Congress responded to evidence that water quality

---

Reprinted by permission of the Union Carbide Corporation, New York, New York. Jackson B. Browning is corporate director of health, safety and environmental affairs for Union Carbide.

in the United States had deteriorated to the point where the Cuyahoga River could catch fire in downtown Cleveland. It passed the Clean Water Act, which promised that, under the watchful guidance of the Environmental Protection Agency and the force of a new amended Act in 1977, U.S. waters would, where attainable, become fishable and swimmable by 1983 and free from the discharge of pollutants by 1985.

It is quite obvious that this millennium is not going to come to pass on schedule. The curious question is "why wasn't it obvious in 1972 and 1977?" Why was it necessary to fund multi-million dollar water projects that in some cases may not have been needed, in others ineffectual, and that in other situations simply fail to work?

I think the answer is that such efforts are dictated by common sense. Common sense is prickly, and often intrudes upon lofty discussion. It never confuses size with importance, and appearance with reality, and that does little for its popularity. Worst of all, common sense tends to like things simple and straightforward.

By way of illustration, consider the following anecdote. It is a quasi-humorous water pollution anecdote, and as such it may be unique in the annals of modern storytelling.

At a fashionable house party in Dublin a few years ago a group of quite well-informed people were talking about the subject that was then all the rage: environment. In particular, they were concerned about the impact the rapid growth of industry in Ireland would have on its unspoiled countryside and trout streams. The government would have to stem industrial pollution.

At that point a silent and taciturn young man butted in. He was a great landowner—in fact, an earl, and well known for having both feet firmly planted in the 19th century.

"T'aint industry you've got to worry about," the earl said, "It's pig sluice that's ruining the country."

People quickly changed the subject, since it is not considered polite to laugh at the backwardness and ignorance of titled gentlemen, even those with no common sense.

Less than a week later the government released its official study on water pollution problems. The most critical problem, the report stated, was intensive pig breeding. That is, pig sluice.

I would suggest that you may find some parallels in the record of EPA's efforts to control water pollution and water quality degradation.

The Record

Let us look at that record. It will perhaps shed some light on why the Reagan administration wanted to carve $1 billion out of the 1981 EPA wastewater treatment construction grant program, and eliminate it altogether in fiscal 1982.

I think it is urgent that we re-examine not only our water quality goals, but the approaches that have been taken thus far to attain them. There is little point in simply continuing to endorse increased federal funding for water treatment, because there is clearly not going to be any such increase in the Reagan Administration. And I think it is equally clear that the billions spent so far by Washington on water quality have not yielded especially good value to the American taxpayer.

If we are to develop a useful and constructive public policy in regard to the nation's water resources, then it is time, I think, that we set about the task of matching priorities with capabilities; that we consider alternatives that might, with imagination and innovation, meet the critical need to return better pollution controls per dollar invested; that we come to terms with the fact that water quality is not so much a political or philosophical issue as an engineering and scientific problem.

To approach such an undertaking, we have to understand where we have travelled so far, and where the successes and failures have been centered. But it is equally important that we determine where we can go from here, and how we can proceed a step at a time. Spelling out water quality standards for the year 2000 is a congenial waste of time. The real task is to come up with a workable and effective program for the next five to ten years.

In the beginning, the 1972 Federal Water Pollution Control Act was conceived as an extremely capital-intensive program designed to spend billions in an accelerated effort to get ahead of water pollution problems that had been accumulating for years. It was, I think, a classical instance of the proverbial tendency of Washington to throw money at problems. I think we might also admit that many of us applauded from the wings. In 1972, you will recall, there were still a lot of people who thought we could buy anything at a price.

The objectives of the act were utopian from the outset, and the dimensions of the problem generously underestimated. The scale of investment required to even aim at the stated targets was mind-boggling. According to most recent EPA figures, it would today cost U.S. municipalities some $120 billion to meet the 1983 treatment requirements mandated under the law, plus another $114 billion to meet storm water requirements.

The national clean water effort further embodied some critical flaws in perception and execution. The problem of water pollution was generally presumed to be static rather than volatile, and to be fairly uniform in its required treatment across all waterways, rather than highly specific to any river or water body. And the allocation of water treatment grants was dictated by Congress according to a political formula, rather than a problem-solving agenda.

A well-operated wastewater treatment facility can remove the bulk of toxic pollutants from wastewater, as EPA's own studies have shown. But unfortunately, not all that many wastewater treatment facilities are properly designed or operated, and even where they are functioning well they may yet be functioning inadequately under the law.

In point of fact, it is estimated that about half of the municipal wastewater treatment facilities built with EPA funding do not meet performance standards. So we now have a situation in which, while industry has across the board performed quite well when meeting wastewater treatment and water quality goals at its own expense, some municipalities have been failing to do so at public expense.

This quite naturally leads to demands that compliance timetables for municipalities under the Federal Water Pollution Control Act be extended, since as a *fait accompli* they are in fact not being met.

The water quality issue presents itself in these terms: first, that federal funding has failed to provide the prescribed benefits in the past, and offers little prospect of doing so in the future; second, that federal funding and EPA's interpretation of its mandate have resulted in a broad failure to prioritize water quality goals—that is, to tackle the most serious problems first and target the optimal return on investment.

Evaluating Our Water Quality Goals

I am convinced as a consequence that we are at a crossroads in determining the direction of the nation's future in terms of water quality. And I think that if we are to have any hope of evolving policies that will achieve the maximum value in environmental protection for each dollar the United States can afford to invest, we have to get all the cards on the table. Environmental quality is an issue that transcends elections. Survey after survey shows that the American people want it and are willing to meet a high price tag for it. These public goals are not subject to any substantial revision—at least not for long. What is at issue is not environmental values, but the fact that to date the public has not been getting enough value for the costs being paid.

The first step that must be taken is to re-think the 1983-85 water quality goals, and to re-think them without animus toward industry or any other sector. These goals are not going to be met, and no amount of rhetoric by the environmental lobbies is going to change that.

This presents an important opportunity. And that is, instead of the usual round of vilification of industry foot-dragging or bureaucratic incompetence, to re-think and re-state our environmental protection goals in toto. During the past decade, these environmental protection goals have gradually been subordinated to the interests of the regulatory process and its perquisites. Most regulatory dollars are not spent meeting goals, but satisfying constituencies.

Only realistic goals can be met, and only against the measure of realistic goals can the effectiveness of regulatory programs be charted. Moreover, since there is now a broad national consensus that we cannot afford everything right away, realistic goals become the basis for program priorities—priorities that must be evaluated not only against the single criterion of environmental quality, but against other societal needs.

Let us consider the problems from what might be called an "engineering" point of view. Today, if you imagine a water treatment map of the United States, you can see four types of situations:

First, in a large number of cases, the public water treatment system mandated for local governments is not in place yet.

Second, there are the municipal water treatment systems in operation, which may or may not be meeting performance standards and which may or may not be adequately treating upstream industrial discharges.

Third, waste water treatment systems for direct industrial discharges are in place, and will—unless the law is changed—have to be expanded by 1984 to remove toxic wastes to EPA standards.

Fourth, industrial plants now discharging toxic pollutants into public treatment systems are now going to have to pre-treat wastes to the same standards as those pertaining to direct discharge, and they are going to have to remove toxics to the extent that the public treatment system is not equipped to do so.

Into this neat little planning world, let me introduce a few questions. How much duplication and redundancy of effort has gone on and will go on, where industrial plants are pre-treating wastes for delivery to public water treatment systems?

If the biosystems in properly engineered and operated public treatment systems are adequate to remove most organic toxic substances, is it wise to require industry to pre-treat to remove these same substances?

If industry has treatment systems in place—and these systems not only tend to have cost less than comparable public systems but to function more reliably—might it not make sense to allocate some federal funds to get industry more involved in the waste water treatment picture?

If we look at waste water as a flow grid—with low volumes and high concentrations generally being discharged by industry and high volume, low concentration discharges from commercial and residential users—the question becomes not "who should be mandated to do what" so much as "where on that grid can waste be treated most efficiently and cost-effectively?"

There may be a number of alternatives depending on each specific situation.

The best solution in one case may be a public treatment facility that is sufficient to handle all industrial discharges without any required pretreatment.

In others, the most efficient path might be for industry to pre-treat its discharges and part or all of the local community waste to a level where an existing public treatment facility will not have to be rebuilt or a new public facility brought on stream.

Getting the Most for the Money

We should not continue to assume that public treatment facilities are the only way to handle wastewater, or that federal water treatment funding should go only to local governments.

In some cases, industry might be able to use some of these dollars to greater effect. With appropriate tax incentives, it might even be possible to induce industries to go into the waste water treatment business.

I think that one of the fundamentals of a market economy is that it is cheaper to let essential services be provided by the most efficient performers of the economy. And I think that lesson may well apply in some stances to water quality control, garbage collection and postal service, to name a few.

Our own experience at Union Carbide is telling. In West Virginia, we operate a model wastewater treatment system which handles the wastes from the local community and from our facilities there. In fact it is capable of handling the wastes equal to that of a city of 600,000 people. And I am quite willing to bet we do so at a cost and with a degree of reliability that few municipalities could equal.

You have to question whether it makes the best sense for the United States economy to fund water treatment solely through the public sector. Tax dollars are real dollars, so industry will pay one way or the other. I'm willing to wager that when effluent producers treat their own waste, a lot less of it is discharged.

If the goal is to get rid of water pollution, then why not reconsider the whole philosophy implicit in our approach to the problems so far—with a view toward determining the most effective, fair and unencumbered path to that goal?

Why not consider cooperative efforts among industrial plants located in any given watershed to treat effluent as cheaply and efficiently as possible?

Why not use the lever of federal funding participation to draw together just such collective undertakings?

Consider the possible consequences of such an approach to water pollution control:

First, so long as federal funds were relatively abundant in specific circumstances, the all but irresistible financial incentive to over-design, over-administer and over-spend on treatment facilities would be curbed by the financial exposure of the business participants.

Second, prioritization of goals would tend to occur naturally. The industrial participants can be counted upon to adhere to cost-benefit principles.

Third, the tendency of the EPA to base water treatment requirements on theoretical models should be countered by industry's and local government insistence that a specific treatment system be built to handle the pollution problems of an actual river in an actual place.

Fourth, industry is not likely to participate in such efforts voluntarily and financially unless satisfied that the problems to be confronted have been identified on the basis of sound scientific data, and not on the basis of EPA internal memoranda promulgated without peer scrutiny. Acquiescence in the face of demands unsupported by sound scientific data and opinion is bought with political handouts.

Fifth, approaching the problem from the point of view of the water that needs to be protected rather than the need to bring each industrial and municipal effluent producer to heel could pay a major dividend. It should quite naturally increase attention to cost-effectiveness by defining the problem as a matrix instead of a series of individual situations. Once we begin to think like this, we might have every hope of resolving the continuous conflicts between varying requirements for air, water and land ecologies and treat them as a whole fabric.

To no small degree, the clean water effort is falling short because its stated goals were utopian. But it is also failing because neither the problems nor the avenues of solution were ever defined carefully and programmed on a step-by-step basis nor could they have been: The goal of water quality got lost in a maze of federal construction programs and money transfers, and in a regulatory process that sometimes gave the actual tasks of pollution control second priority to the exercise of the power to regulate in the search for political support.

As Congress reconsiders the issues of water pollution it can now do so with a perspective that was lacking in its deliberations in 1972: implicit lessons contained in a decade of experience in attempting to find workable solutions to the nation's water quality programs. On the basis of this experience, I think it is clear to critic and advocate alike that, while some EPA thrusts have proven highly effective, others are bankrupt of merit. Now is the time to examine with an open mind all of our alternatives: to keep indeed to reinforce, the programs that have proven effective, and to weed out those that have clearly failed. It is essential that we bring to this the imagination, candor, and ingenuity of all those concerned with these public policy issues. If we fail to do so, we shall bear the price for years to come.

A Balanced Approach to Clean Air

Du Pont offers a detailed evaluation of some of the problems it believes the Clean Air Act has caused for industry.

A Balanced Approach to National Priorities

The Clean Air Act, enacted in 1967 and revised in 1970 and 1977, is riding on a stopgap Congressional resolution. The resolution was passed as an emergency measure when Congress failed to reach agreement on reauthorization last fall. Du Pont believes that it is of critical importance that the Act be reauthorized. The nation's drive to clean up the air must be continued. But reauthorization will not be enough.

What is needed are constructive changes in the Act which will enhance our nation's environment and economy . . . changes that will not weaken the law, but that will streamline and simplify it, thereby speeding progress towards attainment of national air quality goals.

Common sense must be applied. Clean air efforts must be balanced with other important societal needs—the need to provide jobs, the need to achieve greater energy self-sufficiency, and the need to increase industrial productivity. Du Pont believes that clean air need not be sacrificed for economic growth and energy development. Taxpayer and consumer dollars need not be wasted. All that is needed is a balanced approach to clean air.

A Balanced Approach to Industrial Development

During the past decade, the Clean Air Act has had a profound impact on jobs. Seventy million people live in areas where, because of the Act, plant construction may be restricted or banned. Such bans reduce job opportunities. The Act's complex and prolonged permitting process has discouraged industrial growth.

Before a new project can be started, the government has 37 opportunities to approve or disapprove a plan, 24 opportunities to stop a proposal, and 11 chances to cause delays through hearings, studies or reviews. Some construction approval requirements of the Clean Air Act can delay a project from several months to several years . . . or can kill it altogether.

Du Pont believes that reform of the Clean Air Act can be an important and integral part of the nation's program of economic recovery. By eliminating some of the Act's cumbersome restrictions, industrial development can be expanded and expedited. More jobs can be created at a faster rate. A balanced approach for improving air quality, but not at the expense of jobs, is needed.

A Balanced Approach to Industrial Modernization

By impeding the building of clean new plants which benefit from the latest pollution control technology, some provisions of the Clean Air Act have actually perpetuated an industrial base that is older, less efficient, and more pollution prone.

For example, the Clean Air Act contains special rigid emission requirements for the building of new plants in areas where quality does not meet national standards. Due to these requirements, many companies cannot afford to build new facilities or modernize existing ones. They have no choice but to maintain older, more polluting plants. The Act, therefore, is inhibiting industrial development and modernization in the very regions which could profit the most from air quality gains.

Du Pont and industry generally do not support Clean Air Act revisions which will allow plants to be built with no air pollution controls. Rather, we are seeking revisions which will encourage the building of plants with better controls. A balanced approach for creating a regulatory environment which supports the building of new, clean plants and the modernization of existing ones is needed.

A Balanced Approach to Energy Self-Sufficiency

Various provisions of the Clean Air Act have slowed the nation's progress towards energy self-sufficiency. They have restricted America's ability to develop domestic energy resources. The U.S. has sufficient coal resources to supply the nation's total energy needs well into the next century. Yet, it now takes up to 10 years to bring a new mine into production or to build a million kw coal-fired power station. This is because the required studies, permits, and paperwork can take five to seven years to complete.

Moreover, provisions of the Act's Prevention of Significant Deterioration (PSD) program are delaying industry's efforts to convert to less expensive and more stable energy sources. Such conversions free up valuable energy sources which can be used for more important national purposes. The PSD program is not only working against the development of domestic energy resources, but it is also creating needless costs which inevitably get passed on to consumers.

In 1979, Du Pont decided to seek permits for a new boiler at one of our plants. We wanted to switch the operation from natural gas to coal, thereby cutting future energy costs and assuring a fuel supply less subject to interruptions that could cause shutdowns and worker layoffs. Extensive pollution controls that exceeded state requirements were planned for the new boiler. Nonetheless, the Environmental Protection Agency (EPA) decided a full-blown PSD review was required. After six months of preparation, we submitted a 213-page application to EPA, supplemented later by another 236 pages.

The state issued its construction permit in two months; it took EPA a year to approve our permit application. When EPA had taken no official action six months after our application was filed, we decided that further expenditures on the boiler were a poor risk. The project was abandoned; permit uncertainty was a factor.

In this case, the PSD process clearly did not benefit the environment. All important pollution controls would have been included in the project anyway. Moreover, the process worked against energy development.

Cases such as this demonstrate why Du Pont and other companies believe revisions in the Clean Air Act must be made which will simplify the PSD process so that efficient use of energy is encouraged, yet air quality is not sacrificed. In short, a balanced approached for balancing America's clean air goals with its drive for energy self-sufficiency is needed.

A Balanced Approach to a Cost-Effective
Air Pollution Program

No environmental law costs more than the Clean Air Act and no environmental law has had a greater economic impact on the U.S. Its requirements have resulted in costs which equal two-thirds of the total bill for all environmental statutes.

The Council on Environmental Quality estimates that the total cost of complying with the Clean Air Act is $22 billion a year. It is also estimated that costs imposed by the Act over the last decade have been at least $2,100 for every four-person household.

At a time of high inflation, high unemployment, and high interest rates, we must ask ourselves "Can America afford to extend the Clean Air Act without revising it so that it is more cost-effective?" Du Pont thinks not . . . and most Americans agree. A recent poll conducted by the Opinion Research Corporation found that 81 percent of the public (and 78 percent of environmental activists) believe that changes in the Act can be made so that air quality is protected and improved at a lower cost.

Du Pont and other companies recommend that Congress place a higher priority on cost-effectiveness when establishing emission control requirements and the strategies to attain them. We do not believe that control costs should be considered in setting the health-based standards, but we do believe that Congress should insist that government, industry, and the American people get the greatest benefit possible out of every environmental dollar spent.

To accomplish this, changes are needed in the Clean Air Act which promote the use of the effective "best controls," not only in clean air areas, but also in areas where air pollution poses more of a problem. In addition, the EPA should be given some flexibility so that it will not be forced to impose severe economic sanctions on states that have made good faith efforts, but cannot meet the deadlines for national air quality standards.

The price tag of clean air is one that Du Pont is more than willing to pay as long as our efforts are cost-effective and result in better air quality. A balanced approach to improving the cost-effectiveness of the Clean Air Act is needed.

A Balanced Approach to Federal/State Authority Over Air Pollution Programs

In 1967, Congress passed the first major clean air legislation which assigned primary control over air quality to state and local governments. The Clean Air Act and its amendments have shifted responsibility for regulating clean air to the national government where it is centered in the EPA.

A federal presence is essential to coordinate efforts to achieve clean air throughout the nation. But increased federal intervention in state clean air efforts has created red tape and confusion, caused needless delays in enacting air pollution programs, and stifled state economic growth.

The Act requires each state to devise a plan to improve air quality. State plans, however, are based on federal requirements and must be approved by the EPA, which often only has limited knowledge of local situations. All revisions of state plans must be approved by the EPA. This bureaucratic system has caused prolonged and unnecessary delays in implementing state air quality programs. While states were required to file plans by July 1, 1979, [by 1982] only 20 plans have been fully approved.

This two-tiered federal/state review system not only places needless burdens on the regulatory agencies, but it also imposes unnecessary costs and delays on industry. Because of overlaps in federal/state authority created by the Clean Air Act, opportunity to apply EPA's "bubble" policy to control air emissions at one of Du Pont's plants was nearly lost.

Faced with stack-specific limitations on some 100 emission points at one of our plants, we proposed to use incineration for full abatement of several major hydrocarbon emission sources to balance the smaller ones. (In effect a pollution bubble would be created whereby the plant's emissions would be controlled as a whole, rather than on a stack-by-stack basis.) Such a bubble would not only provide better pollution control at a lower cost, but it would also result in far fewer abatement devices that the state would have to monitor.

Although the bubble was provided for in the state's implementation plan, EPA insisted on a separate review. It took 15 months to get the bubble approved. This delay would not have occurred had there not been a two-tiered federal/state permit approval process. Now that the bubble is in place at our plant, we estimate that our capital investment costs will drop from $15 million to $5 million or less.

Du Pont believes that once a state implementation plan has been approved by the EPA, the state should be given more flexibility to manage its own pollution program, without undue interference from the EPA. Revisions in the Clean Air Act should be made so that states can grant variances, exemptions, time extensions, and waivers for such reasons as technological feasibility, economic hardship, and energy considerations as long as progress towards attainment is continuing. A balanced approach to federal/state authority over air pollution programs is needed.

War over the Wilderness

By Niles Howard with Marjorie Siegel

This article presents a well-balanced look at the debate over expanding the National Wilderness System.

The Willard Overthrust Belt, an 8 million-acre tract of rugged terrain where the borders of Idaho, Utah and Wyoming meet, has long been regarded by outdoor enthusiasts as one of this country's most spectacular regions. Millions of years ago, violent earthquakes buckled the earth's crust there, creating mountains so jagged and rivers so swift that even today some of the territory can be reached only by foot.

But in the early 1970s, geologists exploring the area came to an extremely promising conclusion: The same upheavals that created the mountains also formed vast underground deposits of porous sandstone and limestone in which immense quantities of natural gas and crude oil have accumulated. So great is the amount of this fuel, some believe, it could go a long way toward helping the country overcome its dependence on foreign natural resources.

Yet many oil, gas and mining officials are increasingly fearful that a good portion of those possible reserves will never be gotten out. At the urging of several conservation groups, Congress was asked to designate 300,000 acres the government owns in the area as permanent wilderness, thus placing it off limits to all commercial development. Another 300,000 will be set aside for further study. And industry officials consider that these 600,000 acres are among the most promising in the entire area in terms of oil-and-gas potential.

Looming Battle

Many energy executives are furious at the prospect of losing those potential reserves—so much so that they have vowed to defeat the

Reprinted with special permission of *Dun's Business Month* (formerly *Dun's Review*), August 1979. Copyright 1979, Dun & Bradstreet Publications Corporation. Niles Howard was a senior editor and Marjorie Siegel was an assistant editor with *Dun's Review* when this article was written.

measure no matter how long it takes. Similarly, conservation groups make no secret of their intention to insure at all cost that development is banned. The coming conflict will surely be intense.

Yet for all its fury, the battle of the Willard Belt is actually only a microcosm of a much larger struggle that is going on between conservationists and industry over the disposition of the federal government's vast land holding. Over the past fifteen years, oil, gas, mining and timber executives have watched with desperation as the government has placed temporary bans on the development of millions of acres of these lands while it studies how much of it can—and should—be preserved.

Everyone involved agrees these issues are crucial. Conservationists contend that even the most careful development will destroy the delicate ecological balance of these areas, thus depriving future generations of the pleasures and benefits they offer. Energy industry officials, on the other hand, insist that the country has already preserved enough wilderness land and that to set aside more will have disastrous results, virtually destroying any chance this country has of ever reducing its dependence on foreign resources. Federal lands contain an estimated 85 percent of all this country's oil reserves, they say, not to mention a significant share of gas, timber and scarce minerals. And although no one knows for certain how much of these resources are contained on the lands being considered for designation as wilderness, opponents of these measures are clearly worried.

"A price must be paid for wilderness, often in terms of severe impacts on local communities; effects on the price and availability of energy fuels, hardrock minerals, lumber and paper products; and lost opportunities for developed recreation," observes George S. Dibble, a vice president of Husky Oil Co. and president of the Rocky Mountain Oil & Gas Association. "Few Americans recognize the trade-offs—economic and social—involved in wilderness set-asides."

Although the philosophical issues in the debate may seem reasonably clear-cut, the specifics of the controversy are highly complex, and to understand them requires an appreciation of the importance to industry of the federal government's land holdings. Altogether, Washington owns more than 760 million acres in fifty states, fully a third of the country's total land area. Some of this land, to be sure, is intensively and productively used, for military bases, Indian reservations and public works projects. But much of it still exists as vast forests and rangeland.

Over the years, the government's policy has been to lease as much of this land as possible to corporations for mining, oil and gas drilling and timber cutting, and these areas have long been a major source of domestic energy. Last year, for example, more than 50 percent of the country's oil came from land leased from the federal government. Nevertheless, a good deal of these vast government lands remained unaffected by mankind. Too rugged for farming, too inaccessible for mining or energy exploration, for years they lay largely ignored. But about twenty years ago, new geological theories and surveying techniques coupled with rising prices of most resources caused developers to take a closer look, and it began to appear that the very geological forces that made some of the lands inaccessible and spectacular caused them to be mineral-rich—particularly in Alaska and the Rocky Mountain states. Consequently, the government found itself under great pressure to make some kind of decision about the future of these lands.

Creating Wilderness

Responding to the pressure, Congress in 1964 passed the National Wilderness Systems Act, which set aside a relatively small portion of this land—58 tracts totaling 9.3 million acres—as wilderness, decreeing not only that it should remain off-limits to developers, but that it should be entered only by foot or on horseback. Industry was not happy to have any land ruled out of bounds, but most businessmen had feared much worse and were thus reasonably satisfied. What bothered some, though, was a little discussed provision of the bill instructing various government agencies to study the roadless land they managed to determine whether any of it might also qualify as wilderness.

There was pretty general agreement among conservationists that they would be satisfied if the National Wilderness System grew to about 20 million acres by the turn of the century, and over the next few years the Forest Service and the Bureau of Land Management, which manage most of the roadless land, recommended that about 10 million more acres be included in the system, bringing the total to slightly over 19 million.

Then, in 1968, industry got an inkling of what these lands might be worth. Using some sophisticated new surveying techniques, oil company geologists discovered oil in Prudhoe Bay, an area in the uppermost part of Alaska that had been known mainly for its large herds of wild caribou. Quickly, other oil companies obtained exploration leases from the government and began their own drilling programs.

Conservationists, fearing that both the beauty of the area and the caribou would be hurt, mounted various legal challenges to these leases and to the pipeline that was planned to carry the oil out of the area. Their well-publicized fight delayed the pipeline for years, but they ultimately lost. Then they pressed the Forest Service and BLM to withdraw much of the Alaskan wilderness from oil and mineral exploration under the Wilderness Act, but before these agencies moved on the matter, Congress stepped in on its own.

Staking Out Alaska

In 1971, Congress passed the Native Claims Settlement Act, a long-delayed agreement with the descendants of Indians, Eskimos and Aleuts whose land was taken from them after the U.S. purchased Alaska from Russia in 1867. The major provision of the bill was an award of nearly $1 billion plus 44 million acres of Alaskan land. But little noticed by the energy and minerals industries, conservation-minded legislators managed to tack on an amendment, section 17 (d) (2)—d-2 for short—that allowed the Secretary of the Interior to temporarily withdraw 80 million Alaskan acres, pending Congressional action. Congress would then decide, by December 1978, how much of this land was to be designated national recreation areas, national parks, monuments or wildlife preserves.

Interior Secretary Rogers Morton thus withdrew 79 million acres. But Congress, which had to validate or reject this temporary set-aside, soon found the issue to be thornier than anyone had imagined. Conservation groups had their own ideas about which of these lands were to be open to recreation interests and which were to be left as wilderness, and many complained the 79 million acres was not enough, anyway, considering the enormous size of the state—some 375 million acres.

On the other side were businessmen and most Alaskan political leaders, who complained that the government had no right to remove such a big chunk of the state from development, particularly since the government had never given the state title to most of the 104 million acres it had been promised for joining the union in 1959. Repeatedly, bills that would settle the status of Morton's 79 million acres were brought up for a vote in Congress, but the Alaskans succeeded each time in blocking action.

Then, the Carter Administration—responding to conservationist pressure— raised the ante to 93 million acres. The White House was still unable to get a bill through, and it became apparent that the 1978 deadline would pass without action, thus automatically reopening the lands for development. To avoid that situation, the President stepped in personally. Under a 1906 Antiquities Act, he designated 56 million acres of Alaskan wilderness as a National Monument, at the same time instructing Interior Secretary Cecil Andrus to use his powers under the 1976 Bureau of Land Management Organic Act to freeze another 54 million acres for three years. With the stroke of a pen, one-third of Alaska was locked up.

Inspired by the move, House conservationist forces, led by Representative Morris Udall of Arizona, took the offensive and in May 1979 pushed through the House the biggest Alaskan withdrawal yet—125 million acres, an area larger than California. Of this, 67 million acres would be designated part of the National Wilderness System, thus increasing its size fivefold. The remaining 58 acres would be designated for other purposes, mainly recreational, although some mining would be permitted under limited circumstances. Included in the area that would be locked up permanently is the 13.5 million-acre Arctic Wildlife Refuge. Says Jay Mitchell, public lands coordinator for Atlantic Richfield Co.: "If the oil companies had only one more well to drill, that is where it would be."

In the meantime, the same groups may come to battle over another proposal to withdraw from development much of the wilderness land in the lower 48 states controlled by the U.S. Forest Service. Although the Forest Service was instructed, under the 1964 wilderness act, to survey its roadless lands for potential inclusion in the National Wilderness System, the review was almost immediately beset by administrative delays—most notably failure of the agency to agree on the criteria for qualifying land as wilderness.

Then in 1971, the Forest Service announced a sweeping project, the Roadless Area Review and Evaluation, to be completed by 1980, but after six years it became apparent that the program was hopelessly bogged down. Conservationists complained loudly that the review was eliminating from consideration virtually all wilderness lands east of the Rocky Mountains, while business protested that since land under consideration was withdrawn for the duration of the review, it was locking up for years areas that were clearly not wilderness.

Thus, in the spring of 1977, the Forest Service instituted a new program, RARE II, rewriting the wilderness criteria and adopting a system whereby its field supervisors would immediately report on land under their supervision that met those criteria. Soliciting public opinion on these proposals, the Forest Service. . . released. . . a list of 1,921 tracts of roadless land, totaling 62 million acres. Then, in April, 1979, the Carter Administration recommended to Congress that 36 million acres be opened up for timber and mining, and that 15 million acres be included in the Wilderness System. The rest was set aside for further study.

Known Deposits

Criticism of the proposal became intense. Industry was particularly infuriated about what it saw as a failure of the Forest Service to consider the mineral potential of the lands it had recommended for inclusion in the wilderness system. "There are known mineral deposits within RARE II," says Keith Nobloch, a vice president of the American Mining Congress.

Although the Forest Service says it followed the law in obtaining U.S. Geological Survey assessments of all of its land before recommending disposition, mining and energy executives maintain that those reports are invariably superficial and that they routinely fail to turn up big mineral deposits. Industry would like to conduct exploratory drilling operations on potential wilderness lands— "You've got to have drilling if you want some details," says Nobloch—but both conservationists and the Forest Service say such activity would severely disrupt these lands.

Already, though, business is looking beyond both RARE II and Alaska to a third block of government lands controlled by the Interior Department's Bureau of Land Management. With 400 million acres, the BLM controls the biggest share of the government's holdings, and there are growing fears among businessmen that a significant portion of this land could also be declared part of the Wilderness System.

The BLM has embarked on an inventory of these lands with the idea of finding areas that might qualify as wilderness. Given until 1991 to complete the study, it has already narrowed the list of lands with strong wilderness potential to 62 million acres.

It is, of course, too early to tell what will become of any of these proposals, but it appears that the conservationists now have the upper hand in spite of the growing shortage of energy, "Conservationists have a very persuasive argument," says Les Mack, a vice president of the American Petroleum Institute. "They argue that it's better to declare something wilderness now because once it is opened it can never be closed. When we really need it, they say, then we can go in and take this energy out. What they don't realize is the long lag-time involved. It can very easily take ten years or longer before production can begin—after your original discovery."

Needless to say, industry is lobbying heavily against additions to the wilderness system. Businessmen agree that the original act was well-intentioned when it was passed fifteen years ago, but now, they say, it has become a runaway force, gobbling up just about all land on which development has not yet occurred.

They contend that the country already has much more wilderness than it can make good use of, and if the pending restrictions are passed, much of the most promising lands—in terms of natural resources—will be off-limits. As William Dresher, dean of the University of Arizona's College of Mines, puts it, "We're trading away our future, and we're really going to feel the pinch in another ten or fifteen years."

Access to Land: The Gateway to Energy Security

The greatest potential source for future mineral development, according to this article, lies in land controlled by the federal government, and industry should have access to those resources in light of its recent environmental protection record.

A recent story in *The Wall Street Journal* reported a humorous remark made by Les Line, Editor of *Audubon* magazine and vice president of the National Audubon Society. Mr. Line was a passenger on a commercial airline flight which was damaged when it collided with a flight of birds.

"The pilot was very apologetic to me for killing the birds," Line said afterward. "I told him, 'better the birds than me.'"

Few of us—environmental defenders, champions of economic development, or middle-of-the-roaders—would disagree with Mr. Line's sense of priorities.

The question is: can we also agree when the choices—and the issues involved—are less clearly cut? For example, is it possible to develop some sort of national consensus on the controversial question of allowing energy companies access to public lands?

In 1981, the U.S. Department of the Interior announced an accelerated schedule for leasing offshore areas for oil and natural gas exploration and development. As might be expected, there was opposition. However, the energy industry believes that there is a great national need for the U.S. to assess the resource potential of its offshore areas and to increase energy production if possible, thereby reducing our dependence on insecure supplies of foreign oil.

Energy Requires Finding First

The United States has a special responsibility in the area of energy production. Currently, our country consumes about 30 percent of the energy used in the non-Communist world, and if we continue our over-reliance on other countries to meet our petroleum needs, we will tend to keep world oil prices high. That would be extremely unfortunate, especially given the fact that our nation's energy potential—including conventional petroleum, coal, uranium, and oil shale, not to mention synthetic fuels and renewable sources—is far and away the greatest in the Western world.

However, the awesome energy potential of the U.S. will not be realized unless energy companies have promising areas to explore for—and then from which to produce—energy. In short, we can't produce it unless we first find it.

The fact that the Adminstration plan for accelerated leasing has produced a great deal of discussion should come as no surprise. For years, there has been a movement to place vast areas of the country off-limits to energy exploration and production, claiming development would endanger water, air, and wildlife.

Conversely, industry has tried to focus public attention on U.S. energy needs and the potential of public lands for helping increase domestic energy production. Gulf strongly believes that energy production and environmental considerations are compatible. The Reagan Adminstration shares this belief.

In past Administrations, the government's attitude toward land access vacillated wildly from pro- to anti-exploration. At times, the oil industry sometimes felt it was engaged in a bizarre version of the children's game, "May I?" where commands are given to go forward or backward. The contradictory orders—first to advance, then to retreat—frustrated the oil industry's efforts to explore some of America's most promising offshore energy prospects.

For our industry, "stop" is now turning to "go." Whether the green light changes back to a red one later in the 1980s could rest, in large measure, with how the oil industry exercises environmental stewardship in the course of its activities, as well as with the efforts our industry makes over the next several years to reach some sort of understanding with environmental groups.

The opportunity for reaching such an understanding is probably greater now than in years past. The scarred landscapes, smog-laden areas, and salt-choked streams, characteristic of certain sections of the country, give a melancholy testimony to the fact that in the past industry did not always live up to its environmental responsibilities.

A Question of Balance

However, for industry, the errors of the past have been replaced by a heightened awareness of our environmental responsibilities in the present. Clearly, all future development in the U.S., including energy exploration and production, will have to take into account the American people's strong commitment to environmental goals. Opinion polls indicate that a broad consensus exists for sustaining, and improving where possible, our wildlife areas and the quality of our land, water, and air. Gulf strongly supports the protection of those lands already set aside by Congress.

As with most controversial issues, the matter of environmental quality comes down to a question of balance. Specifically, how can we balance the protection of our natural heritage for future generations with the need to make progress in meeting other pressing national needs: to maintain our national security, to reduce unemployment and dampen inflation, as well as to encourage economic growth?

Such questions confront us with a special urgency in the case of energy. Clearly, the nation is still too dependent on foreign oil, even with recent gains in the production and efficient use of energy. Moreover, as the experience of the 1970s shows—with recurrent energy shortages, recession, and inflation—our economic progress as a nation is tied closely to energy.

In the simplest terms, America's energy explorationists cannot find energy unless they have access to lands that hold energy promise.

In the case of land access, the energy potential of enormous sections of the country is at stake. Onshore, the federal government owns 738 million acres in the 50 states—one third of the nation's total land area. Most of these lands are located in the western states and Alaska. In addition, the federal government controls the mineral rights on some 64 million acres of onshore lands.

At the beginning of 1981, only about 15 percent of federally controlled onshore lands had been leased for oil and gas operations.

Offshore, the lease situation is even more depressing. The U.S. controls nearly a billion acres of offshore land. From the start of the federal offshore leasing program in the 1950s, only 19 million acres—about 4 percent of the total—has been leased.

Substantial Reserves Undiscovered

Despite the fact that the U.S. is by far the most extensively explored area of the world, experts believe it still has great energy potential. The U.S. Geological Survey estimates the amount of undiscovered recoverable crude oil ranges from 64 billion to 105 billion barrels. For natural gas, the range is 475 trillion to 739 trillion cubic feet. These estimates do not include oil and gas that might be recovered under more favorable economic and technological circumstances.

By comparison, the average of crude oil estimates provided by the U.S.G.S. represents more than half the oil produced in the U.S. since 1859, when the petroleum industry was born. In the case of natural gas, the average of the estimates is approximately the same as the volume of natural gas produced so far.

In 1981, the American Petroleum Institute unveiled a study indicating that U.S. dependency on imported oil could be reduced by some 50 percent during the 1980s—from 8 million barrels per day of imports in 1979 to about 4 million barrels per day by 1990. Future security of supplies, greater stability of energy prices, a favorable impact on inflation, and higher U.S. productivity are among the many national benefits anticipated if we reach the goal of cutting oil imports in half.

A key element of the goal is multiple use of public lands. This means pursuing a policy that provides for responsible protection of these lands, while allowing natural resource development, recreation and other worthwhile and compatible uses. Congress actually intended that a multiple use policy be pursued, but administrative withdrawals have sharply curtailed resource development.

The vast majority of the untested areas believed to have oil and gas potential are those same areas controlled by the federal government. The U.S. could very well remain a hostage to foreign oil if federal lands continue to be padlocked against resource development. Estimates are that approximately 40 percent of the nation's undiscovered oil and natural gas lies beneath federal lands on and offshore. In addition, recent studies indicate that some 40 percent of the nation's remaining coal and uranium reserves are located on federally controlled properties. In addition, 50 percent of our geothermal resources, 80 percent of our oil shale, and 85 percent of our tar sands are on public lands.

Ecology and Technology Not Exclusive

Clearly, much is at stake, not the least of which is future U.S. security and economic vitality. Ecology and technology are not mutually exclusive. We are not really faced with a choice between birds and airplanes. The choice is not energy production versus protecting and enjoying the great outdoors. Americans can have both.

The genius of America lies precisely in our national disposition not to take "no" for an answer, to achieve the seemingly impossible with striking regularity. In recent memory, we have seen this happen in the energy business. Massive energy exploration, production, and transmission—in Alaska and other ecologically sensitive areas—have taken place in harmony with nature.

If the Reagan Administration is successful in its efforts to increase resource development opportunities on public lands, the petroleum industry will have the opportunity once again to prove that technology and environmental protection are compatible.

Then, perhaps, the environmentalists and the energy developers could reach that long hoped for rapprochement, which would end "stop and go" national land use policies without damage to the environment.

Endangered Species: Should Man Try to Play God?

By Jay D. Hair, Robert O. Anderson,
Christine Stevens, Jerry L. Haggard,
William D. Blair, Jr., and J. Peter Grace

What steps should be taken to prevent the extinction of endangered plants and animals? This article shows constrasting views of business and environmental leaders.

Each day, one of the world's approximately 10 million species becomes extinct. The rate of extinction is increasing so rapidly that by the end of this century an additional one million species will have vanished from the face of the earth. While a vast majority of the public would support any effort to save the bald eagle, whale, or panda, many officials in government and business question whether the barricades to progress and the costs of compliance justify government programs to protect every endangered plant or animal species. The most well-known debate on this issue erupted in 1978 when an endangered three-inch-long fish, the snail darter, was blocking the completion of the Tellico Dam project in Tennessee.

Jack D. Early, president of the National Agricultural Chemicals Association, was quoted recently in the *New York Times* as saying: "Any species is expendable somewhere along the line except man." Mr. Early accused the government of "playing God" and "ignoring Darwinian necessity" by constantly invoking the Endangered Species Act.

We have asked a group of concerned citizens to comment on this

Excerpted from article in Business and Society Review, Summer 1982, with permission from Warren, Gorham and Lamont, Inc., 210 South Street, Boston, Mass. All rights reserved. Jay D. Hair is executive vice president of the National Wildlife Federation; Robert O. Anderson is chairman of the board of Atlantic Richfield Company; Christine Stevens is with the Society for Animal Protection Legislation; Jerry L. Haggard is an attorney and member of the Public Lands Committee of the American Mining Congress; William D. Blair, Jr., is president of The Nature Conservancy; J. Peter Grace is chairman of W.R. Grace & Co.

issue. Specifically, we asked: Do you agree with Mr. Early's belief that some species are expendable? Is it necessary to protect the natural habitat of every living thing? Should the government halt seemingly beneficial commercial projects in order to prevent the extinction of a virtually unknown plant or animal? We received the following replies:

Cooperation Urged: Jay D. Hair

The health of our ecosystems is dependent on maintenance of the complex ecological relationships that exist among all species. Plants, animals, and microorganisms working together in complex interrelationships that are still very poorly understood make up the biosphere and worldwide web of life of which we human beings are a part. As we modify this biosphere to cultivate our crops, raise our animals, and produce products of direct economic interest to us, we simplify the relationships and increase the instability of the system as a whole. As our actions promote the extinction of organisms worldwide, we lose the elements that might have proved later to have been of the greatest interest and importance to our descendants. The extinction of plants and animals worldwide is probably the most significant event that is occurring in the world during our lifetime.

Suggestions have been advanced that only "higher" life forms, such as mammals and birds, should be listed as endangered and that the "lower" forms, such as plants and invertebrates, should not be listed. This type of listing priority is biologically indefensible. The term "lower life form" implies that nearly three-fourths of the world's species are unimportant, but species importance and high taxonomic status are not synonymous. To the contrary, plants and invertebrates often may be more important to ecosystem health than vertebrates. For example, the loss of the peregrine falcon in the eastern U.S. had comparatively little effect on other species, whereas the loss of the American chestnut tree over about the same area and time period adversely affected virtually all eastern forest wildlife.

Wild species are the source of many of the basic necessities of human life and have played major roles in the evolution of human culture. No one can predict which species are ultimately of critical importance to human existence or will provide valuable material benefits in years to come. In the diversity of species, humans have a varied, infinitely renewable supply of food, energy, industrial chemicals, and medicines.

Take just one example: medical chemistry. It has been estimated that fully 40 percent of all prescriptions written in the United States contain as their chief ingredients compounds derived from plants, including lower plants. The Incas discovered the antimalarial properties of the bark of the cinchona tree, from which quinine was later isolated, and the foxglove plant, the well-known source of the heart drug digitalis, was already in medical use in medieval times. But many of the most important plant drugs in current use were only recently discovered, including, for example, some of the anti-leukemic compounds and anticancer drugs such as vincristine, derived from the periwinkle plant and used in the treatment of Hodgkin's disease.

There is no end to the potential for discovery of this sort, because we have only begun the chemical exploration of nature. Two of the compounds mentioned, quinine and vincristine, belong to the major class of chemicals called alkaloids. Thousands of alkaloids are now known, including many that have practical uses. Yet only about 2 percent of the flowering plants—5,000 of some one-quarter million species—have been tested for presence of alkaloids. The majority of these compounds are still unknown, locked away in the unexplored world of plants.

Because few species of plants and animals have been subject to sufficient investigation to determine possible medical, agricultural, or industrial benefits, extinction of any species may deprive mankind of many valuable products. Clearly, we should do everything in our power to ensure that we take every feasible step to prevent the avoidable loss of species.

When I assumed the executive vice-presidency of the National Wildlife Federation over a year ago, I called for improved working relations between industry and environmental groups, a policy that I refer to as "corporate detente." There are two ways to solve problems—through confrontation or cooperation. I am convinced that if constructive dialogue between business and conservation organizations is initiated early on, many of the open conflicts involving natural resource management that result in costly legal battles can be avoided. With adequate safeguards to protect our fish and wildlife resources, development can proceed.

Mutual Prosperity: Robert O. Anderson

When Mr. Early suggests that "any species is expendable somewhere along the line except man" and that the Endangered Species Act ignores "Darwinian necessity," he grossly oversimplifies the relationship between *Homo sapiens* and the many other species that share this earth. We depend on plants and animals for food, materials and even the air we breathe. The world's ecosystems are highly complex and delicately balanced. Even the best biologists cannot predict with confidence the long-term effects of disruptions in these intricate webs of life. Also, we have no way of knowing the value of the world's genetic resources to future generations. Some marine animals, for example, produce substances used in medicine. Under these circumstances, it could be reckless indeed to deliberately eradicate another species, plant or animal.

Of course, it would be naive to think that species don't die. Obviously, they do—it is part of the evolutionary process. The crucial point is that we avoid needlessly causing such extinctions. In this regard, commercial development and the preservation of endangered species are not really in conflict. As a matter of fact, it is rarely (if ever) the case that industrial projects in the United States have been stopped simply because they endangered another species. Sometimes, to be sure, higher expenses have been incurred to protect wildlife, but at Atlantic Richfield, at least we view these as the costs of doing business in modern society.

Recently, for example, a team of our environmental specialists physically transferred young Golden Eagles (protected by federal law) to new nests, safely removed from our coal-mining activities in Wyoming's Power River Basin. Near Bakersfield, California we have established natural habitats on company-held acreage surrounding oil exploration and development activities. Trucks, tools and other equipment are kept off these areas. The blunt-nosed leopard lizard (currently on the endangered list) is one of many animals living on this land.

As a final example, consider oil development in the North Slope of Alaska. In 1969, we asked naturalist Angus Gavin to assess the impact of energy development on the wildlife in this rugged and beautiful part of the world. Despite the efficient development of the greatest oil strike in North America during this time, major changes in animal populations have not occurred.

On one point, Mr. Early is certainly right. Society needs to take advantage of its commercial opportunities. But with proper planning and respect for the environment, commercial development, and wildlife—even endangered species—can prosper together.

Louis XIV Mentality: Christine Stevens

As one who has been fighting to prevent commercial whalers from making the different species of whales extinct, I decidedly do not agree that any species but man is expendable. Dr. Roger Payne, that foremost whale scientist, recorder of the "Songs of the Humpback Whale," observer of the "sailing with trails" play behavior of the Southern Right Whale and other previously undocumented cetacean activities, accepted the Albert Schweitzer Medal of the Animal Welfare Institute with a quotation from Chief Seattle: "What happens to beasts will happen to man. All things are connected. If the great beasts are gone men would surely die of a great loneliness of spirit." He concluded: "If we can fire the imagination of the human world on behalf of non-human life we will be living in a more enlightened world and will not be facing the prospect of dying from a great loneliness of spirit."

The practical reasons are overwhelming for preserving all species, including those at the other end of the spectrum from whales—tiny creatures, with very small brains, ones with nervous systems so different from ours that it is hard to develop fellow feeling for them, plants, some of them recommended by their beauty or strangeness, others less prepossessing, easily overlooked, readily forgotten—all of these in their millions *must*, if we are sensible, frugal husbanders of our earthly paradise, be studied order by order, family by family, species by species. They must all be prevented from becoming prematurely extinct. The future ages of the earth are up to us and the next twenty years are crucial. As the master species capable of wiping out a million other species without even intending to do so, it is our duty to stop the avalanche of destruction being caused by overexploitation. Forests all over the world are being cut at a record rate—a major cause of species extinction, and of loss of unknown and totally unstudied species which may contain within their own particular germ plasm a vital component which, for completely selfish reasons, our species should preserve. Often noted is a member of the primrose family now being found effective against the dread leukemia that causes young children to waste away before the horrified eyes of their parents. Also cited with frequency is a wild species of corn, needed to rejuvenate the domestic species gene pool to help feed hungry people.

Anyone who is willing to "expend" other species is callous to the future of his own species. He suffers from the Louis XIV mentality, the "after me the deluge" point of view which led rather quickly to that ruler's own personal expendability.

The purveyors of agricultural chemicals focus on the destruction of insects of species which, so far from heading toward extinction, seem to thrive on poison—not individually, for they die in uncountable numbers, but their evolution is wonderfully advanced, as the survivors most fit to life in an atmosphere fraught with toxic chemicals, then multiply more rapidly than ever before.

Had agricultural chemical manufacturers not been fought, many vertebrate species would have been even more severely depleted than they are. Ospreys, eagles, pelicans, robins, orioles all suffered heavy losses, and whole species were wiped out in many locations as the result of application of DDT, endrin, dieldrin and other powerful toxicants.

Our country still exports these dangerous chemicals to nations with less restrictive laws than those developed here, after much sad experience. A different attitude on the part of manufacturers of agricultural chemicals is sorely needed.

Conflicting Goals: Jerry L. Haggard

As with much legislation of the 1970s dealing with wildlife, forests, and other environmental resources, the understandable desire to protect those values tends sometimes to produce legislation with inflexible requirements which disregard other important national needs. The American Mining Congress supports the efforts to protect those values by reasonable means which also allow the fulfillment of other national priorities and goals.

Unfortunately, proponents of retaining the Endangered Species Act as it is argue the necessity to prevent the *extinction* of species and suggest that those who propose even reasonable modifications to the Act favor, or are insensitive toward, the extinction of species. These arguments and suggestions are specious. The American Mining Congress does not oppose the use of the Act to prevent the extinction of species. We do oppose the misuse of the Act to prevent the development of needed resources.

An area to which consideration should be given is limiting the listing of species of lower forms or less significant forms of life. We realize that this concept is objectionable to some in the scientific community. And we realize also that ideally, and strictly from the scientific point of view, it may be desirable to protect every living organism including the lowest form of life. But we must begin to realize that our government cannot do everything everyone asks it to do even if it has merit. It must be recognized that financial and labor resources are limited. Once that is recognized, the conclusion must be that priorities must be established so those limited resources may be directed to the areas where they will do the most good.

We recognize that a rational system which can minimize harm to endangered or threatened species and their habitats is a desired national goal. However, this goal must be balanced with other equally important goals which the United States must carry out.

Utmost Social Issue: William D. Blair, Jr.

The preservation of the plant and animal species—through the protection of their habitats, of the ecological systems of which they are part—is a pressing social issue for *Homo sapiens*.

This year we will lose even more of the genetic resources that hold the promise of the future for our agriculture and medicine, for industries known and yet unknown. Science now can recombine genes, but only nature can create them.

And this year more than last, we will be asked to do even less about it: to allocate fewer funds to slowing that dangerous trend, so that more can be spent for other purposes. This is happening because the economy is down; because government budgets are being cut; because immediate humanitarian needs are great and growing too. It's a question of priorities—and the biospheric priority loses.

On a planetary balance sheet, the priorities might look different. Protecting, for ourselves and our descendants, our biological capital—which unlike financial capital cannot be replaced—would surely stand out as our imperative first task.

This is all the more true because we don't fully understand how the global ecosystem works, or what it can and cannot do without. Moreover, we don't know which of the components of natural diversity will prove of vital use to us directly—as new food sources, as new lifesaving drugs, as materials for new industries and for scientific research.

In this country today, our collective approach is highly unbalanced.

Government is drastically reducing its modest investment in habitat and species preservation, and in environmental protection generally (by a projected 69 percent over three years, at the federal level, compared with an average 21 percent reduction for other social programs). And private philanthropy, for which the environment is a relatively new concern, is assigning only about one percent of its annual giving to that cause.

While the older social needs—addressing poverty, hunger, disease—are equally valid, it is hard to conceive that any program of comparable scale will produce equally significant progress toward meeting them. Though preserving the diverse natural systems which sustain us is the basic requirement of human welfare, nearly all public and private funds today are being devoted to other ends. With less than a generation left to protect the most important remnants of our natural lands and waters, and the flora and fauna they support, we need urgently to reconsider our priorities. The species with most at stake is us.

Proper Balance: J. Peter Grace

You are right in identifying the need to balance the benefits of environmental preservation with attendant costs. Certainly we have all seen examples of ignoring this cost-benefit relationship in the past: to wit, the snail darter episode. Of course, there are species readily identifiable whose preservation obviates the need to maintain a vigorous environmental vigilance. Among these I would include the bald eagle, the golden eagle, and the whooping crane.

In conclusion, I would emphasize that what you are asking is a most difficult question to answer categorically, since such investments must include esthetic considerations as well as attention to the food chain. Weighing these factors carefully and thoughtfully would seem to preclude across-the-board judgments.

They Are the First

By Jim Jubak

Many environmental hazards are not immediately apparent to workers and businesses. The health problems posed by asbestos present one of the most dramatic cases of such a situation and illustrate the costly economic consequences, legal complexity, and human suffering that can result.

Ted Kowalski, thin and dapper, stands on his sidewalk, leaning on a polished wood cane, feeding the squirrels as he does every morning.

Each day Kowalski walks his Manville, N.J. neighborhood, talking to the people who are afraid, keeping up the spirits of the people who don't know where to turn. But Kowalski only gets as far as the front door of a few of these neatly painted houses. Some of his friends, ashamed to be seen, have withdrawn, waiting only to die.

Kowalski has asbestosis—a crippling disease that results in a chronic cough, shortness of breath and a high susceptibility to pneumonia and flu. So do his wife and his son. His daughters have refused to have physicals; they don't want to know.

From his front lawn he can call the roll of the victims. "There's Ronnie, her husband died of mesothelioma; she never worked there, she has it. There's Sue, her husband died from mesothelioma. She has it. Carol has it; her husband Steve is very sick. She's been diagnosed as having asbestosis. A lot of people that I personally know. I can go on and on." The "it" he speaks of is asbestosis. Mesothelioma is an almost inevitably fatal cancer caused only by asbestos. An estimated 250,000 people will die of asbestos-related diseases in the United States by the turn of the century.

But these people—and the more than 27 million other Americans who have been exposed to asbestos—aren't just victims of an occupational disease. They're victims of an industry that did almost

---

From *Environmental Action*, February 1983. Reprinted by permission of Environmental Action, Inc., 1346 Connecticut Avenue, N.W., Washington, D.C., a political lobby group. Jim Jubak was an editor of *Environmental Action* when he wrote this article.

nothing to protect its workers from exposure to asbestos, even though evidence suggests industry officials knew about its dangers as far back as the 1930s. They're victims of a workers' compensation system that serves mostly to hold down the expenses of big corporations. They're victims of unions that weren't aggressive enough about protecting their members' health, of doctors who looked the other way and of government officials who administered systems that deprived workers of compensation.

The workers at this Manville Corporation plant are no different from millions of Americans who worked with asbestos or other dangerous materials. They are just first. The catastrophic health problems now associated with asbestos will be repeated in other industries, as the millions of workers who were exposed to the new, highly carcinogenic chemicals developed in the years surrounding World War II start to get sick.

But the steps that are now being taken—the legal precedents and the laws passed by Congress—won't just affect asbestos victims. They'll set the framework for other workers and for deciding who will pay the billions of dollars that this epidemic of occupational disease will cost in coming decades.

Ted Kowalski worked for the Manville Corporation, the largest corporate producer of asbestos in the world, from 1947 until he took a disability retirement in 1967. From 1959 through 1962 he was president of the union, Local 800 of the International Paperworkers.

"I started off working in the shipping department loading box cars," he says. "I was a carton maker in the finishing department. And I was a bandsaw operator. I worked as take-off man on a gang saw. I worked on a crusher. Every job you worked on was dusty."

Asbestos fibers or fragments of them constantly break off as the material is being cut or ground. "The sun would shine in through the skylight. It was like millions of tiny crystals that would float around," Kowalski remembers. "They'd fall in your coffee. The wagon came in with the coffee and you'd drink the stuff. You never knew how much had fallen in. The big pieces that fell in your cup you'd take out. We sat down, a bunch of us to eat our lunch, and the stuff was there falling."

Asbestos is a general term for a group of non-combustible minerals made up of tiny, hair-like fibers. A hundred could fit into an inch. Stronger than steel wire, these fibers are flexible enough to be woven into a fireproof cloth. Asbestos is found in insulation, roofing and flooring, brake pads, clutch plates, fireproof plastics, cement pipe and block and thousands of other products.

The tiny asbestos fibers are easily inhaled, passing deeply into the lungs. Although most are quickly exhaled, a small number imbed themselves in the lungs. Scar tissue builds up, a condition called asbestosis, which can lead to death as the victim literally suffocates.

It takes a long time—anywhere from about 10 to 40 years—before enough scar tissue builds up so that someone notices a shortness of breath. The cancers caused by asbestos have a latency period just as long—usually 15 to 30 years. Lung cancer has been connected to asbestos since 1935; cancers of the digestive system, the larynx and the kidneys have also been linked to the mineral. Mesothelioma, a rare cancer of the lining of the lung or abdomen, is almost always associated with asbestos exposure; there is no known treatment, and the survival rate is less than 10 percent over three years.

Driving through Manville today, the problems that have made workers and their families sick have largely disappeared. The plant looks clean. The company says that dust levels in the plant are well below the federal Occupational Safety and Health Administration (OSHA) standards—and the union agrees. But it wasn't always like that.

If you lived in Manville before 1970, you couldn't escape asbestos. It was on the roads, it was in the air, on cars, on people's clothes. "Years back, you'd be riding down Main Street and the trucks would be in front of you going to the dump and the stuff would fall off onto the road," says Kowalski. "I brought it home on my clothing. My children used to call me 'Daddy the snowman.'"

Early forms of dust collectors in the factory weren't very effective, and respirators weren't required. "They never said you had to wear one," Kowalski remembers. "You'd ask for one and they'd say 'Geez, what did you do with the other one?'" The dust levels were so high that in the heat of the plant, the mask would get clogged with asbestos, which would mix with sweat and harden like cement.

Dr. Lawrence Livornese, one of the doctors who tried to bring the disease rates in the plant to public attention in the 60s, recalls one of his first Manville patients was a "chronic cougher" who had worked making pipe since the 1940s. He'd just had a company physical; they'd told him nothing was wrong. Since Manville Corporation policy in those days was not to release x-rays taken during company physicals—not to outside doctors and certainly not to the workers themselves—Livornese took his own x-rays. The worker's lungs were "a real snowstorm," the doctor recalls, a mass of white scar tissue—the product of years of shoveling raw asbestos.

The Manville Corporation factory has been in Manville, known locally as Asbestos City, since before World War I. Talking with each victim, the question always comes up, "Why did it take so long for people to find out?" Talking to union officials, you ask "Why did it take so long for the union to get involved?" And "What was the company's responsibility?"

My own involvement with asbestos keeps me humble when I try to answer. I worked at the Manville plant for four summers and I can't remember a day when the dangers of asbestos crossed my mind. My father retired from Manville at the end of 1980 after 43 years with the company. His father worked there.

I even walked the picket line in the 1970 strike, the turning point on cleaning up the plant. I thought the issue was money. Most of the time I didn't think about asbestos at all.

Doctor Livornese dealt with this kind of myopia on a larger scale when he and Drs. Norbert Schalet and Maxwell Borow approached the union and the town about doing a mortality study in 1964. The local doctors wanted to compare mortality records in Manville with those in another New Jersey town, one without an asbestos plant. "Surely the town wasn't interested," says Livornese. "The union wasn't." That was the same year Dr. Irving Selikoff, now director of the Mt. Sinai Environmental Sciences Laboratory, published his pivotal study of the health effects of asbestos on insulation workers in Patterson, N.J.

The loyalty of workers, especially older workers, towards the company played a large part in this attitude. Joe Mondrone, whose father worked in the plant as a pipe fitter, is now president of the union local: "Even when I became a vice president and I told him what Johns-Manville [until recently the name of the Manville Corporation] was doing, he was always loyal. He'd say they gave me a job during the Depression when I needed a job."

It became impossible to ignore the evidence as the latency period for asbestosis and cancers drew to a close in the 1950s and 1960s. Almost everybody in the close-knit town knew someone who was sick.

Before the 1970 strike that made working conditions an issue, the union had asked a team of environmental scientists from the Mount Sinai School of Medicine in New York to look at asbestos hazards. A mortality study of 689 workers who had 20 or more years of employment at the plant prior to 1959 confirmed many workers' worst suspicions.

Only 134 workers out of that group should have died—using figures from standard actuarial tables, but the Mt. Sinai team found 199 deaths. Out of that group, 27.8 people could have been expected to die from cancer, but 72 did. Most cancer deaths came from cancers associated with asbestos.

"The dust was so high in the textile department that 40 percent of the sample who had worked there had died of asbestosis," says Dr. William Nicholson, associate director of the Environmental Science Laboratory at Mt. Sinai.

The 1970 strike—a long, bitter struggle that lasted through the fall and into the winter—set up a union/company environmental committee and marked the start of real cleanup at the plant. Workers, including my father, routinely began asking to see their company x-rays. My father filed his first workers' compensation claim for a breathing impairment caused by asbestos in 1970.

It's so easy to blame the Manville workers for not asking the right questions. But it's never been simple for workers to learn about— let alone change—their working conditions. Asbestos carried no product warning. The union had only a rudimentary occupational health program—and it still could be better. Local doctors were all too often afraid to confront Manville's economic power. Although OSHA has made it easier for some workers to gain access to their own medical records, these advances haven't yet reached all workers. The Reagan administration has already started to cut them back.

"Every once in a while, you read about a doctor's conscience being bothered. It's the only time you read anything about how they knew in the 30s and 40s," says Joe Mondrone. For years Kowalski was diagnosed as having chronic bronchitis.

Company doctors didn't want to bite the hand that fed them. Some local doctors simply didn't care enough to fight it out with an economically powerful corporation. And other doctors were simply ignorant. Without some kind of alert from the company or the union they didn't know that they should be looking for asbestosis or asbestos-related cancers.

And it still happens. Only last year, one retired worker with asbestosis was mistakenly diagnosed by a doctor at a local hospital as having tuberculosis. The worker repeatedly told the doctor that he was misreading the x-ray. Much of the medical profession's attitude toward workers came out in the doctor's surprised remark, "You know how to read an x-ray!"

In this situation workers have to defend themselves. Under OSHA, workers now have legally guaranteed access to records on health monitoring in the plants. Under the Reagan administration, however, OSHA has proposed withdrawing a worker's right to examine medical and environmental monitoring records.

Last August the Manville Corporation gambled its corporate future on one roll of the dice. By filing for reorganization under the bankruptcy laws, the company protected itself from the thousands of lawsuits brought by asbestos victims against the company and other asbestos manufacturers and companies that used asbestos. Manville is betting that its dramatic action—the company is still profitable—will force Congress to pass a measure bailing out the industry. But by filing, the company has opened up its affairs to intense outside scrutiny. Many observers believe the examination will conclusively prove what court cases had begun to suggest—that the company along with other manufacturers suppressed information about the health effects of asbestos for 40 years.

Some of the most damaging testimony came in the videotaped deposition of attorney Charles Roemer, given to the New York bankruptcy court hearing Manville's case. At 83, Roemer is one of the last survivors of a 1942 meeting where, according to Roemer, Manville's general legal counsel admitted to him and two others that the company was willing to let its employees die from asbestos exposure rather than inform them of health consequences that could lead to costly lawsuits.

In the 1930s and 40s Charles Roemer's cousin was the physician who gave workers their semiannual physicals at the Union Asbestos and Rubber Company (UNARCO) plant in Patterson, N.J. "One day he came into my law office," Roemer told *The Record* of Bergen County, N.J. in an interview. "He told me that there was something wrong with the lungs of five or six of the workers. He said, 'Charlie, we've got to get these men to leave their jobs or some of them are going to die horrible deaths.' " The company finally agreed to dismiss the men and pay each 400 weeks of workers' compensation.

But Roemer didn't stop there. He and two UNARCO executives visited Manville's general legal counsel, Vandiver Brown, in his Manhattan office. Brown heard them out, Roemer remembered, but only shook his head when he heard about UNARCO's decision.

"He said their x-rays had produced similar evidence of asbestos disease among their workers, but he said it was company policy not to tell the employees about these finds," Roemer told the court.

"I asked him, 'What will happen to these men who continue to work on the job?' And he told me, "They'll work for us until they die.' "

The money involved is no small change. Researchers at Mt. Sinai estimate that as many as 27 million workers—in shipyards, power plants, garages, construction sites and other workplaces—were exposed to asbestos from 1940 to 1980. The total cost of compensating workers exposed to the mineral could run well beyond $40 billion. Currently, the company faces suits by 15,000 plaintiffs and other asbestos manufacturers face similar legal burdens. New suits have been piling up at an average rate of 425 a month. Last year, the average legal settlement cost the company $40,000—half to the plaintiff and half for medical and legal costs. The bankruptcy filing stopped all the suits against Manville dead in their tracks.

Even 10 years ago, Manville would not have faced this volume of suits. The workers' compensation system, set up with the active participation of major industry lobbyists like the National Association of Manufacturers in the years just before World War I, protected companies from suits by workers who claimed occupationally related injuries or illnesses. In most states workers who are injured or get sick on the job are entitled to some portion of their medical expenses and a disability payment based on the degree of injury. In exchange, workers give up the right to sue their employers for further damages. The money for workers' compensation comes from employers through a complicated insurance system.

Management and business-oriented historians have always portrayed the workers' compensation system as a major step in guaranteeing worker safety and rights. In the last few years, revisionist historians like Dan Berman, author of *Death on the Job*, have argued that the system was a victory for business. In its actual operation, the compensation system gave businesses a way to control the costs of compensation—and in most cases to keep these costs very low. Most of the state systems are set up so that the majority of eligible workers never file a claim, these critics point out.

The statistics seem to back up this argument. A 1979 study of disabled textile workers showed that only 5.5 percent received workers' compensation. Only 21 percent of asbestos victims ever file claims. Nearly half the claims are unsettled when the worker dies. Less than half the survivors of these victims receive the death benefits to which they're entitled. Nationally, the average benefit is just $74 a week.

Recent interpretations of liability law have changed all that. First, courts have expanded product liability laws to include workers who used defective products. Workers using asbestos in their jobs have successfully sued asbestos manufacturers claiming the material was indeed defective, since the asbestos industry failed to give proper warning about its use. In other cases the courts have ruled that workers who can prove "willful misconduct" can also sue their employer—whether or not they're covered by workers' compensation. It's here that the issue of what Manville knew and when becomes crucial.

All the hoopla over Manville's bankruptcy filing has obscured a simple but rather vital question. If sick workers aren't getting benefits from the employer-financed workers' compensation system, who's picking up the bill for their illness? To a great extent, the taxpayer is.

The House Labor Standards Subcommittee estimates that up to $3 billion a year that should be picked up by the compensation system is being paid by the federal government in the form of welfare, Social Security and Veterans Administration payments. A bill sponsored by Rep. George Miller (D-Calif.), the subcommittee chair, would shift this cost back to the employers who are responsible. "It would eliminate an unwitting federal subsidy," says Michael Goldberg, counsel to the subcommittee.

Prevention and intervention can save lives. Screening procedures can find pre-cancerous tumors and cancers at an early stage. Found early enough, the tumors can be surgically removed. "We could save half the 10,000 workers who now die of bladder cancer if we detected this early enough," [according to Sheldon Samuels, head of occupational health for the Industrial Unions Department at the AFL-CIO]. These diagnostic procedures wouldn't be that hard to implement through current company physicals.

Along with diagnosis, union leaders would like to see a system to identify and educate exposed workers. The risk for many workers can be lessened by changes in lifesystle and medical treatment. "You've got to teach the family and the worker what has to be done for the rest of the worker's life." And any system has to extend to family members. Mesothelioma and asbestosis show up in the families of asbestos workers. Children who've been born to workers in the lead smelting industry often have birth defects. "Do you say to the children that they don't have an occupational disease?" Samuels asks.

Some union leaders would go even further, believing that all uses of asbestos should be banned. Mt. Sinai's Nicholson agrees. There's no threshold below which asbestos won't cause cancers—reducing the amount in the air lessens but does not eliminate, the risk. "Products exist for replacing asbestos in virtually every use," Nicholson says. Sweden, for example, has instituted an almost complete ban on the substance.

But even a ban on new uses won't stop new cancers, Nicholson cautions. "Our problem for the next 40 or 50 years or even longer is the asbestos now in place in power plants, in brakes, in schools, in ships, etc." He estimates that there is about 1 million tons of asbestos now in use that's capable of causing asbestosis or cancer. The number of people dying of asbestos yearly is expected to increase until 1995.

The people of Manville, N.J. have paid a high price for their piece of the American dream. The hardworking immigrants who settled this town struggled, and often succeeded, in earning the rewards our society promises. They bought houses, raised children and sent them to college. For many, that dream has ended with the cruel reality of oxygen tanks, slow descents into weakness and incurable cancers. And they never made that choice for themselves. "The people I know, they feel bitter," Kowalski says. "When we were hired, they should have said, 'Hey, there's a risk involved. Do you want to take it with the risk?' And you'd have had the option to say no."

"You can restore a product," he says. "You can restore a building. You can never restore a human life."

Technology and the Environment: Who Pays the Piper?

By John P. Mascotte

In this analysis of the problems posed by asbestos, the president of the Continental Corporation argues that it is not always possible to foresee the environmental problems caused by technology and that swift, fair means of settling damage claims need to be established.

I want to talk to you about a growing concern of mine and what I hope will become a growing concern of opinion leaders around the country. I speak of the unexpected, unpredictable, undesirable side effects of technology. The costly, painful, unfair, sometimes calamitous side effects—in human terms—of a technological society caught up in a worldwide competitive race for markets, jobs, profits and the achievement of other national goals.

I didn't come here today to make an anti-technology speech. Quite the contrary. Technology is not our enemy. In fact, it may be ironically true that only technology itself—properly applied—can save us from the undesirable side effects of technology. But our understanding of technology and how to control it, and predict its side effects, is the problem we must master.

Until recent years, Americans have taken a benign view of technology. And well they might, for American industry, as the prime manager of technology, has given us the most advanced and wealthiest society on earth. Until the early 1960's—outside of science-fiction films—we virtually ignored technology's impact on the environment. More recently, however, such problems as brown lung disease, Love Canal, Three Mile Island, kepone, and now asbestosis

---

From *Vital Speeches of the Day*, City News Publishing Company. January 15, 1983. Reprinted by permission. John P. Mascotte is president of the Continental Corporation.

have become synonymous with unnatural and unexpected events that have undermined public confidence in our ability to manage technology safely.

Over the last decade or two, new laws and regulations have come into our lives to help protect us from these dangers. Some of these laws and regulations may have gone too far. But, by and large, the basic laws on the books are needed and effective, and are backed up by a court and jury system that has generally served us well over the years.

Asbestos-related disease, one of technology's unfortunate side effects, is a medical, social and economic problem of far-reaching consequences that has been coming on quietly for over thirty years. It takes decades for the disease to manifest itself. We are not prepared to handle this kind of problem, and the way we are handling it today is making the problem worse.

What we must ask ourselves is this: Can our present court/jury system respond to the challenges of asbestosis, and other similar environmental health problems, which may strike us in the future? Some of us are convinced that the current system cannot respond fairly and quickly to those who are victimized by this tragedy.

Let me examine this issue by giving you some necessary technical background on this difficult situation. Asbestos is a mineral whose unique properties permit its use in more than 3,000 commercial, industrial and personal products. It is an important and probably indispensable part of the modern industrial economy. There is, however, a substantial body of evidence that serious and harmful effects arise from its misuse. It is known to be a causative or contributive factor in certain respiratory and gastrointestinal diseases. It has been estimated that at least 5.6 million persons have been exposed to asbestos and may be at risk—and some say that this number may be conservative. There is no way to calculate how many may die and how many millions of others may suffer disability and a substantially reduced span of life.

Persons suffering from asbestos-related disease are now resorting to that all-American remedy, the lawsuit, in ever increasing numbers. One company alone estimates their current number of lawsuits at about 17,000 in 1982, and this company expects another 32,000 lawsuits in the next 20 years. Now that's just one company! And in most cases, more than one manufacturer is being named as a defendant. Litigation is expected to continue at a high rate until about the year 2010 before diminishing, largely as a result of industry's growing ability to handle asbestos more safely.

The long-term cost of this litigation is now estimated by one study at $40 to $80 billion at 1980 dollar values. Some 260 involved insurance companies will pay claims through workers' compensation or product liability coverage but it will represent only a fraction of the total eventual cost. And hundreds of millions of dollars more are, and will be, sought from asbestos manufacturers and other companies, perhaps involved in the form of punitive and other damages.

I would be remiss if I did not mention that some claimants—according to one asbestos manufacturer I talked to—have "insubstantial or marginal claims and a fair number are highly questionable." Those situations, of course, must be carefully screened.

It is interesting to note that the nation's trial lawyers, a group who could be expected to oppose any proposal to circumvent the court/jury system to solve this problem, is beginning to understand the major predicament we are facing.

From the California Trial Lawyers publication, the FORUM, comes the following quote: "The enormity of the litigation, in terms of the numbers of claims now pending throughout the country and those expected to enter the system, raises grave problems. There are obviously not enough courtrooms in the world to accommodate the trial of each of these filings, should court and counsel fail to arrive at a mechanism for large-scale disposition of cases."

As you may know, The Manville Corporation, Unarco and Amatex have recently asked for the protection of a bankruptcy court. Moreover, under the prevailing tort system, all parties contributing to an injury are jointly liable for damages. Some courts have continued to process cases against these Chapter 11 companies. If the result is to shift their liability to other defendants, then the domino-effect could force many others into bankruptcy as well.

This growing wave of litigation—if not handled in a more sensible way—will have far-reaching consequences for American industry, for the legal system and for the government. Its most immediate impact, as you might imagine, is upon our legal system. More courts, judges, personnel and equipment will be needed to handle these cases and public money will pay for them.

Product liability law is very complex, because the laws of fifty different states are involved. The costs of litigation—for plaintiff and defendant—therefore, will be extremely heavy.

A lawsuit may seem like a costly, even wasteful remedy, given the meager amount of insurance available to compensate the victims of asbestos-related disease. But as the circumstances now dictate, there is no other remedy at hand. The victim may have been exposed to the disease forty years ago, his employer may no longer exist as a legal entity, or it may have merged with a successor corporation. *The problem for the victim has been, and continues to be, to find someone to accept responsiblity—the manufacturer, the distributor, the general contractor, the installer, the insurance company, the government—somebody!*

The search for additional responsible parties goes on at a feverish pace. Courts of appeal in many jurisdictions are beginning to consider this litigation. To no one's surprise, they are coming to widely varied judgments and they are beginning to expand liabilities in the face of the inadequacy of the available insurance coverage. They have created some novel concepts of liability that threaten the established understanding of what constitutes the law, and what the rights and responsibilities of manufacturers, suppliers and consumers will be.

My point is to suggest that our institutions—mainly the law and our legal system—are inappropriate mechanisms to use in handling the tide of litigation that is, and will be, generated by asbestos-related disease.

If we were designing a new system that would work rationally, efficiently and fairly for all, how would it work? How might it be created?

In considering the question, we find the following elements are probably necessary to any workable solution:

1) We start with the victims themselves. We must remember the terrible cost being paid by those people afflicted and their families. This cost is economic and psychological, as well as physical. The present system, when it delivers justice, is costly, inefficient and, above all else, painfully, if not cruelly slow. Justice Holmes once said that "justice delayed is justice denied." How prophetic those words must be to thousands of victims, many in their 60's or older, who urgently need help now.

2) We should seek at all times the equitable and uniform treatment of asbestos victims. The present fault system of litigation is a lottery—some win and some lose—often seemingly unrelated to the merits of an individual's case. Settlements may have to do with

the peculiarity of local law or even the skill of individual plaintiff's counsel or even the whim of a jury.

3) One of our principal objectives ought to be the conservation of available financial resources. It's clear that liability for asbestos-related disease is enormous and that available insurance coverage is limited. The present court/jury system dissipates those resources. For example, defendants and insurance companies are conservatively paying out $2.00 in expenses for every $1.00 put into the hands of the victims, and the $2.00 in expenses does not include the cost to the public in providing judges, juries and other court expenses.

4) And as a corollary to that, we should devise a special system or trusteeship that makes for an efficient distribution of available money to the victims. *The amount of money now devoted to offensive and defensive litigation is staggering.* I say this not as a criticism of the plaintiff's attorneys. I do not entirely share the view, particularly among some in the insurance industry, that there would be no problem but for the greed of the plaintiff's counsel. There are some offenders, true, but the trial lawyers did not create the present system, any more than the insurance companies did. *What we must do now is focus on the problems of the victims and devise a system that delivers promptly the benefits they are entitled to receive.*

5) Another objective of a more efficient, workable system would be an end to most litigation; because it may be destructive of the victim's best interest; because it is weakening the courts and legal system; and because the search for responsible persons to sue is leading to broader use of litigation, and to novel and unsound theories of legal liability. Such a new system, however, would recognize that there would always be some differences of opinion which must be resolved by litigation.

6) And lastly, our objective should also be the conservation of Manville, and other involved companies, and the protection of the rights of their shareholders, workers, suppliers and creditors. Justice is a two-edged sword...a set of scales...and the rights of all parties must be considered in these proceedings.

The petitions by Manville and others seeking the protection of a court in a Chapter 11 bankruptcy, is, at the very least, one of the legal novelties generated by the problem of asbestos-related disease. I find the position of Manville's management, that the viability of the company is threatened by overwhelming asbestos claims, a compelling one. Manville's estimates of its potential future liabilities, backed by an independent study, is—if accurate—frightening. Moreover, corporations are being sued for punitive damages on the basis of what they allegedly knew, or should have known, about the hazards of asbestos thirty or forty years ago.

It cannot be in the public interest for companies to be liquidated to find the money to pay these claims. This is like killing the goose that lays the golden egg. The shareholders, workers, creditors, and suppliers of these companies also have rights to be honored. I earnestly believe that the time has come to end this legal scramble and get on with the main task of compensating meritorious victims as quickly and fairly as possible.

And so the question arises how might this be done?

We, at Continental, believe that the time has come to take asbestos-related disease out of the fault system. This is the only way to bring this litigation nightmare to an end. It is the only way we can conserve the available financial resources—of the asbestos manufacturers and their insurance companies—in order to more fully help the victims.

This means no-fault handling—a worker would need only to prove that he was exposed to asbestos and that he currently manifests the symptoms of disease.

We believe that compensation should cover all the victim's medical expenses; that he should also be compensated for lost or reduced earnings, pain and suffering, and some amount for foreshortened life span, and that he should be compensated for reasonable legal expenses.

What the victims need then is a special fund, created by Congressional statutory action, which would be a vehicle for the disbursement of available funds promptly to all meritorious asbestos-related cases. The fund should have a board of trustees representing the spectrum of involved parties. This voluntary fund would derive its money from negotiated contributions from asbestos manufacturers, suppliers and installers and their insurance companies, and possibly the Federal Government.

We do not rule out responsibility for the Federal Government. A large proportion of persons affected by asbestos-related disease are shipyard workers whose work was carried out for the government in a government-controlled workplace. And remember, a war was on when most were exposed. It is also a fact that the public is already paying part of the victim's expense through medicare, social security, and public assistance. If we properly understand the full ramifications of the asbestos disease problem, resources of both the private and the public sector may be needed as we consider the long-term costs involved.

Congress has been considering several legislative remedies. Congressman George Miller's bill HB5735, "The Occupational Health Hazards Compensation Act," we see as a reasonable vehicle for removing asbestos compensation from the fault litigation system. We support the concept of this legislation as a practical and necessary step toward a long-term solution to this problem.

Such health hazards as asbestos, and the toxic substances found at Love Canal recently, are but two examples of the potential for environmental disruption that are the by-products of our accelerating technology. These problems will always be with us. Our challenge, obviously, is to learn to do a better job of managing technology and its potentially damaging side effects.

Since the 1960's we have learned much about environmental pollution; however, it's apparent that these recurring environmental problems are undermining American faith in industry's ability to manage technology in the public interest. This loss of faith is having growing political consequences. We require the great benefits of technology, so we must help the American public recognize that these benefits do not come without risk and cost.

As we look forward to the twenty-first century, we must contemplate a future where environmental accident and disease may well be the leading public health problem. We solved the public health problems of tuberculosis, poliomyelitis and other dread diseases but we need to know more, through research, to understand and forecast environmental disease before a frightened public decides that public health can be assured only by public control of all technology. And they have a right, I believe, to insist on public control if we in business and industry do not listen more carefully and get our act together.

AN INTERNATIONAL PERSPECTIVE

Pollution Plagues Industrial Firms in Growing Nations

By H. Jeffrey Leonard

A number of less developed countries have experienced growth in industrialization in recent years. Now, strong pro-environmental groups in the LDC's are demanding that greater attention be given to the pollution problems accompanying this industrialization.

Since the Stockholm Conference on the Human Environment in 1972, observers have noted a fundamental difference in the approach to environmental problems of the advanced industrialized nations and of those nations that only recently have begun to industrialize. Development planners, economists, industrialists, and even many environmentalists have contended that countries still in need of rapid economic development should *not* imitate the United States and other industrial nations by passing extensive regulations to con-

Excerpted from the *Conservation Foundation Letter*, August 1982. Copyright, The Conservation Foundation. H. Jeffrey Leonard is an associate with The Conservation Foundation.

trol pollution. "First build up the industry, then worry about reducing the side effects created by it," has been the overwhelming sentiment of those seeking to outline a strategy for increasing the national income of poor countries by stimulating industrial development.

Despite the widespread endorsement of this maxim, pollution problems in some rapidly industrializing nations have become too severe to be ignored or put on the shelf until greater affluence is attained. Specific instances of human suffering and economic disruption caused by industrial-related pollution in many developing countries have stirred public concern and prompted new policy responses by governments. This has been especially true in those countries that have quickened the pace of industrialization through what the United Nations calls the "redeployment" of industries away from the most developed nations. (See box on pages 310-311.)

Even in the face of prevailing international economic problems, the 1970's brought dramatic industrial development progress to a select number of the still underindustrialized countries. Among those that have experienced particularly rapid development are Spain, Greece, and Ireland in Western Europe; several socialist economies of Eastern Europe; Brazil, Mexico, and Venezuela in Latin America; and Hong Kong, Singapore, Taiwan, and South Korea in Asia.

For most such nations, large transfers of technology from the developed countries have figured strategically in the quest to build industrial capacity. Some countries have been oriented toward attracting multinational corporations to locate production facilities within their borders or to establish joint ventures with domestic firms. Other countries have preferred not to depend on foreign ownership of industrial enterprises; they have sought instead to purchase licenses, technology, or even whole plants from abroad.

The spread of a wide variety of industrial technologies around the globe, as well as the speed with which industrial development is taking place in some countries, has tended to alter classical patterns of development that took place in stages. In a world in which technology flows with considerable freedom and in which sophisticated consumers everywhere demand esoteric items, the underindustrialized, less affluent countries tend to specialize in highly sophisticated and consumption-oriented industries before building up domestic technological capabilities or product markets. Many countries, in effect, create "last industries first," as economist Albert Hirschman puts it.

These strategies provide great economic opportunities for countries that do not have the technological sophistication, capital resources, and consumer demand necessary to sustain rapid increases in industrial output. At the same time, however, the internationalization of industry—with its speedup of development and its dispersion of industrial processes—has increased the chances that environmental disruptions will hamper further economic growth or injure public health.

For some rapidly industrializing nations, fears of pollution have been a factor influencing the economic development strategy. For example, the choice of industries to support sometimes has been affected by a country's willingness or unwillingness to accept productive processes that are known to cause significant environmental or public health problems. Some nations have tried to compete for industries from the advanced countries by adopting permissive policies; others have refused to accept industries that appear to be searching for a convenient haven from stringent environmental regulation.*

Ireland presents a good example of a latecomer to industrial development. Its strategy in the early 1970's was based in part on the assumption that participation in the international division of labor depended upon a willingness to accept dirty industries. By the end of the decade, however, Irish officials had become convinced that their ability to compete for new industries was not fundamentally dependent upon granting them a blank check for polluting Ireland's air and water.

Traditionally, Ireland has exhibited the classic characteristics of a country that was "underdeveloped" as a result of its colonial status in the British Empire. Even in the late 1960's, Ireland was experiencing high unemployment and heavy emigration from rural to urban areas, as well as out of the country. An agrarian nation with a very low level of industrial development, Ireland's urban economy

*The examples and quotations cited draw on case study research and interviews by the author in Ireland, Spain, and Mexico between March 1980 and July 1982. Field research in Ireland and Spain was undertaken as part of The Conservation Foundation's Industrial Siting Project, supported by the German Marshall Fund of the United States, the Ford Foundation, and the Richard King Mellon Foundation. The work in Mexico was partially supported by the Institute for the Study of World Politics.

Have Pollution Regulations Caused Industry to Flee the U.S.?

During the 1970's, many observers in the United States expressed concern that the costs of complying with environmental regulations might adversely affect U.S. industry's ability to compete with imported products and in foreign markets. It was expected that regulations would increasingly push industries out of the United States and other advanced industrial nations (the "industrial flight" hypothesis), and the less-developed countries would compete to attract multinational industries by minimizing their own regulations (the "pollution haven" hypothesis). This push and pull combination, it was thought, would exert a powerful influence on international location patterns and on national strategies for industrial development in the Third World.

Have environmental regulations—and public concern—actually affected siting patterns as predicted by economists and public policy analysts? A three-year Conservation Foundation research project has tested both the "industrial flight" and "pollution haven" hypotheses, examining recent international trade and investment figures for evidence of significant change and conducting case-study research in five rapidly industrializing nations—Ireland, Spain, Romania, Mexico, and Brazil.

No major across-the-board dislocations can be attributed to

depended on expensive imports. As a result, Irish leaders embarked on a major effort to encourage multinational corporations to build new production facilities in their country. They assumed that this could only be accomplished if Ireland became a "dustbin" for the United States and Europe. One old Irish politician was quoted as having said:

"All my life I've seen the lads leaving Ireland for the big smoke in London, Pittsburgh, Birmingham, and Chicago. It'd be better for Ireland if they stayed here and we imported the smoke."

Irish officials thought that their industrial development plans would entail major environmental sacrifices. To secure the cooperation of those responsible for approving specific industrial proposals, the head of the Industrial Development Authority (IDA) held a series of closed-

environmental regulations or public opposition, although a small number of industries have been induced to build more production facilities overseas in recent years. These include some industries—such as mineral processing—for which environmental problems have been only one of several factors inducing American companies to branch out worldwide. In addition, a few industries involved in the manufacture of very hazardous and heavily regulated products—e.g., asbestos and benzidine dyes—appear to have been directly pushed abroad by new regulations, litigation, and general public concern.

The important discovery in CF's industrial siting research, however, is that in no instance has a healthy, growing American industry been forced to move abroad as a result of either environmental regulations or public opposition.

Moreover, there is strong evidence to indicate that consciously setting low environmental standards in hopes of attracting new plants may be a very risky economic development strategy for newly industrializing countries. There is a real danger that those few industries likely to find such an inducement attractive are the same ones that manufacture products which are becoming obsolete, extremely hazardous, or subject to consumer standards. These characteristics, in turn, can reduce demand for the products and shrink export markets to the United States and other advanced industrial countries.

door meetings to advise local officials that—for the sake of jobs and the Irish economy—the country would have to accept some of the dirtier facilities from the advanced industrial nations, without insisting on tight pollution controls.

A paper presented in 1972 argued that Irish pollution standards could be less stringent than in the industrialized nations because the country's climate ensured a high assimilative capacity for its air, rivers, and ocean. Only several years ago, the chairman of the Irish National Trust, Phillip Mullally, asserted:

"Of all the economic incentives the Irish government offers to foreign industry to invest here, the most valuable is the permission to pollute."

Contrary to these expectations, Ireland has not become a dumping ground where multinational corporations can locate new facilities without regard for the environment. Like those in other rapidly industrializing countries, Irish officials discovered that they could regulate most new industrial plants to protect their environment without causing significant shifts in investment patterns. In addition, generous tax incentives have enabled Ireland to attract high-technology industries that are free of major environmental problems.

Of course, several special circumstances have enabled Ireland to reject the dustbin approach and become more discriminating. Ireland is a small country with a small population and a small economy. It cannot and need not aspire to build a full industrial base or a complete chemical industry from basic bulk chemicals to finished chemical products; it can pick and choose which industries to develop and which not to develop.

In addition, the fact that Ireland is a European nation with a highly educated and skilled workforce has given it an enormous advantage over many other countries that also would like to be able to "specialize" in high-technology industries.

Most other industrializing countries have not had the luxury of being quite so choosy as Ireland. There appear to be few cases in which under-industrialized nations have spurned industries for environmental reasons if other alternatives were not readily available. Nevertheless, the number of countries willing to accept all comers, no matter how serious the threat of pollution or public health problems, clearly has shrunk in recent years. At the very least, most countries have become much better at negotiating with foreign companies about pollution control measures and at anticipating potential problems in advance of new plant construction.

In Spain, which hosts a wider variety of foreign firms than Ireland, the level of environmental concern among government officials and the general public is not as high as in Ireland. But, when it comes to multinational corporations, both the officials and the public tend to have a markedly different attitude. Alfonso Ensenat, subdirector general for the industrial environment in the Ministry of Industry and Energy, explains one of the reasons why a double standard exists in everyone's mind even if not in the law itself:

"There are two types of technology: pre-ecological ones and ecological ones. We have to be very careful to make sure that a foreign company will use the second type here, because if not, the public opinion will sooner or later turn against the company. Spaniards are very proud people. If we permit *our* industries to pollute *our* rivers, that is our business. But if a foreign company comes here and makes contamination, it is an insult to Spain.''

Mexican government officials are only at a very preliminary stage in attempting to deal with the country's pollution problems. National regulations governing the air emissions and water effluents of industry are still rudimentary, and even these are rarely enforced. The Mexican public, too, is notoriously apathetic about pollution problems, whether because of concern for persistent widespread poverty or the feeling that it is the responsiblity of the government to find remedies.

Yet even in Mexico, there are limits to what companies, particularly foreign companies, can get away with. Industrial development planners in Mexico have become more concerned about pollution and health matters in judging which types of foreign firms Mexico should attract. Mexico recently rejected a proposal from an American company to build a new plant to produce asbestos products in Mexico:

''We did not accept the company's motives for wanting to come to Mexico. We think the problems of asbestos have been exaggerated in the United States, but we do not want to get involved with a company if it is running away from those problems. We are prepared to live with the risks associated with asbestos if it is for our own domestic needs, but we will not accept asbestos companies anymore if they want solely to produce for export.''

One reason why governments in some rapidly industrializing countries have become more assertive about pollution is that public concern at the local level has risen dramatically since the early 1970's. This has induced officials to feel they have a mandate to be more scrutinizing and stringent. Increased public activism also has raised the political penalties for laxness. If the public perceives that a foreign company views it as expendable, that public easily can draw the conclusion that its own government agrees.

A motivating factor for local activism in many countries has been economic. Farmers, fishermen, and others who feel that an industrial proposal, or an existing industrial facility, threatens their livelihood often have joined to protest loudly. Such groups rarely have functioned as more than short-term coalitions united by their immediate economic interests; they typically do not have an environmental motivation or in-depth knowledge about ecological concepts.

A good example of such spontaneous protest arose several years ago when a large alumina plant was proposed by Alcan and a Spanish partner. The consortium originally chose to locate along the northwest Atlantic coast of Spain, near Ponteredra. However, Spanish fishermen—especially musselers and shrimpers—already concerned about the damage to their livelihoods being caused by wastes from pulp and paper plants along the coast, put up an intense fight against the project. Eventually the entire alumina facility, almost identical to one built by Alcan on the Shannon estuary in Ireland, was moved inland to San Ciprian in Lugo Province. Alcan officials insist that the plant, like its Irish counterpart, would have segregated and dried all its red waste mud without permitting any runoff into the sea, but this did not console the beleaguered fishermen.

In Europe the environmental movement has tended to be closely identified with certain political parties and to have much broader political agendas than in the United States. This is especially true in Spain, where most ecological groups have strong biases against the national government and often are closely associated with political forces pushing for regional autonomy or other broad political goals. One Spanish government official says that in Spain, "ecology is almost never just an issue by itself. It is almost always a means to political ends."

In the Basque region of Spain, environmental protest has become an important way to express Basque support for regional separatism. Industrial pollution, particularly in Bilbao, is viewed as a result and a symbol of external control over the Basque economy. Wall posters painted throughout the Basque area—supporting the separatist terrorist group ETA, the more moderate separatist political party Herri Batasuna, or other groups favoring some form of regional autonomy—often oppose nuclear power and decry pollution. Quite frequently United States business interests are singled out in these posters, both for their contract work at Lemonitz (Westinghouse), the nuclear power plant just outside Bilbao, and for their contributions to industrial pollution in the Basque region.

Though they generally are not the worst offenders in the area, since it is one of the oldest and most polluted industrial regions in Europe, nearly every American firm operating a production facility in the Basque region has had to face protests and efforts by local groups to block new construction or shut down existing operations. The protest against Dow Chemical's proposal to produce pesticides in one of its plants near Bilbao was so intense several years ago, for example, that the company eventually switched its plans and now produces the pesticides at one if its plants in the United Kingdom.

A major problem in many countries outside the United States is that the public is generally uninformed about either the operations of industrial plants or their potential environmental problems. It often is difficult or impossible to obtain information from companies or local officials about chemicals or materials that are used and hazards that may result.

This is one reason why environmental groups and the general public sometimes react with rage when pollution or public health problems from a particular industrial operation are revealed. Yvonne Scannell, a law professor at Trinity College in Dublin, says: "Irish environmentalists are largely uninformed. It isn't surprising that they get hysterical over an issue that concerns them, since they haven't got access to the information that would answer their questions."

When a company is perceived as having hidden damaging information in order to establish a new plant in a country, the public backlash may be very serious, as one firm in Ireland recently discovered. The case involved the use and disposal of asbestos by an American firm, Raybestos Manhattan. Raybestos, the largest U.S. manufacturer of frictional products, came to Ireland to produce brake pads, primarily for the European market, during the mid-1970's. At the time, the company appeared to fit perfectly into Ireland's evolving strategy of attracting smokeless, high value-added, export-oriented industries.

The original proposal for the $8 million plant—to be located in the town of Ovens and have a capacity to produce 10 million asbestos disk brake pads per year—was eagerly accepted by both IDA and the Cork County Council. However, at about the time the Ovens factory was nearing completion, press clippings on the hazards of asbestos were widely circulated among the citizens of Ovens. Protests over the plant erupted, but overall local public opinion remained divided. Many people were swayed by the 130 jobs the plant was providing and by assurances from Raybestos that it was one of the cleanest of all manufacturing facilities in Ireland.

The community of Ovens was more united in opposing Raybestos' use of a dump site near the factory for disposing of waste asbestos and reject brake pads; after all, the dump site brought no significant economic benefits or jobs to Ovens. Public protests at the dump finally forced Raybestos to close it down in 1977 and search for a new disposal area.

Japan's Approaches to Dealing with Environmental Pollution

By Joseph A. McKinney

Given the scope of the pollution problems faced by Japan, the nation has made remarkable progress in dealing with them. This article shows how a national environmental commitment evolved between business, labor and the Japanese public.

It is widely known that Japan has suffered severe problems with environmental pollution. What is less well known is that Japan has been among the more successful of nations in dealing with environmental pollution. The purpose of this paper is to summarize briefly Japan's experience in this area and to outline the policy measures which have contributed to its considerable success in reversing the tide of environmental pollution.

Historical Background of Pollution Policy

If Japan has made more progress than most countries in reducing the level of pollution, it is not because the problem was recognized there earlier or that action was taken there more speedily once it was recognized. While there are a few examples of early recognition of the problem, such as the transfer of a copper smelting operation in the 1880s from the mainland to an island in the Seto Inland Sea, in general, Japan's awareness of the problem and willingness to deal with it seemed to lag behind that of the United States and Europe by several years.

During the postwar period, the government of Japan, in conjunction with Japanese businesses, placed high priority on rapid economic growth through industrialization. The environmental pollution which

Reprinted by permission. An earlier version of this paper was presented at the Southwestern Economic Association Meeting, Houston, Texas, April 3, 1980. Joseph A. McKinney is an associate professor of economics at Baylor University.

resulted from this industrialization was especially severe in Japan for two major reasons. First, as Japan proceeded during the late 1950s and the 1960s to move from light industry into heavy industry, the industry mix of Japan became heavily concentrated in such polluting industries as paper and pulp, chemicals, stone and clay, iron and steel, and metal products.[1] Secondly, the density of both population and industrial development in Japan create particular problems for the country. Japan's GNP/inhabitable square kilometer is 18 times as great as that of the U.S., six times as great as that of the U.K., and twice as great as that of the Netherlands. Similar comparisons of industrial production, energy consumption and automobiles per inhabitable square kilometer reveal even wider disparities.[2] Environmental scientists have pointed out that while the natural environment provides for dilution and assimiliation of pollutants in relatively low population areas, these pollutants become exponentially more damaging as population and output increase.[3] Considering the density of Japan's population and the concentration of industrial activity there, it is not surprising that her pollution problems have been severe.

Given its goal of rapid economic growth and its close association with business interests, the government of Japan was at first reluctant to recognize the problem of pollution. Evidence had surfaced in the late 1950s to the effect that Minamata disease, a debilitating disease characterized by aberrant behavior on the part of the person suffering from it, was caused by lead poisoning. Also Itai-Itai disease, which causes extreme pain and brittleness of the bones, was linked to cadmium poisoning. Yet this information was apparently ignored for several years as the polluting industries continued discharging mercury and cadmium into the environment.[4]

A turning point in the public's attitude toward pollution occurred in 1963 when residents of the Mishima-Numaya area organized to prevent the construction of a petrochemical complex in their area. Other movements soon sprang up around the country. In 1968 court cases were filed against polluters by victims of Minamata disease, Itai-Itai disease and Yokkaichi asthma which was caused by pollution of the air by petrochemical producers. The plaintiffs won these cases in the early 1970s and the companies were forced to compensate victims in amounts that ranged from $27,000 to $63,000 per victim. The wide publicity which these cases received and the assessment of guilt to the companies had a profound impact on the attitude toward pollution in Japan.[5]

Pollution Control Legislation in Japan

The first major pollution control legislation was passed in Japan in 1967, eleven years after the first law in the United States. This law, entitled the Basic Law for Environmental Pollution Control, contained a "harmonization clause" which stated that "insofar as the preservation of the living environment is concerned, it shall be carried out in harmony with the healthy development of the economy."[6] On the face of it, this clause seems to reflect a recognition by policymakers of the fact that the benefits of pollution control must be weighed against the costs. However, this provision was attacked by some as an indication that the law had been passed primarily to protect industry from environmental groups and that improvement of environmental conditions would be sacrificed in order to attain more rapid economic growth.[7]

In 1969, the Tokyo Municipal Government passed a law which rejected the idea of a tradeoff of environmental deterioration for economic growth and threatened to stop the water supply to polluting industries. While this law was legally superceded by the national law, the city government of Tokyo stood firm in its determination to take a hard line toward polluters, and in doing so apparently had a significant impact on public opinion.[8]

Due to a groundswell of public concern about environmental pollution a special session of the Diet was held in December 1970 to address this issue. The 1967 Basic Law was revised to eliminate the "harmonization clause" and fourteen other pieces of pollution control legislation were passed. Since that time at least nineteen other laws have been passed dealing with either environmental quality standards or damage relief from polluters, giving Japan "perhaps the most thorough body of national environmental legislation in the world."[9]

Another important step was taken in 1971 with the establishment of the Environment Agency for the purpose of coordinating and directing pollution control efforts. Before the establishment of this agency pollution control policies of the various agencies of the government were not well coordinated and often conflicted with each other. Conflicts still sometimes arise between the Environment Agency and other government agencies such as the Ministry of International Trade and Industry, but there is much more coordination than previously. It is noteworthy that the Environment Agency does not have centralized enforcement powers; environmental laws are actually enforced by prefectural governments. The Environment Agency often pushes for more strict implementation of the laws, but ultimately must fall back on a consensus worked out among the agency itself, the prefectural government and the industry involved.[10]

Expenditures for Pollution Control in Japan

Between 1970 and 1975, investments by private industry for pollution control increased by 570%. At their peak in 1975, these investments amounted to 964.5 billion yen or 17.7% of total plant and equipment investments. As the most needed pollution control measures were finished, these expenditures gradually tapered off to 7.2% of total investment in 1977, 4.5% in 1979, and a low of 3.9% in 1980, and were again on the upswing at 5.3% in 1982.[11] The allocation of these investments in 1978, which is indicative of the proportions in subsequent years, was 58% for air pollution control, 16% for water pollution control, 6% for noise and vibration control, 6% for disposal of industrial waste, and 14% for all other projects.[12]

These very substantial investments in pollution control equipment have been made primarily to attain ambient pollution standards established by the government. But the government has also encouraged such expenditures through taxation policy and special financial arrangements. It is estimated that tax reduction for the purpose of encouraging pollution control projects reduced national tax revenues by 24 billion yen and local tax revenues by 11 billion yen for fiscal 1977. These tax breaks financed a bit less than 5% of private pollution control expenditures in 1977. Such investments are also encouraged, especially in the case of small businesses, by access to loans bearing interest rates lower than those available in private capital markets and also having longer repayment periods. It is estimated that in 1975 the availability of such loans was equivalent to a subsidy of 2.6 percentage points reduction in the interest rate. This compared to a ratio of 4.5% in the United States and 14.2% in Norway.[13]

In contrast to the recent trend in industrial pollution control investments, environmental protection appropriations in the national budget have been steadily increasing and in 1978 amounted to 868.7

billion yen or 1.4% of total budget appropriations. Of this amount, 514.7 billion yen was earmarked for the construction of sewage treatment facilities, an area in which there is much room for improvement in Japan.[14] In addition to direct subsidization of local pollution control projects by the national government, municipal or prefectural bonds for pollution control projects are often taken up by government agencies.[15] According to Remy Prud'homme, anti-pollution investments in Japan are overall higher than in any other country by a substantial margin.[16]

Effectiveness of Policy Measures

In general it can be stated that Japanese pollution control measures have met with a surprising degree of success. The loss from environmental pollution is estimated to have peaked for Japan in Fiscal Year 1970 at 9.4% of GNP or 14.2% of Net National Welfare as estimated by Hisao Kanamori.[17] Despite continuation of Japan's relatively rapid economic growth since that time, the pollution levels of both air and water have been substantially reduced. With regard to air quality pollution, ambient concentrations of such pollutants as sulfur dioxide, carbon monoxide and lead have been reduced by at least 50%. Suspended particulate matter has been steadily reduced in all the major cities. For other pollutants such as nitrogen dioxide, while there has not been an actual reduction in ambient concentrations, the average concentrations have at least leveled off since 1973.[18] Even with the congestion of Japanese cities and extreme geographical concentrations of industrial facilities, the overall air quality in Japanese cities is probably no worse than that in major U.S. cities and may be somewhat better.[19]

With regard to water pollution, there is still much room for improvement in Japan. It is true that there has been a dramatic reduction in pollution by such harmful substances as cadmium, mercury and lead. However, pollution by organic substances, as measured by biochemical oxygen demand, remains a serious problem. The presence of phosphates from detergents and untreated sewerage has caused eutrophication of certain rivers and lakes. An ambitious plan for improvement of sewerage treatment is underway. While the sewerage of 22.8% of the population was treated in 1975, this figure had risen to 31% by March of 1982.[20] There are some signs of improvement in water quality in the last few years, but much remains to be accomplished in this area.[21]

Japan's major approach to pollution control has been the establishment of rather stringent ambient standards at the national level with close consultation between the central government and local governments as to how these standards can best be attained. There can be no doubt that, within the context of the Japanese system, business has had substantial input into the standards which were established. Beyond that, the actual implementation of the policies has involved extensive negotiations between local governments and the affected business enterprises. There has been substantial flexibility and room for compromise as business and government have worked together to meet stringent but mutually accepted standards. There has been a maximum of persuasion and a minimum of coercion in the implementation of the standards.[22] Wherever possible business has been given some latitude as to how pollution standards were met. For example, a plant may be allocated a certain level of permitted emissions but left free to allocate these emissions among the various facilities within the plant.[23]

It is difficult to render a judgment concerning the economic efficiency of Japan's pollution control policies. In general Japan has followed the principle that the costs of pollution should be borne by stockholders of the polluting industry and/or the consumers of its product rather than by taxpayers. This is in accord with the "benefit principle" of equity which has been endorsed by the OECD as the appropriate pollution control stategy.[24] On the other hand, Japan has relied almost exclusively upon direct administrative controls and administrative guidance to implement this principle rather than the taxation of pollution emissions which is generally regarded as more efficient.

How is it that Japan has been able to avoid the rigidities which commonly characterize regulation and the bureaucracy of control? A clue is found, it seems, in the following statement by Edwin Mills and Katsutoshi Ohta. Writing some years ago, they stated that "although the formal structure of the Japanese pollution control program is similar to that of the U.S. program, there is no guarantee that it will work as badly. Much depends upon the flexibility and imaginativeness of its administrators."[25]

From the vantage point of 1984, the Japanese system seems to be working quite well indeed, and its success is in fact largely attributable to the remarkable flexibility and imaginativeness of its administrators. The spirit of compromise and the process of decision making by consensus which so permeate the Japanese system have made it possible to avoid the cost of unreasonable regulation. Although pollution control standards have been stringent, the affected industries have had substantial input into them and have been given some latitude concerning how they were to be attained. The relationship between government and business has not been the adversarial relationship which is so common in the United States, but rather one of striving cooperatively to attain common goals.

Certain characteristics of Japanese society, such as strong identification of labor with the employer and the strong identification by all elements of society with the national goals of Japan, made recognition of the pollution problem difficult so long as the major national goal was economic growth. However, once the problem was recognized these same traits have assured widespread acceptance of national goals for controlling pollution, and have provided the cooperation necessary to make a stringent pollution control policy successful.

Conclusions

Although Japan was slow to recognize the social costs of environmental pollution, she has in recent years been among the more successful of nations in dealing with this problem. Environmental legislation in Japan is perhaps the most extensive in the world, and antipollution investments higher than in any other country. Pollution levels have been substantially reduced with little apparent impact upon economic growth. While pollution control policies may not have been implemented in the economically most efficient manner, the Japanese system has at least been flexible enough to avoid the costs of unreasonable regulations and rigid bureaucracy. So long as improvements in the quality of the environment remain a matter of high national priority in Japan, she will very likely retain a position of world leadership in the development of pollution control technology and in the successful implementation of pollution control policies.

References

1. Sueo Sekiguchi, "Environmental Regulation and Japan's International Trade," *Japanese Economic Studies,* III (Summer 1975), p.108.
2. Remy Prud'homme, "Appraisal of Environmental Policies in Japan," paper

presented at the Fifth World Congress of the International Economic Association, Tokyo, 29 August-3 September, 1977.

3. Allen V. Kneese, "Analysis of Environmental Pollution," in Robert Dorfman and Nancy S. Dorfman, eds., *Economics of the Environment* (New York: W.W. Norton Co., 1972), p. 43.

4. For a more complete account of these cases see Donald R. Kelley, et.al., *The Economic Superpowers and the Environment* (San Francisco: W.H. Freeman and Co., 1976), pp. 180-196, and Ken'ichi Miyamoto, "Environmental Protection Policy in Japan: Brief History and Appraisal," paper presented at the Fifth World Congress of the International Economic Association, Tokyo, 29 August-3 September, 1977.

5. Miyamoto, "Environmental Policy in Japan: Brief History and Appraisal," pp. 6-7. To date corporations responsible for air pollution have made compensation payments of 80 billion yen. See Ken'ichi Miyamoto, "Environmental Problems and Citizens' Movements in Japan," *The Japan Foundation Newsletter,* XI (November 1983), pp. 1-12.

6. Japan Environment Agency, International Affairs Division, *Quality of the Environment in Japan: 1978,* p. 27.

7. See, for example, Miyamoto, "Environmental Policy in Japan: Brief History and Appraisal," p. 8.

8. Ibid., pp. 8-9.

9. Kelley, *et. al.,* p. 243.

10. Ibid., pp. 244-245.

11. Miyamoto, "Environmental Problems and Citizens' Movements in Japan," p. 4.

12. Japan Environment Agency, *Quality of the Environment in Japan: 1978,* pp. 42-44.

13. Ibid., pp. 54-56.

14. Ibid., pp. 45-46.

15. Ibid., p. 56.

16. Prud'homme, p. 11.

17. Hsiao Kanamori, "Japanese Economic Growth and Economic Welfare," paper presented at the Fifth World Congress of the International Economic Association, Tokyo, 29 August-3 September 1977.

18. Japan Environment Agency, International Affairs Division, *Quality of the Environment in Japan: 1981,* p.3.

19. Even in 1972 atmospheric clarity, as measured by ambient concentrations of nitrogen dioxide and high density photochemical oxidants, was much better in Tokyo than in Los Angeles. See Japan External Trade Organization, *The Environmental Control in Japan,* 1976, p. 6.

20. Japan Environment Agency, *Illustrated White Paper on the Environment in Japan: 1982,* p. 9.

21. Ibid., pp. 6-10.

22. Japan Environment Agency, *Quality of the Environment in Japan: 1978,* p. 277.

23. Ibid., p. 281.

24. Prud'homme, pp. 17-19 . Prud'homme contends that in Japan the "polluter-pays-principle" is understood as a "punish polluters principle," and that its economic efficiency is entirely coincidental.

25. Edwin S. Mills and Katsutoshi Ohta, "Urbanization and Urban Problems," in Hugh Patrick and Henry Rosovsky, *Asia's New Giant* (Washington, D.C.: The Brookings Institution, 1976), p. 738.

Polish Ecology Club Risks Government Ire by Battling Pollution

By David Brand

Written prior to the crackdown on the Solidarity movement by the Polish government, this article shows that governments can be "environmental villains" in socialist economies and that there is little "due process" by which environmentalists may seek a redress of their grievances.

Krakow, Poland—A year ago, Krystian Waksmundzki was nothing more than a noisy irritant to the local Communist Party bosses. He had lost his job as professor of geography at Jagiellonian University because of his unfortunate habit of refusing to keep his mouth shut about Poland's appalling levels of air and water pollution.

A year later, Krystian Waksmundzki is yet another of those folk heroes thrown up in Poland's year of quiet revolution. Not only are people eager to listen to him but also he and a group of fellow ecologists have helped close several of Poland's dirtiest factories, including the country's largest aluminum producer, the Skawina smelter just outside Krakow.

He still hasn't got his job back. But now that he can freely air his views in public, he's confident it's only a matter of time. "I'm waiting for justice," he says.

Mr. Waksmundzki is vice president of the Polish Ecology Club, a highly influential group of academics and businessmen that has forced Poland to face up to its deadly pollution problem. The club was formed last fall in the heady days following the rise of Solidarity, the independent trade-union movement, and now has 14 branches across the country with a total of 20,000 members.

The club could perhaps have 20 times that number of members, but the Polish government continues to be nervous about recognizing an organization whose agitation is helping to close plants in a country on the brink of economic collapse. "Until we are registered, we won't admit any more members," says Mr. Waksmundzki. "We are still an underground organization."

Poland's revolt against its dirty air and water is something that the Soviet bloc "has had coming to it for a long time," declares a Czechoslovak-born businessman living in London. "Communist governments' response to pollution control has been practically nonexistent until now," he says.

A Matter of Priorities

The reason is obvious. In the absence of public pressure, industrial development gets priority over the environment. "In the Soviet bloc, you still see factory health problems that we in the West haven't seen in 30 years," says one West European aluminum-industry executive. "It isn't that they don't have the technology for pollution controls; they don't want to spend the money—they just don't want to bother."

Krakow was a natural place for the East European revolt against pollution to begin. The medieval city has a long tradition as a center for naturalists and ecologists. It came as a terrible shock to these scientists in the late 1960's to discover that impurities in the air, such as sulphur dioxide and hydrogen fluoride, were the price being paid for Poland's headlong rush for industrial growth. Corrosive acids were eating away exquisite detail in ancient walls of stone and stucco. Roofs were being weakened. And the Vistula River was becoming gray and smelly.

The problem is partly that Krakow is a river valley; the prevailing westerly winds blow the pollutants over the city, where they often become trapped by temperature inversions. And Krakow's high humidity can turn the pollution into a sulphurous smog. Ecologists say the problem is equally the result of too many factories being built too close to the city.

Haze over the City

But when complaints were made to party officials, "they ridiculed us," reports Ecology Club member Kalmus Alexander, a Krakow architect. "When we held meetings, officials tried to prevent us, and accused us of trying to stop the building of socialism—even journalists met with censorship when they tried to write about it." Mr. Waksmundzki tried to get publicity for his cause by subterfuge, such as speaking out on radio programs that the censors had overlooked.

It did little good because the industrial growth around Krakow continued unabated, with only minimal pollution controls. The Skawina aluminum smelter was the worst offender, but the huge Lenin steelworks at Nowa Huta on the outskirts of Krakow was also spreading a gray haze over the city. "The Lenin steelworks was to have had a capacity of 1.5 million tons a year, but it was increased to six million tons without any consultation," says Mr. Waksmundzki.

Clearly, say the Ecology Club members, production was being put ahead of people. The head of environmental protection at the steelworks was also a member of the local party committee for production. "Party people wouldn't admit there was anything wrong," says Mr. Waksmundzki. "Across Poland, party people in the factories were falsifying their reports" on pollution levels.

Poland's industrial managers had taken some note of environmental demands during the 1960's by ordering plants to control their emissions. But because no standards for pollution control were set, the law was ignored.

Again in 1972, with pollution-related health problems on the rise across Poland, environmental units were formed at all factories in Poland and the order went out to install modern pollution controls. But the law wasn't obeyed, says Mieczyslaw Grzadziel, who was environmental-controls manager at the Skawina smelter. "The government wouldn't give us the money to buy the controls," Mr. Grzadziel says. "Instead, all the investment went into new plants."

As a result, health problems worsened in industrial areas across the country. "It started with bronchitis and allergies," says Mr. Waksmundzki. "Then it got much worse. The incidence of heart disease and cancer started to rise. The pollution was huge. The concentration of dangers was enormous."

Nowhere was the pollution worse than at the Skawina aluminum smelter and in the little town surrounding it. Plant officials now admit that the area had the worst health record in Poland.

Ecology Club members estimate that the plant, which had no filters at all, was disgorging pollutants more than 40 times above the limits set by law. The problem, says the plant's Mr. Grzadiel, was that the 30-year-old smelter was designed to produce only 15,000 tons a year, but by 1980 was producing at the rate of 53,000 tons.

The heaviest pollution really began in 1978 when the smelter's old generators broke down and were unable to maintain a steady supply of electric current. To keep up the yields of aluminum, the plant managers added more flux, in this case a material called aluminum fluoride. That had the effect of lowering the smelter's operating temperature, thus compensating for the loss of current. Unfortunately, the aluminum fluoride increased the emissions of hydrogen fluoride gas, which can have nasty side effects.

"The pollution was terrible," says Mr. Grzadiel. "People really began to feel it. I've been here for 30 years, and I could feel the difference."

Jacek Szostek, Solidarity's representative at the smelter, recalls how hard it was to breathe, particularly on warm days. "It started with a sore throat and then got worse," he says. Why didn't the workers complain? "People didn't like to," he says "The wages here were so high, and people were afraid of losing their jobs." Even workers that Mr. Szostek describes as being prematurely aged by their years at the smelter kept quiet.

Solidarity now knows that the plant's management was well aware of the dangerous level of pollution but ignored it in order to keep up its production quotas. Mr. Szostek says that late last year Solidarity finally obtained the data from the plant's director, who was later fired.

Last November, Skawina residents, supported by Solidarity and the Ecology Club, brought a court action against the smelter's management demanding compensation for the damage to their health. Early this year, after much wrangling, the government in Warsaw ordered the plant closed.

In recent months, a special government commission has been trying to assess the health damage. Mr. Grzadziel, the plant official, says that the findings so far are that every worker with 20 years or more service is sick. Most of the plant's 2,400 workers, he says, will retire on pensions because they are too sick to work anywhere else. "Things are so bad that I have suggested building an outpatients' department just for people affected by the pollution," he says.

Now Mr. Waksmundzki and his colleagues at the Ecology Club are turning their sights on the huge Nowa Huta steel plant. They don't want to close it, but they do want to force the government to replace the old coke furnaces and to build a new generating plant.

"The investment in environmental protection at the steel plant has been 10 times less than it should have been," he declares. The plant does have some filters, he adds, "but they're inadequate and not of the best quality."

The club's officers are aware that although they now are free to speak their minds, they are in a somewhat awkward position in a country that is hovering on the edge of bankruptcy and is facing wide-scale unemployment. "We must be careful not to be labeled as people closing down factories—we don't want that to be used against us," says Mr. Alexander, the architect.

On the other hand, the club does want to get the point across to Poles that the country must take a more sober attitude toward industrial development. "We want to prove to people that there are things more important than material goods," says Mr. Waksmundzki. "Like just breathing good air."

Remember the Amoco Cadiz

By Peter Koenig

In this case study of the breakup of the oil tanker Amoco Cadiz, *we see the magnitude of environmental damage caused by a single disaster and the frustration experienced by individuals who seek to recover for the damages they have experienced.*

"On the morning of March 16, 1978, in 30-knot winds and 15-foot swells, the ship's steering gear broke. The crew could not make repairs. The tanker's master sent out an SOS, and the German salvage tug *Pacific* responded. The rescue attempt was unsuccessful, and fourteen hours after the *Amoco Cadiz* lost its steering, high waves opened its hull on the Portsall rocks."

Because Brittany stands at the mouth of the English Channel, one of the most heavily trafficked sea lanes in the world, it seems illogical that its coast should be as dangerous as the capes off South Africa and Chile. But Brittany's shoreline was etched by glaciers. Reefs extend an unusual distance offshore, and tides and currents are violent. In March, storms blow up almost continually. The super-tanker *Amoco Cadiz,* which on calm days had looked like an imperturbable force over the seas, appeared as fragile and broken as a foundering fishing boat.

Two hundred and twenty thousand tons of crude oil spread over 400 square miles of the Atlantic. The most volatile third of this cargo evaporated, and another third sank to the ocean floor. But the remaining oil coated 200 miles of Breton coast.

The *Amoco Cadiz* briefly made world headlines when it sank in 1978. But the significance of the event rests on what has happened

---

Excerpted from article appearing in *Audubon,* March 1981. ©1981, Peter Koenig. Reprinted by permission. Peter Koenig is a freelance writer whose articles have appeared in *Psychology Today, Barron's,* and *Boardroom Reports.* He formerly worked for *Business Week.*

since—in Brittany, in Paris, in Washington, in the Chicago court where lawsuits stemming from the accident are being heard, in the laboratories of scientists studying oil pollution, in the offices of bureaucrats trying to regulate it, and in the headquarters of the oil companies responsible for it.

The *Amoco Cadiz* began its last voyage on February 4, 1978, at Ras Tanura, Saudi Arabia. It loaded more crude at Kharg Island, Iran, then set out south around Africa, bound for Lyme Bay, England, and Rotterdam, Netherlands. Six weeks later, on the morning of March 16, 1978, in 30-knot winds and 15-foot swells, the ship's steering gear broke. The crew could not make repairs. Pasquale Bardari, the tanker's Italian master, sent out an SOS, and the German salvage tug *Pacific* responded. The rescue attempt was unsuccessful, and the crew was helicoptered ashore. Fourteen hours after the *Amoco Cadiz* lost its steering, high waves opened its hull on the Portsall rocks, ultimately spilling 223,000 tons of crude.

What ensued was an international media event. Within hours of the *Amoco Cadiz* grounding, platoons of journalists, politicians, bureaucrats, scientists, and oil industry representatives descended on Brittany. Next came the cleanup workers. Eight thousand French troops and 2,000 volunteers spent tens of thousands of manhours scraping Brittany's coast, raking its beaches, skimming its tidal estuaries. They removed enough of a mousselike oil and water mixture to fill 17,700 railroad boxcars.

Then the initial toting up of damages. The *Amoco Cadiz* cargo killed hundreds of varieties of marine flora and fauna and 20,000 birds—mostly cormorants, razorbills, and puffins. "The *Amoco Cadiz* spill decimated the local marine environment the way a huge fire would decimate a forest," an on-the-scene marine biologist from the U.S. Environmental Protection Agency said. "There are fish swimming around with seventy percent of their bodies rotted away. There are beaches blanketed with the shells of dead limpets, razor clams, and heart urchins."

The spill caused an estimated $300 million in damages. Much of this sum was spent by the French government in the cleanup. But fishermen, lobstermen, seaweed collectors, and oystermen suffered personal damages as well. Farmers suffered when an oily sea-spray tainted livestock and crops. Local hoteliers suffered when tourists canceled reservations.

And there were accusations and denials. The *Amoco Cadiz* was owned by Amoco Transport Company, a Liberian corporation which is 65 percent owned by Amoco International Ltd., a Bermuda corporation, and 35 percent owned by Amoco International S.A., a Swiss corporation, both of which are wholly owned subsidiaries of Chicago-based Standard Oil Company of Indiana. During the effort to rescue the *Amoco Cadiz,* the ship's master and the captain of the tug *Pacific* became sidetracked in a dispute over the terms of the salvage contract. Via ship-to-shore phone, the two captains got their managements in Chicago and Germany embroiled. When this came to light, the French government accused Standard Oil of Indiana and the German salvage-tug company of causing the spill. Both accused parties immediately disclaimed any responsibility, as did the French government itself.

But both government and industry vowed that everything would be taken care of. Victims would be compensated. All possible steps would be taken to avoid similar disasters. The French government announced a variety of measures it was taking to safeguard Brittany's waters. Standard Oil of Indiana moved to fulfill its limited obligations under international law. It set up a fund in a Brittany court to cover economic damages, regardless of responsibility for the spill. This fund was good for a maximum $16.7 million from Standard of Indiana, plus $13.3 million from a special industry fund—$270 million short of the estimated damages.

At this point, the media event ended and the *Amoco Cadiz* disappeared from the news. At this point, our story begins.

When the *Torrey Canyon* sank off the south coast of England in March 1967, it sparked worldwide interest in the problem of oil pollution of the seas. When the *Argo Merchant* sank off Nantucket in December 1976, it triggered action in Washington which resulted in the reasonably tough Port and Tanker Safety Act of 1978. By the time the *Amoco Cadiz* sank, however, the public was inured to the sight of oiled birds and beaches. The disaster did spur the French to take the lead from the United States in the fight against oil pollution. Otherwise, not much has happened.

There have been studies of the ecological consequences of the *Amoco Cadiz* spill. Since 1978, 125 French and American scientists have been monitoring Brittany's beaches, bays, and estuaries. Their findings suggest it will be ten years before the observable effects of the *Amoco Cadiz* spill disappear—the same length of time it took for the observable effects of the 120,000 tons of Kuwaiti crude spilled from the *Torrey Canyon* to disappear.

But the world public no longer cares. The shock value of supertanker accidents is gone. Scientists have not been able to prove that oil in the seas causes irreparable damage, or that it poses a health hazard to humans.

When the *Amoco Cadiz* disintegrated off Brittany, the local population was outraged. Some of the anger, and the talk one still hears of bombs and sabotage, were prompted by the perceived insult of the spill rather than by an objective assessment of damages sustained. But the grievances of many Bretons are entirely genuine.

Seaside strollers first noticed oil pollution in the 1920's, when they began stepping on tar balls. Scientists first became alarmed about oil pollution in the 1950's. The body politic became alarmed in 1967, when the *Torrey Canyon* went down. Since then, oil pollution has risen and fallen as a public issue, but industry practices and policies haven't been changed significantly.

The basic points of dispute between environmentalists and oilmen are straightforward. Tankers spill oil when they dump dirty ballast water, when they run aground, collide, or explode. Environmentalists maintain that the amount of oil spilled as a percentage of total shipments is too large, and that oil companies should spend some of their profits to improve tanker operating standards.

Oil-company executives maintain that the amount of oil spilled is insignificant. They argue that the cost of improving tanker standards would outweigh the benefits, and that those costs would have to be absorbed by consumers.

Debate over these points might have been dramatic. But it became technical and dull. Environmentalists who rallied against oil pollution in the late 1960's and early 1970's found themselves debating industry experts on the principles of naval architecture and marine engineering. They found themselves locked in battle over the rules of conduct in shipyards and ports and harbors, and on the bridges and in the bowels of tankers. The public was bored.

A brief history: In 1954, delegates to an international conference in London outlawed the discharge of ballast water containing more than 100 parts per million of oil from tankers within 50 miles of shore. Tanker masters ignored this toothless dictum, and in the late

1960s environmentalists began pressing for segregated ballast tanks.

Industry opposes segregated ballast. Exxon has calculated that the cost of retrofitting the world's 1,300 largest tankers would be $4 billion. But, as environmentalists stepped up political pressure after each big spill, industry made two compromises.

First, it agreed to change the method of loading tankers. The new method involved decanting ballast water from the bottom of the tanks, letting the oily residue in the tanks settle, then loading crude oil on top of this residue. This "load-on-top" method helped keep oil and water separate.

Second, industry agreed to wash the tanks with streams of crude oil after every third or fourth voyage. Crude-oil washing reduces the amount of residue in tanks and thus the amount that goes overboard with ballast.

A quarter of a century after environmentalists identified dirty ballast water as a pollutant, separate tanks for oil and water aboard tankers are still a rarity.

Meanwhile, environmentalists and the oil industry also have battled over what to do about tanker accidents. Twice as much oil goes into the oceans via dirty ballast water, but the effects of tanker accidents are concentrated. Eighty percent of tanker accidents occur within ten miles of shore; 30 percent in and around the English Channel alone.

Environmentalists want tankers to be built like airplanes—with backup systems: double hulls, separate main and auxiliary steering gears, twin rather than single screws and rudders, and bow thrusters—reversible screws athwart tanker bows that improve maneuverability. Environmentalists also want more sophisticated collision-avoidance navigational equipment, and shore-based traffic-control systems.

Industry opposes most of these measures as costly and ineffectual. "Human performance is the overriding factor which determines how safe merchant shipping will be," W. O. Gray, an Exxon naval architect, declared to an Oil Companies International Marine Forum in Washington, D.C., in 1978. Eighty percent of tanker accidents, Gray said, are caused by incompetence, inattentive watchkeeping, ambiguous master-pilot relationships, faulty operational procedures, poor physical fitness, excessive fatigue, alcohol abuse, or excessive turnover. Gray concluded that the way to minimize accidents was to upgrade inspections and manning requirements.

Environmentalists agree that human frailty causes most accidents. But they argue that it would be prudent to have as many safety features as possible.

Under pressure, industry has installed some new safety equipment on tankers. But the rate of accidents still increases. In the eleven years between the wrecks of the *Torrey Canyon* and *Amoco Cadiz*, there were 60 major accidents that dumped 1,640,000 tons of oil into the oceans. Since the *Amoco Cadiz* sank, the amount of oil spilled per accident has continued to accelerate.

This history only begins to explain the failure of environmentalists to do much about oil pollution. Not only have they become entangled in debates that grow ever more obscure, they have ended up debating the wrong parties—governmental and quasi-governmental authorities responsible for regulating pollution rather than the polluters themselves.

Port states and coastal states make rules concerning oil pollution. Flag states—the countries where shipowners register their fleets—make more rules. There is the international legal regime developed by an alphabet soup of United Nations agencies, and the 153-nation Law of the Sea Conference which, since 1973, has been trying to balance the rights of coastal states to regulate their territorial waters with the rights of ships to free navigation. Then there is the body of private admiralty law, and the organizations the shipping industry has established to regulate itself.

This fragmentation of authority is one of the oil industry's great strengths. Companies like Exxon and Mobil and Standard Oil of Indiana are global enterprises whose shock troops consist of casual labor—roustabouts and gas-station attendants—but whose generals form an industrial peerage of high sophistication and intelligence. They are able to pit nations against each other the way real-estate developers looking for shopping mall sites pit towns against towns.

The oil industry further benefits from weak enforcement of such anti-pollution statutes as are on the books. The enforcers deal more familiarly with the shipping industry than they do with the public they are supposed to protect. But even if they kept themselves at a greater distance from the industry, their success would be limited. For the sanctions against polluting the oceans, in the main, are laughable.

I learned just how laughable when I called round to the agencies responsible for regulating oil pollution.

First, I reached the American Bureau of Shipping in New York, one of the ship-classification societies established by industry to insure that vessels are fit for their intended service. The ABS had classified the *Amoco Cadiz* a Maltese Cross A-1 Circle E Oil Carrier—one of the best. I got through to Kenneth Sheehan, ABS's counsel. I asked how ABS worked.

"We look at a ship's plans," he said. "We have surveyors in the shipyards. We have surveyors in the steel mills, and where equipment is tested. We have surveyors at the drydock tests. Then at sea trials. Then, periodically after construction, we check the ship. Quarterly for cargo gear. Yearly for machinery. Once every six years in drydock."

I asked what happened when ABS found something substandard.

"The owners know they can't slip anything by on us," Sheehan said. "And they wouldn't want to."

"So you never find anything substandard?"

"Of course we do. Then we issue a report detailing what needs to be done."

"And the ship doesn't sail until the repairs are made?"

"That depends."

"How many sailing days have been lost by ABS-rated ships as a result of your finding something substandard?"

"We don't keep records like that," Sheehan said.

I called Liberian maritime authorities, for the *Amoco Cadiz* had flown the Liberian flag. My first contact was with Captain William A. Chadwick, chief of the Marine Investigation Division, Marine Safety Department, Bureau of Maritime Affairs, Ministry of Finance, Republic of Liberia. Captain Chadwick is an American, and works out of Liberia's office in Reston, Virginia.

"To be honest, you can't enforce the regulations designed to minimize oil pollution," he said. "It's difficult, for example, to tell if a ship is following the procedures for load-on-top."

"What happens when you do find a ship in violation of Liberian regulations?" I asked.

"We detain it," Captain Chadwick said.

"How many ships did you detain in 1979 and for how long?"

"I wouldn't have that information. Perhaps you'd better talk to the deputy commissioner."

Alister Crombie, an Englishman, deputy commissioner of Liberia's

Bureau of Maritime Affairs and also of Liberia's Reston office, did not have precise figures on Liberian ships detained in 1979. He did say that Liberia had fined 18 of the 2,500 ships flying its flag in 1979. The maximum fine for oil pollution, he said, is $2,000.

I called the U.S. Coast Guard, the agency that has primary responsibility for shipping in U.S. waters. In 1977, in response to the public furor over the *Argo Merchant,* the Coast Guard began inspecting foreign tankers entering U.S. waters. Since the boarding program began, the Coast Guard has conducted 5,835 examinations on 1,700 ships, during which 2,857 deficiencies have been brought to light. After making a dozen phone calls, I gave up trying to find out how many sailing days were lost and fines levied as a result of those deficiencies.

When I was in London on my way to Brittany, I visited the Intergovernmental Maritime Consultative Organization, the United Nations agency with primary international responsibility for dealing with oil pollution. IMCO was created by convention in Geneva in 1948. Ten years later, enough nations ratified the convention to make it binding. But IMCO was given no power to regulate. Instead, it was given power to make treaties at conferences. These conferences are influenced, if not dominated, by industry. And two-thirds of the delegates at a conference must approve a resolution before it is included in a treaty. Then each treaty has to be ratified; this takes an average of five to eight years. Then, after the treaty is ratified, it may or may not be enforced, depending upon what the ship-classification societies, flag states, and port states do.

IMCO's headquarters stand on the north side of London's Green Park. There I met Thomas Busha, an American and number two in IMCO's legal-affairs division. After the *Amoco Cadiz* sinking, Busha wrote a definitive paper on the implications of that event for international admiralty law. I wanted to ask him about those implications, and also about IMCO resolution A. 237 (VII) passed in October 1971: "The achievement by 1975, if possible but certainly by the end of the decade, of the complete elimination of the willful and intentional pollution of the seas by oil."

When I mentioned this resolution, Busha said, "Things were more complicated than we thought." I pressed. He grew vague. Fifteen minutes later, his phone rang. Hanging up, he muttered, "My boss wants to see me. Matter of some urgency." Then he vanished.

Over the past five years, the amount of oil going into the oceans via dirty ballast water has remained constant. The amount going in as a result of tanker accident has quadrupled. In 1975, 188,042 tons of oil spilled into the oceans as a result of tanker groundings, collisions, and explosions. In 1979, the total was 752,533 tons.

A trial to determine why the *Amoco Cadiz* went down, who was at fault, and what damages shall be paid to whom will be heard in the U.S. District Court for Northern Illinois. Ten lawsuits filed in various U.S. courts have been consolidated into one case involving seven categories of parties—Standard Oil of Indiana, the Republic of France, various private plaintiffs, the shipbuilders, tug owners, cargo owners, and insurers.

The case is sufficiently complicated to make the chancery suit in Dicken's *Bleak House* look simple. The question of right and wrong has long since been subordinated to the maneuverings of opposing teams of attorneys. When I called round New York admiralty law firms to get help in understanding the case, no one could talk freely because all of the firms were involved in the case. In essence, the victims of the *Amoco Cadiz* spill say that Standard Oil of Indiana did it, and that, to a lesser extent, the shipbuilders and tug owners did it, too. Standard Indiana says that God did it, and that if God didn't do it, then the tug owners did. But not Standard Indiana.

Standard Indiana has vigorously contested all claims for compensatory and punitive damages stemming from the *Amoco Cadiz* oil spill. It maintains, for example, that the French government's claim for $300 million has no merit.

The parties suing Standard Indiana will try to prove that the *Amoco Cadiz* ran aground as a result of negligence, and that the oil company's management knew of the negligent conditions which caused the accident.

In documents filed by Standard Indiana, the company has argued that U.S. courts do not have jurisdiction to hear the complaints, that liability is limited to the value of the *Amoco Cadiz* after it sank, that the *Amoco Cadiz*'s crew tried to repair the ship's steering gear after it broke, that this was impossible due to heavy seas, and that the subsequent failure to keep the tanker off the Portsall rocks was due to the "perils of the sea" and/or "the negligence of others for whom the plaintiffs are not responsible."

The arguments will not be submitted to a jury for many months. The lawyers retained by the various parties, and a second tier of lawyers retained by them, are still taking depositions in Chicago, London, Brest, Genoa, and elsewhere from scores of witnesses. As usual, the suits stemming from the *Amoco Cadiz* oil spill are taking on a life of their own.

But the case in Chicago is worth environmentalists' attention. First, the private suits against Standard Indiana represent an attempt by a handful of local citizens to get their day in court against a giant oil company. This is no easy task. After the *Torrey Canyon* sank, English citizens suing that ship's owner, Union Oil Company of California, never did make it to court. They never got a penny. The governments of Britain and France, meanwhile, settled out of court with Union Oil for $7.5 million—about $20 million less than total estimated damages.

Second, the French government's suit incenses the oil industry. "By God, if the French want to fight, we'll give them a fight!" Claude Walder, director of the Oil Companies International Marine Forum, exclaimed during an interview. It is not the amount of money at issue that is upsetting. Standard Indiana's liability is indemnified under the Tanker Owners Voluntary Agreement Concerning Liability for Oil Pollution, and under a policy the company holds with the London Steamship Owners Mutual Insurance Association, a self-insurance club to which 250 shippers and oil companies belong. Standard Indiana's annual reports reassure shareholders: "The suits are not expected to have a material adverse effect on Standard's consolidated financial position."

What upsets the oil industry about the French government's suit in Chicago is the tear it makes in carefully tailored arrangements to handle major oil spills. Oil executives argue that France should have sued in French courts, not American ones. If France refuses to play by the rules, others may also refuse, and this amounts to a loss of control by the oil industry.

Oil pollution of the seas is going to get worse, not better. To make this prediction, one need only glance at the economics of the tanker business. There are currently 4,000 tankers plying the oceans. Thirty-four percent are owned by oil companies; 6 percent by governments; the remaining 60 percent by independent operators. In an ideal world for the oil industry, the oil companies would turn a nice profit on their own tankers, while the independents thrived too, providing the extra carrying capacity needed at times of peak shipments, and absorbing some of the overhead costs of keeping the world's tanker fleet ready when oil shipments were down.

That ideal world existed for about 20 years—from the closing of the Suez Canal in 1956 until the Arab oil embargo of 1973-74. Over that period, the world's tanker tonnage increased seven-fold. During that period, too, the oil industry established the flag-of-convenience concept with the blessing of the U.S. government.

Flags of convenience are good for shipowners. Incorporation in flag-of-convenience states is a mere formality. Flag-of-convenience ships can be built and repaired anywhere. Their crews can be of any nationality; by contrast, the crews of U.S.-flag ships must be 75 percent American. Most important, flag-of-convenience states impose no income tax on profits earned by tankers.

But flags of convenience are bad for the oceans. Ships sailing under the Panamanian, Liberian, and Cypriot flags have accident records that are much worse than those of ships sailing under U.S., British, and Japanese flags. American seamen tell horror stories about flag-of-convenience ships. To qualify for a mariner's license from a flag-of-convenience state, all one need do is produce a license from another maritime state. Mariners' licenses are easy to forge, and so there are many unqualified officers in responsible billets aboard flag-of-convenience ships.

Furthermore, flag-of-convenience ships operate under lax safety regulations. For example, U.S. ships go into drydock every two years; Liberian ships every four or five years. U.S. seamen may spend no more than six months a year at sea; Liberian seamen, 11 months.

Until the Arab oil embargo, owning tankers had been extremely profitable. Since 1974, when OPEC began levering-up the price of oil, there has been an industry-wide depression because there are too many tankers. There are too many tankers because owners did not foresee that rising oil prices would flatten world demand for crude. Current tanker capacity now approximates 300 million deadweight tons, while the demand for tanker capacity is only 200 million dwt. Ten percent of the world's tanker fleet is mothballed in Norwegian fjords and elsewhere; 10 percent lies idle in port at any one time; while 30 percent is "slow-steaming," operating below capacity. At the same time, tanker operating costs are multiplying. In 1973, fuel cost $20 a ton; in 1979, $180 a ton.

These economics mean that few new tankers are being built, which means that the world's tanker fleet is aging. Naval architects estimate that the metal used to build tankers lasts ten years before it begins to fatigue. Since most of the fleet was built prior to 1974, the seaworthiness of many tankers will become increasingly uncertain after 1984. "There has been a serious spate of tanker accidents in the last eighteen months," J. C. S. Horrocks, secretary-general of the International Chamber of Shipping, admitted in an interview. "It is difficult to say that the depressed state of the market is not connected with this fact."

Faced with this trend, environmentalists can forget about oil pollution—chalk it up as a victory for industry—and rush to the battles more recently in the news, such as Love Canal or Three Mile Island. Or they can pause to reflect, and assume that their failure to prevail on this matter may portend failure on other issues unless they join the struggle to make control of the Earth's resources more democratic.

Counting the Cost of Acid Rain

By Ross Howard and Michael Perley

The major barrier to implementing a policy for dealing with acid rain is the cost of such an undertaking. This article by two Canadians shows that doing nothing about acid rain is also very costly.

To date almost the only discussion of acid rain in economic terms has focused on the cost of turning it off. In surprisingly short order, governments and industry have been able to project frightening multibillion-dollar expenditures needed if acid rain sources are to be curbed in North America. One recent prediction runs close to $5 billion over a decade for Canada alone.

There's much to suggest that such sums are exaggerated, based as they are on traditional technology and corporate analyses, but much more important, these costs are grossly deceptive. They loom as large as they do—casting shadows of galloping inflation, corporate bankruptcy, job loss and skyrocketing consumer prices—because they stand alone. The other cost of acid rain—economic damage—has been left unconsidered.

The task of calculating acid rain damage is admittedly far more intricate than the abatement estimates, and governments and decision-makers have so far chosen to ignore the question because they don't know its exact dimensions. But there is already some evidence that the cost of acid rain is so enormous that it could undermine the financial stability of entire regional and national economies. And while the detailed damage reports are still unavailable, there is much to gain by recognizing the enormity of what is at stake. The case of the Canadian sport fishing industry illustrates some of the costs of acid rain.

Excerpted from *Acid Rain* by Ross Howard, published by McGraw-Hill, New York, $6.95. Copyright. Ross Howard is the environment editor at the Toronto Star, and Michael Perley is executive director of the Canadian Environmental Law Research Foundation.

Operators of the 1,600 lodges and road's end resorts across northern Ontario are none too optimistic these days. As they told provincial northern affairs ministry researchers in a 1978 study, their costs were being driven up and their resources, such as the yellow pickerel, northern pike and brook, rainbow and lake trout that attracted the Americans (who make up 65% of the clientele) were declining. Nearly 85% of those Americans who traveled, on average, 700 miles to the north and spent $675 per visit came for only one reason: the fishing. Those Americans, and Canadians, generated more than $120 million in annual direct and indirect revenue, creating more than 10% of the 200,000 northern jobs available.

As the government report also noted, the further east across the wilderness of Ontario the researchers moved, the more and more discouraged they found the fishing-lodge operators. The report did not mention that the northeast was the area most heavily rained upon by acid, and preferred to attribute fish decline to cyclical populations, over-fishing and unspecified urban and industrial pollution. The report offered numerous recommendations for more studies. It suggested increased fish restocking, as well as a public-relations campaign to remind us all that our aquatic resources are under stress. It also included the ominous warning that "fishermen are going to have to accept declines in quality standards."

But as one fishing-lodge operator discovered in 1979, much more than just quality was at stake. Jerry Liddle, a young operator whose family runs three lodges in the northern Wawa area, approached the Ontario Ministry of the Environment in 1978 for funds to conduct a major study of acid rain and its implications for his industry. As Liddle correctly suspected, nothing like this had been considered in any detail by the provincial government (and certainly not by the northern affairs ministry study).

However, Liddle received only a few thousand dollars, and not from any of the policy-making, long-range research divisions of the environment ministry but from the already alarmed and overburdened fishery and water quality team. The money barely covered Liddle's costs of duplication and postage for a simple questionnaire, but it was enough for him to come to some rough conclusions by late 1979. His fishing-lodge colleagues knew little or nothing about acid rain—but they knew their fishery was declining. As he summarized, "The trend is toward smaller and smaller fish, a lack of large or spawning fish, and increasing difficulty in catching fish."

His summary bore remarkable similarity to the conclusions University of Toronto researcher Harold Harvey reached exactly a decade earlier concerning the Killarney lakes of near-northern Ontario, lakes that had been killed by acid rain.

"The quality of the resource base has been going downhill, especially in the last 10 years," Liddle added. Drawing from environment ministry data on the beleaguered lakes of northeastern Ontario, Liddle concluded that almost 600 fishing lodges could go belly up within 20 years if the acid rainfall continued, killing about 6,000 jobs and $28 million of annual income in the area. The environment ministry received his report with little comment, but Liddle had uncovered the tip of an iceberg. The fishing lodges he studied serve only 12% of the more than 16 million fishing "occasions" that take place in an average year. According to government statistics, almost one out of every two Ontario male residents and one out of three females go fishing, spending an average of $154 a year on their hooks, rods, bait, hipwaders and so forth. Combined with the Americans who come north, these fishermen spent an incredible $450 million in 1975, a typical year. There are already five people fishing for every available fish in the northeast. And this is where acid rain is falling most heavily, on the 140 lakes already known to be acid-dead and on the estimated 48,000 lakes similarly jeopardized.

In early 1980, the Ontario government commissioned its first study on the financial impact of dead lakes. By then the six-million-acre Adirondack state park to the south of New York , where equally intense acid rain was being monitored, offered indications of what Ontario might find. Each year, until recently, at least 1.7 million fishing trips were registered in the park, generating an estimated $16 million in the local economy. But in 1976, after the confirmation of more than 100 acid-dead lakes, state park researchers estimated that nearly $1.5 million in fishing expenditures had been lost.

A more detailed study in 1978 based just on the dead lakes—the total had risen to 170—showed a direct annual loss of $370,000. Applied to all 3,000 lakes in the park, the economic loss was estimated at "probably much higher than $1.7 million a year," the parks commissioner Anna La Bastille reported.

But the Adirondack figures are only a foretaste of what Ontario soon could be paying for the acid in its 48,000 threatened lakes. Tourism is the second-largest industry in the province, directly accounting for $5 billion in annual revenue and 470,000 jobs—nearly

6% of the total gross provincial product and 11% of all the jobs—
and nearly $900 million of this is spent just in the area from the
Bruce Peninsula to the Muskoka-Haliburton boundary and all of the
northeast. Much of that area is the most acid-vulnerable too. It's the
cottage heartland of Ontario, containing almost two-thirds of 250,000
such getaway retreats, which foster 50 million person-days of relaxation each year (the equivalent of 7 million people each spending
one week "at the cottage"). Those cottagers directly spend $200
million a year in the area.

It's not easy to quantify what a lake with no fish means to a person with a $40,000 investment in his cottage. But for 70 years city
dwellers have been spending massive amounts of money for the
privilege of owning a piece of nature by an unspoiled lake. The most
popular tourist activities of Ontario residents are cottaging, boating,
fishing and camping.

The full value of this near-northern wilderness exceeds dollar
statistics. Consider Gord Mewhiney, spokesman for the Federation
of Ontario Cottagers Associations, in his summation to the legislative
committee on resource development in 1979: "What is happening
in front of our cottages? We were once told of water pollution, then
we were told not to eat the fish because of mercury and now we
are told that our lakes simply don't have a hope in hell. Our northern area, our lifestyle, it's all jeopardized. Put a plug on acid rain,
now before it is too late."

Treasurer of Ontario Frank Miller may offer multimillion-dollar
enticements to automobile manufacturers to build factories in the
south, but he is also the first to face delegations of worried resort
owners from Muskoka. After all, he got his start operating a Muskoka
resort (and still does). Muskoka is his constituency. He knows the
value of the industry. And his counterpart ministers at the provincial industry and tourism department know it; they've lent more
than $56 million to the industry since 1966 to build it up. By 1979
tourism loans, particularly for resort rejuvenation, were taking up
20% of all annual business development loans. The Ministry of Industry and Tourism boasts that its good works are "synonymous
with economic growth" in Ontario, and projects that by the year
2000 "Tourism will be Canada's leading contributor in income,
employment and export earnings." Under existing policies, acid rain
will continue to fall unabated until the year 2001.

Ontario's environment minister, Harry Parrott, once tossed off an unexplained estimate of $500 million a year as a possible acid rain damage cost, when he spoke before the legislative committee. But the economic effects of acid rain on tourism could, almost like the physical effects of acid rain, begin unnoticed and be attributed to something else.

Ontario tourism operators objected to newspaper reports about acid rain in the late spring of 1978, calling it the worst possible publicity for the beginning of the tourist season. Who can blame them? And yet, future seasons may never happen if the conspiracy of silence continues. Dr. David Schlinder of the federal Freshwater Institute feared the worst when he told the committee in early 1979: "There's been much talk of the jobs lost if major polluters are forced to curb their emissions. But I hope somebody is thinking of the thousands of tourist operators who will be out of business in 10 to 15 years if there are no controls on emissions."

Nearly 5,000 miles to the northeast, across the Atlantic in Sweden, there are details on exactly what is at stake in waters washed with acid. A 1978 government study, for example, calculated that Sweden faces a $16.5-million annual loss in inland commercial fisheries owing to acidified waters. Sport fishing and tourism losses total another $50 million annually. Coastal fishing for species that spawn in fresh water (like Atlantic salmon) wasn't calculated in that report, beyond a note that 85% of the migration to the sea would be affected. The report was based on the assumption that the productivity of the fish "sooner or later in principle will be zero if the deposition of acid continues at the present rate." And, as the report dispassionately concluded, in the most heavily acidified regions "the disappearance of incomes from fishing and tourism can jeopardize the possibilities for the people to exist and make a living in these areas."

At a UN conference in Stockholm in 1971, the Swedes also considered the damages to forests, property and human health, in dollar terms. Based on the unfortunate likelihood that acid-rain source emissions, particularly from Europe, would remain the same as had been measured in 1965—a condition the Swedes admitted "is thought to be the most realistic"—by the year 2000 Sweden will suffer a 13% decline in forest growth. "A direct estimate in monetary terms (of such a condition) hardly does justice to the nature of the damage," the report added, but "the most informative figures are probably that 7% of the raw material base of the country's forest and pulp industry will have disappeared by the year 2000." And that would equal a minimum cost (loss) of $40 million a year, by the year 2000.

More than forests are at stake. Agricultural crops are worth $8.9 billion per year in Canada. There is strong evidence that what grows in the soil is affected by the acid rainfall. The extensive experiments by the US Environmental Protection Agency (EPA) at Corvallis, Ore., and others at Oak Ridge, Tenn., Hawaii and the experimental tobacco plots north of Toronto all show damage to crops such as radishes, beans and tobacco. Matching direct damage with subsoil degradation may take years of research before precise answers are available. For now, the only sure conclusion is that untold millions of dollars worth of agricultural crops are at risk. And yet, to date there are no Canadian or American policies to counteract this risk. It wasn't until October 1979 that either country formally acknowledged that "there is every indication that acid rainfall is deleterious to crops."

Not all of the economic calculations of acid-rain damage need be based on too few studies and "reasonable predictions." There is one aspect of the damage that is clear-cut now, and enormously expensive—property damage. Long before Sweden concluded that sulphur dioxide and associated air pollutants were costing $20 million a year in metal, stone, and wood corrosion, engineers and scientists around the world had charted rates of air pollution damage. To cite only one example, Cleopatra's Needle, the stone obelisk moved from Egypt to London, has suffered more deterioration in the damp, dirty, and acid atmosphere of London in 80 years than it had in the preceeding 3,000 years of its history. Cement, concrete, metals, paints, even fabrics are victims—flags fade faster and are tattered sooner in cities such as Los Angeles or Chicago than in cities of cleaner air. In 1978 the US president's Council on Environmental Quality estimated property damage due to acid rain at $2 billion a year. In 1977 the National Research Council of Canada reported that sulphur emissions in air cause an estimated $285 million in damage per year in building deterioration, including $70 million in exterior paint damage alone. The distinction between direct damage by air laden with local sulphur dioxide and wind-blown sulphuric acid from distant sources is not clear yet, but the total damage due to sulphur emissions in one form or another, is obvious. As the International Joint Commission reported in 1979, 50% of the corrosion of cars may be due to acid rain.

And finally, there are health costs. One study estimated that at least 5,000 Canadians may die each year because of acid-rain-related sulphates; other researchers put the figure at 187,000 deaths a year in the US. The dollar value of life in North America is inestimable on an individual basis; on a national basis economists and health care professionals estimate that premature death causes an average of $80,000 loss in income alone. As the professionals are the first to admit, such calculations are "highly insensitive" to such factors as spouses who don't earn income, and medical costs and lost income not directly attributed to illnesses leading to death. But the American EPA, by calculating time and productivity lost, and hospital and compensation costs, estimates that air pollution is costing the country more than $10 billion a year. The Council on Environmental Quality estimates that sulphur dioxide alone causes $1.7 billion worth of health care costs each year in the US. The costs will almost inevitably be higher by the time research has pinned down exact totals.

No one knows exactly what acid rain is already costing North America, or will cost if the problem increases. Future costs, however, go well beyond the merely economic. As biologist Tom Hutchison of the University of Toronto told the Ontario legislature committee, "Deterioration of our lake environments, of the fisheries and the recreational aspects that go with it, is going to hit a lot of people very hard . . . If we allow our short-term solutions to problems to devastate that environment, as we are on the way to doing now with acid rain, I think we are going to have to do a lot of answering to a lot of people in 15 to 20 years' time."

Unfortunately for Hutchison and that environment, 15 years' time is beyond the normal vision and term of office of those making the decisions now.

Chemical Warfare

By Ross Howard

This author argues that the regulatory and political pressure experienced by Canadian chemical companies has been caused largely by their failure to mount a creditable public relations and consumer education effort.

There's a dirty, dishonest conspiracy afoot in Canada. If successful, it will cost Canadians billions of dollars, lay plagues upon the land and destroy decades of trust and tradition. Or so says the chemical pesticide industry of Canada. And with bellicosity reminiscent of bygone industry-environmentalist wars, the 60 member firms of the Ottawa-based Canadian Agricultural Chemicals Association (CACA) have gone on the offensive.

The "meddlesome environmentalists" and public health advocates, according to the CACA, are spreading vicious rumors about the industry's product. They're challenging the safety and wisdom of using an annual $250 million worth of chemical insecticides, herbicides and disinfectants in the nation's homes and gardens, farms and factories. The mostly urban guerrillas have "a dedication to having the chemical industry legislated out of existence," says the CACA. Should they succeed, Canadians would face soaring food prices and plummeting crop production, a decline in foreign income and another 2,000 or more workers on the unemployment rolls.

The CACA takes the issue and its combative stance very seriously. Its September 1980 annual meeting in St. Andrews, New Brunswick, was not unlike a Vietnam-War-era council of generals and hawks. Outgoing president James C. Bartlett of N.M. Bartlett Inc., a Beamsville, Ont., chemicals firm, hinted at deeper alien motivations behind the "wild-eyed campaign" of the critics and "prejudiced, ill-informed activists and by the entourage of exploitive journalists, commentators and just plain crackpots they attract." He warned of

Excerpted from "Chemical Warfare," *Canadian Business,* Vol. 54, No. 6, July, 1981. Reprinted by permission. Ross Howard is environment editor at the Toronto Star.

the enemy's "domino strategy" of first knocking one vulnerable chemical pesticide off the market and then using its demise as precedent for attacking others. It had already happened in two cases. He criticized bureaucrats and legislators too timid to stand up against the trend, and to thundering applause declared it was time to "get right into the arena with the activists."

Incoming president Alexander D. St. Clair, then of Diamond Shamrock Canada Ltd. of Toronto and now president of St. Clair Consultants Ltd., launched the association into a program of stepped-up appeals to farmers to fight for their chemicals, intense political lobbying and a media campaign for the hearts and minds of "our urban womenfolk" unduly swayed by critics' claims that their food was chemically poisoned. "We're ready to confront any group on any facet of agricultural chemicals issues. . . . Not only reasonable environmental people but also cultists of all degree of irrationality," St. Clair averred. He didn't specify which was which among the critics, which include the Toronto Board of Health, Saskatchewan Environment, the Canadian Environmental Advisory Council, the Canadian Environmental Law Association and occasionally the US Environmental Protection Agency (EPA).

But the unusually aggressive campaign by a still-powerful and prosperous industry whose agents and representatives are in every community, has been fraught with setbacks. Seven months after St. Clair's declaration, another six pesticides had been pulled off the market as dangerous and the most widely used herbicide in the country, 2,4-D, was facing new restrictions. The CACA was back in its Ottawa foxhole, having withdrawn from a commitment to discuss pesticide safety at a St. Lawrence Centre public forum held last March in Toronto by the Toronto Department of Public Health and the Canadian Environmental Law Association.

In part the industry was betrayed by one of its own kind: an American firm that allegedly miscalculated or falsified vital tests used to validate pesticides' safety. In part the industry hides behind a constrained and ill-equipped federal Canadian bureaucracy that learned of the disturbing test errors in 1977 but only reluctantly speaks of their implications today. And in large part the industry's vehement assertions of pesticide safety are betrayed by the fact that about 100 specific pesticides—nearly 25 percent of the total in use—are on the market in Canada now with no assurance of their long-term safeness for people and the environment.

It began in 1977 with what's known as the IBT affair. Industrial Bio-Test Laboratories Inc. of Northbrook, Ill., one of the largest of 70 private toxicological laboratories on the continent, was discovered by the EPA to have serious "deficiencies" in tests it had conducted on 123 pesticides for possible links with cancer, birth defects, nerve damage and metabolic problems. The tests, done for 31 manufacturers and two US agencies, had been used alone or in conjunction with other tests to gain EPA approval for the pesticides.

Private labs are typically the second and critical screening through which manufacturers run their products, at a cost of as much as $10 million each over several years, to determine the pesticide's toxicity. The reports attesting to the safety of prescribed use are a major determinant in US licensing procedures. The EPA used a total of 4,300 IBT test reports to mid-1977 in its approval process.

Many of the first 123 products validated by suspect IBT findings are manufactured by a lot of familiar companies, including Abbot Laboratories Ltd., Chemagro Corp., Chevron Chemical Co., Dow Chemical Co., Penwalt Corp., UpJohn Co., and even the US Department of Agriculture. Their uses range from aerosol house and garden sprays to wheat treatments, bacterial poisons and common flea collars. The EPA ordered manufacturers to review and clarify the accuracy of the suspect tests, warned that more could be added and triggered an on-going grand-jury investigation into the IBT testing.

Several other countries, including Canada, have based their own licensing decisions on IBT data. According to the CACA, 96 percent of active ingredients in pesticides in use in Canada are imported; the industry simply blends them; only one firm—Uniroyal Ltd.— actually makes raw product; the majority of chemical firms in Canada are foreign-owned. And the US and Europe are the main suppliers of the raw toxics. In Canada, the procedure for approving their use is doubly based on trust. Federal agencies routinely accept Canadian firms' safety tests that, in turn, use information or approvals based on tests conducted by US parent companies or labs such as IBT. Ottawa sets general standards for maximum dosages, but it is the companies' responsibility to determine that the products aren't dangerous.

The IBT controversy revealed a breakdown in the honor system. Health and Welfare Canada issued a brief statement in 1977 acknowledging the US discoveries and announcing an investigation. No chemicals were named. It wasn't until June 1980 that Ottawa had anything more to say on the affair, and by then the environmentalists were way ahead. They were armed with US information and fortified with examples such as Agent Orange, a forest defoliant used in Vietnam that has produced liver and skin damage, cancers and mutagenicity among US Vietnam veterans who were exposed to it. Two ingredients of Agent Orange, 2,4,5-T and 2,4-D, were on the Canadian market. The critics argued that IBT-tested products could be on the Canadian market with no assurances of safety. Farmers and the pesticide industry termed such accusations groundless and irresponsible. The critics pressed to know what the regulatory agencies and the industry knew about IBT.

Some provincial agencies weren't interested in knowing it themselves. "We were aware of the IBT problem almost three years ago," admitted Alex Chisholm, executive secretary of the Ontario-appointed Pesticides Advisory Committee, in mid-1980. "But it's not our function to ask. That's up to the Ontario environment ministry." Chisholm's committee advises the provincial environment ministry on pesticide safety and usage. John Onderdonk, head of technical support services in the pesticides control section of the provincial environment ministry, declared, "We rely on the Pesticides Advisory Committee and the feds."

Surprisingly, it was Saskatchewan, the province most dependent of any on agricultural chemicals, that pushed the federal government hardest. In June 1980 provincial environment minister Ted Bowerman's repeated criticisms of Ottawa for withholding the IBT list finally prompted federal health minister Monique Bégin to release a list of 97 IBT-tested chemicals licensed for use in Canada. She did not reveal why 92 pesticides were still considered suspect. The list gave products by brand name only, unlike the detailed chemical component list available from US EPA, which totaled 123 pesticides. But, Bégin insisted, "There is no evidence to demonstrate that these pesticides represent a health hazard to [farmers] or [to consumers] as residue in food." That argument would itself soon be proven invalid.

The man caught in the middle of the pesticide and propaganda war is Dr. Alexander Morrison, assistant deputy minister of the Health Protection Branch of Health and Welfare Canada. The branch makes the key recommendations about the safety of pesticides to Agriculture Canada, which in turn licenses them. Morrison says there are solid reasons for keeping most of the information confidential, even from provincial officials: for one, the pesticide manufacturers would sue the pants off Ottawa. Details of questionable chemical tests are proprietary information—their and the government's secret. Apparently, revealing the problems in the chemicals tested by IBT could involve mention of the key ingredients of the pesticides, an open betrayal of commercial secrets.

That stance infuriates the environmentalists, including Dr. David Penman, senior health consultant with Saskatchewan Environment. "When people ask us what's wrong with these chemicals," he says, "the answer is, ridiculously enough, "We don't know." And we can't find out."

The CACA says that the most dangerous antipesticide allegations threaten to undermine the federal regulatory system and wipe out the industry. Yet some of the CACA's members have not been overly prompt in wiping out any doubts about the safety of the chemicals they defend so vigorously. In January 1980, two years after Health and Welfare and the EPA ordered all companies to reevaluate the IBT tests used to register their products, R.O. Reid, the chairman of the federal Canadian committee overseeing their progress, complained directly to the CACA that many firms "have still failed to submit the information" originally requested in 1977. The process was admittedly time-consuming and costly. In one case more than 17,000 pages of micro-filmed data needed careful evaluation.

Although Alexander Morrison is not prepared to discuss what's been found [suspect IBT-approved] he readily admits that much of the information he can't release is available in the US thanks to freedom-of-information legislation or simple phone calls to the EPA.

Without being too specific—"I've had a practice for 10 years of not being involved in public debates with media people," he adds— Canada's top watchdog for public health will admit that "Yes, the tests on the 100 chemicals are still all invalid. At this time we do not have normal assurances of their safety." Twenty-seven of the IBT-endorsed pesticides have been found in the environment or in food in Canada, although none exceed the permissible safe level—a level assumed safe at least partly because of IBT data.

But if Morrison seems restrained about what's out there in the field and whether it's safe, much of the problem lies with his department's second-class status in ruling on pesticide safety. It's Agriculture Canada that ultimately decides on the registration (approval, with any possible limitations) of pesticides as safe. Not unexpectedly, that department is an unabashed promoter of products that increase agricultural productivity including pesticides. Officials are quick to point out the economic benefits of chemical weed killers, insecticides and bacteria suppressants. Officially, Health and Welfare, and to a lesser extent Environment Canada, Labour Canada and other agencies are called in to advise Agriculture of what, if any, toxic effects exist for "non-target organisms" such as plants and human beings. Those effects are assessed by limited testing in those departments and heavy reliance on the tests of chemical producers and private laboratories such as IBT.

"What happens if Agriculture ignores our advice? We try to use sweet reason, and, if necessary, take the matter to our minister," says Morrison. "And eventually some political decisions have to be made." The federal health minister is not obliged to ban a chemical deemed unsafe or suspect. Morrison says he's unaware of any case where strong health ministry objections have been ignored by Agriculture Canada, but adds, "I'm not about to tell you what I tell my minister. We civil servants are the technicians who advise the politicians. They bear the ultimate responsibility. I don't."

There have been cases of dubious advice. Back in 1977, a special nine-member subcommittee of National Research Council scientists, chaired by Patrick McTaggert-Cowan, reexamined studies and decisions permitting the five-year dousing of New Brunswick with fenitrothion to kill spruce budworms and allegedly save the forests. McTaggert-Cowan concluded that the fenitrothion approval, which included the sanction of Agriculture Canada, involved "stupidities, deliberate and otherwise . . . scientific work [lacking rigor], planning and control. . .[and] brute force and educated ignorance." But New Brunswick, which is heavily dependent on the forest industry, is still using the pesticide with the endorsement of Agriculture Canada, although Nova Scotia, Maine, and Ontario have banned it because of its dubious effectiveness and possible risk to human safety.

"Political decisions" may not reflect the "best scientific" recommendations Morrison says his department tries to make to Agriculture Canada. And even those recommendations, he adds, involve "judgment calls" because of the complexity of modern chemicals and the "sometimes incomplete, contradictory scientific information." And he quickly points out the economic implications of banning a major pesticide. "To make that kind of recommendation without evidence that it's needed is going to disrupt the production of food in North

America in a gigantic way." Making the safe recommendation with evidence that it's needed would, of course, have the same disruptive effect.

The economic argument in favor of pesticides is powerful and is not easily criticized by the 95 percent of Canadians who depend on the labors and chemicals applications of the 5 percent who farm so productively. From only 7 percent of Canada's land mass, the agriculture industry produces an annual $10 billion worth of food products, $6 billion of it exports. Without chemical pesticides and herbicides our intensive farming would collapse, and home, garden and industrial pests would proliferate, argues the CACA, which says it now sells $250 million worth of products a year. Morrison Says there are "about 400 registered pesticides in Canada—100 of them in common use."

But they have to be there; they're vital, says CACA. "Chemical pesticides represent only about 2 percent of a grower's input costs; yet at a conservative estimate they increase the amount he harvests by some 30 percent," the industry says in a 1980 position paper. Without the chemicals, "Some authorities predict the immediate first-year effect could be an overall reduction in yield of 50 percent." CACA president Alexander St. Clair says the result could be "a 200 percent to 300 percent increase in food prices." What St. Clair and other industry spokesmen don't make clear in such sweeping claims is that they're talking about the implications of eliminating virtually all of the farm pesticides, something the industry's critics don't yet dream of.

James Hay, director of the Agriculture Canada research station in Saskatoon, says a total ban with no replacement controls would not mean a 50 percent crop loss: "Our figures are a 15 percent yield reduction due to weeds," the major problem in the province. "We think that farmers will soon be able to reduce the amounts of weed killer by 25 percent with more efficient equipment and application," Hay adds.

And there are nonchemical alternatives, ones that avoid the growing tendency of pests to develop immunity to chemicals. The leading alternative today is called integrated pest management (IPM), and it uses the following multitactic controls: fungi, parasites and bacteria specially bred to kill specific pests; mixing and rotating of crops to repel them; and synthetic sex stimulants to drive bugs crazy.

IPM is touted as the safe future for farming. But short of the future, there remain the doubts about the chemicals currently in use. The CACA argues that it's impossible to establish any pattern of human illness or mortality related to the increased use of chemical pesticides. Excluding lung cancer not related to pesticides, cancer rates "haven't increased significantly in 40 years in North America," the association states. The claim may be invalid. Last year the US National Cancer Institute (NCI) reported that US cancer rates had risen for the first time in 25 years—at least 11 percent since 1970. The US magazine *Science* has reported that the NCI's former director of science policy concludes that less than half the increase is due to smoking and that chemicals may be to blame for the other half. Chemical-industry scientists, of course, dispute the findings.

What alarms the pesticide critics is that mortality studies of pesticides can take years to confirm or rule out a health hazard. And if the studies ultimately prove the chemical *is* hazardous, new victims have already been added to the list. Critics want proof there's no link. Morrison concedes that his department is "very much concerned about the possibility of subtle effects. . .we're not so likely to see acute episodes of sudden deaths. . .but for the long range . . . perhaps the next generation, the implications are frightening."

It has already happened. The birth defects among the children of US soldiers exposed to Agent Orange, the aborted pregnancies of residents of the Love Canal area and other chemical horror stories are quickening public recognition of the risks of environmental contaminants. The Science Council of Canada was scathing in its 1977 indictment of federal officials and agencies for their ignorance of or disinterest in long-term hazards of low-level exposure to chemicals in general. The federally funded Canadian Environmental Advisory Council, in another bitter critique in 1979, warned that science's capacity to invent new complex chemicals—at the rate of about 1,000 per year—has far outstripped the toxicologists' ability to unravel the longterm, synergistic and still undetectable hazards. Government specialists are few; hence the reliance on industry and private labs such as IBT.

The critics aren't satisfied with the pace of the retesting of the IBT-validated chemicals, the Health Protection Branch's interim actions or the industry-dominated testing process. Moni Campbell, a researcher with Pollution Probe, a Toronto-based public-interest group, says, "The nonessential, almost cosmetic, chemicals on the IBT list should be banned until proven safe, and those most essential to agriculture given urgent reevaluation.'' She points to the ban and phase-out of 2,4,5-T, which the industry vehemently opposed but admitted would cause little agricultural inconvenience. Saskatchewan member of Parliament Simon de Jong, several environmental advisory boards, and the Science Council argue for the establishment of government-funded but independent testing and toxicology centres, and an end to policies barring access to pesticide information. Morrison says such centres would cost millions of dollars a year.

But he concedes that "the IBT situation is potentially terribly frightening." He says his department gets more letters about food additives, chemicals and perceived deterioration of the environment than anything else.

The CACA says the public has been terrorized by environmentalists' allegations about pesticide risks, even to the point of stampeding politicians into banning valuable safe pesticides. CACA past president James Bartlett argues, for example, that although 2,4,5-T "is a relatively unimportant product to agriculture or our industry," it had to be defended to prevent the "domino strategy" of activists seeking to topple one chemical after another. That "domino strategy," whether it's an environmentalist plot or sincere, scientifically motivated pressure, has seriously undermined the CACA's campaign for public credibility. Last October the EPA announced plans to ban almost all uses of the chemical lindane, used in pesticides, seed treatments and dog and cat flea collars. It causes cancer among humans—not often, but enough to make it worth eliminating, the EPA argued. Ottawa so far has declined to act.

Lindane was on the original IBT list. Also on the list was the insecticide disulfoton. Last Dec. 22 Agriculture Canada banned the sale of six brands used for house and garden products, saying that the products could constitute a potential health hazard. By January Ottawa had followed US leads and ordered a ban on a range of uses of pentachlorophenol—in wood preservative, weed killer and disinfectant. It contains dioxins of possible carcinogenic risk.

Other scientific reappraisals are reinforcing the perception that pesticides are dangerous. Although 2,4-D was on the US IBT list but declared safe by virtue of other tests, according to Morrison's department, late last year Agriculture Canada announced its own discovery of dioxins in some formulations of 2,4-D. Despite the CACA's protest that the dioxins 'are so mild they are harmless,' Ottawa has ordered a halt to the offending formulations (about 25 percent of the 8 million lbs. used per year)—in 1982, when stocks are depleted.

The IBT revelations are probably not over. Of the 100 IBT-tested chemicals still on the market in Canada, captan fungicide (used on 720,000 acres of corn and beans in Ontario alone) is known to have been poorly examined for carcinogenicity. Sweden banned it two years ago. And apart from the IBT 100, there's still the question of those pesticides tested by other private laboratories. "We still don't know if IBT was an aberration. We haven't had a chance to look at other laboratories' results," he says. "There has been a belief that private industry could be trusted."

Once upon a time there may also have existed a belief that government could be trusted to regulate industry with reasonable effectiveness and—where public health is concerned—with reasonable dispatch. But in May 1981, when Alexander Morrison's department suddenly concluded that the IBT-tested fungicide captan deserved banning or severe restriction, Agriculture Canada decided to convene a new committee to mull over the idea. One should not be hasty in removing a potentially hazardous agricultural product from the market, argued Deputy Agricultural Minister Gaetan Lussier. The chemical industry, the provincial governments, the farmers and the consumers need to be consulted first. Otherwise, Canadians could find themselves hungry, he insisted. The environmentalists argue that properly conducted, post-IBT testing of captan shows Canadians could find themselves dead.

But government is not alone in failing to build a credible image. Across town in the CACA command post, the promised launching of a media and information blitz on urban womenfolk to win them back from the environmental guerrillas has been abandoned. Executive director Jacques Chevalier laments that "It's well-nigh impossible to educate the urban consumer. Our real customers are several stages away at the farming level." Indeed, it's especially hard to sway a group when their side seems to have the larger supply of facts. These days, almost nothing flies very far on blind faith and rhetoric alone.

SECTION THREE
Setting Policy: Closing the Gap

Introduction

Pinpointing environmental problems and agreeing to take some remedial action only begin the process of protecting the environment. A more difficult task is developing policies to solve the problems.

Designing policies to protect the environment engenders areas of disagreement. The first concerns the level of protection; that is, how clean is clean? With general agreement that it is impossible to totally eliminate pollution, what targets or goals should be set? And since pollution takes many forms, from the chronic problems of carbon dioxide buildup to the acute problems of dioxin and heavy metal poisoning, and affects many media (air, water, and land), the range of complex policies to be established is enormous. Obviously ample occasion exists for conflict between the business and environmental communities in quantifying pollution guidelines. And absent an unarguable standard for most forms of pollution, the policy decision arrived at must ultimately be a political one.

A second conflict area in policymaking is more technical: selecting policy instruments for controlling pollution—policy instruments that best combine effective control and lowest cost. This is the least-tested area in the environmental protection process, hence the area of greatest experimentation. Is it best to levy pollution taxes, set physical limits on emissions, establish markets in pollution rights, require environmental audits of firms, use the "bubble" approach to limiting emissions, or any number of other alternative means of controlling pollution? While many different groups may have opinions about the best way to implement environmental protection, they recognize that designing optimal policy tools to achieve environmental goals is still in its infancy.

Environmental policymakers are just beginning to learn ways of measuring the effectiveness of environmental protection policies. Although it might seem simple enough to measure the success of policies in preventing pollution, disagreement over pollution measurement methods and over interpretation of these measurements is pervasive. What characteristics of air and water to measure remains a question; and only the beginning of a body of historical data exists by which to measure progress in controlling pollution. Measurement and interpretation problems become even greater when international environmental issues are involved.

The remainder of the twentieth century is likely to be a time of "learning by doing" in the area of policy development. In most cases, the wisest policies will be those that set allowable levels of emissions but leave the means of control up to individual firms. This will encourage innovation and take advantage of the creativity and inventive systems of the marketplace. In the mid-1980s, more flexible, localized decision-making approaches seem to be in the prevailing wind.

The articles in this section reflect the change and experimentation that characterizes environmental policymaking today. It is common to think of "environmental policy" as an area in which government will make most of the decisions, but this is just not the case. The vast majority of pollution-control decisions are made by thousands, perhaps even millions, of business people, engineers, consumers, and other private individuals who daily pull the levers, inspect the filters, tune the engines, and handle the chemicals and materials that make the difference between a clean or polluted environment.

Laws and regulations and guidelines matter, but there will never be a large enough environmental police force to insure environmental protection in an economy and society as decentralized and individualistic as the United States. For environmental protection to work there must be a widespread ethic or belief in the importance of the goal of environmental protection and a feeling that the rules and guidelines are reasonable, necessary, and not economically crippling to individuals or firms. For these reasons, environmental protection policies must both follow and lead public opinion. If government policies are too stringent or too far advanced for public opinion, nonobservance renders them meaningless. If they are perceived as fair and reasonable and the public supports them, then the need for government enforcement is greatly diminished.

One of the themes in this section is the importance of selling pollution policies. The business community has to be sold or convinced that pollution-control devices will not ruin profitability. Plant engineers have to sell the idea that they sometimes have better ideas and techniques than the EPA for achieving environmental goals. Labor unions have to "buy" the argument that pollution controls do not lead to job exportation. And the public has to be sold on how important the whole process is to its long-run welfare—a not inconsequential task. But selling always has been a critical ingredient in the political and economic processes of democratic capitalism. It is an aspect of American society with which those in the nonprofit sector often feel uncomfortable, but it is an aspect of our system that policymakers at all levels ignore at their own peril.

Environmental Values Are Economic

By Alfred E. Kahn

The former chairman of the President's Council on Wage and Price Stability argues that there can be substantial economic benefits to society in environmental protection and that we must look at these benefits as well as the more frequently discussed costs of the programs.

I think we need to distinguish two different kinds of regulation: the ones that protect particular economic interests against competition, by limiting price-cutting, market entry, or the free flow of goods and services; and the ones that have as their purpose such goals as protection of the environment, health, or safety.

Protectionism and restrictions on competition typically mean higher prices and diminished pressures for efficiency, which we can ill afford. The other kind of regulation—environmental, occupational, and product safety—is very different. No one in his or her right mind could argue that the competitive market system protects the environment. It doesn't.

Economists have long recognized the inefficiency that results when production or consumption activities in a market economy have so-called spillover or external effects on third parties, effects that do not get taken into account by the producer or consumer, the seller or buyer. These may be favorable: if you buy soap and use it freely, I may find you a more congenial traveling companion on public transportation; if you have an apple orchard next to my property and I keep bees, my honey business will profit from the pollen you provide. Bell Lab's research and development of transistors, paid for by telephone subscribers, conferred enormous, free benefits on makers and users of pocket calculators and television sets.

Excerpted from article appearing in *Challenge,* May/June 1979. Reprinted with permission of M. E. Sharpe, publisher, Armonk, New York, 10504. Alfred E. Kahn is the former chairman of the Council on Wage and Price Stability.

The more familiar externalities are the unfavorable ones: if your factory spews out smoke, it will probably increase my laundry bills and the number of times I have to paint my house; if it dumps waste in a river, it may reduce my fishing catch or ability to swim downstream from you, and it certainly will cost me to recondition that water so I may drink it.

Unless the government intervenes in some way to impose these external costs on the activities that cause them, the results will be economically inefficient. The activities will not bear all the costs that they impose on society, and will therefore in effect be subsidized. In consequence, the products or services in question will tend to be oversupplied, and they will tend also to be inefficiently produced. Their producers will have no incentive to hold down the costs that they can slough off on to others. As a result, they will refrain from making any expenditures, no matter how small, to cut down on those external costs, no matter how large.

Competition in these circumstances, in the absence of regulation, becomes competition in the degradation of the environment. These observations apply as much to consumption as to production activities: an obvious example would be the congestion and inconvenience that private automobiles impose on the center of cities during rush hours, or the exhaust that they spew into pedestrians' lungs.

With our recently enhanced recognition of the many ways in which unrestrained economic activities may impose damage on the environment, these ideas have now become commonplace. And it is widely recognized that economic efficiency alone requires that all pertinent social costs, internal and external, be levied in one way or another on the particular acts of production or consumption responsible for them. This will eliminate the subsidization: by confronting consumers with prices reflecting the full social costs of supplying them, it will ensure that no activities will be carried on whose *total* incremental costs exceed their benefits. And it will ensure, also, that production will be carried on by methods that minimize *total* costs, rather than only those costs that happen to fall on the producer.

Although the economics is not the same, many of these observations apply also to occupational and product safety: we as a society are not willing to leave these to the operation of the free market any more than we're willing to do it with airline safety.

Some businessmen and economists have criticized the spread of

environmental, occupational, and product safety regulation in recent years, asserting that it has contributed to inflation of the costs
of doing business and to the distressing decline in the rate of our
productivity growth.

Yet obviously, measurement of these costs alone tells us nothing
about whether they were worth incurring. It does not even tell us
whether a particular regulation, or indeed all of them taken together,
were or are actually inflationary: that, again, would depend on
whether the costs exceeded the benefits. And the contribution to
diminished productivity growth could well be apparent only in a
reflection of the failure of traditional calculations of productivity
changes to include external costs.

By exactly the same reasoning—that it is irrational to try to assess
these regulations in terms of their costs alone without looking also
at their benefits—it is irrational to decree that society must bear those
costs without having made one's best judgment that the benefits do
indeed justify doing so.

The popular conception that we must make choices between
"economic welfare" and environmental protection is simply wrong.
Environmental values are economic values; it is in principle just as
important, in the interest of economic efficiency and therefore
economic welfare, to conserve our limited natural resources, to make
wise and sparing use of our limited clean air, water, and living space,
as it is to economize in the use of labor and capital; and using some
of our limited economic resources to preserve or restore an acceptable environment is just as much a contribution to economic welfare
as devoting them to travel, shelter, or national defense.

It is equally essential for us to understand that the values associated
with what we think of as economic welfare are no less important
in philosophical, ethical, or aesthetic terms than the values achieved
by environmental protection; and that the extent to which we pursue environmental goals must therefore be subjected to the same
kind of economic—that is, cost/benefit—tests as the extent to which
we supply the people of this country with food, housing, medical
care, museums, education, and police and fire protection. And make
no mistake about it: we do subject *all* of these to economic tests
and limitations.

There can be little doubt that we have not always applied this kind
of test to our environmental and safety regulations in the past. The

anti-inflationary program, not to mention the recognition that many American people are not getting all the food, shelter, and medical care we would like them to have, quite properly requires that we begin to do so now.

Nearsighted Leaders, Long-Range Challenges

By Russell W. Peterson

The president of the National Audubon Society calls for long-range environmental planning and argues that "biological capital" is as important as financial capital and does not lend itself well to guidance from a market system.

No greater problem faces our nation than the government's inability to make accurate projections of global trends in population, resources, and environment, to analyze their social and economic implications, and to integrate this information into federal decision making.

The most significant attempt has been the *Global 2000 Report to the President,* a million-dollar study by 13 federal agencies completed in 1978. But the report itself notes that "the executive agencies of the U.S. government are not now capable of presenting the president with internally consistent projections of world trends for the next two decades." It added that "each agency has an idiosyncratic way of projecting the future based on its own responsibilities and interests. These different approaches were never designed to be used as part of an integrated, self-consistent system."

Much of the attention attracted by *Global 2000* focused on the alarming consequences predicted by the turn of the century if current global trends continued—some people called it a "doomsday report." Yet its real message was that life for most people in the year 2000 would be more precarious "*unless* the nations of the world act decisively to alter current trends." If we look at the report as a vehicle for making us aware of the need to redirect government policies to avert disastrous consequences before it is too late, *Global 2000* can be seen as a document of hope.

Reprinted with permission from *Technology Review*, Copyright 1982. Russell W. Peterson is president of the National Audubon Society.

Whither the World?

But how can we adequately read the trends and make appropriate decisions if the government has no system dedicated to such a complex assignment? It is puzzling that the United States, with the most sophisticated data-processing systems in the world, a high degree of computer-modeling expertise, and unexcelled policy-analysis capability, has so long resisted establishing even one group for conducting global analysis and planning at the highest level of government, where it is needed most.

This lack is especially strange because it is considered perfectly splendid, indeed necessary, for industry to conduct long-range planning. But for government to do so becomes somehow unsavory—smacking perhaps of communism or, at the least, socialism. Recognizing this unfortunate connotation, we might substitute the term "foresight capability." What we are talking about, of course, is not a planned society, but rather the use of planning by our democratically selected leaders to meet society's needs.

There are many examples of how foresight capability could help steer our national course. One concerns today's serious problem of hazardous wastes. The nation is laced with thousands of hazardous-waste dumps. Through leaching and wind erosion, these are spreading toxic chemicals throughout our ecosystems and poisoning water supplies, farmlands, and building sites. If a government "forecasting agency" had existed several decades ago, it probably would have foreseen—in light of the chemical industry's rapid growth—the need to ensure safe and practical disposal methods for the thousands of new chemicals being created annually. It's likely that the federal forecasters would also have ensured that the users of the new chemicals paid for appropriate disposal, rather than passing such costs on to future generations. Given this kind of sound economic consideration, some hazardous chemicals would certainly have lost out to other materials in the competitive marketplace.

Today, we exhibit similar but more serious negligence, failing to bring foresight to bear on the nuclear-waste problem. Even though we are in the early phases of the nuclear era as projected by its promoters, a frightening array of wastes has already accumulated, including mountains of uranium mill tailings, billions of cubic feet of low-level wastes, deadly high-level wastes temporarily stored in dozens of locations, and abandoned radioactive facilities awaiting the nations' decision to spend almost as much to dispose of them as it did to build them. We obviously need to consider the implications of the accelerated buildup of such wastes over the next decade.

Another argument for the establishment of foresight capability in government is that the rate of change is escalating, leaving us less and less time to alter a threatening trend once it is recognized. For example, many biologists tell us that increasing human activities—propelled by more people trying to improve the standard of living—are alarmingly accelerating the extinction of other species. To ignore the long-term impact of such trends is foolhardy.

The faster we move, the more important it is that scouts tell us of the problems and opportunities ahead. The military has traditionally used such scouts. Now, when we have threats to our national security every bit as serious as military threats, we sorely need more comprehensive scouting. One such threat is the political instability that often grows out of a nation's limited capacity to meet the demands of its people for food and natural resources. Advance knowledge of how growing population will affect available resources, and how environmental impacts may affect resource supply, may be significant in national security decisions. And importantly, such insight may help in developing the best ways to aid hard-pressed nations.

There have been a number of attempts over the years to establish some foresight capability in government, but most were short-changed and short-lived. Our myopia—when we focus on the present and worry about such things as how many dollars we can make this year or how to get reelected—blinds us to global and longer-term considerations.

To use Herman Kahn's words, we muddle our way into the future. In so doing, human beings—the "ultimate resource" as Julian Simon calls us—have in some ways made great progress. And for many humans progress will continue, unless we muddle our way into a nuclear holocaust or irreversibly befoul or deplete the planet's natural systems. But I believe that many of the hundreds of millions who die prematurely or suffer severely from hunger, disease, and war—and much of the inestimable natural riches that are recklessly squandered—could be saved with a little foresight.

The Risks of Muddling

Fortunately, as the rate of change escalates and the margin of error for avoiding a catastrophic mistake narrows, many individuals are demanding that we think before we act—that we analyze the long-term and global implications of our actions and consider available alternatives.

The nation took an important step in this direction in 1970 with passage of the National Environmental Policy Act. NEPA required federal agencies to prepare environmental impact statements for all major actions. This meant examining alternatives to the proposed action (including no action), and required public involvement. Despite its imperfections, NEPA has had profound effects across the nation and has been copied by many other countries. It represents the beginning of wisdom in the way we deal with nature.

The environmental impact statements brought into the open the perennial conflict between exploiters of our natural resources interested in making a buck today and those who focus on the broader and longer-term interests of society. The National Audubon Society was created early this century to fight such an issue—to stop commercial plume hunters from wiping out plumed birds—and stop them it did. But the plume-hunter mentality still plagues us. This mentality is the dominant view in the Reagan administration and is devastating the advances made in the 1970s toward protecting the environment.

Fortunately, citizens are well ahead of their current leaders on environmental issues. Their message, a hopeful one, was recently delivered to Congress by pollster Louis Harris: "By a massive margin of 80 to 17 percent, the public wants no relaxation of existing federal regulation of air pollution." He added that most people vehemently oppose any attempt to reverse the environmental gains of the past ten years, and stressed that this feeling has strengthened during the past year. "This message on the deep desire of the American people to battle pollution is one of the most overwhelming in our 25 years of surveying public opinion."

In a major effort to catalyze public action, 54 citizens' organizations with over 5 million members have formed the Global Tomorrow Coalition. Our purpose is to promote continual monitoring and awareness of global trends that threaten our life-support systems, and to promote action to alter such trends.

We have unanimously petitioned Congress to establish a permanent federal mechanism to provide foresight capability. We are calling for a broad, constantly updated system for gathering trend data, analyzing global implications, and presenting alternatives to both the general public and government decision makers. By systematically using foresight, we can more likely identify and pursue life-supporting paths into the future rather than life-threatening ones.

The government's current position calls to mind a statement by Robert Hamrin, an economist by training, an educator by inclination, and a specialist who takes a broad view: "It is ironic that the new guiding philosophy, supply-side economics, focuses solely on financial capital, neglecting completely the ultimate supply center, matter and energy. The time has come for economists to acknowledge the very crucial fact that although the books of the market system seem to balance and record economic progress, the books of nature, which render the real accounting for the human race, run increasing deficits. If we are to have a true supply-side economics, it will have to incorporate the fact that biological capital is equally as important as financial capital for achieving long-run sustainable growth."

Economic Approaches to Air Pollution Control

By Armin Rosencranz

The pros and cons of alternative ways of dealing with air pollution are explored in this article, with emphasis being placed on the economic consequences of the various approaches.

As early as the 1920s, British economist A.C. Pigou observed that pollution occurs because the sources of pollution are not required to take into account the "social costs" of their actions.[1] In other words, there is no marketplace for environmental quality. The pollution control systems that have been established throughout the developed world have attempted to compensate for this deficiency through bureaucratic regulation.

As economists have noted, regulatory approaches to pollution control are economically inefficient in that they require the same proportionate reductions in emissions from sources with varying control costs, rather than requiring greater reductions from sources able more cheaply to abate pollution. Moreover, regulation creates weak incentives for research and development.

Additionally, the regulatory approach offers no incentive for sources to reduce emissions *below* the levels required by law. Indeed, regulations often encourage sources to lobby for cutbacks or delays in order to avoid large compliance costs. Yet, as economic growth continues, an ever-increasing percentage of pollution removal will be necessary to retain a roughly constant degree of environmental quality.

So environmental strategists in the United States and elsewhere are once again looking toward the marketplace for solutions to environmental problems. While many of these economic approaches still have not been tested, they may shortly take a prominent place

Reprinted by permission from *Environment*, Vol. 23, No. 8, October 1981, pp. 25-30, a publication of the Helen Dwight Reid Educational Foundation. Armin Rosencranz is a lawyer and political scientist from Inverness, California.

among the control options available to the market-oriented Reagan Administration. Economic strategies may also be adaptable to the problem of transnational air pollution, in that they tend to substitute a rational, objective model for the national self-interest considerations that ordinarily dominate transboundary pollution control decisions. They may, correspondingly, be less likely to engender international legal disputes.

Ideally, an economics-based approach to air pollution control would provide financial incentives for industry to pursue the most cost-effective means for reducing pollution. How the incentives should be structured depends on their specific purpose. Incentives in their purest form would be based on air quality *results,* allowing the producers to select the most cost-effective abatement approach.

In a more limited way, incentives could be designed to foster specific pollution-abating behaviors: for example, selection of fuels, selection of industrial processes, use of pollution control technology, or selection of products. They could stimulate the production of salable by-products, or induce a shift toward the production of less polluting goods.

A variety of economic strategies can be employed in controlling air pollution. Some of these are discussed below.

Subsidies

Since the start of pollution control efforts in the United States, federal and state regulatory systems have included economic incentives through such programs as government subsidies, low-interest loans, and outright grants to industry for the purchase of pollution abatement equipment. Taxing authorities have allowed accelerated depreciation for such expenditures. These provisions, however, are geared solely toward decreasing *disincentives* to the use of pollution control technology. They do not stimulate creative marketplace responses.

Penalties as Incentives

Economic incentives have generally been introduced as an adjunct to a regulatory program. Noncompliance penalties, for example, which are assessed in terms of the economic benefit gained by the polluter from noncompliance with pollution control requirements, are somewhat akin to economic incentives.

The State of Connecticut pioneered this approach in the mid-1970s with a system of civil assessments and sureties designed to remove the financial advantages an industry gains from delaying compliance.[2] Similar provisions then were incorporated into the 1977 federal Clean Air Act amendments. These systems provide, in addition to the basic fine for noncompliance, a penalty based on the profit that accrues to the polluter by failing to meet emissions standards.[3]

Taxes as Incentives

The administrative simplicity of taxes, combined with the public revenue they can generate, makes them attractive tools to achieve a variety of social purposes. Numerous tax-related proposals have been offered since the inception of federal pollution programs, although no major legislation of this type has yet been enacted in the United States. The Nixon administration in 1971 first proposed a tax on the sulfur content of fuel.[4]

Norway has employed, since 1971, a basic tax on each unit of oil, plus an additional charge based on its sulfur content. The system was refined in 1976 to provide rebates to polluters in proportion to the amount of pollution abatement achieved by them.

The Netherlands also employs a fuel tax. The Dutch system, however, is not designed to provide direct incentives to use low-sulfur fuels. Instead, it funds the implementation of their 1972 Air Pollution Act. The taxes are based on the type of fuel (gasoline, light fuel oil, heavy fuel oil, coal) and not on the sulfur content of the fuels.

In the United States numerous other tax measures have been considered or proposed as means of creating disincentives to pollution. These include a tax on the purchase of new vehicles with excessive pollution ratings, or a tax on gasoline sales based on an automobile's emission rating.

Tax measures, when designed as incentives, can have an impact on a wide range of behavior such as manufacturers' product designs (for example, for automobile engines), consumers' selection of products, industries' and homeowners' choices of fuels, use of pollution control technology, and levels of fuel consumption (for example, consumers' driving habits). While such tax measures can be helpful, they nevertheless are piecemeal, and each addresses only a segment of the pollution problem.

Emissions Charges

Broader in scope and more significant in its impact on market forces is the concept of emissions charges. The economic theory involved and the experience to date with pollution charge systems in various countries are treated in the recent OECD [Organization for Economic Cooperation and Development] publication, *Pollution Charges in Practice*.[5] This OECD undertaking in itself suggests an awakened international interest in economics-based pollution abatement strategies.

The salient feature of the charge system is that it can both foster cost-effective redistribution of funds and create incentives for voluntary pollution abatement.

An emissions charge differs from a penalty fee in that it is generally imposed on *every* source that emits more than a given amount of the substance on which the charge is levied.[6] It differs from a tax in that the "product" for which the charge is made is pollution itself. The charge not only raises funds to carry out socially desirable pollution control activities but creates a broad incentive for polluters to abate their pollution, employing whatever strategies they find most cost-effective.

However the charges are calculated, they ought to encourage all sources to seek better and cheaper ways of reducing emissions. Charges should induce polluters to develop and use progressively more efficient techniques for abating pollution, including reduced fuel consumption, the substitution of lower sulfur fuels, more efficient production processes, and emissions reduction.

In 1973 East Germany established an emissions charge system that encompasses more than a hundred different polluting substances. Producers are prohibited from passing the charge along to their customers, which increases their incentive to reduce the level of their emissions. The program is administered on a regional basis, and the proceeds are used within the region for environmental planning and administration and for compensating victims of pollution.[7]

Compensation is the major purpose of a charge system implemented in Japan, also in 1973.[8] The charge is calculated by *estimating* (not directly measuring) emissions through the sulfur content of fuels used and the amount of desulfurized flue gases. The total amount of charges to be assessed is divided among all major pollution sources, with those inside a high-risk pollution zone paying more than those outside it.

According to the aforementioned OECD report, charges, to be politically acceptable, should be simple to calculate[9] and the revenues

should be redistributed to support any or all of the following:
- anti-pollution research and development;
- monitoring networks;
- compensation for health damage;
- compensation to firms in financial difficulty resulting from their pollution control activities;
- costs of administering and implementing the pollution control program;
- pollution control expenses of polluters;
- collective pollution control facilities.[10]

The difficulty of making the necessary quantitative judgments appears to be a major obstacle to broader application of charge systems in the developed countries.

Creating Pollution Markets

This is the most radical, market-oriented, and conceptually challenging of the economic approaches to air pollution control. In its purest form it involves the issuance of marketable "rights"— licenses to pollute. Under this system a ceiling is established on the level of permissible pollution, and a limited number of permits to pollute are then issued and traded on the open market. Theoretically, sources able to control emissions at least cost will do so, and will purchase more rights. This system should provide continuing incentives for pollution abatement since any reduction by a producer could be sold to another source seeking to build or expand or could be "banked" for later sale or use in plant expansion.

To enter the system, new sources must purchase rights or offsets equivalent to or greater than the amount of pollution that they will produce. As economic growth continues and competition builds for the available rights, their value and the incentives for existing sources to reduce pollution—or even to cease operations in order to sell their rights—will increase.[11]

A system of marketable pollution rights appeals to free-market economists not only because the market itself would set the price but because the system would require minimum governmental involvement. There are drawbacks, of course. The pollution permits would have a market value only marginally related to pollution control costs. Permit holders could have greater impact on regional development than public planning authorities. Those who could afford it might purchase more rights than they intended to use in an area—perhaps all of the rights—to keep out competitors or curtail the demand for scarce resources. If this hoarding or cornering of pollution rights should occur, the market would cease to operate, as it does in other such situations.[12] Finally, the system might actually forestall rather than encourage pollution abatement: there would be no incentive for voluntary abatement if there were no demand for pollution rights; also, the more rights available in a region, the less they would bring in the pollution market.

A modified pollution rights market has been in effect in the United States since 1977, namely, the "offset" policy formulated by the Environmental Protection Agency and endorsed by Congress in the Clean Air Act of 1977. This policy, designed to avert a complete halt in development in areas unable to attain the air quality standards required by the Clean Air Act, allows a new source of pollution to be established if it controls its emissions *and* if other sources in the area reduce their emissions more than enough to offset the added pollution—that is, if there is a net reduction in air pollution.

To date most offsets have been between different units belonging to the same company—such as between two utility plants in the same region. There are instances, however, in which producers with common interests have been able to negotiate offset arrangements. The Volkswagen corporation, for example, negotiated an offset with the State of Pennsylvania to achieve their common purpose of bringing a VW plant into the state. Similarly, Oklahoma oil companies granted offsets to General Motors, enabling G.M. to build a new Oklahoma factory (an arrangement facilitated by the Oklahoma Chamber of Commerce).[13]

The European Reaction

As in America, there are no taxes, charges, or fees anywhere in Europe on air pollution emissions. An OECD environmental official observed that "it seems conceptually and administratively difficult to apply pollution charges to air pollution."[14]

Other economic strategies, such as marketable permits, offsets, noncompliance penalties, and fuel taxes may be easier to implement, enforce, and regulate in Europe than are pollution charges.[15] Pollution charges depend on the accurate measure of emissions; the other strategies do not.

Because of large emission monitoring costs and other administrative costs associated with pollution charges, European environmental officials seem to agree that charges (or fees or taxes) are only practical when levied on fuel.[16] Unlike a pollution charge, however, a tax on fuel offers polluters no strong incentive to install control technology.

West Germany, France, the Netherlands, and Italy all have systems of charges on water pollution, and one might therefore suppose that at least these four countries—and perhaps the rest of the European Community (EC) of which they are a part—would be receptive to charges levied on air pollution. But EC and OECD environmental officials doubt that there is any such receptivity, except perhaps in the Netherlands. According to one official,[17] the French Electricity Board (EDF) would never agree to such a charge nor would the large French petrochemical plants. In any case, no charges on air pollution emissions have been seriously considered to date in any of the EC countries.

Transboundary Air Pollution

Emissions charges would seem to be more difficult to implement internationally than nationally because of the problem of calculating the appropriate contribution of each emitting country. For any such system to work, each participating nation would have to cede sovereignty to a multinational, decision-making executive body which would redistribute the funds.

Such cessions of sovereignty seem highly improbable. Moreover, an applicable, understandable, and acceptable economic approach toward transboundary pollution must be *very* simple—relying, for example, on a direct link between emitting and receiving countries. Such links are sometimes difficult to establish even in the field of water pollution, and the multiplicity of sources in the case of transboundary air pollution would make any charge system unworkable—at least until tremendous strides are taken in tracing and tracking emissions.

Outlook

The current political and economic climate in the United States suggests that economics-based alternatives to regulatory strategies may emerge surprisingly soon.[18] Various state pollution control and economic development agencies appear to be developing proposals for a market in pollution rights,[19] and the National Commission on Air Quality held a public meeting on economic incentives in February

1980 at which then-Assistant EPA Administrator William Drayton advocated economic approaches to foster greater air pollution control and compliance. He stated that controlled trading of pollution rights—through "bubble" mechanisms, offsets, banking and brokerage systems—would aid both the regulators and the regulated and would leave to the regulated the problem of devising efficient and cost-effective pollution control.[20]

The adoption of a marketable permit or offset system on a regional, continental, or even international scale offers a means of maintaining air quality in tandem with continued economic development. A major problem with this approach, however, is the advantage that it gives to existing sources over new sources. In addition, many U.S. environmentalists object to the notion that pollution rights can be bought and sold. Many also fear that establishing a market in pollution rights guarantees pollution up to the established regional ceiling. But with or without economic approaches, air pollution will continue to be a problem. Relying exclusively on the regulatory approach insures that a significant portion of the costs of pollution will be paid for by its victims.

Economic approaches to air pollution control may best be viewed as a complement rather than an alternative to regulation. Direct regulation may be better suited to certain conditions than are economic approaches. But brief U.S. experience with various economic approaches have been sufficiently cost-effective to warrant further experimentation.

Notes

1. See James E. Krier and Robert B. Bell, "Old Economics and New Environmental Controls," Stanford Lawyer 15 (1980): 16.

2. See Frederick R. Anderson et al., Environmental Improvement through Economic Incentives, 1977, pp. 54-55.

3. Ibid. A proposal that passed the House of Representatives but not the Senate in 1976 would have based pollution fines on the cost to the producer of achieving the specified emission limits, rather than on the benefits derived from not meeting them.

4. See Material Relating to the Administrative Proposals for Environmental Protection, House Committee on Ways and Means, Print H-782-9, February 1972.

5. Pollution Charges in Practice, OECD, 1980.

6. Ibid., chapters 1 and 3. Much of the following discussion draws on the materials presented therein.

7. See Peter H. Sand, "The Socialist Response: Environmental Protection Law in the German Democratic Republic," Ecology Law Quarterly 3 (Summer 1973).

8. Anderson, note 2 above, pp. 49-51.

9. The OECD report (note 5 above) urges that charges be based on emission factors comparable to the flat-rate estimates used in water pollution. Among such factors are the weight of SO_2 per ton of fuel used or per ton of output, modified by a "treatment coefficient" designed to take into account the control activities actually carried out by the plants concerned.

10. Ibid., pp. 65, 66, 118.

11. Krier and Bell, note 1 above, p. 17.

12. Correspondingly, conservation groups could conceivably buy up all available permits or offsets to insure improved air quality.

13. Krier and Bell, note 1 above, p. 19.

14. Interview with Jean-Phillipe Barde, OECD environment directorate, May 22, 1980.

15. Ibid.

16. Interviews with Michel Poitier and Henri Smets, OECD environment directorate, April 1979.

17. Interview with Jean-Phillipe Barde, April 21, 1979.

18. The move toward alternatives to regulation may receive added impetus from Bruce Ackerman and William T. Hassler, Clean Coal/Dirty Air, Yale University Press, New Haven, 1981. The book explores some anomalies of EPA's requirements for new coal-fired power plants.

19. See for example, "Maryland Proposes That Firms Buy and Sell Air Pollution Rights," Washington Post, July 30, 1980.

20. See "Witnesses at NCAQ Hearing Agree Economic Incentives Show Promise," Air Waves, National Commission on Air Quality, March/April 1980, p. 2. Krier and Bell, note 1 above, p. 18, report that at one New Jersey chemical plant, Dupont expects the bubble approach to result in 89% removal of hydrocarbon emissions at a cost of $5 million, whereas traditional controls would achieve only 84% removal at a cost of $20 million.

A Simpler Path to a Cleaner Environment (Section 2*)

By Tom Alexander

The author suggests policies for dealing with environmental problems in an economically efficient fashion. Special attention is paid to the EPA's "bubble" concept.

The biggest environmental policy that is needed today is for Congress to give up the pretense that costs don't matter. The major philosophical flaw in both air and water regulations has been the tendency to require that sources reduce emissions or effluents uniformly, with the technology often specified. This approach takes insufficient account of the variation in the cost of curbing the same pollutant at different sources. The cost varies by industry, by plant, and even within a given plant. While superficially there is a certain appearance of equity in requiring all polluters to cut back by the same percentage, the equity question becomes more debatable if the cost of doing so would bankrupt one industry and leave another relatively unscathed. If, instead, enforcement were targeted upon the sources that are cheapest to control, it would be possible to clean the air with less money.

Until a few years ago, unfortunately, this approach seemed to be ruled out by the administrative facts of life. Government regulators seldom have enough information to discriminate wisely among the thousands of differing cost situations that exist in the real world. The best judges of how to do that are the polluters themselves. The problem has been to find a way to elicit their cooperation rather than their resistance.

The Birth of the Bubble

In the last couple of years, though, there have been some signifi-

---

* "A Simpler Path to a Cleaner Environment (Section 1)" begins on p. 78
 Tom Alexander is a member of the board of editors of *Fortune* magazine.

cant advances in this direction. The EPA has been encouraging states—which under the Clean Air Act are charged with enforcing air-quality standards—to experiment with giving industry more latitude and employing economic incentives. The idea grew naturally out of the "emission offsets" policy, under which air pollution from new facilities must be compensated for by reductions from existing sources. One result was the EPA's "bubble" approach. In concept, it's as if a gigantic bubble enclosed all of a plant's chimneys, with one master-chimney leading to the outside community. The polluter can spend money where it does the most good, namely on sources that can be muzzled at the lowest cost per ton emitted. (See "A Brave Experiment in Pollution Control," *Fortune*, February 12, 1979.)

By now, more than 70 of these "bubbles" have either been approved or are being developed, with potential savings estimated at nearly $200 million. The agency has already extended the principle by allowing bubbles with two or more plants owned by different companies, as well as bubbles that include additions to existing plants.

The EPA is also encouraging states to extend the bubble principle through the time dimension by allowing companies to "bank" emissions offsets in the form of so-called emission-reduction credits. That is, if a company closes an existing plant or reduces its emissions below the level actually required, it can bank the credits for its own later use in another plant in the same area, or even sell them to another company. So far, formal emissions banks have been established in the San Francisco, Louisville, and Seattle areas, and other states and metropolitan regions are preparing to set them up.

The banking idea is not without problems. For one thing, companies have proved reluctant to close an old plant in order to bank the offsets lest the authorities confiscate them as a painless way to meet the attainment deadlines. There are political problems too: local citizens near one plant can't understand why *their* air has to get dirtier even though air somewhere else is getting cleaner.

Brokers Wanted

Finally, the whole mechanism of offsets and increments—with its complex requirements for monitoring, modeling, and multiple permits—has proved baffling to many potential buyers and sellers. One consequence is that the EPA has been trying to encourage a whole new profession of knowledgeable "brokers" who could bring potential buyers and sellers together and steer them through the maze of the offset market.

Despite the difficulties, the popularity and limited success of the basic idea—creating salable rights to emit pollution—has captured the imagination of many regulators. Some of the enthusiasts are in a group established within the EPA by Douglas Costle, the agency's chief during the Carter Administration, to study innovative reforms. At the moment, the variation that's stirring the most interest is "marketable permits."

A Ticket to Pollute

Under this scheme, which is really just an extension of bubbling and banking, a limited number of permits to emit a certain tonnage of a pollutant would be awarded to existing emitters in a region in proportion to their present emission tonnage; alternatively, the permits might be auctioned off to all comers. Collectively, these "tickets" would allow only a fixed percentage of present emissions. Thus, if the authorities wanted a 25 percent overall reduction, all the permits added together would allow only 75 percent of the present overall tonnage. Exactly how the polluters in the area cut back to this level would be determined by open-market trading in the permits.

The advantage, say the proponents of marketable permits, is that the cleanup burden would be shifted automatically to those factories that can be cleaned up most cheaply. Assume, for example, that the local authorities wanted an overall reduction of 25 percent in nitrogen dioxide. It costs plant A, because of its age or its industrial process, a relatively high $10,000 in capital and operating costs to cut nitrogen dioxide by one pound per hour over the plant's remaining life. But plant B can achieve the same reduction for only $1,000. If the market price for permits in the area was $2,000 per pound, plant A would benefit by buying up extra permits and continuing to pollute at the present level. Plant B, on the other hand, could come out ahead by cleaning up by more than 25 percent and selling its unneeded permits.

It might even be possible for groups of ordinary citizens to buy up some or all of the permits and hold them, thereby depriving polluters of the right to emit the tonnage covered by the tickets. What economists like about that idea is that it would reveal what people are willing to pay for pollution control. As things stand now, people enjoy the benefits of a cleaner environment without a true awareness of the costs. According to economic theory, this arrangement tends to create an infinite demand for more cleanliness.

Economic incentives all have the advantage that they concentrate decisionmaking in the hands of those with the most information and the most interest in economic efficiency, such as plant managers. Unlike the conventional regulatory approach, moreover, economic incentives tend to stimulate the development of innovative pollution control technology.

Apostles of an Old Idea

But while bubbles, banking, and marketable permits are the incentive approaches most favored by the EPA and some industry spokesmen, the one that some economists cling to is the old idea of an emissions charge: levying a fee to pollute. This approach, say its apostles, if the most efficient in balancing environmental and economic values, and it provides some incentive to reduce pollution all the way down to zero. The regulators are less enchanted; they profess not to know how to set the tax level to achieve health-protection goals. And many businessmen fear that after they have already spent so much on meeting mandatory standards, emissions charges would represent an open-ended requirement to spend more.

One recent EPA study furnished some enlightening insights into the relative costs of various economic incentives. The study focused on the cost of controlling short-term concentrations of nitrogen dioxide, an air pollutant that is expected to get worse in many sections of the country and that is increasingly being linked to various respiratory ailments. No national short-term air-quality standard for nitrogen dioxide has yet been imposed.

The Command Scenario

The EPA study looked at the Chicago area, where 146 plants spew most of the nitrogen dioxide. In one hypothetical case, based on the present command-and-control approach, EPA analysts assumed that the three major industrial sources in the area—coal-fired boilers, oil-and-gas-fired boilers, and process units—were ordered to install the highest level of emission controls to bring nitrogen dioxide concentrations at all locations in the area below a short-term standard of 250 micrograms per cubic meter of air. The researchers calculated that the annual cost of that approach would be $130 million.

Next, the study explored the consequences of imposing a uniform emissions charge set at a level designed to induce industry to attain the same standard. That approach proved far more expensive than the first, costing some $719 million a year—$414 million of which would go to emissions charges and $305 million of which would go into control equipment and operating costs. The explanation for the high cost of this approach is that only a few locations in the Chicago area routinely violate the 250-microgram short-term standard. Yet certain polluters in some of those locations, such as coal-fired boilers, are very expensive to clean up. It would take an extremely high emission charge of about $15,800 per pound per hour per year to give these heavy polluters sufficient incentive to install the necessary equipment. The trouble is that this uniform fee would induce other polluters to clean up far more than is necessary to meet the standard, resulting in wasteful overkill.

Custom-fitted Fees

The overkill could be reduced if the emissions charges were varied to take account of the differing costs of controlling different types of sources. If, say, all oil-fired boilers paid one rate, all coal-fired boilers another, and industrial processes still another, the total cost would drop to $155 million. If, however, the fees could be custom fit to each and every source of nitrogen dioxide, taking into account variations in local air quality and control costs, the total bill would plunge to a mere $13 million a year, or just 10 percent of the conventional command-and-control approach.

The catch is that administrative and other costs under this customized approach might eat up most of the savings. The task of analyzing all the various sources and their control costs, and modeling their environmental impacts, plus all the delays, uncertainties, and political and legal challenges that would likely be involved, could prove daunting for any bureaucracy. It might create as much red tape as the "prevention of significant deterioration" regulations do now.

Most of the red tape could be avoided with a marketable permit system, which the EPA also tried to cost out. The researchers were unable to arrive at an exact figure, since the cost would depend upon who is the best negotiator, how well the market works, and the market prices of the permits. They concluded that the cost would lie somewhere between the $130 million required under the conventional regulatory approach and an absolute minimum of $13 million.

In the case of pollutants with apparent thresholds for health effects, then, a marketable permit system probably represents the simplest, most cost-effective approach. And even when the evidence in support of thresholds is shaky, as it is for most pollutants, nationwide air-quality standards make economic sense. If they could be based upon the concept of acceptable risk, taking costs and other factors into account—not the case at present—they would serve a useful purpose in preventing pollution abatement from becoming an open-ended drain on the economy. So, in the case of the familiar local pollutants such as carbon monoxide, lead, nitrogen dioxide, and ordinary particulates emitted from smokestacks, all of which lend themselves to the standards approach, marketable permits seem the way to go.

Where Toughness Is Needed

But in the case of the pollutants that move over long distances—carbon dioxide, chlorofluorocarbons, the sulfate and nitrate precursors to acid rain, and the carcinogens—a totally different approach is called for. Health-related national air-quality standards would be inappropriate and impossible to enforce, and the best way seems to be to apply steady economic pressure upon industries to keep on reducing those emissions. In a situation like that, emissions charges shine.

The fees would no doubt have to be determined by the political process, balancing, for example, damage to the Northeast's lakes from acid rain against damage to the Midwest's industrial economy from curbing the ingredients in acid rain. The charges could be altered from time to time, depending upon new scientific information and upon whether the situation was found to be getting better or worse. In setting the fees, of course, costs and the effects on other national goals should be taken into account.

The present Clean Air Act would allow the wider use of economic incentives, but bars them in many instances. What's needed, therefore, is for Congress to remove the obstacles and provide a clear mandate for the regulators to forsake the present command approach and march down the incentive path. Congress could do something else: recognize at last that the total elimination of risks is expensive and just plain silly.

Ben Wattenberg of the American Enterprise Institute has recently pointed out one of the larger curiosities of the environmental movement. Based as it is on the notion that we live in a society hazardous to your health, it flies in the face of an astonishing demographic discovery. That is the remarkable rate of increase over the last dozen years in the life expectancy of the average adult American citizen, an increase greater than in any similar period in this century despite all the supposedly dangerous substances in the air and water.

Many people might argue that environmental improvements have played a part in this development and perhaps they're right. But it is hard to escape the conclusion that most of the explanations for longer life spans—and even for the powerful appeal of the environmental movement itself—is that our wealthy society can afford them. Thus, a prudent environmentalism should take care lest its actions damage its own economic underpinnings. "Richer is safer," says political scientist Aaron Wildavsky—and, he might add, healthier, cleaner, and, on balance, happier.

Will John Barker's Bubble Burst?

By Greg Johnson

One of the most promising alternative solutions to environmental problems is the "bubble" concept. This article shows the pioneering work of one individual and one company as they sought to implement this environmental innovation.

The caricature on the handpainted coffee mug bears a striking resemblance to John E. Barker, corporate director of environmental engineering at Armco Inc., Middletown, Ohio. Sitting snugly between two piles of paperwork on Mr. Barker's desk, it identifies him only as "Bubbleman," an unlikely name for a super hero.

But "Bubbleman" isn't interested in leaping tall buildings or wrestling with powerful locomotives. He does, however, face an equally challenging task: "Bubbleman" Barker wants to change part of the way the U.S. Environmental Protection Agency (EPA) does business.

Specifically, Mr. Barker wants to convince EPA that the so-called "bubble policy" is as effective as—but far less expensive than—the traditional air pollution control program mandated by EPA to control particulate emissions at Armco's Middletown steelworks in southern Ohio.

If Mr. Barker is successful, Armco will spend only $4 million to $5 million to implement the "simple and logical" bubble—and clear the way for other companies to use that new air pollution control strategy. If he is not successful, Armco could be forced to spend an additional $15 million to install the traditional controls that EPA would normally require to reduce the particulate emissions.

In the early 1970s, Mr. Barker realized that EPA's air and water pollution control strategies were growing increasingly complex and costly. As an engineer he felt restricted by EPA's "command and

Excerpted from article in *Industry Week*, September 29, 1980. Reprinted with permission. Copyright 1980. Penton/IPC Inc. Greg Johnson is an associate editor with *Industry Week*.

control" regulations that gave him little or no leeway to develop innovative control alternatives. When the Solomon Task Force reported to the President in 1977 on problems facing the steel industry, it suggested that EPA and industry representatives join forces to review "tools" that might help cut the cost of environmental protection. Mr. Barker was chairman of a working group investigating what is now the bubble policy.

The first job for Mr. Barker's group was to determine just what emissions remained after major EPA-mandated control equipment had been put in place. Some emissions were obviously caused by hard-to-control steelmaking processes. But others were known to be generated by heavy vehicle traffic on the Armco mill's miles of mostly unpaved roads, and by the handling of the mountains of raw materials needed. "Everybody recognized the problem," Mr. Barker recalls, "but we didn't have any way to quantify it." The task was compounded because EPA regulations addressed only the process emissions—not the windblown "fugitive" emissions.

But Mr. Barker and others of the same persuasion suspected that windblown fugitives were a major reason that the air quality control regions surrounding many steel plants were often designated as "nonattainment" regions for particulates. They believed that controlling the fugitive emissions might help solve part of the problem.

The germ. "What we found amazed even us," Mr. Barker says. "Sixty percent of our remaining emissions [after major controls were installed] were these so-called windblown fugitives." Only 9.9 percent were process emissions. In those facts lies the germ of the bubble idea; and the reason Armco "wanted to develop a program to control those windblown emissions."

The bubble plan developed for use at Armco's Middletown Works is based on a "trade-off" of process emissions control for control of windblown fugitives. Mr. Barker believes that the bubble will cut particulate emissions 4,000 tons per year—six times as much as traditional process controls, and for one-third the cost.

To understand the bubble approach, picture a single smokestack on the top of an imaginary bubble that encompasses the entire Middletown Works. Any pollutant would have to exit through that stack. This approach contrasts with the individual stack and process control tack which EPA has traditionally relied upon.

No cars. When Mr. Barker escorts visitors through the 2,600-acre Middletown Works, he points with pride to the massive environmental protection expenditures that Armco has made since 1950, the year when the corporate environmental engineering department was created.

Armco completed work on the bubble in July, and Mr. Barker hopes to have air quality monitoring data in hand by October, to prove that his simple and logical plan does work. Key points of the plan, which Mr. Barker devised, include a massive road and parking lot paving program; the installation of spraying systems (not unlike those found in Florida orange groves) to wet raw material storage piles; and the use of road vacuum cleaners and tank trucks to keep unpaved roads and cleared areas free from dust that could be swept up into the atmosphere.

Perhaps the most difficult part of putting the Armco bubble to work was the "forced busing" of 6,000 plant employees from new perimeter parking lots to their individual workstations.

But when Mr. Barker first received corporate approval to implement the bubble, changing the daily routine of 6,000 workers was not his major worry. Since the idea of a bubble was a new one in air pollution control, he had to convince EPA that it was a viable solution to the rapidly escalating costs associated with pollution control.

In early 1978, armed with the emissions statistics and a brief slide show that explained what the bubble entailed, Mr. Barker set out for Washington to meet with EPA officials. "We wanted to show them that we had a tool that the Solomon report had pointed to," Mr. Barker says. He followed up the Washington visit by seeking support from his environmental counterparts in the steel industry.

But while Armco was busy spreading the new "gospel," EPA startled Mr. Barker by proposing a bubble policy that most industry representatives found far too restrictive. The January 1979 proposal specifically banned tradeoffs involving process and fugitive controls.

On the road. "We at Armco took it upon ourselves to go out on the roast beef and green pea circuit to take the story around the country and try to build the grass-root support we needed," Mr. Barker says.

"John Barker became a spokesman, an advocate, a lobbyist, and even a circuit rider, to gain support for the bubble," says C. William Verity, Armco's chairman. "John didn't give up."

In addition to refining his speaking style, Mr. Barker also learned how to lobby in Congress. An associate of Mr. Barker's suggests that this was the long-time Armco engineer's most difficult learning experience. Mr. Barker agrees: "That's something I had to learn in this job. It's something they don't teach you in engineering school, and I'm not sure you learn it in any school. But it's a part of the real world we live in today, and you have to learn to do it, whether you like it or not."

Mr. Barker's "circuit riding" paid off in December of last year when EPA issued its final bubble policy. Although the policy has been criticized by industry leaders as still being too restrictive, it did give Armco enough flexibility to continue work on the Middletown bubble.

Corporate backing. While Mr. Barker has had to work hard to convince congressmen, EPA officials, and environmentalists of the bubble's merits, he has received consistently solid backing from his Armco bosses and the board of directors.

Since 1950, Armco has spent $185 million on pollution abatement technology in its various plants, and since 1966 Mr. Barker has had complete responsibility for corporate pollution control activities. His work on the bubble, however, has taken up nearly one-quarter of his working hours in the last two years. "During the last two years I spent a very significant amount of time trying to get out the message," Mr. Barker says, "but today that activity is pretty much over. My time today is spent sitting down with EPA people in Chicago, Washington, and Research Triangle Park (N.C.), working out the nitty-gritty details."

Armco's corporate environmental engineering department has compiled an excellent pollution control track record. Mr. Barker notes that six "scrubber" systems were installed on Middletown's open hearth furnaces even before the Clean Air Act of 1970 was signed into law.

Taking the risk. Consequently, Mr. Barker realizes the risk involved in trying to bypass traditional EPA controls and opting for the as-yet unproved bubble. "The risk could be spending $4 million or $5 million that you don't need to spend under the law."

If Armco's bubble is rejected by EPA, Armco could be forced to install expensive and energy-intensive "baghouses" (which function like huge vacuum cleaners) to control process emissions that now escape into the atmosphere. Mr. Barker believes that that massive construction project would take nearly three years—which would put Armco far beyond the Dec. 31, 1981, compliance deadline it is expected to meet.

"The other risk," Mr. Barker adds, "is that if we are successful— and if some extremely hard-line environmentalist is successful—the EPA might say, 'Well that's great. Now do both. Do both the baghouse and the bubble.' "

An extensive air quality monitoring system (EPA, Armco, and an independent consultant have measuring devices scattered throughout Middletown) will provide the facts that will determine if the bubble is successful.

But even if the data do prove that the bubble is a success, there will be at least one more hurdle standing between Mr. Barker and his goal: EPA's present bubble policy limits bubble use to "attainment" (clean-air) regions only. The Ohio EPA has classified the Middletown air quality control region as nonattainment, based on data gathered at a monitoring station located just a few city blocks downwind from the Armco plant. The station has consistently shown the area to be in violation of the particulate emissions standard. Complicating the situation is the fact that the prevailing winds cross directly over the plant—and directly at the monitor—nearly 65 percent of the time.

But Mr. Barker argues that Ohio EPA has misinterpreted the regulation that places the area in a nonattainment category, and believes the region will eventually be reclassified as attainment, clearing the way for the bubble.

More bubble. If EPA approves the bubble, Mr. Barker believes the air quality "tool" will see more use by U.S. industry. "I think if we get this one approved, you'll see a lot of companies dig in and do the work that needs to be done."

But even some steel industry representatives remain skeptical. "Most companies in the steel industry see no way they can use the current bubble policy," says Earle F. Young, vice president for energy and environment, the American Iron & Steel Institute, Washington. "The EPA has imposed a crust of extremely rigorous procedures . . . [that] include such complex demonstration requirements that long and costly delays in even applying for approval of a bubble are inevitable."

"Some people say that the bubble is absolutely useless because of the restraints that are built in,'' Mr. Barker says. ''But I personally don't share that view.''

If Mr. Barker meets with success—and he says ''logic'' dictates that he will—Armco will most likely begin planning bubbles for other Armco facilities. And, he suggests, he might begin pushing for a bubble approach in the regulations regarding water pollution control.

Mr. Barker ties his work with the bubble in with the work Armco's Mr. Verity does as chairman of the U.S. Chamber of Commerce. ''Mr. Verity's goal is to develop a better working relationship between government and industry in general, not just in pollution control but in the whole regulatory scheme.'' Proving that the bubble works, Mr. Barker suggests, is a step in that direction.

Environmental Confrontation: The War that Companies Can't Win

By David Clutterbuck

This article outlines a detailed strategy for responding positively and minimizing conflict when a company finds its products or policies under attack by environmentalists.

It can happen in any industry, to large and small firms alike. One day sales are good, production problems are few and far between and, apart from some apparently inconsequential barracking from environmental pressure groups, the business future looks rosy.

Within a matter of months, however, the company suddenly finds itself cast in the role of villain in a set-piece environmental conflict.

To its horror, the company finds itself accused, for example, of harming wildlife, threatening the health of children or wasting scarce mineral resources. Its image suffers, the public begins to boycott or avoid not just the product in question, but anything made by the firm. Sales figures begin to drop and everyone wants to know why.

One of the reasons, according to Dr. David Ford, a management researcher at the University of Bath in the UK, is that few companies learn from the mistakes of others in dealing with environmental issues. Another is that even fewer have planned strategies for avoiding environmental conflict.

Ford, who has undertaken a detailed study of how companies react to environmental pressures, has found that companies have three main choices in dealing with environmental conflict.

They can maintain an aloofness, on the grounds that anyone can see that the environmentalists do not know what they are talking about, and hope that the nuisance will eventually go away. They can take the offensive, attempting to sway public opinion before the environmental lobby does so. Or they can bend with the wind, accept that some concessions are inevitable and attempt to avoid conflict altogether.

Unfortunately, the first of these options is both the most common corporate reaction and the one likely to do the most harm to a company.

"Managers usually don't appreciate the size of the environmental lobby or that it won't go away," Ford says. "They tend to regard any difficulties for their products created by environmentalists or other public interest bodies as unfair competition. Their first reaction is to stonewall, issuing bland denials. Before long the situation progresses to an unequal battle.

"It's quite clear from all the cases I have examined that a company can scarcely ever win by assuming an opposing stance. But that doesn't mean to say it has to give in."

On the contrary, he maintains, the company that has a well thought-out strategy for coping with environmental conflict can profit from the experience.

Ford maintains that individual companies and whole industries involved in environmental conflict pass through several or all of five stages: *peace, skirmish, conflict, defeat and victory from defeat.* However, those who plan their reactions properly, says Ford, can by-pass the last four stages with what he calls a *pre-emptive strike*, in which they respond to alarm signals before an organized environmental campaign can be launched against them.

In the *peace* stage there are only the faintest rumblings that an environmental conflict may be on the way. One of the signs is that another company with a similar product is coming under attack from environmentalists.

For example, says Ford, all chemical companies ought now to be planning how to react should environmental groups in their countries mount a campaign against herbicidal lawn weedkillers containing the defoliant dioxin. Public action on this issue has already become strong in North America, Australia and Scandinavia. Evidence from Australia suggests that the wives of 25 percent of soldiers exposed to the chemical in Vietnam have given birth to stillborn children, says Ford.

Yet some large Western European chemical companies have not even begun to discuss the issue with environmental groups. By delaying acceptance of the reality of the threat, maintains Ford, companies frequently find it is too late to prevent a harmful clash with public pressure groups.

While no company can be expected to drop a product or process at the first hint of a health or environmental scare, says Ford, it should use this time as a period of grace to prepare for the worst and attempt to salvage as much as possible. "You won't have time to have considered reactions if the problem strikes unexpectedly," he maintains. "Decisions taken in the stress of the moment are most likely to be wrong."

Thomas Thomas of the US research organization SRI International, Inc., who has been helping US companies predict and formulate responses to environmental change, advises "Don't follow your initial reflexes—they are part of the system that blinkered you before. Talk and listen to people two or three layers down who are saying 'I told you so'."

The *skirmish* stage settles who, if anyone, a company is going to get on its side. The usual reaction from a company under siege, Ford says, is either silence or complete denial. This soon turns the initial concern of the public interest groups into outright hostility. If the media are unable to get satisfactory answers, then they too will be forced into a hostile stance.

Ford quotes the example of the Royal Dutch/Shell Group, which marketed a fly-killer called Vapona. Normally a relatively open company to the media, it responded defensively when a Swedish biochemist suggested that a constituent of the product, dichlorvos, was a danger to health. The company answered queries from the press and other interested bodies by saying that it had published safety data and could see no problem.

The company's unwillingness to discuss the issue or even accept the possibility it was wrong, according to Ford, led the media and environmentalists to pursue it in full cry. Sales were quickly affected, especially after Italian newspapers claimed the product harmed the infirm and young babies in hospitals.

By the time the company changed to a more open, cooperative stance, the damage had been done. Restrictions on the chemical were discussed in several countries and eventually implemented in Italy. The controversy over the product still continues 11 years after it began, although the company feels it has amply demonstrated that the attacks were unfounded.

In addition, Shell damaged its relationships with much of the media for a long time afterwards, claims Ford. "It was never in control of events until it gave out complete information," he says, "and by then it had lost its good image and much of its sales of the product. Some technical journalists felt they could never trust the company again."

The strategy Ford advocates during the skirmish stage is to admit that there is or may be a problem and involve all the interested organizations in a problem-solving exercise. "Invite the relevant government bodies, the media, and the environmentalists to help find practical, economical solutions," says Ford. "Otherwise you will get them all on the opposing side."

A benefit of this approach is that a company will usually then be able to distance itself from the product or process that is causing the problem. It becomes a "pollution problem" rather than an issue of an allegedly irresponsible company.

Unless a company seizes the initiative in the skirmish stage, it will start being hurt, says Ford. By the time top management starts to calculate just how much the conflict will cost their company, maintains Ford, in most cases the sums involved are already getting out of hand. The time to examine the costs of conflict, Ford insists, is during the skirmish stage.

Occasionally, companies wake up to the harm that the conflict is inflicting on their business in time to avoid disaster. "Shell eventually defused the conflict by trying to start again," says Ford. It invited the press and environmentalists to work with it in assessing the dangers. Even so, much damage had already been done.

In most cases, however, conflict escalates, with greater public pressure forcing governmental intervention and eventual defeat for a company. The company involved either completely withdraws the product under fire, or modifies it to meet at least partially the environmentalists' objections. In very few cases is the public pressure group defeated.

If a company manages to modify its product till it is relatively or fully acceptable to the environmental lobby, then it usually takes advantage of the opportunity to proclaim its social responsibility. This is the stage Ford calls *victory from defeat*. He explains: "A company will fight tooth and nail not to do something the environmentalists demand. But as soon as it has done it, it will advertise the fact."

However, the costs of modifying a product at this late stage may be high. "Very often, companies only start to look seriously at alternatives when they realize they are not going to win. They should have started planning for this right at the beginning, in the peace or skirmish stages," says Ford. A gradual introduction of modifications is likely to be cheaper and will at least spread the costs over a period of time.

Examples of companies which have made a virtue of necessity right from the beginning and earned themselves credit by working with the environmental lobbies are rare. One such case, however, says Ford, is US chemicals manufacturer Monsanto Inc., which discovered that its polychlorinated biphenyls (PCBs), used widely in paints and electrical equipment, were coming under strong environmental attack. PCBs were said to leach into the ground, accumulating in the food chains of wildlife and interfering with breeding cycles. Because they were not biodegradable, the compounds could not be destroyed naturally.

Once the hazard was recognized, the company immediately carried out a broad investigation, with outside help, to discover the dimensions of the problem. It then abandoned all those applications, such as paint, where it could not ensure that the spent compounds would be returned for recycling. It also started a major education programme to encourage customers to make sure all waste PCBs were returned or incinerated.

Ford estimates that this action cut sales of the product by about 50 percent. But its open and effective response avoided conflict with the environmentalists and meant that PCBs did not follow other non-degradable poisons into a total ban.

Another company which has learned how to defuse environmental conflict is UK shoe manufacturer C. & J. Clark Ltd. At first it was all set for a clash with the anti-whaling lobby, which, according to a company spokesman, "started harassing us about using leather cured with sperm whale oil in about August of 1978." The company blandly told the protesters that the oil was used by tanners, over whom it had no control as it bought its leather supplies on the open market.

Then a petition was sent to the company chairman, Daniel Clark, who recognized the harm that a prolonged environmental conflict could have on sales. As a predominantly one-product company, Clark was particularly vulnerable to the threat of a public campaign not to to buy its shoes.

In April 1979 the company took the initiative and sent a revision of its buying contract to its many leather suppliers. In six months time, the letter said, no leather containing sperm whale oil would be accepted. Three months later another letter informed the suppliers that Clark had bought an electrospectrometer to test each batch of leather delivered. Virtually all the suppliers decided to accept the ultimatum. Clark claims its shoes are now free of sperm whale oil. "All of the organizations which petitioned us beforehand have been equally vociferous about praising our action," claims a company spokesman.

The other alternative initial course of action, a well orchestrated offensive by the company, seems to work less well. Among its strongest proponents in the US are the plastic bottle manufacturers. They were attacked by environmentalists first because they were allegedly using up scarce energy resources and later because non-degradable plastic bottles were a litter problem. Instead of concentrating on finding solutions to these problems, the industry has embarked on a massive public relations campaign to swing the public to its side.

The campaign includes instruction kits for use in schools and a team of 20 top executive speakers from 13 companies who tour the US talking to groups of journalists and environmentalists.

The executives are taught to represent the plastic bottles as borrowed energy and deliberately to bring up contentious issues such as the leaching of chemicals used in the plastic, should no one in the audience do so. The aim is to convince the audience that the industry is doing all it can to resolve these problems.

This campaign has undoubtedly muted some of the criticism levelled against plastic bottles by giving the media a better idea of the difficulties the industry faces in finding solutions to the litter and energy problems. But it has certainly not defused the conflict, nor removed the pressure from environmental groups.

Research by US social psychologist Paul Slovic suggests that it is only worth a company's while taking its case to the public if it has a very good case to start with. While better than keeping silent, attempts to educate the public to the corporation's way of thinking can easily backfire, making matters worse by pushing the subject further into the public eye.

"People's perception of the dangers rises according to how easy it is to imagine the worst case. The more discussion on the subject, the more their imagination works," Slovic explains. "Consider an engineer arguing the safety of a nuclear reactor by pointing out the improbability of each of the ways radioactivity could possibly be accidentally released. Rather than reassuring the audience, the presentation might lead them to think 'I didn't realize there were so many things that could go wrong'."

Slovic points out, too, that once people have taken a point of view on the risks involved, subsequent information on the subject is distorted to fit. The near disaster at a nuclear power station at Three Mile Island in the US, for example, "proved the possibility of a meltdown to some people and the reliability of containment systems to others," he observes.

Slovic and some research colleagues have carried out a number of studies into how people perceive the risks involved in corporate activities. Very rarely did the statistical risks coincide with people's instinctive assessments. People felt, for example, that the chances of dying were 1.5 times greater from nuclear power pollution than from riding a motorcycle, although radiation deaths are extremely rare and motorcycle deaths very common.

Slovic and his collegues have demonstrated that people make mental trade-offs between the perceived benefits and the perceived risks attached to a product or process, and that this trade-off determines their attitude towards it. The benefits of vaccinations outweighed the risks by 1,100 percent in one survey; the risks of aerosol spray cans outweighed the benefits by over 400 percent.

Slovic suggests that the most effective way for a company to reduce public opposition to its products is to increase their perception of the benefits. "People are generally prepared to accept increased risks for increased benefits," he says.

What all this boils down to is that the public fickleness that companies in the fashion industry, for example, have long ago learned to live with and profit from, is a factor that all companies should take into account in their strategic planning. However illogical and unreasonable it may appear to a chief executive that his company's products may be singled out for attack on health or environmental grounds, the possibility should be considered and broad contingency plans made.

"Almost any corporation is liable to find itself under this kind of attack," says SRI's Thomas. "It is not the company that attracts the assault in most cases. What happens is that some group of people starts to consider that some aspect of the dominant set of values in society is insane." If the company does not change its own values it is at first caught in the squeeze between two competing ethics, then left behind.

Unfortunately, Thomas maintains, the rate at which these sets of values can change is increasing. Moreover, the time period between when society expresses a wish for change and when the change is forced through is also dropping. Hence companies will have less and less time to react to environmental pressure.

Fortunately, however, social forecasting has been much more successful over the recent decade than economic forecasting. Thomas urges companies to make their planning processes more receptive to such issues. He suggests that they automatically include sociologists on project teams. "If you can foresee a problem with a pressure group, you can usually circumvent it," he claims.

Andrew Cawdell, of the UK branch of environmental activists Friends of the Earth, suggests that companies also make more attempts to "get to know environmentalists." He believes that companies should carry out environmental audits of all major products and processes to determine if they have any potential for environmental conflict. The companies should then throw open the audits to an environmental group to criticize on a confidential basis, if they wish.

To this end, Cawdell also suggests that companies should compile an index of environmental issues that impinge upon their activities.

Cawdell claims to have been rebuffed by the UK packaging industry when he tried to provide it with such a tool. He was able to condense the audit to four questions which could be asked concerning each product:

Is the product being sold in a throw-away pack when it could be sold in a returnable container?

Is the package made in such a way as to make separation and recycling of its constituent materials difficult?

Can the product be packaged in a different material that will have less effect on the environment?

Could the product be sold loose or in greater bulk?

Both Ford and Thomas foresee the rapid strengthening of environmental pressures which are currently in the skirmish stage. Says

Thomas: "Areas of potential impact include anything related to energy or to health. The choices people make will hit nearly everything they consume. We can predict a steady movement towards more durable, less flashy goods and towards food with more nutritional value." Public action against low-nutritional snack foods is already gathering strength in both developing and developed countries.

Ford suggests that companies pay particular attention to any of their products which correspond to one of the following criteria:

Does it have a permanent effect on people or the environment?

Does it alter symptoms rather than causes? For example, most air fresheners do not affect the air. They simply reduce the nose's ability to detect odours.

Is it artificial? For example, food colourings and additives.

Is it wasteful? More especially, does it use up scarce minerals, natural products such as wood, or energy, including heat?

If the answer to any of these is yes, then now is a good time to start looking for substitutes.

The SEC's Pollution Disclosure Requirements: Are They Meaningful?

By Martin Freedman and Bikki Jaggi

The Securities and Exchange Commission now requires certain firms to make pollution disclosure reports available for potential investors. This article explores the quality and usefulness of these reports and makes some suggestions for change.

The Securities and Exchange Commission is empowered to establish rules and guidelines concerning the registration of publicly held companies. Included as part of this charge is the power to require these companies to disclose information that is considered relevant to the needs of financial statements users. One of the SEC's new requirements concerns information about pollution abatement. Despite this requirement, an analysis of financial statements indicates that management is not enthusiastic about disclosing pollution information. A probable cause for the lack of enthusiasm relates to the perceived usefulness of this information. Several studies have examined different aspects of the usefulness of social information in general and pollution information in particular and have provided conflicting evidence.

This article reevaluates the need for pollution by focusing on three aspects of pollution disclosures: Is there an economic rationale for pollution disclosures which can make them useful? Do investors perceive pollution information as being useful and react to pollution disclosures? Do pollution disclosures reflect actual pollution performance, so that they can be considered useful?

© 1981 by the Regents of the University of California. Reprinted from *California Management Review,* Vol. XXIV, No. 2, pp. 60-67 by permission of the Regents. Martin Freedman is an assistant professor of accounting at the State University of New York at Binghamton. Bikki Jaggi is a professor at the College of Business Administration, Kent State University, Kent, Ohio.

Development of Disclosures Policies

Prior to 1973, some companies voluntarily disclosed pollution information in their annual reports and registration statements, but there was no SEC requirement for such disclosures. In 1969, the National Environmental Policy Act was passed, and one of its provisions required the SEC to consider environmental effects in its disclosure requirements for publicly held companies.[1] As a result of this requirement, the SEC from 1971 to 1973 issued a number of releases concerning environmental disclosures.[2] The 1973 release is very important in this respect; it required disclosures of any material effect on pollution abatement activities.[3] Although some firms failed to comply with this regulation in 1973, most firms did, but they did so in a myriad of ways in different degrees.

Later, environmental groups brought suit against the SEC to require the mandating of more extensive pollution disclosures (*Natural Resource Defense Council, Inc.* v. *SEC,* 1974). As a consequence of this action, the SEC held hearings and issued a number of releases clarifying pollution disclosure requirements.[4] This process culminated in a release in September 1979 in which the SEC required firms to disclose, in addition to the 1973 requirements, estimated future capital expenditures for pollution abatement, any violations and potential violations of the pollution laws, and the extent of any fines.[5] Furthermore, the SEC stated it would forcefully enforce the pollution regulations, and it demonstrated this new approach by publicly criticizing U.S. Steel for not adequately disclosing pollution information in its filings with the SEC from 1973-1977.[6]

A group of companies and an industry association also intervened in lawsuits brought by environmental groups to rectify the alleged failure of the Environmental Protection Agency to implement several provisions of the Federal Water Pollution Control Act. One of the rulings of the Federal Court of Appeals related to pollution disclosures in which the court decided that in enforcing the water pollution act, the EPA does not have to inform the public of its investigatory activities nor to comment on these activities. The implication of this ruling will probably be that the enforcement process will be speeded up and that public disclosure of pollution information by the EPA will be slightly restricted. However, this ruling should have no impact on the SEC's pollution disclosure requirement.

Despite the restrictions on pollution disclosures, there has clearly been a shift in the SEC's policies from reluctance to encouragement for requiring pollution disclosures. An apparent reason for the SEC's earlier reluctance stemmed from their belief that financial statement users were not looking for pollution information and that, therefore, its inclusion in annual statements was not essential. However, the developments during the 1970s, including the emphasis on the need for corporate social responsibility and the enactment of environmental laws, made pollution information relevant to investment decisions and forced the SEC to change its policies to require disclosure of information relating to corporate activities concerning the environment. The success of the SEC's new policies depends upon the usefulness of pollution information, which is influenced by the content and format of disclosures. If pollution disclosures provide investors with additional information in a form which can be reasonably interpreted by them, these disclosures will be useful.

Economic Rationale

In the 1960s, firms did not consider it their responsibility to get involved in pollution-related activities, and the issue of pollution disclosures did not receive much attention. Even if some firms did undertake certain environment-related activities on a voluntary basis, this disclosure was not considered important. Developments in the 1970s changed the situation with regard to corporate social responsibility. Now corporate social responsibility is well recognized and several rules and regulations have been developed to require corporations to avoid polluting the environment beyond certain levels. This new perspective raises the issue of whether information on pollution-related activities should be disclosed in an appropriate form so that investors can evaluate the social performance of the firms. Theoretically, arguments for and against such disclosures can be presented.

Arguments in favor of pollution disclosures are based on the grounds that any information affecting corporate earnings should be disclosed to enable investors to make an informed judgment, so that the optimal allocation of resources takes place. Since pollution expenditures are likely to be substantial in amount, they will have an impact upon corporate earnings. It has been argued that in the short run the effect on earnings would be negative, that earnings, rate of return, and dividends would decline. This argument is supported by a study of the seven largest American steel producers.[7]

This study estimated that if the steel companies made the appropriate expenditures for pollution abatement for the years 1972-1976 and were unable to fully pass these costs to consumers, their earnings per share and dividends would be severely reduced.[8] The validity of this argument is also apparent from the fact that large amounts of capital expenditures raised through equity or debt are not likely to result in a positive return in the early stages of the pollution abatement program.

Despite the negative effect in the short run on the earnings performance, the pollution abatement expenditures are believed to have a positive impact on the performance of the firm in the long run. It has been argued that pollution expenditures would result in the use of more modern equipment. This modernization process may lead to greater productivity and higher earnings in the long run.[9]

The above arguments relating to the short-run and long-run impact of pollution expenditures on the earnings performance of firms demonstrate that pollution information is important for investment decisions. Without this information investors will not be able to evaluate the short-run or long-run performance of the firm. These arguments support the disclosure of pollution information in an appropriate form.

Another argument in favor of disclosure of pollution information relates to the ability of this information to reduce risk. Firms belonging to highly polluting industries are required by law to restrict pollution to a specific level. If they are exceeding the pollution limits and violating the laws, they risk legal sanctions in the form of fines and heavy capital expenditures for cleaning the environment at a later date (U.S. Steel's agreement is an example of this). In the worst case, there may be a possibility that certain plants will be closed down because of their negative impact on the environment. Thus, disclosure of pollution information, especially information on meeting the emission standards, will enable investors to evaluate future risk. Nondisclosure of such information will increase uncertainty, and investors will not be able to evaluate a firm's future liabilities.

Arguments against the disclosure of pollution information are based on the grounds that the cost to the firm of providing the information exceeds any benefit that users of the statement might obtain. The cost/benefit arguments can be presented both from the perspective that the costs of generating the information are prohibitive and that the information that can be generated is useless.

Another cost that management may claim they incur relates to putting a disclosing firm at a competitive disadvantage. The management of the disclosing firm might feel that information disclosed on pollution abatement might be detrimental to the firm because another firm may be able to assess efficiency and long-run plans based on the pollution disclosure.

A major argument supporting the premise that pollution disclosures are useless is based on the efficient market hypothesis. If capital markets are efficient, it can be argued that there is no need to formally disclose pollution information because information on corporate pollution-related activities is fully known to the market long before it is disclosed in an annual statement.

Most of the above arguments against disclosure of pollution information are similar to arguments that are made about any information included in annual statements. They may be valid under certain circumstances, but the main thrust of the SEC rules and regulations lies in disclosing as much information as possible in a formal way so that investors are equitably informed. The arguments in favor of pollution disclosure indicate that pollution information is important for return and risk evaluation. Therefore, despite some arguments against disclosure of this information, a strong theoretical justification exists for disclosure of this information.

Do Investors Need It?

In view of the potential of pollution information to enable investors to better evaluate the risk and return of a firm, it can be expected that information will be needed by investors, especially institutional investors. Several institutional investors, such as religious and nonprofit organizations, consider social and environmental problems in their investment decisions. For these decisions they need information with regard to social performance of firms in which they invest.

The demand for social information by investors has also been examined by B. Longstreth and H.D. Rosenbloom. The authors surveyed institutional investors to determine whether they needed social information for their investment decisions. Several institutional investors indicated a need for social information, but there was no clear indication that most institutional investors were concerned with social performance of firms.[10]

The findings of other survey studies do not clearly support the expectation that social information in general and pollution information in particular are being demanded by investors. These results may be due to the fact that questions for demand of pollution information were either not included or were not properly formulated. Another reason could be that the need for pollution information was not greatly felt at the time the surveys were conducted. On the basis of survey results, it is difficult to evaluate the SEC's disclosure requirement for pollution information.

Another method to determine investors' need for social information is to analyze investor reaction as soon as this information is disclosed. It can be expected that disclosure of pollution information will trigger investor reaction. This aspect of disclosure was first examined in 1975 by A. Belkaoui.[11] He concluded that investor reaction to firms disclosing social information was different than their reaction to firms which did not do so. The findings of this study need to be interpreted with caution because of its methodological problems.

We examined investor reaction to pollution disclosures in a 1980 study of firms from four, highly polluting industries: chemicals, oil refining, steel, and paper pulp. The results relating to the total sample did not show statistically significant differences between investor reaction to those groups disclosing pollution information and those who did not. We then divided the disclosers into extensive and restricted disclosure groups. The results indicated that investor reaction to firms disclosing extensive pollution disclosures was different than their reaction to those with limited or no disclosures. We concluded that extensive pollution disclosures are likely to trigger investor reaction because such disclosures will enable investors to evaluate a firm's pollution performance.[12]

On the basis of the above studies, it can be said that the expectation of investor reaction to disclosure of pollution information will be valid only if investors are able to use information to evaluate social performance of a firm. This evaluation is possible if detailed information is disclosed. The detailed information may include the degree of compliance with pollution laws, plans to reduce the pollution, and the expected amount of future capital expenditures to meet the pollution standards. No reaction can be expected if disclosures are not detailed enough to enable investors to evaluate a firm's social performance.

Pollution Performance and Disclosures

The analysis so far indicates that pollution information should be in demand because it is likely to be useful for evaluation of risk and return of the firm, but the empirical studies do not clearly support the demand for pollution information or investor reaction to pollution disclosures. One way pollution disclosures can be considered useful is if they reflect pollution performance of the firms. If there is no association between pollution performance and disclosures, disclosures may be difficult to interpret.

Disclosures vary with firms at present, since no specific disclosure format is widely accepted. However, certain important items for pollution disclosures can be identified. Based on the importance of each item, a disclosure index can be developed, and we have attempted to develop such an index.[13] After developing the pollution disclosure index, we correlated pollution disclosures of a firm with its pollution performance, as indicated by an index developed by the Council on Economic Priorities. We found no significant correlation between pollution disclosures and pollution performance of firms.

This absence of association is perceived by the investors, and they ignore disclosure of pollution information because they find it difficult to interpret. It can be concluded from these findings that it is not pollution information per se but the present form of disclosure that renders pollution disclosure information useless. In order to improve the effectiveness and usefulness of this information, proper disclosures need to be developed.

In the absence of strict monitoring procedures, it can be argued that several factors other than requirements influence management decisions to disclose pollution information and the extent of such disclosures. An important factor in this regard is likely to be the economic performance of the firm. Depending upon performance, it could be decided whether disclosure of extensive information would be in the best interest of the firm.

In a previous study, we examined the association between economic indicators and pollution disclosures. Our findings for the total sample did not indicate any statistically significant association between the disclosure index and economic indicators. We then segmented the sample on the basis of the size of the firms. For the segmented sample, we found that large firms with poor economic performance made extensive disclosures compared to the rest of the sample. A logical explanation for these findings is that large firms with poor economic performance attempt to justify performance on the basis of their enhanced concern for the environment and indicate to investors that this concern reduces uncertainty about the future.[14]

The discussion in this section shows that disclosure requirements are not being followed by all firms. Only a small segment of firms choose to disclose extensive information. This may be either due to ambiguity about the disclosure requirement or the lack of enforcement with regard to compliance with this requirement. Whatever the reason, pollution information is not being fully utilized by investors.

Improving Disclosure Requirements

In order to improve the effectiveness of pollution disclosures, the following expansions of the disclosure requirements are suggested.

- We believe that the usefulness of pollution information will be enhanced if firms disclose their expenditures for each major class of pollution. Currently, most firms disclose the total expenditure for pollution abatement and do not separately report on air or water pollution or solid waste disposal. A separate reporting would enable investors to better evaluate the pollution performance of the firm. A detailed report on each pollutant would enable sophisticated users of this information to make a better evaluation. Furthermore, it would be helpful to users of this information if any special problem concerning each pollutant were reported separately.
- Firms should be required to report on the technique (in either general or specific terms) that they use to abate pollution in their plants. A firm may use a number of techniques. Broadly speaking, these can be divided into stopgap measures (such as catalytic converters in smokestacks) or modernization programs. Stopgap measures will probably not lead to long-term improvements in either productivity or pollution abatement. However, a modernization program should result in long-term benefits. The reporting of techniques will enable sophisticated users of this information to better evaluate the potential effectiveness of the pollution abatement program.
- If a firm has an overall pollution abatement program including

a long-range plan, the plan including past and expected accomplishments and the current status of the program should be disclosed. In many firms, the long-range pollution abatement plans provide the basis for determining capital expenditures for pollution abatement and for determining the current standards permitted by the EPA. Knowing the plan, including its current status, should enable the reader to make a more informed judgment on future pollution and economic performance.

- Many firms decide that plant modernizations are the best way to achieve improved pollution performance and productivity increases and to make the firm more competitive. Although improved pollution performance may be an indirect effect of the modernization program, it is a consideration in these programs. Firms should disclose the current status of these modernization programs, including when the expected pollution and productivity improvements will be achieved. If readers were made aware of when these improvements would occur, they would be better able to assess the future performance of the firm.
- Finally, firms should disclose both positive and negative effects of pollution abatement. The SEC disclosure guidelines required the reporting of any material effects of pollution abatement on the firm. Firms have interpreted this as meaning that negative effects should be reported. This requirement should be expanded to include any material effect, whether it is negative or positive.

A number of firms may claim that the disclosure of all this information may put them at a competitive disadvantage. However, we believe this argument is spurious. If all firms in a highly competitive industry are forced to disclose this information, then no company should be at a disadvantage. Only companies not making a serious effort to abate pollution may be hurt, and these companies have to disclose potential violations of the pollution laws and the extent of any fines, based on the 1979 SEC pollution disclosure guidelines.

Although these suggestions do not alleviate the measurement problem directly, they do provide a basis to aid the investor in evaluating the riskiness of the firm's pollution situation. It is quite difficult and costly to try to measure the effects of pollution. However, by providing information on the liability of the pollution program, which is now required by the SEC, and by enforcing the suggestions recommended here, a better measure of pollution will be created.

If investors do use pollution information in making investment decisions, as the empirical evidence tends to indicate, then meaningful pollution information should be provided. The SEC made major steps in the 1970s to require the disclosure of pollution information. It should continue to require the disclosure of more extensive pollution information so that investors and stockholders can make intelligent decisions based on the best available evidence.

References

1. Securities and Exchange Commission, Securities Act Release Nos. 33-6130 and 34-16224 (27 September 1979).

2. For example, see Securities and Exchange Commission, Securities Act Release No. 5170 (19 July 1971); and Securities Act Release No. 5386 (20 April 1973).

3. Securities and Exchange Commission, Act No. 5386.

4. For example see Securities and Exchange Commission, Securities Act Release No. 5704 (6 May 1976).

5. Securities and Exchange Commission, Act Nos. 33-6130 and 34-16224.

6. *New York Times,* "U.S. Steel Disclosure Criticized," (28 September 1979).

7. J. Cannon (J. Halloran, ed.), *Environmental Steel* (New York: Praeger Publishers, 1974).

8. Ibid., p.144.

9. For example see C. Canty, F.G. Perry, Jr., and L.R. Woodland, "Economic Impact of Pollution Abatement on the Sulfite Segment of the U.S. Pulp and Paper Industry, *Tappi* (September 1973), pp. 52-55; and J. Bragdan and J. Marlin, "Is Pollution Profitable," *Risk Management* (April 1972), pp. 9-18.

10. B. Longstreth and H.D. Rosenbloom, *Corporate Social Responsibility and the Institutional Investor* (New York: Praeger Publishers, 1973).

11. A. Belkaoui, "The Impact of the Disclosure of Environmental Effects of Organizational Behavior on the Market," *Financial Management* (Winter 1976), pp. 26-31.

12. M. Freedman and B. Jaggi, "The Relationship Between the Types of Pollution Information Disclosure and Investors' Reaction," *Proceedings,* the Southeast Regional Meeting of the American Accounting Association (1980).

13. B. Jaggi and M. Freedman, "An Examination of the Association between Pollution Disclosures and Economic Performance of Firms," unpublished manuscript, 1980.

14. Jaggi and Freedman, "An Examination."

Environmental Concern: A Phillips Tradition

How do corporations view their environmental efforts and communicate their views to the public? This article by the Phillips Petroleum Company is an example of the literature being published by corporations which is designed to communicate to stockholders and the public the company's environmental protection activities.

The Overview

Safeguarding the environment and conserving natural resources are high on the list of Phillips priorities.

Long before pollution became a universal concern, Phillips was making strides toward preserving the environment. The same Phillips Environment Conservation Committee that was formed almost 20 years ago is still operating today.

"This says something about the company's commitment to pollution control," John Moon, chairman of the committee, said recently. The committee is responsible for reviewing all major pollution control plans and projects. It is a forum for environmental matters, a medium for exchanging new information.

Phillips believes that all actions to protect the environment should take into account the socio-economic costs to the consumer as well as the potential environmental benefits. Within this framework, the company's specific objectives for the protection of the environment are:

To plan and conduct all company operations so as to protect the environment.

To ensure that company operations comply with all federal, state and local environmental laws.

To encourage open communication between local groups, conservation and industry organizations, and the general public about

---

meeting environmental needs in ways satisfactory to the company and the community.

To include environmental protection as an essential part of the development of new manufacturing processes.

To conduct research into more environmentally acceptable products.

To continue research in pollution control technology and conversion of waste streams into useful products.

To provide employee training and information programs on environmental design and operating techniques, regulatory requirements and prevention of accidental release of pollutants.

To cooperate fully with governmental agencies in gathering information that will lead to fair and effective conservation standards, and to provide company experts to serve on government-requested study groups in the field of environmental protection.

The company's Environment Conservation Committee helps to ensure that environmental protection isn't an isolated activity restricted to a specialized group.

"The concern cuts across all organizational lines and requires the participation of virtually all portions of the company," says Moon.

"We try to draw together the best knowledge available on pollution control, then transmit that know-how to where it's needed in the company," he explained. Information and findings go to nine committee members, each representing a major company segment.

"Our effort at Phillips is directed at protecting the environment not only in the best way we can, but also economically. This is so there is less cost impact on the consumer," Moon said.

To accomplish this goal, each of Phillips major operating organizations has established an internal network of environmental coordinators located in plants and offices. Those coordinators work with other corporate staffs, particularly the company's centrally based Environment and Consumer Protection Division.

This division of Corporate Engineering, headed by Moon, provides environmental services and consultation throughout the company. The staff is the company's contact with governmental agencies and industry groups on environmental matters.

Where the Deer and the Elk Play . . . and the Fish Bite

The magnificent Wasatch National Forest in northern Utah is the home of deer, elk, icy streams and snowcapped mountains. It is also the home of miles of underground pipeline and a network of producing oil wells.

"A visitor wouldn't be able to tell there were wells out here unless he was right by them," says Paul Armstrong, a 32-year Phillips veteran who supervises the company's operations in the Bridger Lake area. "This is the best place to work. The beauty here hasn't been disturbed at all." That's because of a Phillips conservation effort that began 10 years ago—before any of the wells were drilled and the pipeline laid. The first phase of that conservation effort was to find the best methods of developing the resources without disturbing the environment.

Today, the only signs of man's intrusion at the well site are a wellhead, a small gravel pad around the well and a one-lane access road. The ground around each well is grassy, level and terraced.

An alarm system signals Armstrong if there has been an oil spill, ruptured equipment or a sudden release of products. When this alarm goes off, checks are made and corrective action taken.

"I believe we are on top of environmental control here. We've never had a spill," says Armstrong. "I think we're doing the best we know how, and if anything better comes along we'll make use of it."

Since Phillips established an operation in the forest, campers have had access to the picturesque area. "Every couple of weeks my men and I even pick up the litter left by the public," he says. "We clean up the cans and bottles left behind because we want the forest to stay clean."

Because of this kind of effort, Phillips received a commendation from the Bonneville chapter of the American Fisheries Society for an oil field in harmony with its environment.

The water from the stream that runs just a few yards from the plant is crystal clear and the fishing is very good. "Phillips has taken care of the forest and the wildlife," Armstrong says. "The deer and elk graze right up to the plant area. I really enjoy being so close to these wildlife neighbors, and I'm glad we're protecting them."

A Fail-Safe System Prevents Oil Spills

In hard hat and overalls, Charlie Fewell stepped off the pier into a swaying crew boat headed toward two Phillips oil and gas producing platforms four miles out in California's Santa Barbara Channel. A large sign flashed a bold reminder: "No Pollution."

For Charlie Fewell, that message is about as necessary as one telling him to tie his shoelaces in the morning."No pollution—no exceptions" is a rule Fewell has lived by every day he has been field supervisor for Phillips operations in the Santa Barbara Channel.

Not so much as a paper cup goes over the side at the Hogan and Houchin platforms. When it rains, every bit of moisture is collected off the three-deck platforms and channeled into processes that remove traces of oil. Sewage from crew quarters is treated.

The most critical concern, of course, is preventing oil spills that can occur during drilling or while the oil is being produced from the 60-odd completed wells on the two platforms. An eyewitness to the Santa Barbara oil spill of 1969, triggered by drilling from another company's platform a few miles away, Fewell is determined that nothing like that will occur in his operations.

"The word is—if there is any danger of a spill, no matter how small the possibility, operations are shut down," Fewell explains.

Any serious production abnormality causes alarm panels to light up and horns to sound. And if the problem is not corrected immediately, automatic shutdown devices go to work, closing off pipes and vessels, and turning off production equipment. Producing wells can be closed off by safety valves at the surface wellhead or by "down hole" valves 200 feet below.

When drilling is in progress, a two-story high blow-out preventer assembly is placed at the wellhead below the drilling deck. Although blow-out—a rush of oil and gas up the drill hole—is a rare occurrence in offshore drilling, the preventer shut-off valves are tested daily.

Each day the platform crews also check the operation of critical components of production equipment and pollution safeguards. Over a 30-day cycle, some 400 mechanisims on each platform are tested and examined. With pride, Fewell points out that this equipment check system he helped develop has proved to be so effective that it has been adopted as a standard accident-preventive procedure in the industry.

Taking the Shaft Out of Coal Mining

Surface mining of coal became controversial because the industry was not sensitive to environmental and reclamation problems. That's why Shawn Sorrell, environmental director for Phillips Coal Company, is working to ensure that the company's mining and land reclamation operations are "clean."

Sorrell knows firsthand how careless reclamation practices can cause adverse effects. He grew up in the heart of West Virginia coal mining country. Now he's assessing land near the Red River south of Shreveport, La., where Phillips holds leases slated to be mined for lignite coal.

"We're planning on mining 150 million tons of lignite over the next 30 years," says Sorrell. "My work here is to ensure that Phillips can reclaim the land, leaving it not only as good as its original state, but even better in some ways.

"We've done tests on top of tests in this area to determine what the environmental impact will be, and the measures necessary to minimize those impacts," he says. An initial one-year baseline study examined virtually every environmental aspect of the area: soil, vegetation, air, ground water, surface water, wildlife and even possible archaeological evidence. Results of the study are being evaluated by the coal company and governmental authorities.

"We're not likely to run into reclamation problems here in the South," says Sorrell. "Both the soil and the rainfall conditions are ideal for vegetation.

"The biggest concern here seems to be whether farmers will be able to grow crops when we're done and, if so, whether production will be as good as before. Our tests show the answer is yes," Sorrell says.

Since mining activities occupy only a portion of the project area, owners can continue farming and grazing on some of the land. Crops, trees and grasses can be replanted within two or three years after mining begins.

When reclamation is complete, the mined land will drain better and possibly will be more productive than before mining.

Air quality will not be adversely affected by mining. And streams in the path of the mine equipment are rerouted, then restored to their original location once mining ends. Disturbed wildlife habitats will be reestablished, or other suitable wildlife provided, and any significant historical or archaeological sites that are encountered will either be protected or relocated in cooperation with state authorities.

Sorrell says, "We're certain that not long after we mine it, the area will be as good or better from land use and environmental quality standpoints than it was before we touched it."

The Economics of Energy and the Environment: Good News for Consumers

By Roger W. Sant

This author argues that substantial profits can be made by entrepreneurs who provide innovative ways to solve our energy problems in a way that is compatible with environmental protection.

The government, the business community and the media generally have been painting a grim picture of America's energy predicament today and through the 1980's and 1990's. There is plenty of energy "bad news" to be worried about. That is not even arguable. But what is arguable are comments like, "it will only get worse;" or, "we are powerless to do anything;" or, "the Government has things so messed up that we'll never recover;" or "the only 'practical' solution is to encourage much greater conservation." We appear to be a nation waiting to be led, but unwilling either to follow or do much on our own.

What I would like to do is look behind the grimness, not because I choose to be optimistic, but because I think the data now provide some basis for "good news," for consumers, the environment, our energy future, and the economy.

The best information and analysis suggests that economic forces are now strongly pushing us toward an energy solution. That doesn't necessarily say that the market, as it is, is tending toward a solution, but rather that the pure economics all indicate directions that would provide us a stable energy system. And furthermore, the transition underway appears to be opening up some of the best markets in a long time. To some that may say only that we're through the

This article was printed in the January, 1981, issue of *Energy Consumer*, which is no longer published by the Department of Energy. The information contained in this excerpt does not represent current energy programming or policy. Roger W. Sant was Director of the Energy Productivity Center of the Carnegie Mellon Institute when he wrote this article for the *Energy Consumer*.

worst of it, but I prefer to take the view that the 1980's will, in fact, be a decade of major energy opportunities, not a continuation of the 1970's crisis. I'm sure some will say "how can you come to that conclusion?"—particularly as the Persian Gulf instability continues and gold krugerrands threaten to become the only acceptable currency at gasoline stations. The answer, I think, lies in shifting our focus from that of scarcity to availability and from production to marketing.

Most marketing people instinctively understand that for 220 million Americans, energy means a whole range of services that we enjoy—comfortable rooms, light for reading, heat for cooking food, and mobility. Fuels and electricity are just a means of providing those services, and then only a partial means. Furnaces, insulation, boilers, automobiles, water heaters, appliances, etc., are every bit as important.

Industrial managers agree. What they need is the means to form steel, or the shaft power to run machines, or the heat for a distillation process. Yet most of us connected with the politics of energy have looked at the problem, not in terms of these services, but through the wrong end of the telescope—trying to manipulate supplies or restrict the consumption of various Btu's, kilowatt hours, or barrels of oil to reduce imports. If one really pays attention to consumer needs, our dependency on imported oil is only one of several indications that the existing energy system is not serving those consumers very well and is not the real problem. From this perspective, the problem is more fundamental than imports. It is that our system is not providing the energy services people want at the lowest possible cost. A high level of oil imports is only one symptom of that imbalance. Attempting, as we have, to eliminate that import system is like prescribing aspirin for a broken arm. Let me explain further.

I only recently discovered that no more than 40 percent or so of the cost of all energy services results from buying fuel. The balance comes from amortizing, maintaining, and operating the equipment necessary to convert fuels into useful services. In 1980, for instance, the cost of energy services in the U.S. economy was roughly $4200 per person—a whopping 43 percent of the per capita gross national product. But, only $1700 of that expenditure will be for fuel; all the rest will be for the systems needed to make fuels useful.

The largest portion of that $4200 will pay for mobility, the bulk of which is short distance travel. What we might call comfort and convenience—space conditioning, hot water, and appliances—will cost each of us an average of $1100. Freight will run about $750 per person, and only $400 or so will be spent for manufacturing functions and production feedstocks. The rest is for miscellaneous uses.

As one would suspect, the fuel portion of the cost of energy services was much higher in 1980 than it was in 1972. In that year, only about 25 percent of the cost of energy services resulted from fuel and electric costs—compared with 40 percent in 1980. That means in an 8-year period there was a big shift upward in the fuel component of energy services, reflecting the well-known rise in energy prices. But the interesting part is that it appears that a fuel proportion similar to the 25 percent we experienced in 1972 was much closer to the 1980 lowest cost case, given the existing prices of fuels, electricity and equipment.

In other words, the energy system is out of balance primarily because we have failed to invest enough in improving the equipment, structures, and vehicles that convert fuel and electricity into useful services. In 1978, we at the Mellon Institute asked ourselves, "What would have been the result if the least-expensive energy supplies and end-use devices had been combined to supply our energy services?" To answer this question we made a detailed study, the results of which were startling, at least to us. We are now updating those figures, and find that if we want to minimize cost to consumers, we are going about it with great determination *in the wrong direction*.

The data show that, contrary to most pronouncements, all of the oil we import is more expensive than our other energy services options. This means that if everyone's economic self-interest were fully accommodated, we would not be purchasing any foreign oil. In other words, our national paranoia about imported oil is ill-founded. We have cheaper options.

And, contrary to conventional wisdom, we found that utility-supplied electricity is not one of those cheaper options. It also appeared relatively uncompetitive at 1980 prices. The quantities of domestic oil, coal and gas we use would appear about right, but the findings indicate they should be used in very different ways—to supply different energy services than they now supply.

The really good bargains are the thousands of devices that improve the amount of services consumers get for each unit of fuel or electricity used. Double-paned windows, automatic flue dampers, electronic pilot lights, sophisticated thermostats, small units that generate electricity and usable heat simultaneously, and diesel engines in automobiles are all examples of very inexpensive options. With few notable exceptions, the two most popular Washington solutions, solar and synthetic fuels, are not even in the running and probably won't be for some time—unless major technical breakthroughs occur.

In order to get these results, we compared two cases: the way we actually were supplying energy services in the United States in 1980, and a hypothetical best-technology 1980 case that would have resulted from perfect least-cost decisions. We attempted to determine how the lowest-cost situation might have departed from the actual in regard to additional uses of energy-efficient products and to different "mixes" of fuels. We assumed throughout the study that the energy services in both cases would be identical; only the means of providing those services would have differed. And, as I have indicated, they would have differed considerably.

All of the shifts called for would have reduced the cost of energy services by about $350 each or a little under $77 billion for the whole economy. In other words, these calculations indicate that using the lowest cost available products and technologies would have reduced energy service costs by about $1400 a family in 1980, and that's conservative.

It is important to note that in this hypothetical case improved efficiency would not reduce demand, but satisfy it. That is the key to the overall concept of an energy service market. Improved efficiency is undertaken to satisfy the demand for services at lower cost, not to reduce the demand for fuels. Therefore, our assumption was that energy services would be identical in the two cases. This is in contrast to the traditional brand of conservation—lower thermostat settings, smaller homes, less driving, less manufacturing, etc.—which depends upon using lower levels of energy services and therefore requires some sacrifices by consumers.

It also should be underscored that we are making no claim about the precision of these numbers. The results obtained, however, clearly tell us that there are some large markets for products and technologies that, in effect, can compete with fuels in providing energy services.

Development of these markets, along with using oil and natural gas in different ways, would reduce consumer costs. In addition, of course, developing these markets would improve the nation's security and environment by reducing consumption of imported oil and more environmentally hazardous fuels; those results are secondary effects of reducing costs.

The only claim I would make for this hypothetical case is that it justifies aggressive pursuit of some different opportunities. I think this pursuit will bring about a complete shift towards the marketing of services, not fuels and equipment. Customers will be offered the opportunity to buy comfort and convenience rather than natural gas and electricity; mobility instead of gasoline; and manufacturing process functions instead of fuel oil.

Let me summarize what I think all of this will mean in the 1980's. First of all, our analysis and the U.S. experience of the last few years make clear that economic forces are now heading us in the direction of an energy solution. They will continue to do so throughout the eighties. Scarcity will not be a factor except through temporary political disruption, which can be effectively dulled with the strategic petroleum reserve filled up.

Second, all of the oil we now import is a downright bad buy. We should not be using it because we have less expensive options, regardless of the national security benefits that might be gained from using less.

Third, at current costs, most new central power generation is too expensive to compete in the energy services market place. Electric utilities are experiencing this problem now—and it should become more evident in the early part of this decade. Fortunately, we will be able to take advantage of current excessive generating reserves along with better utilization of power throughout the day and season; this should make utility power a better relative buy later in the decade.

Fourth, the most significant energy opportunities in the next ten years are going to be in marketing the products that improve energy efficiency. That's not because of anyone's moral ideas about conservation, but rather that's the direction costs will push us.

Finally, perhaps the most significant change will be that traditional retailers of oil, gas, coal, and electricity gradually will become energy wholesalers because of organizational and recruiting problems. The retail role will be taken over by new marketers of energy—in the form of light, heat, and motion instead of kilowatt hours, therms, and gallons.

Honeywell, General Electric, IBM, Carrier, General Motors, Johnson Controls and many others, large and small, will compete with the utilities, especially if the utilities are slow to change their strategies or are prevented from changing by regulators. The new retailers will provide heating and lighting services including furnaces, insulation, and light bulbs, and fuel at the lowest package cost. Instead of requiring the customer to balance fuel, structural, and equipment costs, the energy services company will provide improvements that make economic sense, and will charge the user one low monthly price for the complete service—the cost of fuel, a monthly charge for equipment, and perhaps a management fee.

These five conclusions mean that real entrepreneurs should have a field day with energy markets in the 1980's and least-cost energy choices will result. The risks may be high, but the rewards will be higher. In this environment, the most successful government policies should be those that encourage wide-scale competition, not in further subsidies or regulations. If both of these things happen, the consumer will be the biggest beneficiary because we will get to live in a world of energy choices again, and this will lead to lower costs.

Citizen Participation in Power Plant Siting: Aladdin's Lamp or Pandora's Box?

By Dennis W. Ducsik

Will greater participation by citizens in the siting process speed up or slow down the completion of new power plants? Despite the utilities' resistance, the author says citizen involvement may lessen the companies' problems.

For over a decade now, one of the most intractable problems on the energy-environment scene has been rancorous political opposition to the construction of big power plants. Born in the late 1960s at places like Storm King Mountain, Turkey Point, Bodega Head, and Four Corners, the resistance movement has snowballed to the point where it is now rare for a major project involving an electric generating facility to go unopposed. This lack of public acceptance has even been institutionalized in the form of national organizations such as the Environmental Action Foundation, to which groups all over the country turn regularly to help in fighting utility expansion plans.[1]

Although the reasons for political resistance to power plants are many and complex (especially in the case of nuclear reactors), concern over the choice of site and its environmental and social implications usually plays a key role. Indeed, with the possible exception of "No to Nukes," the most familiar cry to a utility executive's ears is almost certainly "Don't Put It Here." It is a cry, moreover, that seems likely to be heard with increasing frequency throughout the '80s and beyond. Electric companies are already hard pressed to come up with locations that are technically capable of develop-

Excerpted from article in *Journal of the American Planning Association*, 47, 2, April 1981. Reprinted by permission. Dennis W. Ducsik is director, Program on Science, Technology, and Society at Clark University, Worcester, Massachusetts.

ment as well as suitable on economic, environmental, and political grounds.[2] As the tradeoffs involved become even more acute in the future, it follows that confrontation between the industry and affected interest groups can be expected to intensify as well.

The ultimate source of difficulty, of course, is that no large-scale power facility can be designed to completely avoid imposition on a landscape, an airshed, or a body of water in its vicinity. The laws of thermodynamics together with engineering and economic realities simply preclude it. Nor is it realistic to think that siting disputes are a thing of the past in light of recent progress in reducing the nation's consumption of electricity. Even load growth at the modest annual rate of two percent translates into a significant need for additional generating capacity, and there will always be older plants to replace irrespective of the rate of increase in demand. Some would argue, in fact, that it is desirable to accelerate the retirement of certain oil-fired units as a means of reducing dependence on foreign petroleum products and improving air quality in cities, where many of these units are located. Thus, a sizable complement of new sites must still be found in the years ahead.

Can anything be done to avoid the grim prospect of more disruptive conflict over the location of power plants? In this author's view, the time has come to give serious consideration to an idea that has actually been around since the early '70s and found useful application in fields such as highway location and water resources development,[3] but not to any significant extent in the electricity sector. This is the concept of "open" planning, which calls upon electric companies to voluntarily incorporate some form of citizen participation into the site selection process. Many variations are possible, but the key feature of this approach is that interaction with concerned citizens should take place during the process of elimination that is commonly used in the evaluation and choice of alternative locations. Such collaboration should occur, moreover, well in advance of the regulatory process which now provides, in the form of licensing hearings, the principal opportunity for persons affected by a siting decision to influence it directly. Under the participatory scheme, a formal public hearing would mark the end point of dialogue between the company and the public at large, not the beginning.

Over the years this notion of citizen involvement in site planning has gained the endorsement of prominent individuals and organizations outside of industry circles,[4] and has even been written into proposed legislation. On the whole, however, it has yet to penetrate the thinking of those in the best position to initiate new approaches to the politics of siting, i.e., the utilities themselves. Instead of reconsidering the longstanding policy of keeping sites confidential until license applications are ready to be filed, most companies take the position that legislative reform is needed to ensure that siting disputes will be settled more expeditiously within the framework of federal and state certification procedures. As to suggestions that the company might try to get together in a constructive fashion with environmentalists and other citizen advocates, typically these have either been greeted with the utmost skepticism or dismissed as altogether outlandish.

With the climate of alienation that has long prevailed between utilities and their ardent antagonists, this attitude on the part of the electricity industry is perhaps understandable. The problem, however, is that for several years now the idea of collaborative siting has been so negatively prejudged that very few companies have been willing to experiment with it, even on a limited basis, and there has been practically no careful evaluation of it in the industry literature.[5] As a consequence of this unfortunate lack of attention, very little is really known as to whether citizen participation might be a viable means of stemming controversy over where to put future power plants, or, for that matter, any major energy facility likely to engender serious environmental opposition.

The principal objective of this article is to develop a realistic and balanced perspective on the matter, one that accounts in particular for issues that are important from the standpoint of the power industry (who, after all, must take on the bulk of the risks before any benefits can be realized).

The Rationale for Collaboration

The source of consternation from the utility standpoint is that intervenor groups, capitalizing on the procedural complexity of the regulatory system, have turned such proceedings into the "marathons among legal track meets."[6] The resulting delay and uncertainty can wreak havoc on facility planning efforts which, because of the technical complexity and vast financial commitments involved, must proceed in an orderly fashion. Equally distressing to the industry is the tendency for disputes to wind up in the courts, before judges who are ill-equipped to engage in technology assessment and who are inclined, therefore, to base decisions on strictly procedural considerations instead of the substantive merits of the project.[7]

Environmentalists, too, are disillusioned with the traditional hearing process. Coming as it usually does at the end of the licensing process—which itself does not begin until after facility plans are ready to be consummated by the utility—the hearing is widely regarded as an exercise in futility.[8] This breeds frustration, distrust, and anger on the part of concerned citizens, who sense quite rightly that many important options have been foreclosed[9] and that their involvement comes too late to have a meaningful influence on the project (except perhaps to stop it altogether).

Such difficulties have precipitated much discussion and debate as to how the rules of practice governing hearings might be modified to make them less vulnerable to dilatory tactics on the one hand,[10] and to facilitate effective contributions from intervenors acting in good faith on the other.[11] The basic problem, in other words, lies not so much with what goes on during the hearing itself, but rather with what does not transpire in the way of communication during the earlier stages of the planning process.

It is against this background that suggestions arise to the effect that citizens be invited to participate directly in site selection, beginning at a time when options are open and plans can be developed in a way that accounts fully for environmental and social concerns. In theory, this creates an opportunity to avoid a great deal of unnecessary conflict and to take corrective measures well in advance of the eleventh hour, when changing plans can result in a dramatic escalation of overall project costs.

There is another and probably more important benefit that could accrue to a utility in the wake of a successful interactive endeavor, i.e., an increase in its general credibility in the public's eye. If nothing else, a more open process would seem to be a good way to ameliorate problems of misinformation and confusion that so often in the past have served to erode public confidence.[12] The resulting goodwill might even spill over in the long run into the arena of price regulation, where any relaxation of political tensions would be a most welcome development to beleaguered utility executives attempting to secure timely rate relief.

At least on the surface, these and other exhortations on behalf of citizen participation appear perfectly logical and reasonable. Why, then, has the concept yet to be embraced by the electric utility industry? Before attempting a judgment on the matter, it seems advisable to try to appreciate the misgivings of those most familiar with the particulars of how the siting process operates in practice.

The Nature of Utility Concerns

As any utility planner or consultant will readily attest, finding sites that are capable of development and potentially licensable—in engineering, economic, and environmental terms—is an exacting task that takes several years of effort, costs millions of dollars, and often produces documentation which occupies an entire bookcase.[13] Further complicating the situation is the fact that site selection has become almost as much a political process as it is a technical one.

The general misgivings on the part of utility respondents can be translated into six distinct statements of concern.

Concern no. 1: Will early disclosure of planning information put the company at a political disadvantage, and thereby prejudice its ability to purchase and/or license a preferred site?

Concern no. 2: Can environmentalists behave in a rational and constructive manner and be willing to accept compromise solutions?

Concern no. 3: Can laypersons participate effectively in a complicated planning process without having the skills and qualifications normally required of the technical professional?

Concern no. 4: Will environmental advocates recognize that there are no perfect solutions, given that planning operates in the presence of numerous constraints and ambiguities?

Concern no. 5: Is it possible to keep the focus on site selection when many environmentalists are more interested in large, generic issues such as need for power and the future of nuclear technology?

Concern no. 6: Will the company get burned in the end anyway, due to the impossibility of achieving universal happiness with the outcome of the planning process?

All in all, if the above reactions to the concept of public involvement in siting were to be characterized in a single word, that word would have to be "dubious." To most respondents it seems palpably irrational to attempt to build a collaborative relationship when there is little hope of arriving at accommodation but a very real possibility of creating chaos and intensifying conflict. Would this not, in effect, be playing right into the hands of one's enemies? Thus, it is the prospect that open planning could well turn into a Pandora's Box that stands as the major disincentive to its use by the electric utility industry, for whom citizen participation is simply too much of a gamble.

Political Objections Evaluated

Of the six basic concerns articulated by utility respondents, the first two are closely related and reflect a basic fear that going public at an early stage would somehow backfire in a purely political sense. Without confidentiality, it is argued, opposition to potential sites will be stimulated before the company is ready to meet it, and intransigent activist groups will simply have additional opportunities for disruption.

Consider first the assertion that premature disclosure will give rise to unnecessary public concerns and embarrassment on the part of an ill-prepared utility. While this is certainly a plausible scenario under business-as-usual conditions, it seems unlikely that anyone would expect the utility's data and analyses to be anything other than preliminary.

This is not to say that advance notice of conceivable facility locations would be received by the public with total equanimity. Nevertheless, at least there is an opportunity to deal constructively with the public's fears and mistaken impressions. It is difficult to imagine how such an effort could give rise to anything like the anxiety engendered by the conventional "decide—announce—defend" process, in which dialogue tends to polarize shortly after affected persons learn of the project.

A second argument that seems less than persuasive is that site planning information must be kept secret lest it eventually be used against the company in some manner. First of all, it is hard to see how this might pertain to the case of environmental data, considering that extensive impact statements are required in connection with the regulatory process at both state and federal levels. Also seemingly overdone is the fear of speculation, insofar as even a two or three million dollar increase in land cost—which is often occasioned by rumor in any event—is quite small relative to overall project expenditures. While this is by no means an insignificant amount, neither is that which the utility loses for each day or week that a new power plant is delayed as a result of public opposition that might have been avoided.

A second major type of political concern identified in this study is that having to do with the alleged motives and behavior of "extremists." With environmentalists expected to exploit every available opportunity for subversion, it is understandable that the industry would see little to be gained (and much to be lost) in attempting a collaborative siting process. The obvious question to be raised here, however, is whether the problem of extremism is as widespread or as threatening as the statements of utility respondents make it seem.

It is important to note at the outset that some respondents seemed to view the environmental community in terms just as monolithic as environmentalists have always viewed the power supply establishment. Indeed, many of the adjectives chosen to characterize intervenors (intransigent, self-serving, irresponsible, and so on) seem borrowed from the very lexicon activists have long employed with reference to utility actions. Any sociologist will confirm that even the most docile citizen can be transformed into an activist if the circumstances are right; witness, for example, how parents angry over the busing of school children and farmers aroused by governmental food policies have taken to the streets in recent years. In this light one might argue that much of the extremism decried by the utilities is really a natural response to a perception that unless they resort to unorthodox tactics their strongly held values will be excluded altogether from the decision process.

Still, it would be naive to suggest that the problem of extremism will disappear altogether. Some will undoubtedly enter the participatory arena bent on opposition, and there will be others for whom no amount of interaction in the spirit of accommodation would make a difference. What is to prevent such persons from disrupting an otherwise useful process of interaction among parties willing to seek compromise?

At first glance this appears to be a Catch-22 situation: without certain parties, participation won't materialize, and with them it can only degenerate into confrontation. What is being overlooked, however, is the possibility that the open planning process itself might create an unfavorable climate for extremism. Both regulatory officials and members of the judiciary, who are not unaware of the prevailing political climate, may be much less sympathetic to continuing challenges in the face of an obvious good faith effort by the utility to incorporate all views and suggestions into the siting process. This is particularly true if a negotiated settlement has been reached, in which case the company would have the support of a constituency much broader than it had enjoyed in the past in connection with its siting decisions.[14]

Technical Objections Evaluated

Proceeding in a manner similar to that of the foregoing section, there are a number of points that can be made in response to the third and fourth concerns utilities seem to have about citizen participation. Here the prevailing view is that the process could just as easily break down in the technical sense, either because of an inability on the part of concerned citizens to grasp analytical complexities of the subject matter, or because of an unwillingness to accept the ground rules by which site selection normally operates. Is it not impossible, respondents ask, to "democratize" an endeavor that is complicated and needs to be conducted in a very structured and orderly fashion? To begin with, consider the argument that because the siting process is highly technical, it should be reserved for technical professionals who have acquired the necessary experience and expertise. Obviously, one cannot expect citizens to participate directly in the sort of detailed ecological or meteorological studies that utility specialists carry out. But this is far from the real objective of participation, which is to incorporate a broader set of values and perspectives into the siting process.

One topic a utility staff might not be completely familiar with, for example, is that of socio-cultural conditions related to land use, which often have significance. Further, most planners would readily admit that the site tradeoffs are at root a matter of judgment and even intuition. Here it is the purely technical methods of analysis that tend to break down, and it is also where collaboration with affected interests—a dialectic inherently capable of operating on subjective information—could be most advantageous.

Establishing that concerned citizens have a legitimate role to play in siting, of course, says nothing about how participation should be structured to be workable. One point which needs to be brought out is that collaboration does not necessarily connote a joint effort. What seems most important is that the public not be totally insulated from the technical work; it is essential that lay participants at least be informed of what is being done, and be encouraged to make whatever observations or suggestions they feel are appropriate (e.g., as to new lines of inquiry, the criteria to be applied in making tradeoffs, and so on). Beyond this baseline the degree of interaction can vary considerably as a function of what is expected from the participants, what sort of capabilities they exhibit, or where their major interests lie.

The hope, of course, is that citizens working on a cooperative basis with the utility would come to realize that decisions are never made under ideal circumstances, and that it is necessary to bound the problem and even muddle through on occasion in order to maintain a timely and efficient evaluation process. Realizing this goal is still not easy, however, and much will depend on the extent to which a spirit of give and take develops in the course of interaction.

To encourage this the utility must first ensure that the project schedule allows sufficient time for planner-citizen interaction, recognizing that environmentalists might be inclined to approach the impact assessment process in a more cautious manner than experienced site planners. Planning lead times already span a couple of years or more, and as long as participation begins at an early point this would seem to allow the necessary breathing room.

In addition, it is important that the utility be sensitive to the fact that if the alternatives presented are not sufficiently broad to present real choices, participation will be suspected of being a thinly-disguised effort to market a decision that has already been made (even if it has not!). If such a perception is to be avoided, attempts must be made to broaden the range of options to the point where there is room for compromise. It might be desirable, for example, to begin with a reconnaissance of broad regions of interest instead of narrowing the focus immediately to evaluation of a small number of final candidate sites.

Yet, it will not be so easy to relax other types of constraints or to remove certain ambiguities from the impact assessment process—what then? Here it would seem that the utilities' attitude toward such difficulties, and not the difficulties themselves, is the most important factor in determining the viability of the collaborative approach. It may well be, for example, that having a wide range of options available may not be so crucial if the company shows it will actively seek to develop new alternatives and to ease particularly burdensome constraints. What seems essential is that participating citizens come to feel that the company is keeping an open mind and is trying, in the face of imperfect circumstances, to be responsive to environmental and social concerns. If this can be achieved, the notion of blending citizens into a highly technocratic planning process seems not so disquieting after all.

On the Search for Common Ground

Several arguments have been made to the effect that constructive interaction between utilities and concerned citizens is not a wholly implausible scenario. Nothing has been said, however, about whether the process can actually converge on a mutually acceptable course of action. Respondents noted in their fifth and sixth concerns that discussions could founder at the very beginning—over nonsiting questions like need for power or choice of plant technology. Thus, if the parties involved will never see eye to eye and impasse is inevitable sooner or later, why bother with collaboration at all?

In light of strongly held sentiments, it seems clear that questions of power demand and alternative means of supplying it must be dealt with somehow if a collaborative siting process is to proceed. Ideally, such questions should be debated and resolved in a separate forum and at a more appropriate level of policy making.

It is conceivable, however, that existing forums for consideration of long-range plans will prove unacceptable to citizen advocates in some respects. What then? In this case, perhaps the only way to keep the focus on the issue of location is to start with a plant that seems least likely to raise the hackles of the environmental constituency. It certainly seems unwise, for example, to apply a collaborative approach for the first time to the siting of a nuclear reactor. One need not be so pessimistic, however, over the prospects for effective cooperation in the case of other major facilities such as coal-fired or hydroelectric plants, which at least do not suffer from a deep-seated mistrust in the basic technology that is employed.

With a basic strategy of working up to the more controversial projects, one begins to wonder if it might not be feasible after all to address, as an adjunct to the site selection process, the questions of need for power and alternative supply strategies. Certainly there is no a priori reason why some issues like, say, the validity of load forecasts or the prospects for purchasing power cannot be scrutinized in an open forum, at least to some extent. This author, for one, is not about to underestimate what can be accomplished if only the present atmosphere of hostility and suspicion can be dispelled.

This is not to say that compromise solutions will be easy, and this brings us to the final issues, i.e., the problem of honest disagreement.

It is often possible to achieve substantial agreement on a course of action without reaching consensus on underlying goals and values. The history of decision making in our pluralistic society is fraught with examples where those with seemingly irreconcilable differences at the level of broad principles have come to terms within a context of specific proposals. One must take care to remember, in addition, that universal happiness is not the criterion upon which any process of conflict resolution should be judged. The ultimate goal, rather, should be to avoid unnecessary conflict and seek accommodation wherever possible, and to have all participants feel comfortable with the way the process was conducted. The hope is that those whose interests suffer will not only be fewer in number, but also more equitably treated and less inclined, therefore, to turn their disagreement into overt resistance. Is this not, after all, the classically conceived essence of democratic methods for managing the clash of opposing views?

References

1. See R. Morgan and S. Jerabek, "How to Challenge Your Local Electric Utility: A Citizen's Guide to the Power Industry," Environmental Action Foundation, Washington, D.C. (March, 1974).

2. See, e.g., G. A. Brown et al. *Power Plant Site Considerations at Charlestown, Rhode Island,* University of Rhode Island, Marine Technical Report No. 23, Kingston, Rhode Island (1974); see also R. H. Ball et al., *California's Electricity Quandary: II. Planning for Plant Siting,* Rand Corporation Report R-1115-RF CSA, Santa Monica, California (September 1972).

3. See, e.g., A. K. Sloan, *Citizen Participation in Transportation Planning: The Boston Experience,* Ballinger Publishing Co., Cambridge, Massachusetts (1974); J. O'Riordan, "The Public Involvement Program in the Okanagan Basin Study," 16 *Natural Resources Journal* 177-196 (January, 1976).

4. See, e.g., Committee on Power Plant Siting, *Engineering for Resolution of the Energy Environment Dilemma,* at 12, National Academy of Engineering, Washington, D.C. (1972); Special Committee on Electric Power and the Environment, *Electricity and the Environment: The Reform of Legal Institutions,* at 8-9, Association of the Bar of New York City, New York, N.Y. (1972).

5. One of the better pieces on the subject that has appeared in recent years is an interview with Robert I. Hanfling of the Department of Energy, "Utility Decisions: What Voice for the Public?," *Electrical World* (December 1 and 15, 1977).

6. T. J. Dignan, "Licensing Hearings: A Modest Proposal," *Nuclear News,* at 45 (May 1974).

7. For a good discussion on this point, see Barton, "Behind the Legal Explosion," 27 *Stanford Law Review* 567 (February, 1975).

8. See, e.g., Ebbin and Kasper, *Citizen Groups and the Nuclear Power Controversy*, MIT Press, Cambridge, Massachusetts (1974).

9. The necessity of committing to studies and making equipment selections for a given site prior to knowing whether that site would be acceptable is described in J. L. Leporati, Envirosphere Company, "Expanding Role of States in Power Plant Regulation," presented at the 47th Annual Executive Conference, New York, NY (October, 1976).

10. One measure that is often proposed, for example, is the use of a res judicata standard to preclude the rehearing of issues for which there was a prior opportunity for hearing.

11. See, e.g., Boasberg, Hewes, Klores, and Kass, *Policy Issues Raised by Intervenor Requests for Financial Assistance in NRC Proceedings*, NUREG 75/071, Nuclear Regulatory Commission, Washington, D.C. (July 18, 1975).

12. The inverse relationship between public confusion and public confidence has been documented by Clark and Brownell in *Electric Power Plants in the Coastal Zone: Environmental Issues*, American Littoral Society Special Publication No. 7, Highlands, New Jersey (October, 1973).

13. See Nagel and Vasseld, "Power Plant Siting Requirements," *Planning*, Vol. 39, No. 2 at 24 (February, 1973); Brown, "Power Plants—Picking the Sites," *Consulting Engineer*, Vol. 40, No. 3, at 133 (March, 1973).

14. As it was put nearly a decade ago, "a political compromise with expert and responsible ecology groups capable of representing the public's interest would be a large step toward securing a solid mandate upon which to rest long range construction plans." D. Jopling and S. Gage, "The Pattern of Public Political Resistance," *Nuclear News*, at 32 (March, 1971).

Building in Environmental Costs

By David Gordon Wilson

The problem of solid waste and some rather innovative proposals for dealing with it are discussed in this article by an engineering professor at MIT.

W here there's muck there's brass" is an oft-quoted Yorkshire expression supporting the popular belief that environmental pollution ("muck") is a necessary accompaniment to economic betterment ("brass," or money). I grew up in the English Midlands just east of where much of the early Industrial Revolution took place. We would travel west to Wales through the Black Country, an area that seemed almost devoid of trees or other vegetation—unending heaps of mine wastes, separated only by ancient factories and foundries with belching smokestacks, and rows of houses thrown up to accommodate urban immigrants forced out of their rural villages by inhuman legislation.

Despite this horrible spoliation of natural beauty wrought by industry in many parts of Britain, the environmental disasters we have brought about more recently seem likely to rank as far more serious. Atomic testing in Nevada and the Pacific, contamination of animal feed with polybrominated biphenyls (PBBs) in Michigan, and the dumping of toxic wastes in Love Canal are well-known examples in the United States of what ultimately will be many instances where human actions, ranging from the well-intentioned but misguided to the criminally callous, have resulted in health and environmental effects tragic to the point of disaster.

The situation in the Third World is, ironically, especially hazardous because of the partial success of environmental movements in the industrial countries. Restrictions or bans on many substances have led producers in developed countries to look for markets

Reprinted with permission from *Technology Review,* Copyright 1981. David Gordon Wilson is a professsor of mechanical engineering at MIT.

elsewhere—mainly in nonindustrialized developing countries with few restrictions. A prominent example is tobacco, a major factor in cancer, heart disease, and other serious ailments. According to government estimates, the use of tobacco leads to a quarter-million premature deaths yearly in the United States alone. Yet the U.S. tobacco industry employs slick advertising abroad to promote smoking as one of the keys to the American way of life, and has greatly increased sales (aided to some extent by U.S. government programs) in the last decade.

Likewise, other products, from pesticides to dielectrics, found hazardous in the U.S. (and in some cases banned from sale) are sold widely in developing countries without strong environmental-protection legislation or enforcement. There are no reasons why substances considered hazardous in the U.S. should not be equally hazardous elsewhere. Strict environmental laws are urgently needed everywhere to prevent massive future disasters.

Confusion over Legislation

In some ways, substances so hazardous that a total ban is required are the easy cases. Of more interest are those pollutants that, though unpleasant or unhealthy, are an inevitable consequence of desired activities and can be tolerated up to certain levels. I believe much confusion over environmental legislation results from not recognizing the role of "externalities" in the modern world, and the legislative steps that can be taken to control and channel them.

Externalities are unintended costs imposed on groups or individuals as a result of actions taken by others. Someone opening a fast-food restaurant may make a substantial profit from the enterprise, and customers may appreciate the low prices and quick service. However, neighboring businesses may continually have to clean up litter thrown away by the fast-food customers, and heavy traffic may hinder their own customers. These neighboring businesses pay the external costs of the fast-food restaurant.

In simple societies, the scope for impossible externalities is very limited. People travel by foot and cultivate fields by hand. Any damage to someone else occurs, and is usually handled, on a personal level. Technology has greatly extended our interactions and the possibilities of external damages have become vast and complex.

We can travel long distances at high speeds to places with fragile ecologies, causing irritation and danger to others, threatening the existence of whole species of living things, and using up the earth's limited resources at an accelerating pace. For example, as we consume our petroleum reserve, that oil is not available to our descendants. They will face additional cost, and—because they were not parties to our decisions to use the petroleum—those costs are truly external. Also, our methods of production have become so efficient that when one of our gadgets malfunctions, it is often cheaper simply to throw away the broken component, or even the complete unit, and buy a new one, rather than attempt to repair it. The discards become external costs borne at least partly by others.

Some Modest Proposals

Economists generally agree that externalities should be "internalized" so far as politically practicable. I would like to suggest ways of legislating this internalization, focusing on solid wastes.

Disposal Tax. Final disposal of solid waste is generally not the responsibility of the person discarding the waste. Normally it is deposited in an appropriate receptacle and a service provided by the local government removes the refuse for treatment. A solid-waste-disposal tax has been proposed as a means of including the cost of hygienic disposal in the cost of an item. The average cost of pickup and disposal for the country could be estimated: in the United States it is currently three to four cents per kilogram. This per-kilogram amount would then be imposed as a national tax on material or individual items destined for pickup and disposal by local-government services. Principal candidates are glass, plastic, steel, and aluminum used in food and drink containers; newspapers and magazines; and paper, cardboard, and plastics used for containers, wrapping, and shipping. The total money collected would be distributed among municipalities in proportion to the solid wastes collected by each.

Litter Tax. Some people do not dispose of their solid waste in appropriate receptacles, but instead drop it wherever they happen to be. Other people, usually municipal workers, then pick up the litter. Exact internalization of the costs of litter pickup and disposal—by fining every person who litters—would be fair. However, this would require an unacceptably large police force and judicial system, and most communities instead choose to make exemplary fines on the few litterers caught and convicted.

A closer degree of internalization than provided by charging the costs of litter pickup to the total community would be achieved by putting the cost on the chief offenders via the marketplace. Twice a year a careful sampling of the litter picked up in representative areas should be made. The litter could be divided into soft-drink containers, liquor containers, cigarette litter, newspapers and magazines, and food wrappings. The number of pieces, weight, and volume of each could be recorded, and a formula devised that reflects the relative costs of litter cleanup. A tax could then be levied on each commercial category to pay for litter cleanup nationwide. The tax should be displayed on each product, so that purchasers realize proper disposal of the discards would reduce the tax allotted and cut the price of the product.

Promotion of Local Recycling. A principal benefit of local recycling of paper, rags, and bottles is that the materials are removed from the waste stream, reducing the costs of pickup and disposal of the remaining solid wastes. In my community of Cambridge, Mass., we recently passed an ordinance changing the status of firms known, disparagingly, as "scavengers." They would pick up newspapers from trash containers (many people from long—and good—habits still bundle their newspapers). Previously, removing materials from trash containers was outlawed. Now the city council recognizes that scavengers (now called recyclers) reduce the costs of trash pickup and disposal, and seeks not only to license them to pick up newspapers in certain areas of the city each week, but has offered to pay the difference whenever the local purchase price drops below $15 per ton. If successful—the concept has been adopted by the industry-sponsored Corporation for a Cleaner Commonwealth—this might be extended to bottles and cans.

Promotion of National Recycling. On the national level, recycling is desirable when scarce resources must be conserved. To some extent, the amount of recycling is a function of relative wealth— the poorer the society, the more recycling occurs. But recycling is also greatly affected by national policy. In the United States, there is relatively little recycling of wastes even for energy, despite the energy shortage, because national policy has kept energy prices low. Energy is consequently wasted on an enormous scale. The imposition of a tax on all energy from scarce resources, such as petroleum and natural gas, would have very desirable consequences in stimulating both conservation and recycling. (The energy obtained from waste would, of course, be tax exempt).

Other scarce resources—chromium, tin, lead, zinc, and so forth—

should also be taxed when first imported or mined. There would be no tax on these substances when they are recycled, thus providing an incentive for recycling. Water should likewise be taxed in dry areas if the existing price is low enough to encourage waste. All taxes from scarce resources should immediately be recycled as reductions in income taxes, or negative income taxes, in equal increments to all adult residents.

Facility-Siting Compensation. In countries where local communities are given a degree of autonomy, there is usually widespread opposition to the siting of solid-waste-treatment facilities such as landfills, incinerators, and recycling centers. This opposition is understandable because even if such a facility is neat and quiet, it will attract a stream of noisy and refuse-laden trucks, bringing danger and congestion to the streets. So the community should be compensated.

One method for determining fair compensation is the following: The central authority would select all possible sites for the new facility and draw up tentative plans for each site, including the designation of access routes for truck traffic. Community leaders would then be informed that besides paying all local taxes and observing all local ordinances, the authority would pay a bonus for each ton of wastes processed. The communities could use the proceeds of the bonus to compensate local residents—for instance, by reducing or eliminating local taxes. The authority could suggest a bonus of say, ten cents per ton, and increase the offer by ten cents every week until one or more of the communities agreed to host the facility. The communities could well negotiate for improvements in the proposed facility—for a new access road to protect an area in which children play, for instance.

This approach also allows for private enterprise. In California, compensation is paid by Sunset Scavengers, the company collecting wastes from San Francisco, to the city of Mountain View, where the wastes are put in a sanitary landfill. The city also negotiated for the construction of a marina and other recreational facilities on the filled land. Payment was originally about one dollar per ton, giving Mountain View citizens a very substantial tax benefit. Across the country, Massachusetts recently passed a law (largely because of efforts by several M.I.T. faculty members) to provide compensation to communities agreeing to accept treatment facilities for hazardous wastes.

I could cite many other cases in which such legislation would prove beneficial: reducing sulfur-oxide pollution from power plants, noise pollution from airports, and river pollution from hot or chemically laden discharges. The common feature of these approaches is that they seek to internalize externalities. They involve taxes that flow in a tightly controlled loop, providing compensation to affected communities and incentives for producers to reduce environmental pollution at the source.

SECTION FOUR
The Common Ground

Introduction

In recent years, there has been a conspicuous "reaching out" to one another by the environmental and business communities. The debate between the two groups no longer centers on whether the environment should be protected but rather on how best to do so most efficiently.

As the articles in this section demonstrate, there is no doubt that the American business community accepts the challenge of environmentalism. Business is now trying to determine responses to the challenge that will give the nation a clean environment while sustaining its economic health.

The spirit of compromise and pragmatism, so successful in American society, would be violated if, after essentially winning the debate over the importance of environmentalism, the environmental community were not willing to cooperate in establishing environmental policies that also recognize the need for maintaining a viable economic system. Some environmentalists, of course, still see the business community as the enemy, believing the only proper relationship with business is adversarial. Fortunately, uncompromising, adversarial attitudes are waning in the mainstream of the national environmental movement.

A decade ago the urgent task of awakening people to the dangers posed by a lack of environmental policies may well have required intransigence and direct conflict. Under the circumstances, loud voices may have been the only way to dramatize the issues. Now, having aroused the nation's concern, most environmentalists recognize the need to embrace more constructive and cooperative tactics.

The search for common ground is a search for compromises. Environmentalists must continue to ensure that environmental concerns are kept before the national consciousness. But they also must help develop policies that bring the goal of environmental quality into harmony with other social and economic ends. The harmonizing tactics and methods are far different from those dictated when the challenge was only public awareness. The current level of public support for environmentalism would not be so great if the public perceived that the only way to achieve a clean environment were through a substantial deterioration in the nation's standard of living.

The business community, on the other hand, faces a different challenge. Taken as a whole, no more powerful private entity operates in American society than the nation's business community. But to maintain profitability, influence, and freedom, business must be sensitive to the concerns of the public—not just in terms of the price and quality of the goods it produces but also in terms of protecting the environment from which it draws its resources and livelihood.

The changing view of the responsibilities of business will greatly complicate business decisions in the last quarter of the 20th century. That business accepts this challenge is reflected in the statements of the nation's business leaders in this section. No hesitancy or reluctance is sensed in their attitudes. They do plead for a recognition that achieving environmental goals will take time and cost money but their attitude is not one of opposing the objective.

People in business like to refer to the bottom line or the profitability of their enterprise. In the United States, a new bottom line has been defined for society during the past two decades. That bottom line rests not only on the level of national income but on producing that income in a way which preserves our natural environment, protects human health, and provides for the right of future generations to enjoy a similar level of affluence, health, and natural amenities.

America is a pluralistic society, and, as any biologist will tell you, there is strength in diversity. However, this diversity also means that Americans are never likely to achieve a unanimity of opinions on public issues. In the quest for a clean environment it will be necessary to accept a progressive compromise—progressive in the sense of moving continually toward improvement while balancing the diverse goals and interests of society.

Continued conflict is inevitable—even desirable—on some environmental issues, and some pollutants are potentially so harmful to human health that there will be no room for compromise. But absolutist attitudes, attitudes of "all or nothing," are no longer workable and are not likely to be influential for either side.

Attitudes and institutions have changed. A new generation of corporate executives educated in corporate social responsibility now hold the reins. A new generation of environmental leaders, whose emphasis is more technocratic and issue oriented, act from the need to work with, not against, the business community.

It is too early to say that the war on pollution is won, but it is not too early to say that numerous battles have succeeded. Environmental quality is a goal for which people have decided to pay. Much progress has been made, but there is still a need for further reconciliation—for greater cooperation between the business and environmental communities. All of the signs suggest that this reconciliation will continue during the next decade and that the commitment to a clean environment will grow stronger in this society.

Healthy Environment Needs Healthy Economy

By James R. Dunn

Contrary to popular opinion, this author argues, industrialization and technology have made environmental protection possible.

I do not see why love of nature leads so often to hate, or to a perspective which appears evermore immoderate—a perspective which rarely tolerates alternate views. To an increasing extent, I have become alarmed at the tone of so many of the articles I read about wilderness and the environment.

There is another conservation perspective, however. It is not polarized as anti-industrial nor is it puristic. And I believe it should be heard: *A healthy economy and a healthy environment are interdependent—environmental conservation has only been, and can only be, practiced by affluent societies.*

It is difficult for me, considering limitations of time and money, to get to most of the areas about which I read. Yet where I live, about 12 miles east of Albany, New York, I have a little piece of wilderness which I enjoy and appreciate every day. From my perspective it is far superior to what it was in the past. I look across the lake on which I live at hills which are heavily wooded and abound with wildlife. Many of the species are more abundant than when the Europeans first came to North America.

My landscape has changed enormously in the past few decades. Many old paintings and photographs tell me that a hundred years ago the hills were stripped and used for agriculture, the only trees bounding farmers' fields. The New York State Department of Environmental Conservation's *Conservationist* magazine tells me that deer and turkeys were non-existent and other woodland wildlife faced extinction. As a geologist I see evidence that erosion rates were unacceptably high over the whole area. And privacy was difficult

---

Reprinted by permission, James Dunn is chairman of Dunn Geoscience Corporation in New York.

because all of the land was being used. Now we have a paradox: with far more people it is easier to be alone—to commune with nature. Now nature, including deer and turkeys, is out my back door or a short walk into the wild country across the lake. The hundreds of shrubs and trees which I have added to my own woods to attract and feed wildlife make me optimistic that my little part of the world will improve even more as a wildlife habitat. Most important, this wilderness is available to enjoy and to be grateful for every day of my life.

What I see is not rare in upstate New York; some variation of what I see is the usual situation in this section of my adopted state.

It is clear to me that the things I enjoy in my environment are results of our industrial system. Trees are no longer the only source of thermal energy. The steep, inhospitable, bouldery farmland is no longer needed for food production. Glass and iron that depended on local energy resources a century ago are now produced efficiently elsewhere and the remnants of the mills, furnaces, and farms are rapidly disappearing, often marked only by interesting stone ruins, by unexpected lilac bushes in deep woods, or by the ubiquitous stone walls that mark the boundaries of formerly tilled fields.

When I consider our environmental gains here, as well as in all industrialized countries, and compare them to the absolutely devastating environmental deterioration of the non-industrial nations, it is obvious to me that environmental conservation and wilderness could not exist without industrialization and the wealth it produces. Our ability to set lands aside for wilderness and keep them wild is itself a spinoff from industrialization. For contrast, look at the many so-called "paper parks" in the developing nations, where wilderness areas suffer so much from the encroachment of populations which need the wildlife and the land for survival.

I fear that our tendency to look for the obvious blemishes of the industrial system has obscured our powers of observation. I have long suspected that if we successfully slow the industrial system enough—as we may already have done—we could reverse our environmental gains; and the wilderness areas we now enjoy could become "paper parks" as they are in other less developed nations.

Perhaps, most importantly, industrialization has given us a freedom which we rarely think about: the freedom to take or leave nature—the freedom from nature if you will. The lives of about 58 percent of our labor force in the 1860's—the farmers—were directly tied to the cycles of nature and the vagaries of the weather. To survive, most people got up before daylight, worked until after dark and found vacations and traveling impossible luxuries. They were truly slaves to nature, an oppressive master which punished those who through ignorance or bad luck ran afoul of its laws.

Of course, most of our ancestors in the 1800's only lived a short time, so even if they really enjoyed their hard lives, there was so little time for their pleasures. Yet, as all generations have in our country they left us a better world, a world where freedom from nature is so accepted that most of us seem to have forgotten that our ability to enjoy nature is, itself, predicated on an ability to protect ourselves from its vagaries.

I think that it is mandatory, when we try to correct the environmental deficiencies of industrialization, that we be aware of its environmental and human benefits. Not to do so could result in destruction of many of the things we most appreciate. I am sure that over-correction of the negatives associated with industry will jeopardize in several ways the environment which I enjoy. For example, John Mitchell, in an article in the March, 1981, *Audubon*, described the pressures on the northeastern woods of the chain saw and high energy prices. And trees are now being stolen from my woods while, in fact, wood poaching has become a major problem in state and national forests all over the United States. I wonder about the extent to which we who are environmentally concerned may have helped to create the high energy costs which now threaten my woods by blocking the development of so many energy sources other than wood in the United States.

For these reasons, I object to the tone of many articles on the environment. I object because they may prove counter-productive in environmental terms; and I very much fear that endless repetition of such unscientific opinions have the potential for damaging the environment which we are trying to protect.

The "environment" is a very complex system. Saving it and improving it requires a clear, non-emotional understanding of our interrelationship with our environment. Seeing environmental problems is easy; solving them is difficult After all, the Spartan General Pausanias described the damage from deforestation of western Turkey nearly 2500 years ago, and the problem is still not solved. Turkey's deforestation problems are not the result of ignorance or lack of sensitivity. They are the result of economic and technological conditions.

Their deforestation problem can only be solved when they can produce more food from less land and have better sources of energy
than wood for the average citizen.

I see the emotional writing so prevalent in the environmental
movement largely as a polarizing influence, and possibly an impedi-
ment to truly improving our world. If industry is visualized only
as an enemy, and our economic system is truly shackled, we may
become more like the less developed nations—in order to survive
we would have to destroy the environmental benefits that we so
recently gained.

I fear that much too often environmental judgments stem from
political philosophies rather than scientific study, and may not
necessarily help the environment we all wish to protect. Can a meaningful dialogue among the environmentally concerned be started?

Toward a Cleaner America: A Progress Report

In contrast to gloomy environmental forecasts, this article states that great environmental progress was made in the 1970's and that prospects for the future look good.

Introduction

It has taken almost two decades. But since the 1960's, when public concern over the environment began to spread, the United States has made substantial progress toward protecting the quality of the nation's air and water, toward assuring that the present and following generations will live in a clean and healthful environment.

National advances in reversing deterioration of the environment has been documented by six successive Administrations—half Republican and half Democratic. It began with a growing perception that man's activities were changing, sometimes damaging, our air, water and land. That realization spurred research, analyses and decisions as both the public and private sectors sought practicable ways of easing man's impact on the environment and of reversing deterioration of valuable resources. The challenge was clear: clean up the environment, but do not declare a moratorium on economic growth.

The challenge was met by the public, by government and by industry. The United States, once again, is demonstrating its remarkable capability to balance high-priority goals. It is proving its ability to resolve a massive problem through judicious—and often voluntary—commitment of capital, technology and creativity.

Today our air is cleaner. Our water quality is protected and improving. While there are persistent environmental concerns, the outlook is a very positive one. The progress of recent years is a promise for future years.

A Retrospective

Origins

While environmental protection began to surface as a major trend

---

Reprinted by permission of The Business Roundtable.

in the early 1960's, the year 1970 marked its establishment as a for-midable, persistent and complex national concern. It was in 1970 that the first Earth Day was held, demonstrating the sophistication and militancy of activism born out of a decade when civil rights and the escalating war in Vietnam sparked both aggressive cause espousal and broad confrontation over national policies. It was in 1970 that the federal government marked the emergence of environmental protection as a national priority with the National Environmental Policy Act.

Public attention was focused, in 1970, on "smog", plumes from industrial smokestacks, polluted water discharges, and automobile exhausts. In 1970, the Environmental Protection Agency calculated that almost 74 million Americans were being exposed to particulate matter levels above the air quality standard as required by the amended Clean Air Act.

The state of the nation's water was reported to be equally discouraging. Congress accepted studies which found 90 percent of the watersheds in the U.S. to be polluted. The press graphically recorded the story of the Cuyahoga River, so clogged with pollution that it caught fire. Headlines reported each oil spill and fish kill. And fears of toxic chemical poisoning were fanned by Rachel Carson's *Silent Spring*.

Public concern over environmental protection reached a peak in the early 1970's. In industry, there was a growing perception not only of this public concern, but of the complexity and massiveness of the problem; it had already devoted millions of dollars and large resources to protecting the environment in pre-1970 years. A complicating factor, too, was the emergence of factions that saw environmental protection as a simple, black-and-white issue; you were either *for* the environment or *against* it. There were those who demanded a moratorium on industrial progress—even a roll-back. On the other hand, there were those who saw environmental protection as a passing fad or who resisted full compliance.

Commitments

Fortunately, the majority of those in the public and private sectors were ready to make practical commitments to the new national priority. They were persuaded that environmental protection and industrial progress—given the national aptitudes for technological innovation, economic planning, and cooperative effort—were compatible.

The measurable and remarkable progress made in the years since 1970 shows they were right. The nation's air and water have been significantly improved, and positive progress is being made toward resolution of other environmental problems. The statistics are evidence of the progress in environmental protection. But numbers also give some dimension to the national commitment which brought such progress.

In 1978, the Council on Environmental Quality endeavored to place a price tag on pollution control measures. It estimated that the nation, as a whole, had spent $40.6 billion in combined capital and operating costs for pollution control in 1977, about $187 per American. A year later, CEQ set the price at $47.6 billion, or $215 per American. Subsequent estimates have, of course, continued to rise. The specific CEQ numbers have been challenged by some economists and by some businessmen. But they do suggest a major degree of voluntary response to the national goal of environmental protection. For example, in discussing the 1977 expenditure, CEQ said "only $18.1 billion is in response to environmental legislation." The commitment has been—and will continue to be—costly. But what of the results?

Breathing Cleaner Air

Indicators

Three principal measurements enable federal, state and local environmental agencies to gauge air quality: the composition of ambient air, the effectiveness of controls of specific emission sources, and the frequency of "alerts" triggered by combinations of airborne pollutants and meteorological conditions.

Better Ambient Air Quality

In analyzing ambient air quality, day-to-day measurements are compared with national ambient air standards—"primary" standards related to human health and "secondary" standards concerned with human welfare. The standards are set for "criteria" pollutants that have been assigned priority for control: total suspended particulates, sulfur dioxides, carbon monoxide, ozone, lead, and nitrogen dioxide.

Since 1975, the U.S. Environmental Protection Agency has reported a steady decline for five of these major air pollutants. During the period 1975-81:

- Total suspended particulate levels decreased by 3 percent—a deceptive measure, to a degree, since the major reductions in this pollutant occurred prior to 1975. Between 1970 and 1975, population exposure to particulate levels above the standard was cut by about 30 percent.
- Sulfur dioxide levels decreased by 27 percent.
- Carbon monoxide levels declined by 26 percent.
- Ozone levels were cut by 14 percent.
- Lead levels decreased by 14 percent.

For the sixth criteria pollutant, nitrogen dioxide which results from both mobile and stationary fuel consumption, EPA measures a five percent increase over 1975-81. But an important milestone has been reached, the concentrations appear to be coming down with 1981 showing an eight percent decrease in nitrogen dioxide over 1980.

In 1981, then, for the first time *all* criteria pollutants were down.

A federal study recently published in the *New England Journal of Medicine* added a dramatic footnote to the reduction of lead in the air. During the period 1976-80, reported the survey, the level of lead found in human blood was reduced by 37 percent.

Reduced Emissions

Still another survey, commissioned by the New Mexico Environmental Improvement Division and released in 1983, showed that sulfur dioxide in the state's air had decreased to levels comparable with those of the 1940's level. New Mexico also measured reductions in state air levels of hydrocarbons and carbon monoxide.

Measurement of emitting sources show equally positive progress. In a 1982 overview of the environment, The Conservation Foundation observed that "emissions of most major pollutants have continued to decline, at least as estimated by EPA. Data from 23 metropolitan areas show that particulate emissions dropped 56 percent between 1970 and 1980, partly because of a decrease in the burning of coal and solid waste. With a 24 percent decline in ambient sulfur dioxide levels from 1974 to 1980, most urban areas have now reached EPA's primary, health-based standards."

CEQ, in its annual report for 1981, was supportive. "Automobiles produced in 1980 emitted 90 percent less hydrocarbon and carbon monoxide and 75 percent less nitrogen oxide than models produced in the 1960's." Turning to stationary sources, CEQ concentrated on 6,000 sites characterized as "major"(capable of emitting 100 tons of a criteria pollutant annually). Of these, by 1981 over 90 percent had installed pollution control equipment designed to bring them into compliance with air emission standards. Most of the remaining stationary sources were on a schedule for compliance.

Fewer Air Alerts

As a third measure of air quality, the declining number of unhealthful air alerts is a valid indicator. In recent years, EPA has applied a "pollutants standards index" (PSI) to 23 selected municipalities. The PSI translates ambient measures of criteria pollutants into a number of categories ranging from good to hazardous. Published CEQ data show that, with the exception of 1979, there has been a steady drop in the number of days in the hazardous ranges.

The Conservation Foundation added some specifics: "Some cities have demonstrated remarkable progress. For example, the number of days in the three highest risk categories in New York City was 270 in 1975 and 131 in 1980 (a drop of 51 percent)".

The progress in air quality is clear: cleaner air and better emission control.

Protecting the Nation's Waters

Cleaner Water

How much cleaner is the water of 1983 compared to the water of 1970? The evidence of water quality improvement on a grand scale is evident across the country. According to the CEQ, the nation's water cannot be said to be improving at the same rapid rate as the nation's air, it is—at the least—not deteriorating any further despite population growth and increased Gross National Product (GNP). The Conservation Foundation echoed that cautious conclusion, saying "even to hold the status quo is an achievement in the face of significant economic and population growth since 1970. Moreover, there is episodic evidence across the country that some of the worst pollution problems may be easing." It is the "episodic evidence" that presents clear signals of major progress in water quality improvements.

Success Stories

Said The Conservation Foundation: "Salmon have reappeared in New England rivers. Eutrophication (aging) of Lakes Ontario and Erie has slowed. And the ecological productivity of some estuaries—for example—near Pensacola, Florida—is returning." CEQ adds to the list: "the Willamette River in Oregon, the Penobscot and Winooski Rivers in the northeast, the Cuyahoga River in Ohio, the Great Lakes in general, the lower Savannah and Chatahoochee Rivers in the southeast, and the Potomac River south of the nation's Capitol—all have shown substantial improvement over the quality of 10 to 20 years ago."

Five cases histories show the substantial strides taken in water quality improvement over recent years . . .

- In 1972, Maine's Haley Pond was a good place to avoid on hot days when the stench of dead fish and decaying algae filled the air. The problem was an inadequate municipal waste water treatment plant on adjacent Rangely Lake. Cooperative action by EPA and local citizens resulted in the plant being upgraded at a cost of $500,000. It was the first advance municipal waste treatment plant in Maine. And today, both the lake and pond have been restored to a condition that rates state promotion as a scenic and recreation attraction.

- In New York, the problems of the Mohawk River go back to 1890 and 1891 when it proved the source of typhoid epidemics that killed hundreds in bank-side cities. Overused as a transportation corridor and as a waste water dump by growing cities, the Mohawk River received no curative treatment until the early 1970's when state and federal funds were dedicated to its revitalization. An early sign of good health was the reappearance of fishing. By 1977, all industrial discharges were being treated effectively. In 1980, Utica eliminated its last raw waste water discharge. Today, the state of New York has declared the Mohawk "swimmable and fishable."

- For the first time in more than fifty years, the Potomac River is no longer a visible embarrassment to politicians and residents of the nation's capital. Gone now are the mats of algae that clogged the river and clouded it with a noisome aroma. Bass have reappeared in the Potomac. Waterfront renewal has taken hold. River recreation—from sailing to rafting to angler's derbies—is on the increase. Swimming, banned since 1925, may soon be possible. This small miracle is due to a $1 billion program of new and upgraded treatment plants—and a victory over bureaucracy in productively harnessing the efforts of the federal government, two states, the District, and several municipalities. Business, too, played a key role. For example, a local utility spent $17 million for waste water treatment systems in the Potomac Basin and another $6 million for biological studies of river water.

- In the 1970's, Lake Erie presented editorial writers with a new word: "eutrophication." Defined, it simply meant that pollution was accelerating the aging, and ultimate death of the lake. The symptoms were obvious: closed beaches, curtailed sport and commercial fishing, and local drinking water which smelled and tasted bad. A cooperative effort by the governments and industries of the United States and Canada sharply reduced pollution of the lake. Today, Lake Erie has come back to life. Beaches are open. Commercial fishing is making a comeback and a record walleye population is attracting sports fishermen.

- By the 1970's the Houston Ship Channel was an environmental horror story. The Channel had one of the world's heaviest concentrations of industrial and municipal waste discharges. One 1960 study found dissolved oxygen levels of zero for 16 miles. The equivalent of a waste water load of 2 million people was dumped into the Channel every day. Thanks to cooperative efforts by industry, government and concerned citizens in an $800 million revitalization program, the lower channel now has a new lease on life. The now thriving fish population has sparked a profitable commercial fishing business. Even the sensitive oyster has reappeared and is being harvested on a limited basis.

Encouraging Monitoring Results

While broad national measurement of water quality remains difficult, what The Conservation Foundation describes as "the only coherent nationwide information on water quality" is provided by an ambient monitoring system established by the U.S. Geological Survey over the past seven years. The 500-station monitoring system is the National Stream Quality Accounting Network (NASQAN). The NASQAN stations endeavor to monitor five conventional pollution indicators in local water. Reviewing NASQAN data in its 1982 "State

of the Environment'' report, The Conservation Foundation made the
following observations:

- Dissolved oxygen—"nationally, a majority of the stations are
  showing improvements . . .''
- Bacteria—"The last seven years appear to have seen virtually
  no change in the extent to which surface waters suffer from
  bacterial pollution.''
- Suspended solids—"Analysis of trends. . .shows improvement
  at a majority of the stations.''
- Total dissolved solids—". . . when the original data are
  adjusted to take account of variations in streamflow, the number
  of trends showing improvement is about equal to the number
  showing deterioration.''
- Phosphorus—". . . phosphorus concentrations are decreasing.''

The NASQAN data suggest the opinion that if the across-the-board
quality of the nation's water may not be uniformly improved, it *has*
stopped deteriorating.

Looking Down-Range

For the future, national progress in protecting the environment
since 1970 should serve as an encouragement. It is concrete evidence
that however massive and complex the task, it *can* be tackled and
progress realized. But to sense that the public now will accept a wind-
down of efforts or a qualification of ultimate goals, would be foolish.
There are newly identified problems, more complex ones. Witness
toxic substances and hazardous wastes.

By 1976, attention had been concentrated on such substances as
vinyl chloride, polychlorinated biphenyls, chloroform, and
trichloroethylene as water pollutants. The press brought the tongue-
twisting chemical substances to public attention and linked them to
other new words like "carcinogenic.''

The 1978 report of CEQ said it well. "Bringing toxic substances
under control is more easily said than done. Hardly a week goes by,
it seems without another report of a newly discovered hazard—
definite or suspected—in the marketplace or the workplace, in the
air, water, or some other part of the environment.''

This is an observation that remains true in 1983 and probably for
the immediate future. The public has a clear expectation that the
private and public sectors will respond to its concerns about toxics
and will provide solutions.

For the future, then, there will be no great lessening of challenge. For the public sector, it will remain the refinement of laws and regulations, balancing practicability against impatience. For the private sector, it will be the need to continue to find the answers to environmental concerns and also to continue to serve a spectrum of public demands ranging from job creation to the maintenance of a high standard of living, from consumer responsiveness to the requirements of stockholders and special interest groups.

The outlook is positive. For example:

- The Chemical Manufacturers Association has contracted for a $1 million independent study to provide scientific data to help government develop sound public policy on health and hazardous waste. To begin in September, 1983, the study will be completed in 1984. It will be conducted by a consortium of 15 major universities.

- EPA notes a dramatic decline in the level of polychlorinated byphenyls (PCB's) found in human tissue—only one percent of the population had more than three parts per million of PCB's in 1981, compared to eight percent in 1977.

- Scientific progress is noted in the laboratory identification of micro-organisms that can decompose toxic wastes, a step in biotechnology that began with decomposing oil spills and now raises hopes for biodegrading herbicides and toxic chemicals.

- Experience gained with EPA's "bubble" policy—under which the agency sets one overall reduction target for pollutants in an industrial complex rather than enforcing limits on each emission source within the complex—is showing that the concept often has a dual advantage. One chemical plant reduced total "volatile organic compound" emissions by 99 percent but, under the bubble concept, it saved $10 million. Steel and power plants are also reporting success with the bubble approach.

- The "acid rain" debate is reported, but now there is increased concentration on scientific determination—not just of cause and effect—but the nature of improved controls which may be needed to protect sensitive areas. The effort involves both the public and private sectors. The EPA has launched a new and intensive study. The Electric Power Research Institute, through 1982, has spent $16 million in acid rain research; it will spend another $68 million during 1983-87. On the technological front, such complexities as the "limestone injection multi-state burner" are being reviewed as a potential means of reducing sulfur dioxide and nitrogen oxide emissions. It is becoming more evident that, like most major pollution problems, the issue of acid rain has progressed from concern to awareness—and is now moving into the "action" phase.

The retrospective is encouraging. Environmental protection and industrial growth are proving to be amenable partners in progress. There is reason to expect that the record will continue to demonstrate the compatibility of these two national priorities.

Reconciling Mineral Development and Environmental Quality: The Need for a Constructive Partnership

By William K. Reilly

While speaking on behalf of continued mineral exploration and mining, the president of The Conservation Foundation calls on the minerals industry to recognize that the American public also wants the environment protected during the extraction process.

The question I will address today is "Can we continue mineral development and still maintain environmental quality?" There is an implication in this issue, as it is cast, that mineral development and environmental quality are somehow mutually exclusive. It is indeed quite possible to see them that way. It is possible to define mineral development in such a way that the environment is so little protected and so severely despoiled that people who value the environment might come to oppose mineral development. By the same token it is possible to define environmental quality in such a rigorous, abstract, purist fashion as to preclude the possibility of natural disturbance. It seems to me it is in the interest of all of us as well as in the interest of the people of the United States to avoid such stark and exclusive definitions.

Some years ago when the nation was divided and our public institutions buffeted by the Watergate scandals the uncommonly large number of lawyers implicated in those scandals was commented upon and criticized. What kind of ethical training could those lawyers have

Excerpted from *Vital Speeches of the Day,* May 15, 1982, with permission from City News Publishing Co. William K. Reilly is the president of The Conservation Foundation.

received to have so cavalierly disregarded the public interest? Where was the ethical dimension in their formation at law schools? The legal profession particularly in the law schools reacted seriously to criticism directed at lawyers during that time and responded by adapting the curricula of law schools to assure a more broadly responsible public-concern dimension in law school education.

Out of the professional soul-searching came new emphases which stressed the broad responsibilities to the courts and to society even at the expense of the time-honored emphasis upon *winning* and serving a client's objectives. The ultimate outcome of that period of professional soul-searching in the legal profession was, I think, productive and useful. In the same way, it seems to me other professions including the mining profession need periodically to reexamine their assumptions, reconsider their values and adapt their preparation and training accordingly.

There has been no equivalent Watergate scandal in the mining industry or mining profession. In fact, I think it fair to say that the record of the mining industry has improved significantly during the past 50 to 60 years. Last November, I spoke on a platform with the President of the American Mining Congress in Denver. A questioner in the audience asked Mr. Allan Overton why are people, why is the Congress so down on the mining industry? Why is the industry's image so negative? Mr. Overton responded by saying that he thought that Americans generally failed to recognize an important relationship between "things" and "stuff." Americans value "things," he said, which they see on the counters in their shops and stores, but they forget that "things" are made out of "stuff" which is torn from the plains and the prairies and the mountains by miners. And they forget that without the "stuff" there are no "things." Overton suggested in sum that we have become too disconnected from the sources of our wealth, too far removed from the realities of our material affluence.

Mr. Overton also suggested a second reason why the mining industry has had a somewhat negative presumption in the Congress. He said that many of the congressmen in critical positions come from places like Brooklyn, and from other large cities to whom mineral development and mining are matters of indifference if not misinformation.

I was asked to comment on Mr. Overton's answer to that question and I found myself agreeing that the American people probably do fail to connect "things" with "stuff." I was struck by the similarity in Mr. Overton's view and the view of a David Brower or even a Rachel Carson. They also believe Americans need to get more in touch with the basic resources and systems upon which our lives depend. David Brower would recommend the wilderness experience as a particularly moving and effective way to get back in touch with reality. A visit to a modern mining site can also be instructive on the point.

But I had to disagree with the second part of Mr. Overton's answer. The perceptions of the people in Brooklyn and Washington and much of the rest of the country about mining have been formed by books and movies and newspaper accounts of experiences which have not always reflected well either upon your profession or on the mining industry.

My own early exposure to the history of American mining came from college course accounts of the development of Appalachia. I recall being moved by the book *Night Comes to the Cumberlands* by Harry Candill which recounted a story of neglect of nature, abuse of people, destruction of communities and disregard for the future on the part of scores of mining companies which marched uncaring with their lawyers and their broad leases through the heart of Appalachian mountain towns and hamlets many years ago, leaving behind a culture of poverty, dependency and scarred land.

What I have learned about much modern day mining suggests that stories told in *Night Comes to the Cumberlands* may be ancient history. Shortly after joining The Conservation Foundation I invited Robert Cahn, a Pulitzer Prize-winning journalist and former environment editor of the *Christian Science Monitor* to join us and write a book about corporate responsibility toward the environment. I think it safe to say that the corporate hero of that book is a mining company, the American Metal Climax Corporation and its experience in designing and building one large molybdenum mine in Henderson, Colorado. The planning, analysis, care and consultation which characterized AMAX's efforts to build that mine set a new high standard of excellence in reconciling mineral development with environmental protection. The Atlantic Richfield Corporation has proudly drawn attention to some of its achievements in restoring surface-mined areas. Sun Oil Company has invited attention to its mines to demonstrate experiences where soil productivity has actually been enhanced after the conclusion of mining. For these corporations, and there are no doubt many others with which I am less familiar, their environmental performance is not a subject about which they are secretive or embarrassed but a facet of their public relations, an achievement to which they point with pride. These are positive and powerful experiences. They demonstrate a new philosophy and a new commitment on the part of serious and important mining corporations. If the approach of these corporations becomes the rule and not the exception the answer to the question "Can we continue mineral development and maintain environmental quality?" will be quite simply and unqualifiedly "yes, indeed."

Obviously, we do need minerals and mining. They are vital to our country's economic and strategic interest. We will develop these resources here in the United States. I hope that we will develop them with ever greater sensitivity to the environment. So my concerns about mining and mineral development are not with whether but rather with how. For there is now as a result of the election of President Reagan a new element in the equation. The Reagan Administration believes that environmental protection measures have imposed unacceptable burdens on the economy, particularly on industry. The Administration has worked to ease regulatory requirements affecting industry and to assign high priority to mineral exploration and extraction in the management of the federal lands. The Administration looks to the private market and to state and local governments to assume many of the planning and regulatory functions eliminated at the federal level. For many environmental programs, however, it was the failure of the private market that led to government action in the first place and failures or inaction of state and local governments that led to federal intervention. Although federal efforts have themselves merited criticism there is need to determine in each case whether the private sector or states or localities will in fact act more effectively.

First, the private sector. There are indeed things that the market can do well. Energy pricing can and probably should be left to market forces. The Conservation Foundation was among the very first environmental organizations which publicly advocated deregulation of energy prices in the mid 1970s. A freer energy market will foster greater production and more efficient energy use which is to say more conservation. It is not at all clear that the market will work effectively for such important energy users as rental housing and commercial office space where those who make the decisions about design, insulation and heating and cooling systems are not the ones who pay the fuel bills. There is, however, no market for clean air or water or for wilderness and no market is likely to develop. The market quite simply has failed to provide many societal needs.

As for state and local governments most now find themselves financially strapped and the reduction in federal assistance will increase citizen demands and at the same time reduce state and local budgets and staffs. Few of these governments are in a position to replace federal expenditures for environmental and resource protection or to establish regulatory standards that may be perceived as driving prospective economic development to other jurisdictions.

The Reagan Administration's initiatives have placed environmental institutions under great stress. A sweeping reorientation of policies has occurred at the Department of the Interior. The personnel level of the Office of Surface Mining was proposed to be cut almost in half and the office was reorganized to reduce its functions. The Bureau of Land Management focused much of its efforts on disposing of federal land and encouraging fuel and mineral exploration and extraction. I dwell on changes in the federal policies toward the environment because they have important implications for mineral development. They translate full speed ahead. The drillers and diggers have come to power and their priority is clear.

But that is not and cannot be the end of the question. The key question is how will this new priority be carried out. Given the severe inhibitions which afflict our environmental agencies at the federal level and the financial and tax limitations affecting states and localities the burden falls to private corporations and their mining professionals to assure responsible development of minerals. Rarely before at least in recent history has so much latitude rested with an industry. Rarely before has there been such a direct connection between the decisions taken by corporations and the kind of environment that will result from those decisions. The ball is very much in your court and the nation will watch closely to see how you play it.

Americans want the products and benefits that mining make possible. Where there is consumer demand there are opportunities for industry to create jobs and generate wealth. We must take constraints on economic development seriously if we are to improve our international competitive performance, reduce inflation and bolster economic status of all Americans. But the way in which we do these things is crucial.

I do not accept some of the more expansive claims made to justify

a program of crash development of minerals. I am not persuaded
that the country faces a crisis of strategic proportions in minerals.
Secretary Watt and others have spoken of our high national
dependence on imported strategic minerals: manganese, chromium,
cobalt, tin, nickel, cadmium and so on. The Secretary therefore
injected a new element of urgency about insufficient mineral production in the United States. There is probably some realistic basis
for watching closely the markets and political developments in places
from which we receive an uncommonly large proportion of vital
minerals. But the case has not been made for a crisis response.

Our economy is not as hooked on minerals as it is on oil. What
role can recycling, stockpiling and substitution play in meeting
strategic U.S. mineral needs? Would these in some instances be more
cost-effective than priority development alternatives? If we pursued
the development option aggressively would our refining capacity
be adequate, could we provide it at a realistic cost, and even if we
were to achieve self-sufficiency would that end dependence if our
allies in Europe and Japan still had to rely on imports?

Clearly it is a good moment for linking your star to national defense
and strategic interest. If I could think of a way to link clean air or
national park conservation policies to the nation's strategic interests,
I would not hesitate to do so but any conclusion that our national
security is undermined by inadequate U.S. mineral production should
come only after a careful analysis and should not be a jumping-off
point for debate.

The injection of strategic concerns into the mineral debate risks
justifying the relaxation of a carefully designed network of environmental protections built up over many years, protections which I
believe are vital to the continued public confidence and acceptance
of mineral development in the United States.

Let me turn now to the subject of the environment. I do so as
a conservationist. Someone pointed out recently "We conservationists are no longer at bat," and to some it would seem that we
not only are not at bat, conservationists are not even in the ball park.
In 1981, it appeared that concern for the environment might suc-
cumb to the new preoccupation with economic productivity. Critics
of the environmental policy reforms of the 1970s portrayed those
reforms as obstacles to productivity growth by diverting investment
and adding costs. According to the critics environmental protection
put a brake on the economy, held back productivity, aggravated infla-

tion and contributed to the nation's decline in international competitive performance. Although the dampening effect of environmental programs on the economy is far less than groups like the Business Roundtable have suggested, it nevertheless appeared for a time that concern for the environment might come to be seen as well-intentioned, visionary, expensive and finally muddle-headed. The environmental reforms of the 1970s, it seemed, might go down like the War on Poverty, idealistic but in the last analysis, unaffordable.

Subsequent years brought good news. It hasn't happened. The basic legislative charter for the environment remains intact and now looks increasingly secure. Public issues from acid rain to wilderness protection stay highly visible in the face of near overwhelming concern with economic recovery. Membership in environmental organizations grows along with the shrillness and stridency of the attacks on environmental laws. Poll after poll confirms a deep and abiding popular concern for protecting the environment *even at a considerable expense.* Citing strong and consistent support for air quality, pollster Lou Harris has commented "clean air happens to be one of the sacred cows among the American public."

This isn't to say we won't see some trimming around the edges. We probably will see changes—in some cases significant changes—in the ways clean air and other long standing environmental goals are pursued. We undoubtedly will see more efforts to find alternatives to the traditional tools of federal spending and regulation. We will see more involvement by state and local governments. We will see new emphasis by environmentalists on efficiency and cost-effectiveness.

The conservation community already has some credentials on these matters. We are not strangers to arguments for efficiency and cost-effectiveness. I look for us to make further contributions in this era of concern for economic productivity. We are searching to make our case effectively and responsibly with full regard for the social and economic realities this country faces. But we do so also fully aware that the American public shares our values, supports our goals and stands with us in wanting to see our economy grow and our environment protected.

I have tried in these remarks to make the case for continued mineral exploration and mining and I have tried to make the case for continuing to take the environment very seriously. Not because the federal government wants the one over the other but because the American public wants both. If I am correct in that assumption the task lying before us is one of reconciling interests.

In addressing the issues before us, greater attention must focus on a series of technical issues—where and how carefully developments are sited, how extensively adverse impacts are mitigated, how feasible land restoration efforts are, and related matters. These determine what lasting impact mineral and energy development will have on the environment.

Environmentalists monitoring the reports out of Washington these days might get some discomforting messages about how carefully and how seriously these technical issues will be addressed by industry exploring for and developing mineral and energy resources and by federal agencies with oversight and mitigation responsibilities.

I cannot minimize the serious consequences that may follow from the changes occurring in federal agencies created to monitor and protect the environment. Yet there is room for hope. Increasingly, the attitudes of people at the state and local level make a major difference in environmental protection and every indication is that state and local determination to protect the environment is very strong.

As research under way at The Conservation Foundation tells us, more and more, states and localities not only are finding ways to protect the environment, but, when it comes to addressing the technical issues of siting, mitigation, restoration, and the like, to reconcile development and environmental quality. They are recognizing and addressing the *real* "environmental" hurdles to industrial and mineral development.

Some of these processes provide for the use of mediation and negotiation in settling disputes. Provided the premises are realistic, the parties consider themselves relatively balanced, and all sides appreciate that their real interests will be advanced by agreement, cooperative problem-solving is an innovative way of addressing differences.

Some states, especially those rich in energy and mineral resources, now use severance taxes to provide local governments money to prepare for the environmental and social impacts of mineral and energy development. Montana, for example, has enacted a steep coal severance tax that not only collects general tax revenues, but also funds payments to localities where mining activities will require new roads, schools, police, fire, and health services. Half the revenues are set aside in a trust fund. The state legislature must vote to pay money out of the fund.

In Colorado, Western Fuels, Inc. signed an agreement with Rio Blanco County some estimate to be worth $100 million. The firm will provide roads, schools and other requisites for orderly growth to meet the needs created by its large-scale venture in oil shale development. This agreement came about because officials and citizens in the County insisted that if it were to be done, the development would be done right—without destroying or overwhelming the community.

I don't underestimate the challenge facing states, counties, and towns. The West today is the scene of widespread and far reaching change: growing population, increasing urbanization, new lifestyles, new values. The political alignments are changing as well. As the 1980 Census confirms, there is an unprecedented migration of Americans, in record numbers, to the forests and plains, small towns and rural areas, especially in the West and Southwest. The attitudes of Americans now repopulating the countryside favor land amenities, recreation, the conservation of natural beauty, of forest and wildlife, clean water and pure air, and other environmental values. From some quarters the message is that a cabal of Eastern elitists and Washington bureaucrats have conspired to stalemate the development of Western energy and mineral resources. It's not that simple. There is more than one Western point of view.

The conflicts we see between mining and environmental quality are part and parcel of the changing Western landscape. They result from fundamental conflicts in values and lifestyles among the many long-term residents and newcomers—ranchers and farmers and hunters and fishermen and recreation advocates and environmentalists and miners and so on.

These groups must seek accommodations. The task ahead is to integrate the need for environmental quality with the need for mineral and energy development, to do it practically with attention to details of corporate organization, analysis, reporting, consultation, and communication.

Now as seldom before the times cry out for responsible private leadership. The burden falls to a profession and to an industry to police itself, to develop and apply innovative technologies and to set a new high standard of private environmental ethics. Now as seldom before the need is for constructive partnerships between industry and professional and environmental and local government interests in the common task so much in the interest of all of us: strengthening our economy and conserving the natural systems on which all else depends.

Stewardship in a Finite World

By Bruce Smart

The chief executive of the Continental Group says that the market-place is not comprehensive enough to stand as the sole arbiter of today's problems and that we must find a balance in the conflict between stewardship and personal self-interest.

W hen it comes to choosing between the economy and the environment, many Americans have convictions that are deeply and passionately held, whatever side they may be on. The theme of this paper is that no responsible citizen, certainly no environmentalist or businessman, can safely continue to be blindly committed to a single side of these great issues.

The conflict between man's activities and his environment has been building for centuries.

Around 300 B.C., the Chinese philosopher Chuang Tzu recognized that conflict when he observed: "In the day of perfect nature, man lived with birds and beasts and there was no distinction of their kind. Destruction of the natural integrity for the production of articles, this was the fault of the artisan."

Much later, but in a similar vein, the poet Wordsworth wrote: "Getting and spending, we lay waste our power, little we see in nature that is ours." And most recently, *Silent Spring, The Limits of Growth* and other warnings have been sounded by intellectuals—only to be disputed by the proponents of economic growth.

The return to the past seems both idyllic and possible for some Americans. Yet the forces that propel man to seek economic enhancement are rooted in his genetic makeup, for homo sapiens is after all one of the world's ten million species of living things and responds as they do to biological laws of competitive evolution.

Excerpted from remarks delivered at the Town Hall of California, Los Angeles, California, February 9, 1982. Reprinted with permission. Bruce Smart is chairman and chief executive officer of Continental Group.

Like all species, man has an inborn drive to expand his numbers to fill the available habitat, reaching equilibrium only when some other species or some event gains parity in competing for some mutually necessary resource.

Unlike other species, man has used his reasoning power to alter his habitat to his benefit and so his contest with the others is an uneven one. First through agriculture, later through accumulation of scientific knowledge, he has increased the efficiency with which he provides food, shelter, energy and other advantages. With the human environment thus improved, his numbers have multiplied. At the time of Christ, the world's population was about 140 million people, as it had been for several thousand years. By 1650, about the time of the Renaissance, it had expanded to a little over 500 million, crawling up at an average rate of less than one percent per decade during those 16 or 17 centuries.

Between 1650 and 1800, the population almost doubled, and between 1800 and 1930 it doubled again, those increases coming at a rate of about five percent per decade. In the last 50 years, we've increased 19 percent per decade. We're presently 4.5 billion, headed for 6.2 billion by the year 2000.

Environmentalists make a compelling case that this population growth is unsustainable over the long run. Less is said about a companion fact: A growing population produces more people and thus there are more creative minds around who have new ideas, develop better processes and solve problems.

Each good idea eventually benefits all men. If a group of 100 people originates one good invention, all people benefit. If instead the group numbers 200 people, the same rate of creativity results in two good inventions. Since each person benefits from each invention, there will be twice the benefit per capita. Thus, a larger population provides a larger reservoir of intellectual capital to be used to solve the very difficulties created by its greater numbers.

The point at which the problems of density outstrip man's ability to solve them does not yet seem to me to be evident. As we expand, we also consume greater quantities of natural resources. Oil is a popular illustration. In 1930, annual world consumption of oil was 7/10ths of a barrel per capita. By 1980, it had reached almost five barrels. In the United States, it totalled 28 barrels. Projecting the U.S. standard of living across the current world population, we can hypothesize annual usage of 125 billion barrels per year—a rate that would consume all known reserves in just five years.

Thus our rising population trend, accompanied by demands for rising living standards, is geometrically increasing pressure on finite natural resources.

Social demands for economic progress, often translated politically into rights, are difficult to resist without risking moral outrage, instability and conflict.

Before we are forced to choose between the environment and social justice, consider the proven ability of market forces and technology—the product of those numerous people—to shift from oil to other energy sources, to find substitutes for scarcities, to move from a conventional resource to a new one. Impending shortages of key materials have been foreseen regularly over the centuries but no real shortage has yet shut the world down or even significantly retarded its economic development.

In the eyes of most businessmen doomsday isn't yet on the calendar. Somewhere, of course, there must be a point of equilibrium. Nothing can expand indefinitely on a planet of fixed dimension. This equilibrium will be reached either by man striking some balance with nature or, as with other population explosions, by a disaster-related crash back to some lesser, sustainable level of human activity, including conceivably extinction of our species.

No one knows for sure where the limits are—whether they are far in the future or perhaps have already been exceeded.

But it is time for all of us, environmentalists, government officials, scholars and businessmen to reduce the stridency of our arguments, recognize our shared responsibilities, increase our understanding of the forces with which we are dealing, and lengthen our perspectives. If we do, we can hope to insure a future of quality and meaning for our descendants. If we do not, we risk dooming them to the fate of other species which have expanded beyond the carrying capacity of their habitat.

I come to this conclusion from the perspective of a businessman whose company is active in packaging, forest products, insurance and energy. Continental Group's actions contribute to man's needs for food, shelter, heat, clothing, hygiene, health care and financial peace of mind, among other benefits. As part of the total economy, we apply labor, resources, technology and the principles of capitalism to better the material condition of homo sapiens. Like most professional businessmen, I look at what we do as a necessary and constructive contribution to society.

Through the mechanics of the marketplace, with its premier tool of pricing, we direct our energies and the resources entrusted to us towards those ends that most of us want. By responding to the free will of its participants, the market has proved an effective mechanism for providing more goods, more services, more health, more education, more culture, more leisure and more personal security. We tamper with it at the peril of wasting resources through the inefficiency inherent in more regulated systems.

And yet, the market is not comprehensive enough to stand as the sole arbiter of today's problems. It does not always consider the impact of its actions on third parties or on future generations. Unfortunately, our productive activities do create conditions that affect third parties, conditions that are not improvements to our habitat and not paid for in the marketplace. We discharge unwelcome substances into our air and water. We erode fertile lands. We cut down natural forests, destroying the habitat of other species. Our products end up as solid waste and litter.

In the past, these externalities did not seem very significant, certainly not harmful enough to require costly modification of our industrial processes. As we have produced more and learned more, our society has been persuaded that this laissez faire approach to the externalities of economic activity is both unacceptable and unwise.

In this, the environmentalists have been a prod to conscience, to understanding and to action. In good part because of their warnings, the majority of responsible American businessmen now support efforts to internalize the environmental cost of their actions and, if this cannot be done, accept reasonable laws that regulate the impact of their activities on society. The reverse side of this coin is that all must recognize the cost imposed on society by these new restraints.

Our economic resources are limited, as are our natural ones. What we spend in time and treasure to solve one problem is not then available to solve another. Despite what some may hope, the costs of environmental protection will not be borne by business or by stockholders or by the rich. They will show up in the price of products to be paid by users. If pollution is expensive, the market will opt for less of the products that cause it just as surely as the higher price of gasoline has led to more fuel-efficient cars.

When we add costs to one product or business or one nation, however justified, we damage its ability to compete with other products or businesses or nations not so burdened. As businessmen, we must bring these calculations forward in credible fashion, not as arguments for continued license, but as contributions to consensus solutions. In the final analysis, society will decide the tradeoff between the environment and the economy, either through the market mechanism or through laws.

Some environmental questions are quite amenable to cost/benefit resolution. Recycling is a good example, but it's not a new one. The Prophet Isaiah predicted that men would beat their swords into plowshares and their spears into pruning hooks because the swords and spears were no longer necessary—or perhaps worn out from hammering on the heathen—and they provided a cheaper source of plow-making metal than did virgin ore.

Latter day recycling is more sophisticated. Our modern paper mills recover, reconstitute and reuse the chemicals required in the pulping process rather than dumping them in the river. If they didn't, paper would be prohibitively expensive, leaving out consideration for the downstream fish.

Elsewhere in our own company, we collect and recycle almost three billion aluminum cans. We know this is environmentally sound. It saves a lot of energy, saves virgin resources, reduces solid waste disposal, lessens litter, and is also economically very attractive. The point is, I think, that as raw material costs rise and disposal costs are internalized, used products become more and more attractive as a source of raw materials. Some may believe that a drive for recycling should be founded on legal, ethical or even moral underpinnings. My own view is that it must and will be driven by economic forces, by cost. But the result will be the same. As pressure on resources grows, recovery and recycling will increase and both the environment and the economy will be well served.

On the other hand, some problems defy easy cost/benefit analysis. Take the complex environmental concern with endangered species, a subject that received much publicity in the case of Snail Darter vs. Tellico Dam. It has been estimated that man-made changes to the planet are removing animal species at a rate of one per year—and are escalating as compared to the one per thousand year rate during the period when the dinosaurs were dying off. Plant extinction rates are similarly elevated by man's destruction of their natural habitats.

To understand this subject one must reach beyond the aesthetics of protecting visible and dramatic endangered species such as the Bald Eagle. While effective as rallying points for public support of environmental goals, they may also serve to oversimplify the problem and weaken general understanding of it.

Each of the earth's species contributes its activity and its genetic pool to the diversity, stability and preservation of our eco-sytem. Man depends totally on these species for the habitability of the planet. In his article "Variety is the Key to Life" Paul Erhlich points out the public services collectively performed: moderating the weather; maintaining the quality of the atmosphere; operating the hydrologic cycle; producing and preserving the soil; recycling nutrients; disposing of wastes; controlling pests of crops and causes of human disease; and maintaining a vast genetic library from which come new domesticated plants and animals, antibiotics and medicines. Once lost, a species cannot be replaced and its unknown future value is lost with it.

Americans have in the past tended to look at environmental problems on a local or national basis, as having domestic origins, and susceptible to control by state or local government action. This problem is, of course, global.

Most of the earth's ten million species reside in tropical rain forests, where for millions of years they have been sheltered from the harsher effects of climatic cycles such as the ice age. Now the clearing of this rain forest for timber and farmland threatens many of them. Yet the economic needs of the developing equatorial countries are pressing, and world demands for tropical resources are strong. It is relatively easy to justify forest clearing in short range social and economic terms.

The long term future of the eco-system, on which the survival of man's own genetic pool depends, may be affected by today's seemingly logical and beneficial actions. Obviously, a much wider general awareness of tradeoffs is needed, based on data which society has only begun to collect. I believe that study will convince even the most skeptical that there is a limit to many current forms of economic expansion, and to sustainable human population, and that eventually growth in the quality of life will have to be sought principally in aesthetic, cultural and spiritual terms, a conclusion reached long ago by most great religions. I am not, however, persuaded that these limits are yet upon us in the form of inadequate energy, or a shortage of food, or other forces.

In the past the marketplace has been extremely clever in disciplining our use of scarce resources and encouraging the discovery of substitutes. And the world's food supply—if not its distribution system—has so far kept up with its population, though continuing to do so seems somewhat less certain.

I'm inclined to think the earth will reach its limits of population growth, its equilibrium point, because of crowding, reduced tolerance for each other's proximity, if you will, and the natural and economic forces that stem from that condition. The large increases of the recent past have sprung from rapid declines in mortality around the world. As sanitation and education complete this beneficial process, population change will become more a function of fertility rates. These are already declining. The crude birth rate of the world was 36 per thousand in 1950. Today it is under 30. Many developed countries have experienced fertility levels that indicate zero or negative growth. There is a positive correlation between this low fertility and affluence, education and the availability of means to prevent conception.

Fertility trends are down in developing countries as well. Once the presence of children turns from perceived economic advantage to disadvantage, couples seem to have fewer of them, perhaps another manifestation of Adam Smith's invisible hand of the marketplace.

As a result, world population projections of the recent past have been scaled back. Forecasts 100 or more years ahead are risky. But the United Nations estimate of world stability at 10 to 12 billion seems reasonable. Such a figure would imply a world population density only slightly higher than California's today.

The social and environmental problems that must be solved, along with the economic ones, should not be dismissed lightly. But there does seem to me to be more reason for hope than for despair. Meanwhile, if we want this crowded but hopefully stable world to be worth living in, we must agree on some priorities and concentrate our present efforts on the most important ones. Here rhetoric and accusations will not serve us particularly well. Scientific understanding, coupled with a careful and objective cost/benefit analysis can be a much more valuable tool. There can be and should be much debate over these priorities. Not all will agree with my weighting even if they accept the general thesis. But here's how I line them up now.

First, I think we must strictly control those conditions that are not correctable by nature, conditions that create permanent irreversible scars on the habitability of earth. Possible examples of these would include toxic wastes—including nuclear wastes, for my presumption of adequate energy assumes retention of the nuclear option—agricultural land destruction, and species extinction.

In these areas we act not for ourselves, but as custodians for future generations. As a second priority we must continue to seek cost effective control of physically damaging but reversible conditions represented by such situations as the bulk of air and water pollution.

Finally, I believe that those degradations of the environment that are essentially nuisances, which impair the aesthetic quality of the surroundings but pose little lasting threat to the future, deserve to be addressed as the annoyances that they are, with particular reliance on cost/benefit based resolution. Examples in this category would include solid waste and litter, urban sprawl, and, perhaps, noise.

The setting of these priorities must eventually be done by laymen acting through the political process. Their choices will balance environmental protection with other social and economic goals.

The wisdom with which we respond to our social and environmental problems will be in proportion to the skill with which the costs and benefits of each action are defined and presented by scholars, environmentalists and businessmen, working for consensus rather than for advocacy. Encouragingly there have been a number of recent initiatives with bi-partisan analysis and action. The National Coal Policy Project Study teams, composed of environmental, industry and academic representatives, have already reached 200 consensus agreements on how to develop specific mining sites. The Toxic Substances Control Act of 1976 was the product of the combined effort of environmentalists, industry and government. By accepting the need for legislation, and cooperating in its drafting, industry assisted in producing a law that was both economically reasonable and environmentally responsive.

Recently the National Wildlife Federation has made a welcome declaration of corporate detente, and is soliciting corporate input in an effort to reach common understanding.

The Nature Conservancy has been uniquely successful in protecting habitat by enlisting corporate aid rather than denouncing corporate motives.

Continental Group, and I believe many other corporations, applaud this trend. We are anxious to join responsible environmentalists in objective research on subjects important to us, such as litter recycling and solid wastes. Adversary research, which has characterized much of the battle over these issues, does credit to no one and clouds public understanding of complex issues.

So far industry and environmental cooperation has been local or national in scope. Once well-rooted here, the United Nations, environmental groups, multinational corporations, and perhaps other worldwide agencies must address the complex matter of global application.

Problems of increased population and use of resources are worldwide. Destruction of U.S. farmland denies sustenance to people who import our food. The depletion of Mid East oil impacts Western standards of living. Power plants in England, France and Germany contribute to acid rain in Scandinavia. We all live in one biosphere.

No business can be successful in a world whose eco-system has broken down. And no environmentalist can be content with an environmentally protected world torn by social upheaval rooted in economic distress. We are all in this together across the globe. There are no vocational, geographic or cultural boundaries that isolate us from each other. So the equilibrium that we predict and the stability we seek must also be global.

To reach that equilibrium in a benign fashion we must address a major political issue. Less affluent or developed societies, including segments of the U.S. population, desperately want the fruits of material progress. Over time they will achieve the political power and the technology to have them, but as their material progress expands the world's GNP, it will also multiply the drain on resources and further strain the global habitat.

We can deal with these problems more clearly if we cease looking at each other as adversaries and begin to think of each other as intellectual resources that share a large stake in the future. I would urge the concept of stewardship as the guiding principle. Education, knowledge, organizational rank, political power and wealth all carry with them an expanded opportunity to influence the world's affairs for good or evil. Those that hold this power do so through no God-given personal right but because it has been entrusted to them by others and they have accepted that trust.

Exercising stewardship requires overcoming the inherent conflict between the steward's role and personal self-interest or peer group approval. It demands that each of us act to the broader benefit of society as a whole, now and in the future.

Generations not yet born do not vote, so protecting their interest cannot always help a politician to stay in office. They buy no products, make no markets, perform no work and return no profit. They belong to no organizations, hire no environmental spokesmen, join no protest marches. They support no view, popular or unpopular, in today's marketplace of ideas.

But in a biological sense they are us. They will carry our genes down the path of time. What we are, they will be, tempered by the conditions of the world we leave them and the heritage of our actions.

The great story of our times will be the success with which we arbitrate the many competing claims on our environment. It will take the best from each of us—environmentalist, businessman, scholar, and politician—citizens all, to give that long story a happy ending.

Business and Environmentalists: A Peace Proposal

By Christopher Palmer

Arguing that neither side has a monopoly on virtue, the author tries to identify areas where environmentalists and business can form alliances for dealing with environmental problems.

Environmental groups are not perfect. We have flaws, as does business. By candidly examining the flaws on both sides, we may be able to defuse the destructive animosity and mutual misunderstanding, and even find areas where we can make common cause. Let me first focus on the weaknesses, both real and perceived, of environmentalists.

One of our problems is that we tend to assume a tone of arrogance when talking to business. When we environmentalists act as though we talk to God and as though we have all the answers, then industry, even those business people who are inclined to be sympathetic, will be irritated. We call ourselves "public interest" groups—the implication being that we look after the "public interest" while everyone else is pursuing his own selfish goals.

This tendency is matched by a tendency to be rigid, unwilling to compromise or negotiate. Environmentalists sometimes are afraid to bend and be flexible. We think the arguments made by industry are totally self-interested and exaggerated.

Too often environmentalists think of profits as dirty. We don't always appreciate the effectiveness of the free market. Too few of us have ever worked as entrepreneurs and, consequently, lack all appreciation of just how hard it is to succeed in business. We are much more expert at grantsmanship.

Some environmentalists are—like business people—probably not concerned enough about the harsh impact of high prices on poor

Reprinted by permission. Christopher Palmer is director of energy and environment in the Washington office of the National Audubon Society.

people. Few of us know anything about the degradation and pain of poverty. While the image of us—in Michael Kinaley's words—as a "clique of rich people attempting to protect their backyard" is an exaggeration, nevertheless we are probably oversensitive to the desires of the upper and middle class and insufficiently sensitive to the desires of those less well off.

Environmental goals should not be pursued without regard to their consequences elsewhere. Preserving wilderness is important, but it is only one of a number of important national goals. For example, energy policy should not be based on environmental values alone. A clean environment is just one of many results we want in an energy policy, not the central driving force. Environmentalists have to accept the fact that occasionally—ideally, rarely—they may have to compromise some environmental goals for more important ones, such as jobs.

This brings me to economic growth and productivity. Too often environmentalists give the impression of wishing economic growth would somehow go away. But economic growth and increased productivity are needed to create new jobs, to increase our investments in energy efficient housing and our investments in new less-polluting industrial processes.

And finally, environmentalists, like other human beings, can suffer from parochialism. A recent issue of a major environmental magazine contained a long and detailed editorial on how domestic cats are not a threat to birds. We voraciously consume each other's newsletters but tend to neglect Business Week, Forbes and Fortune.

Let me now turn to steps that business could take to gain a better understanding of us and to help win our confidence and trust.

There should be a greater realization on the part of business of the extent to which future growth and profits depend on efforts to preserve land, air and water. Erosion control aims at maintaining the productivity of soils, essential to sustaining U.S. agricultural output. Forest conservation and reforestation are essential to the protection of soils and watersheds. Reduced pollution and environmental protection make direct contributions to economic productivity.

Another step that business could take would be to show greater appreciation of the tremendous market opportunities in energy conservation, solar energy and pollution control. Business Week reported in its April 6, 1981 issue that the market for energy conservation investments was growing phenomenally fast and could reach $30 billion by 1985. An article in the November/December 1980 Harvard Business Review concluded that alert companies can turn pollution prevention into profit and make economic growth and environmental protection go hand in hand. There are now over 600 companies in the business of manufacturing air and water-pollution control equipment, including cooling towers, scrubbers, precipitators and catalytic converters. These firms constitute a multi-billion dollar industry employing hundreds of thousand of people around the country.

There are three broad areas where we could form alliances with business. First is the area of lobbying. Recently, United Technologies and the Audubon Society formed a lobbying team to promote increased federal funding for fuel calls. Why can't we do this on other issues, such as adoption of user fees, establishment of rational natural gas pricing or elimination of unnecessary government bureaucracies like the Synthetic Fuels Corporation?

The second area is in defining public policy. The National Coal Policy Project, led by Larry Moss, a well-known environmentalist and former chairman of the Sierra Club, and Jerry Decker, of the Dow Chemical Company, is a good example of an attempt by both environmentalists and industry to explore common ground in their conflict over coal policy.

The third way environmentalists could form alliances with business is to enter into business partnerships. Is there any reason why environmental groups have to be limited to testifying, writing and lobbying? Why shouldn't they help to market pro-environmental products? Audubon has recently established an arrangement with an energy management company to promote energy efficiency in commercial buildings. We have just helped to sell a $100,000 system.

The opportunities for business partnerships are immense. Why shouldn't we, for example, work with manufacturers of water-heating heat pumps to develop a packet of information that would help our half million members— especially those in the South, who heat their homes with electricity—to become more familiar with this technology? Why shouldn't we produce an investment newsletter that contains information about profitable companies in solar, conservation and pollution control equipment, which Audubon members could use in purchases and sales in their own portfolios? If we were to sit down with business and industry, we could probably come up with many more projects that could help both of us.

There is much on which we can make common cause, and business people should seek out those in the environmental movement with whom they can work. Environmentalists, in turn should not treat industry as a monolith.

We should all be seeking the right kind of growth, growth that does not degrade the environment that others must share. Environmentalists are not opposed to business enterprises, nor to those who seek a return on invested capital. We are only opposed to mindless growth that demands a narrow advantage regardless of social costs.

Conservation in the 1980's: Building on a Firm Foundation

By William K. Reilly

After outlining an agenda for the environmental movement in the 1980's, the author calls for a change in tactics and greater cooperation with former adversaries in achieving common goals.

The 1970's were years of steady progress in conservation and environmental improvement. The air and waters of many of the industrial cities have not been so clean before in this century. The "environmental decade" of the '70's compiled a remarkable record of laws passed, agencies created, and awareness of natural values heightened and translated into action.

In the 1980's, amidst gloomy and dispiriting news about the economy, about Iran and Afghanistan, it is worth remembering that this society achieved a very substantial success during the 1970's. Conservationists reflecting on this success—on *their* success in the 1970's—are anxiously wondering whether past gains will hold against continued economic buffeting in the years ahead.

Conservationists need to recognize that the heady days of the early 1970's are gone, and with them some opportunities that will not soon recur. But the years ahead bring their own, quite different opportunities for effective action.

What are those opportunities? How can conservation priorities and strategies best be adapted to respond to the society's new preoccupations? I see three critical priorities for the years ahead.

First, the new decade presents an opportunity for the conservation community to return to its historical concern about resources, and to clarify the central role of resource conservation to the long-

Excerpted from *Vital Speeches of the Day,* October 1, 1980, with permission from City News Publishing Co. William K. Reilly is the president of The Conservation Foundation.

term health of the society. Never before has resource conservation been so essential to the national well-being.

Public officials dared to take the chance. Now, as public opinion has shifted, now the key pieces of a realistic energy policy are finally falling into place. It is reassuring that the United States is now moving—in industry, automobile manufacture, home building, and energy pricing—to use less oil. The mix of public policies necessary to achieve energy conservation opportunities, promote shifts away from oil, and ultimately, stimulate innovations in solar and renewable energy technologies will require constant analysis, adaptation, and explanation.

Another critical resource priority in the years ahead is to reverse the degradation of the nation's productive agricultural resources. Last year, 61 percent of the food grains moving across international borders originated in the United States. What Saudi Arabia contributes to the world's energy needs, the U.S. contributes to the world's food supplies. And, like Saudi Arabia's oil, America's food-producing capacity is being depleted.

Almost half the topsoil in some of the most productive middle-western farmland has washed away. Fence-to-fence cultivation, impaction by heavy equipment, cultivation of marginal lands, elimination of shelterbelts, urbanization—all are taking a heavy toll of America's uniquely productive endowment of soils.

The various threats to U.S. agriculture are not limited to soil loss but include: rising energy costs, which translate into bigger bills for grain drying, irrigation, fertilizers, and truck and tractor fuels; monocultures; too few seed stocks to sustain the huge corn and wheat surpluses in the event of a viral or bacterial attack on one or more seed variants; and, in growing areas of the South, Southwest, and West, the steady depletion of groundwater for irrigation.

A billion people will be born in the next 11 years. A great many of them have a crucial stake in American food production, one third of which is for export. A great many of them also have a stake in U.S. energy conservation, essential to moderate world oil use. Wise use of American resources is a matter of utmost national and international interest, a moral imperative worthy of the best efforts of conservationists and everybody else.

As world population grows and as other nations continue to acquire equivalent levels of technology, skills, and capital, what distinguishes this nation and confers upon it a special destiny will be its natural resources. Conservation of agricultural resources was not a success story during the 1970's. We must make it one, along with conservation of energy, during the 1980's.

Our most important legislative gains during the "environmental decade" were in pollution control and government processes such as environmental impact assessment. These present a second area of opportunity for the 1980's.

At first glance, these opportunities may not look very great. A chorus of interests is calling for rollbacks of "unaffordable," "wasteful," "ineffective," and "bureaucratic" environmental controls. Everything from the nation's competitive capacity in international trade to the national security is being asserted as a reason to weaken environmental protections, particularly those of the Clean Air Act, the National Environmental Policy Act, and the Surface Mining Control and Reclamation Act. Some people who never did get the environmental message see the changing context of the '80's as an opportunity to undo its effects.

In practice, however, wholesale rollback of environmental protections will rarely, if ever, be the issue. Thanks to efforts in the 1970's, most of the needed laws are in place. Public awareness of environmental needs is so well-established that massive retreat seems sure to remain politically unthinkable.

Our task in dealing with pollution and governmental processes in the 1980's will be to consolidate these past gains—to secure effective performance even from programs that have thus far cost more and achieved less than we had hoped. Securing performance will now be made easier by the economic troubles and foreign entanglements of the '80's.

The increasing complexity of environmental problems will also make matters more difficult. A number of environmental solutions devised during the past several years followed a pattern: they identified a single problem, developed a control process and a standard for a pollutant or set of pollutants, and proceeded to tighten the standard over time. Mountains of sludge now accumulating from water pollution control plants were not anticipated nor was their disposal planned for when the water pollution program began. Now, however, these wastes rich in cadmium and other toxic materials present a new set of problems, and no disposal option is ideal—not burning, not depositing on crops, not dumping at sea. Solutions will involve other media than water and they will entail trade-offs. In the years ahead, society will have to deal with problems such as these in their entirety, and reconcile many interests and objectives in resolving them.

Consolidating environmental gains in the new context of the '80's requires attention to the details of how programs are working, how they can be made to work better, and how they can be refined to accommodate multiple national goals. Let me suggest the kinds of things conservationists can and should do:

- We can explore and publicize the benefits of environmental programs. Cost-benefit analyses often place excessive emphasis on the costs of pollution control because costs are relatively easy to quantify: the price of stack scrubbers or of preparing environmental impact statements, for example. But the benefits—many of which are intangible—are more difficult to assess. These benefits must not be overlooked, for they are real and no calculus of costs is complete without them, as we must constantly remind the business leadership, the Congress, and the public.

- We can give particular emphasis to health-related benefits. Dirty air has a direct effect on the health of thousands, perhaps millions of Americans. Even during the most severe economic troubles, health concerns are likely to remain high among public priorities.

- On the cost side of the balance, we can assure that costs are not exaggerated. Were jobs really lost because of environmental controls—or were the controls a convenient scapegoat? Did pollution controls force the plant to move—or was its equipment obsolete and uncompetitive?

- Finally, we can work to assure that environmental programs are effectively and efficiently implemented. The widespread complaints of regulatory overlap, complexity, and uncertainty, for example, reflect real problems with real consequences. We can help to see that those problems are addressed in ways that effectively reconcile conflicting objectives.

Tasks such as these call for a style different from that of a decade ago, quite different from the media stereotype of an environmentalist. Four years ago, when I first reported the need for attention to consensus-building efforts in quiet cooperation with other sectors of society, including business and labor leaders, I wondered whether that condemned The Conservation Foundation to minority status within the conservation movement. Now I don't think so.

A message that once seemed out of step is, I think, increasingly accepted. Cooperative research and communications and consensus building, while hardly the only tools being used by conservationists, have a critical role acknowledged by many. The tasks of consolidation entail different needs, require different skills and styles, than the tasks of legislative enactment.

Many Americans are discouraged about the ability of government—particularly the federal government—to satisfy public needs. Too many federal programs seem costly and ineffective. Too many public officials have proven untrustworthy. The call is out for less government spending, less government intervention in the lives of citizens.

This public mood has already led to a lessening of federal willingness to address environmental problems in new and imaginative ways. Conservationists should not infer that environmental problems have therefore become unsolvable. Rather, we should respond by focusing more of our attention on state and local and private action. This is a third priority for the decade.

Many of the problems that we face in the 1980's are most amenable to small-scale, fine-grained solutions. This is particularly true of many resource management problems. Energy waste, groundwater pollution and depletion, piecemeal urbanization of prime farmland, and degradation of coastal lands and waters represent an accumulation of thousands of small decisions. I don't question the usefulness of federal incentives and requirements in addressing some of these issues. It is clear, however, that federal actions would be insufficient even in the best of times. State and local and private initiatives and experimentation are essential to obtain finely tuned solutions to the diverse resource management needs of a very big country.

Emphasis on state and local and private initiatives can also help the process of consensus building that is needed to consolidate the gains of the 1970's. Too many of our detractors—and even a few of us—have come to believe that environmental action comes only after an adversary process has produced legislative or judicial decisions that compel federal action. It has become too easy to focus attention on the compulsion instead of on environmental needs. Focusing our attention on state and local and private action can help to create the support necessary to solve environmental problems that are seen to be real, near at hand, and susceptible of resolution by familiar and accessible people and institutions.

Any reform movement faces risks when it tries to follow up early successes. The environmental movement that was the cutting edge in the 1970's could become dull in the 1980's—pursuing strategies that no longer work, failing to address new problems. None of this will happen, however, if we pursue the important opportunities that are opening before us. Building upon success, we are entering the 1980's well positioned to espouse the enduring message of conservation to a society that has rarely if ever been more in need of learning it.

Environmentalists and Utilities: Let's Get Together

By Brock Evans

A former vice president of the Audubon Society offers a conciliatory hand to the utilities in this article calling for a lowering of rhetoric and a seeking of common ground.

There is a great mistrust which is all too prevalent now between many environmentalists and many in the utility industry, or their supporters, wherever they may be. And it's not just between the utility industry and environmentalists, it's there from many other quarters too. For example, some months back the *Washington Post* reported what happened when a lobbyist from the Sierra Club visited Congressman Gene Chappie from California. The conservative congressman grabbed him by the necktie and said, "Listen, wimp, if you ever set foot in my office again I'm going to break your bones!"

Another story which made headlines was an article reporting that a memorandum from a senior official in the interior department had contained the following statement: "Words such as disturbed, devastated, defiled, ravaged, gouged, scarred and destroyed are words used by the Sierra Club, Friends of the Earth, environmentalists, homosexuals, ecologists and other ideological eunuchs opposed to developing mineral resources."

There's a lot of other material like this . . . we've all seen it; and to say that there exist right now barriers to effective communication between environmentalists and these segments of the business community or their conservative supporters is to put it rather mildly.

We all want to lower these barriers. We environmentalists believe that it is not useful to dwell upon whatever may have occurred between our two interests in the past; the great events and forces now dominating and affecting our national life together—the state of the

Excerpted from *Vital Speeches of the Day,* April 1983, with permission from City News Publishing Co. When this article was written, Brock Evans was vice president for national issues, National Audubon Society.

economy, pressures of foreign competition, a tumult of social change—all are far too important to let whatever may have been in the past between us blind us to the opportunities of the future.

In the past twenty years, there has been clash after clash, conflict after conflict between those who were sincerely seeking to provide new energy sources for the American people and those who just as sincerely sought to protect the American environment from the impacts of these programs: dams in Hells Canyon, Grand Canyon, Glen Canyon, Dickey-Lincoln in Maine . . . coal fired power plants and associated surface mining in Utah, New Mexico, Pennsylvania . . . nuclear plants, it seems, almost everywhere . . . the list is long, and it is an intense, passionate, yet somehow sad chronicle of two interests, each with equally valid claims, struggling to resolve differences, all too often in the political and legal arena, instead of face to face—which is clearly the preferable alternative.

I am here today to say that we have much to discuss, that the time is long come—indeed, perhaps it is long since past . . . and to say that we should have more such exchanges, and do much more to understand each other.

I also think we have much more in common than many sometimes think; I know that to be true from my own personal contacts with many of you and other representatives of the utility industry over the years. After all, you are in the environmental business, dealing with the nitty gritty, nuts and bolts of environmental protection right there on the ground. And you have the same concerns as other Americans: you want clean air too, clean water, a life for your children which is hopefully healthier than our own . . . you love to hunt and fish in the outdoors, you care about wilderness and wildlife too.

And we in turn, we environmentalists, consume electrical power the same as any other American. We want a strong utility industry to provide us with reasonably inexpensive lighting, air conditioning and power to run our appliances . . . all the things you have provided so well for us over the past decades. We have more understanding yet to do about the particular problems of your industry as you attempt to meet and balance consumer and environmental goals, but we are trying.

I should candidly admit that we environmentalists are by no means perfect. We do have our flaws and our faults, and it would do us good to look at them. One of our problems, I think, is that we can tend to take on a tone of holier-than-thou when we speak of our goals and values.

We don't usually mean it that way, but my friends in business tell me sometimes that's how it comes out.

For example, we call ourselves (and the press also calls us) public interest groups—the implication being that we alone guard and look after the public interest while everyone else pursues selfish things.

Now, there is a slight truth in this—in the sense that the goals that we pursue do not return a monetary profit to us—there is no economic return to us in having a good Clean Air Act, more wilderness, regulation of toxic wastes, energy conservation and so on. But those aren't the only values in society—and it's wrong for some of us to assume as I am afraid we might sometimes do, that those who disagree with us are just greedy or misinformed.

We do not have all the answers . . . we do not hold all the truth in our society; no one else does either. But we environmentalists could probably do a little bit better at acting as if we do not, either.

I think there is a tendency sometimes also for us to see certain issues as basically simple—"pollution or not pollution . . ."—when in fact there is often a large gray area out there.

I have to say that industry, including the utility industry, does this too, by too often saying "it's jobs or the environment . . ." when in fact there is a lot wider range of choices than that.

For example, I read a utility ad in the *Washington Post* of December 1, 1982 entitled: "Energy Equals Jobs," which then went on to claim that the Senate version of the Clean Air Act could eliminate new energy sources and severely affect jobs and the economy.

Now we're not going to ask you to make our arguments for us . . . but I think that people who have studied the Clean Air Act would agree that the issues are a lot more complicated and not as drastic as that.

But to continue with this critique of environmentalists, I should also say that not many of us have been in the business world—and we do not always understand the pressures on business and how hard it is to succeed—pressures on you as you struggle to deal with the financial problem of scarcity on the one hand and the desires of many of your customers to cut down electrical use on the other hand. In this kind of context, not to mention the many other pressures you deal with, it is quite legitimate to be concerned about the complexity of the regulatory process—and too often, environmentalists may not always acknowledge that as a real problem for you.

These are areas in which we could do better to increase our understanding of you and your problems. But I think that business in general, and the utility industry in particular, could also do better. There's a lot of rhetoric about "elitists" just trying to take away honest peoples' jobs for the benefit of the privileged few . . . and that doesn't help the dialogue very much.

And I think too that there could be more attention paid by the utility industry in its publications and public statements as well as actions . . . to the extent to which your future growth and profits may depend on a healthy resource base. We think history does show that you cannot have a healthy economy in the long or medium term unless we have successful efforts to protect land, air and water.

For example, forest conservation and reforestation are essential to protecting soils, so that trees can grow back and be cut again and so that watersheds can be protected.

Or, good surface mine regulation means that when the mining is done, the land will be able to produce crops of wood or food to benefit other sectors of society and other needs. . . .

Or, reduced pollution means fewer worker days lost due to environmentally-caused illnesses, and fewer and lower payments into medical care plans . . . and on and on.

We think business or the utility industry could do more publicly to acknowledge that pollution control programs are really not a burden on the economy, and not only do they bring positive economic benefits in terms of public health—they are also good business. They have helped to create a whole new business—the business of manufacturing and servicing control equipment. There are now over 600 companies in the business of manufacturing air and water pollution control equipment, including cooling towers, scrubbers, precipitators and catalytic converters. Firms producing air and water pollution control equipment constitute a multi-billion dollar industry employing hundreds of thousands of people around the country.

We must learn to listen to each other's arguments and concerns, and above all, learn to recognize them as valid and important, made by sincere and well meaning people who love their country and want only the best for it. A beginning way to do this is to be able to criticize ourselves a little bit, to look at ourselves and what we say with a healthy skepticism and frankness.

There is something else too: I think it is important to understand where we environmentalists come from. A famous statesman once said, "You cannot understand a people unless you understand their history. . . ."

I certainly think that applies to environmentalists, or any other group in our society too. We environmentalists do have a long history—environmentalism wasn't something that came around on Earth Day . . . it's been here since the beginning of the Republic, and it's taken many different forms. But there has always been, binding us all together throughout this long time, a consistent set of philosophy and beliefs.

It all began as far as we can tell when a botanist named William Bartram traveled through the virgin forests of the Southern Appalachians in 1775, wrote about their beauty, lamented their passing, and pleaded for their protection. His concerns were picked up around the turn of the 19th century by writers such as James Fenimore Cooper and William Cullen Bryant who wrote about the beauty of the American wilderness, and said it is something special that makes us a unique people, something to be proud of and to care about.

These growing feelings of love for the American land as opposed to the desire to simply exploit it were given philosophical expression by Emerson and Thoreau in the mid-century, especially when Thoreau voiced the opinion that "in wildness is the preservation of the world. . . ." A number of journalists from the Northeast also picked up the cry, saying "we should not let all the land be developed for commercial uses . . . some of it should be protected, set aside as it is. . . ."

And so it was in 1872, after nearly a century of development of a philosophy that perhaps the wilderness was worth something, perhaps there were other values than development/commercial values, that these ideas were given their first political expression: when a conservative Republican president named Ulysses S. Grant signed into law legislation creating Yellowstone National Park, then a vast wilderness far more remote to them than anything in Alaska is to us today.

Things were a little quieter in the 1920s and 30s and 40s, and it wasn't until the post-World War II boom years of the 1950s that the movement became very active again.

The present form of environmentalism arose in the 1960s in reaction to what we perceived as the excesses of the 1950s and the 1960s: increasing tons of pollutants and poisons poured into the air and water with existing laws doing nothing about it . . . . millions upon millions of acres of our best farmland and wildlife habitat paved over by subdivisions, freeways, shopping centers—when better planning could have given us the same benefits without so much destruction . . . . millions of acres of wilderness lost to logging and to energy exploration and development—when effective conservation programs or even more benign extraction methods could have saved much of it. . . .

The result was that the American people rose up in the late '60s and early '70s, into what we now call the environmental movement:

They demanded that their representatives do something to control the pollutants and the poison—and they got the Clean Air Act, Clean Water Act, Toxic Substances Control Act, Safe Drinking Water Act, Resources Conservation and Recovery Act, the Superfund. They demanded that more lands and wildlife be protected—and got millions upon millions of acres added to the great protective systems: parks, refuges, wilderness areas, rivers.

And so that's how we see ourselves—as reformers of the system to make it more responsive to environmental needs—to have cleaner and better air, protected lands, and water . . . reformers who care about their country and want it to do better to protect not only our basic life support systems, but also the things that make life worthwhile. We have never lost faith in our political system or in our economic system . . . and that's why we work within both, we believe in them.

We also believe we can have the benefits of our economic system and values of a free society and at the same time protect our environment. That's who we are, that's what we try to do, that's how we see ourselves.

What would we like from the utility industry, and how would we like to work together in the future? I'd like to try to suggest a few specifics in what I know are sensitive areas, but I feel driven on by the conviction that the times somehow are right for us to step up a dialogue . . . to come together where we can. So I'm going to discuss areas of current concern between us, and share our thoughts and perspectives with you . . . to try to see if there is some common ground toward which we can move.

What I want to say is said with great respect—for you, your expertise, your vast economic clout, your enormous importance to our society's well being. In a sense, perhaps I'm speaking to you today as an ambassador from one power center in our society, to another . . . and speaking as an ambassador, I am bringing the desire of our people to find out where there may be common ground for peace. Twenty years of war is quite enough!

Let's start first with maybe the toughest issue—clean air, and the Clean Air Act. We are deeply divided over the Clean Air Act and its amendments. The conflict, especially over issues like acid rain, will probably continue. But we environmentalists see three new factors for your industry, which at first blush may seem like more dangers—but in reality may be more in the nature of new opportunities for you.

We see several new factors at work now in the Clean Air Act/acid rain area which in our judgment have greatly altered the political equation—in favor of environmentalist views.

—First: even though it is accurate to say there was a standoff on the Clean Air Act this last year—it was we who were the underdogs. Those who wanted to change the Act had the Administration, control of the Senate, the powerful House Committee Chairman, and the financial resources on their side. I can assure you that even a standoff under these conditions—just about the worst possible from our standpoint—was considered by us as a great victory.

—Second: the 1982 elections were a resounding success for environmentalists. Nearly everywhere it was a major issue, environmentalists won. Obviously there were many other factors too . . . but the fact remains that 10,000 individual environmentalist volunteers—more than any other sector except labor—pounded the precincts for environmentalist candidates this last election. And the fact now is that there are many more environmentally sympathetic members in Congress and in key committees.

—Third: We think that many in your industry and in others are now realizing that they perhaps misread public sentiment about the Clean Air/acid rain issue after the 1980 elections. They saw these elections somehow as a repudiation of environmental values, as much as a statement about the economy or our national defense . . . when in fact, as all the polls and public outcry since have shown—it was not, it was very much the other way.

But this misconception, I believe, led advocates of big changes in the Clean Air Act to go beyond just the notion of "streamlining"; they chose instead to back the wrong horse—the horse of the proposal of the Reagan Administration and its agents, which in our view went far beyond any simple notion of "regulatory reform," or "fine tuning." They went to the heart of the Act itself, and its basic purpose to get the air cleaner; they were going to make it dirtier.

And those who shared this misperception, we believe, backed another wrong horse also—the idea that "we don't know enough about acid rain to know what causes it or where it goes . . ." so we need more studies. Or, the idea even that—as Energy Secretary Edwards has said—"it's not really a problem at all."

We think these are wrong horses for you to continue to back, because frankly they have very little credibility—and as we deal with the issues in the next Congress, the situation is not likely to get any more favorable for you. The evidence is too conclusive the other way, we think.

I realize all these may sound like dangers too, but I say again: they could be opportunities for you as well.

We believe that it is in your interest much more to talk about the ways and means of making acid rain controls more palatable to you, and to no longer ride these dead horses of "we need more studies . . ." It is much more in your interest to work with us and the Congress on adjusting rate designs, job impacts, various mitigation strategies than to oppose it—for eventually acid rain controls are going to come, just as they have done quite recently, and very suddenly, in West Germany.

And thus, your opportunity—our opportunity—the opportunities for not just environmentalists and utilities, but for our whole people is *now* to sit together and see what can be worked out in the fastest and more equitable way possible.

Continuing on sensitive ground, let me try another issue: nuclear power!

This has been the obvious scene of clashes over the years, and is probably not going to go away in the near future, even though new plants, plants on order, and plants under construction are being cancelled and costs are going up and up.

As many see it, the costs of building nuclear plants are not likely to ever come down, even if the various "streamlining bills" now being advocated do pass. We believe it is almost certain in this Congress that they will not even get out of committee, or if they do, will probably be so loaded down on the floor with controversial amendments that they will be unacceptable in any event. Perhaps this tells us that we should consider reevaluating where we are in the question of nuclear power.

I learned something interesting about the role of utilities in the nuclear business the other day, from talking to a friend of mine, a business school professor, who started his career as a nuclear physicist. He said he was going over his notes from a college course, and came across this statement from his teacher: "In the early days, most utilities were opposed to nuclear power, because they thought it unreliable and too costly. But the government was promoting it, and there had been a long history (in the 1950s) of severe labor problems in the coal industry, and also rising environmental pressures from the burning of fossil fuels.

"So in the late 1950s and through the 1960s—in response to environmental concerns; in response to labor unrest; in response to heavy government promotion . . . utility executives did opt for nuclear power." Now this was news to some people like me who always thought that your industry was a strong promoter of it from the very beginning.

But it shows us another opportunity now and for the future, I think. For now we have had 20 years of experience with nuclear power—it has not been a great failure by any means and I don't want to say it is; nuclear power has made its contribution. But it's terribly costly, in an era when we all know it is difficult to justify any new plant construction at all. And because of public fears about safety, it will always be subject to overwhelming government regulation, interference, and public scrutiny on a vast scale—all the advertising and public relations in the world can't change that.

The opportunity here for you is now to truly reevaluate your industry's commitment to nuclear power . . . to consider the payoff on continued heavy investments in this controversial and costly power source when cheaper and safer sources are available. Now is the time!

This examination of issues and opportunities for both of us leads me into the area that I think represents the greatest potential opportunity . . . not just for environmental and utility interests, but for our whole society; and that is the whole area of energy conservation. Many of your utilities on their own, and some of your regulatory commissions, have already initiated aggressive programs here. You've done a lot to be proud of so far, and we thank you.

But there's a lot more yet to be done. I'm not presumptuous enough to try to tell you how to conduct your business. You are the ones that have the headaches and the difficulties—of wondering how to pay for facilities built in an era when demand projections were vastly different . . . of struggling with rising fuel costs on the one hand, and increasing consumer and environmental pressures on the other.

The answers aren't easy and they aren't universal. We all know that in growth areas with little generating capacity, conservation is a much cheaper way to develop new energy and avoid much higher costs of construction of expensive new facilities.

But in areas of little growth, conservation may be the answer for different reasons—to reduce costly oil consumption, or to reduce peak demand.

And in some areas, we would agree, conservation may be no solution at all; we may have to build new facilities.

We strongly believe that there still remain great opportunities for you in the environmental services and conservation field. Why shouldn't you get the money that is to be made from making homes more energy efficient . . . why shouldn't you get the money from financing cogeneration . . . why shouldn't you get the money from financing solar and other renewable energy sources? After all, you are energy corporations—no one knows more about this business than you do. It is time to look to the future; to make use of this vast wealth of technological knowledge and access to financial resources that you have and consider getting into these fields in a bigger way.

We want you to make a fair return, and we pledge ourselves to do everything possible to assist you before the appropriate regulatory authorities to make sure that your financing efforts become part of your rate base.

I want to make an admission here and now—that we environmentalists were wrong, 8 to 10 years ago, when we and others argued against the large involvement of utilities in the solar and conservation field. We were afraid that you would take it over and then inhibit its fair growth. Now we realize that there is much you can do in these new areas to your benefit and to ours, to all of us.

Finally, we'd like to see you move into the energy from garbage field . . . some utilities are doing this right now. It takes a large institution to match up the energy problem with the garbage problem, and only you can do it adequately.

We know there isn't much money in it, but it is certainly a public service . . . and at least you won't lose any money. Here again, we'll work with you to give you a fair rate of return.

These are some of the things we environmentalists suggest you in the utility industry could do . . . but that's not enough—it can't be the end of it. We have an obligation also to understand better your situation, to know better the many pressures on you—how you always seem to be getting pulled in different directions simultaneously. On the one hand there are the environmentalists who want you to emphasize solar power and renewable resources; and on the other, the consumers who want you to hold costs down. We recognize the frustration when you look at solar or wind power, see how expensive they are, and then even with the best intentions in the world, throw up your hands.

Perhaps it's time that we environmentalists sat down with the consumer groups too; after all, we share basically the same values and it's just a matter of specifics as to how they are accomplished. We environmentalists need to understand that utility executives are environmentalists and consumers too . . . but you just march to different rules: rules of the market place, such as what to do with your excess capacity, built a decade or more ago on demand projections of 7 percent per year, plants that now have to be paid for with demand growth between 2 and 0 percent per year.

I've spent a lot of time talking about your business and what you ought to do—a presumptuous exercise I know. We environmentalists have obligations too; and it would not be a fair bargain unless we can honestly acknowledge them and try to work at them, on our part.

We have an obligation to understand better your situation, to know the many pressures you face from all sides.

We have an obligation to understand better the rules of your market place, such as the need to pay for generating facilities built in a different era, or the regulatory hurdles you face, or how to pay for rising fuel costs.

We have an obligation to not just give lip service to conservation and renewable energy, but to sit down with your experts within your framework of market place rules and government rules, to realistically devise practical real world measures that will work and will give you a fair return.

And finally, we have an obligation to work more closely, not only with our own local chapters and groups, but also with others such as consumer interests, minorities, the elderly, the poor. We have an obligation to work with all the others, including our government bodies, who are also part of your framework. That is our obligation too . . . and we will try to do it better in the future than in the past, as our part of the bargain.

I have spoken about the dangers of pursuing the old past course of conflict, and spoken about the opportunities ahead of us to work together on many areas—even some of the most controversial questions that now divide us. I have talked about the need for all sides to lower the rhetoric and to work toward a dialogue and I have talked about the obligations that each of us have . . . fundamental human obligations if this is to succeed: to listen to each other, to understand each other's concerns, to give them the same respect and validity that we give our own. We must start here.

I look to the future then, and I see hope: a hope that our two powerful interests, clashing so often in the past, can now at least grasp the essence of a new time, and realize that the best way, not only for all of us, but for our country, is to start working together.

Should This Marriage Be Saved?

By Geoffrey O'Gara

This article points out that not all environmental groups are united behind the idea of working with business in seeking compromise on environmental issues. Some groups oppose any idea of compromise, arguing that an adversarial posture will allow them to come closer to achieving their goals.

It looks impressive. A fat set of rust, green and flesh-colored books with the title *Where We Agree* and shiny black press packet stuffed with laudatory reports about a new marriage between industry and environmentalists. The 60-member roster of participants includes the former president of the Sierra Club side by side with corporate heavyweights from the coal and electric utility industries. Their purpose: to show that long-time adversaries can work out differences on environmental issues in a cooperative, friendly atmosphere.

The National Coal Policy Project (NCPP), which produced *Where We Agree,* is the most prominent of several attempts to get industrialists and environmentalists to lay down their legal and rhetorical weapons and talk peacefully on neutral ground. The results are dramatic: NCPP participants settled their differences on such traditional environmental battlegrounds as air pollution and stripmining.

Their sources, heralded by a well attended press conference in Washington, made headlines in *Fortune* magazine ("A Promising Try at Environmental Detente . . .") and on the front page of *The New York Times.* "Probably never before have so many industrialists and environmentalists found common ground on such an array of issues," *Fortune* gushed. What seemed to fascinate the press even more than the various agreements reached by NCPP participants was the way

---

Excerpted from article in *Environmental Action,* March 1978, by permission of Environmental Action, Inc., 1346 Connecticut Avenue, N.W., Washington, D.C. 20036. Geoffrey O'Gara is a Washington, D.C.-based freelancer who specializes in coal-related issues.

they reached them: they sat down together, got to know each other, accompanied each other on trips to the coal fields and tried to relate as individuals. Nobody called anybody names or threatened any lawsuits; they just shared information and tried to work out compromises. Astonished reporters gaped at the love feast and wrote about the New Cooperation as if they were covering a wedding.

But for all the media bouquets, the project has ignited a serious controversy among environmentalists. Many Washington-based public interest lobbies believe that the adversary role they play is essential in dealing with industry. They are not comfortable with the notion of building coalitions with their old enemies. Furthermore, they are alarmed that the conclusions of a handful of environmentalists and industrialists, meeting privately over a period of two years, might be mistaken by Congress and the public as the last word on evolving coal policy issues.

In terms of the project itself, you have on one side Louise Dunlap of the Environmental Policy Center (EPC) and Richard Ayres of the Natural Resources Defense Council saying that the environmentalists who participated may have been duped into compromises which industry will use to weaken present environmental protection laws. On the other side is Larry Moss, former president of the Sierra Club, defending the idea of environmentalist-industry alliances and accusing Dunlap of "foaming at the mouth."

EPC, which played a major role in lobbying for the surface mining bill passed by Congress last year, is specifically concerned about provisions in the NCPP's mining task force report that would, among other things, allow "high-walls"—the exposed vertical rock faces left behind after stripmining—to remain uncovered in some Western farm regions. NCPP members concluded that more farmland might be kept productive if highwalls didn't have to be covered and graded. EPC says this would undermine the new federal law and open a major loophole for stripmine operators trying to avoid reclamation requirements.

Ayres is equally incensed by the conclusions of NCPP's air pollution task force. He points out that the group's willingness to allow tall stacks rather than emission controls on older coal-burning plants would be a step back from the clean air law now on the books. Tall stacks merely disperse pollutants over a large area; emission controls reduce pollution at the source. But Ayres' response to NCPP goes beyond its specific policy recommendations. In an angry letter to Larry Moss last month, Ayres said, "I decided not to participate [in NCPP] because I disagreed with the proposition that [this] would be a more appropriate or productive means of resolving major issues of public policy than the constituted processes of our government. . . . [NCPP's recommendations on air pollution] do not represent a 'legitimate consensus' on these issues. They were not, and would not be, supported as compromises by the thousands of individuals and hundreds of organizations across the country who spent years working on proposed amendments to the Clean Air Act."

Ayres and Dunlap list these and other complaints in pointing out that snazzy NCPP reports are likely to be misconstrued by legislators and federal officials. The "consensus" opinions reached by NCPP participants was, as Ayres put it, "private discussion among a small group of privately selected people."

The notion that industry and the environmental movement should make friends and work together has numerous adherents on both sides of the fence.

Industry, in particular, has a lot to gain by a "friendly" working out of differences with the environmentalists. Over the last 10 years it has become increasingly clear that big business almost never "wins" an environmental argument; even when a court rules in industry's favor, public sympathy will generally go to the environmental Davids who, under-paid and outgunned, stood up to the profit-minded Goliaths.

This, at least, is the view of Milton Wessel, a New York University law professor whose book, *The Rule of Reason,* is the Bible of the New Cooperation. Wessel points to General Motors' fight with Ralph Nader as a perfect example of what happens when a big corporation brings out heavy artillery to stop a crusader carrying the banner of public interest. GM eventually had to pay numerous injury suits for Corvair accident victims, stop producing the car because of poor sales and endure a sharp decline in public approval of the company. Ralph Nader became the nation's leading consumer advocate. That, says Wessel, is what industry has learned using the old adversary approach of trying to beat the opposition at every quarter.

Instead, Wessel recommends, let both sides put all the facts on the table, get to know each other and look for areas of reasonable agreement.

It is not just the industry side, however, that now wants to settle differences amicably. Many environmentalists see it as a possible shortcut around the expense of litigation and a way to combat flagging public support which has been their lot in drawn-out environmental battles.

William Reilly, president of The Conservation Foundation, recently declared a "new era" of "environmental integration." In an article in the *Council on Foundations Reporter* last December, Reilly claimed the "informality and flexibility"of private, constructive meetings between environmentalists and industry may "serve the best interests of all parties."

Using funds supplied by the Rockefeller and Mellon Foundations, The Conservation Foundation has been gathering information over the past two years about business and environment and publishing reports about successful negotiations between the once-hostile forces.

The Foundation has also put together a group of about 10 industry representatives and environmentalists to discuss implementation of the Toxic Substances Control Act, a law pushed through Congress by labor and environmental groups after five years of powerful industry opposition. The toxics group, a smaller and less ambitious undertaking than the NCPP, has been meeting for about a year under the directorship of Samuel Gusman, a former assistant to the president of the Rohm & Haas Company, a leading chemical concern. Gusman and representatives from such companies as DuPont, Dow Chemical and Monsanto meet with environmental experts (the Environmental Defense Fund, Environmental Action and the Natural Resources Defense Council represented among them) every other month to talk about enforcement of the toxic substances law.

Participants in the group have addressed only two aspects of the issue so far. They started out with the "apple pie" issue of how best to develop an expert toxicology staff at the Environmental Protection Agency (EPA), which both sides favor and hope to encourage. Since then, however, they have moved into the more controversial area of pre-market testing. The group expects to make recommendations to EPA, which must establish rules for the pre-market testing of chemical products, in a few months.

Gusman thinks his low-profile approach and his avoidance of "global issues" will make this project work. "If we're going to succeed at anything, I think it's because we're modest in our ambitions," he says.

Policy-oriented groups such as this one differ—both in approach and in impact—from the kind of environmental mediation that takes place at the local level, where a single, development-related issue often requires compromise among local interest groups. Here, the cooperative method has chalked up some successes.

One often-cited case involved a proposed department store in Montgomery County, Md., a wealthy suburb outside Washington. Federated Department Stores first expressed interest in opening a Bloomingdale's in the area in the late 60s. The company found a site and asked the Montgomery County Council to change its zoning from residential to commercial in order to allow construction of a shopping center.

Neighborhood groups kicked back, and a long-running battle ensued between a battery of experts and lawyers working for the store and an equally adamant group working for the residents. In 1971, the County Council refused to rezone.

The company then hired a planning advisor, Malcolm Rivkin, to help smooth things over. He began a long series of meetings aimed at involving local citizens in the planning and development of the shopping center from its earliest stages. It worked.

Bloomingdale's is now blooming in Montgomery County, because citizens were given leverage in deciding how and where the store would be built. Special setback requirements and height limitations were imposed. More important, the developers agreed to guarantee that the owners of adjacent property would receive at least the value of their property before the shopping center went in if they decided to sell after it was built.

But that kind of success with a local land use problem does not dispel the fears of environmentalists that projects like the NCPP will be used to achieve entirely different goals. The coal project, for example, encompassing a wide range of policy recommendations, is viewed by at least some environmental lobbyists as a sophisticated public relations tactic that will be used by industry to lobby for weaker environmental laws.

Moss, the former head of the Sierra Club who led the environmental slate at NCPP, calls this argument a red herring. "No one proposed that we try to supplant the legislative process," he says. "But it's a mistake to rely exclusively on the adversary process if we can agree, if we can stake out a common interest."

What everyone on all sides agrees is that the NCPP is something of a test case. Greg Thomas, a Sierra Club official who served on the transportation task force, admits, "There is always the danger that the output could be perverted and used for political purposes." But he and Moss see mostly good coming from their cooperative efforts. "It has to be appreciated that trench warfare on every issue that comes down the pike is very expensive for us," Thomas adds.

John McCormick of EPC went to some early NCPP meetings, saw "all the heavies" from coal and coal-related industries around, and left convinced that it was an industry attempt to co-opt environmentalists and give the industry more lobbying credibility.

At the bottom line, NCPP sources admit that most of the project's funding comes from industry. A long list of utilities, coal producers and coal-burning industries such as Dow Chemical, U.S. Steel and Union Carbide have contributed funds, along with the federal Department of Energy and the Ford and Rockefeller Foundations. Industry representatives include Gerald Decker, the energy manager at Dow Chemical who started the project, John Corcoran, former chairman of Consolidated Coal, and Jackson Browning of Union Carbide, who contribute their efforts on company time. Participating environmentalists are paid by the Project.

To avoid the appearance of conflict-of-interest, environmentalists are paid from foundation funds, a cosmetic touch when one considers that the whole project is predominantly industry funded. Offices are located on the neutral grounds of Georgetown University's Center for Strategic and International Studies.

Moss is naturally concerned that the project not look like an industry ploy. He points out that industry as well as the environmentalists made numerous concessions: they agreed that coal mining should be concentrated in Appalachia and the Midwest, and underground, rather than in the fragile stripmining fields of the Northern Plains; they agreed to fines for pollution control emissions from stationary sources; they agreed that mine permits should require present and subsequent control of acid water drainage; and they agreed to support the imposition of waterways user fees to pay the cost of maintaining inland waterway transportation routes.

J. James Roosen, environmental affairs director of the Detroit Edison Company, insists that the industry participants are taking flak for their concessions, too. In exchange for environmentalists agreeing to support simplified and streamlined planning and permitting procedures for the siting of new plants, industry members of the air pollution task force agreed that industry would help pay the expenses of environmentalists participating in the siting process.

This upsets some industrialists for whom, Roosen says, "financing your opposition is un-American." However, he added, industry could swallow the idea if it meant an end to the "guerilla warfare" with environmentalists that has slowed down siting procedures for years in the past. Whether such an agreement could stop rebellious citizen groups from tying up siting plans in the courts remains to be seen, however.

Larry Moss says every effort is being made to keep environmentalists' concessions wedded to industry's concessions. "It's a two-way street," he says.

But Richard Ayres thinks there is already evidence that while industry participants were making concessions in the NCPP meetings, their lobbyists were still pushing hard for the old hard-line positions on Capitol Hill and with the regulatory agencies. "[The NCPP] is not the right kind of forum for resolving these issues," says Ayres, "and it should not be portrayed as a meeting of all the people who matter." He prefers the legislative lobbying approach because "when you know it's going to be binding you work things out, count votes and make compromises that stick."

Dunlap of EPC also dismisses the notion that it saves the environmental cause valuable resources if they can work things out amicably in private. She says it stretches manpower between legislative lobbying and private mediation practices of questionable value. She also says too many people who have a valid interest in environmental problems get left out.

Moss counters a bit angrily that Dunlap avoided every effort to give her group a voice in the NCPP, and that when he belatedly heard her objections he made some changes in the report to at least partially mollify her.

In time Moss, Dunlap, and others who have taken sides over the New Cooperation will probably take a more conciliatory turn. As EPC's McCormick points out, "There aren't enough of us working for environmental or public interest organizations that we can start to attack each other."

But the debate over environmental mediation will rage on. Industry clearly likes the idea, foundations are interested, and various groups are springing up around the country, such as RESOLVE in California and the Office of Environmental Mediation at the University of Washington,* to run the show.

Few disagree that discussions between industries planning to build new plants and citizens in the area they plan to build in could save a lot of expensive and emotional confrontation later on. And on the federal level, now that industries are resigned to living with environmental regulation, they are in just as much danger as the environmentalists of being hurt by poor enforcement, which cuts both ways. Both stand to gain by working together for improvements in this area.

But there are problems. Though no one would accuse the environmentalists who joined the NCPP of being bought off by industrialists, some of their conclusions would, in the eyes of many, turn back the clock of environmental law if put into effect. NCPP environmentalists say the compromises they made were reasonable and point to the considerable concessions that industry was willing to make in exchange.

But trade-offs made by the NCPP participants are not cemented in law, and there is no assuring that an industry lobbyist will remember to mention financing for environmental lobbyists when he tells a congressman how the environmentalists agreed to allow tall stacks on old power plants. Only the good faith of industry participants and the vigilance of environmentalists preserves the linkage between concessions by either side, and some question whether industry lobbyists ever got the message at all.

But publicity surrounding the NCPP has spurred talk about trying the mediation route in fields like power plant siting, energy pricing policy and even nuclear power controversies.

Industry has been convinced to try in part because businesspeople, too, worry about the water they drink and the trails they walk. In larger part, though, industries are involved because they think the process may be cheaper and more productive than the old adversary way.

So environmentalists are watching the process carefully, wary of pitfalls. At this point, no one knows quite where cooperation crosses the line into collaboration.

---

* RESOLVE became part of The Conservation Foundation in 1981, and the Office of Environmental Mediation is now known as the Mediation Institute.

Let's Try Cooperation Instead of Confrontation

By Louis Fernandez

The chairman of the board of the Chemical Manufacturers Association challenges the chemical industry to demonstrate to the world that its products and operations are compatible with protecting human health and the environment.

The chemical industry today is faced with an issue that overshadows all others in terms of its future well-being. It is how we are going to demonstrate to the public, and the world at large, that our products and operations are compatible with protecting human health and the environment.

This is a particularly appropriate time to speak on this issue, because I sense a fundamental change taking place in the chemical industry's approach to its public health and pollution-control responsibilities. We have passed the period of making excuses and pointing fingers. We are now being moved by a new determination to play a leading role in solving the environmental problems in which we are involved. The former CMA Chairman, Bill Simeral of DuPont, captured some of this spirit when he said: "It's not enough to do what the law says—we must anticipate problems and become leaders in the effort to solve them."

Let's face it, though, more than just chemical industry leadership will be required if we as a nation are going to pick up the pace in meeting the environmental challenges that confront us. The quagmire of abandoned waste sites illustrates this best. This problem is too big—and the scientific and engineering demands it poses are too complex for any one sector of our society to tackle it successfully alone. We must all pitch in—the entire business community, federal and

---

Excerpted from speech delivered at the Semiannual Meeting of the Chemical Manufacturers Association, New York, November 7, 1983. Reprinted by permission. Dr. Louis Fernandez is chairman of the board of the Monsanto Company.

local governments, environmental groups, and all concerned citizens. Cooperation must become the new theme of this country's environmental efforts.

The alternatives of continued bickering, continued pulling and tugging at the regulatory agencies, and finally, continued litigation are simply more expensive than any of us can afford and more time-consuming than the public will tolerate.

Let me tell you what the chemical industry is doing for its part to bring about a more enlightened environmental era. I'd like to do so against the backdrop of a recent action that reflects a renewed commitment to solutions the Chemical Manufacturers Association Board's endorsement of a basic set of principles to guide our public-health and pollution-control conduct.

The essence of this statement is as follows:

- to produce only those chemicals that can be manufactured, used and disposed of safely;
- to continue complying with all laws and regulations;
- to cooperate with government officials in dealing with problems related to waste disposal practices;
- to conduct or sponsor studies to increase our understanding of the effects of our processes, products and wastes; and
- to foster continuing dialogue with citizen groups concerned about the effects of our activities.

Together they add up to a program of progressive environmental stewardship, and I doubt that its parallel can be found among many other major industries. What these principles say, in summary, is that we are serious about improving our environmental performance; and that we urge the American public to measure our deeds against our words.

Let us consider some of these deeds beginning with a new CMA survey that documents what we've been doing to responsibly manage our hazardous waste. This survey, by the Environmental Resources Management Company, covered the vast majority of wastes generated, treated and disposed of by the chemical industry during 1981 and '82. Five hundred and thirty-five plants from 70 chemical companies participated in the study.

The results reveal an industry on the move toward better waste management—and one whose current practices don't square with some misinformed opinions about them. For example, many people believe the chemical industry is responsible for practically all of the hazardous waste disposed of in this country. In fact, the survey shows that the chemical industry accounted for only one third of the hazardous wastes disposed of in 1981. Let me hasten to add that a third of all hazardous wastes disposed of still is too high a figure, and industry-wide efforts to reduce these wastes will push this percentage downward. Indeed, the survey shows that the plants responding reported a 42 percent reduction in hazardous waste disposed of on a dry weight basis between 1981 and 1982.

Another encouraging finding is that chemical firms on a dry weight basis landfilled 59 percent less hazardous waste in 1982 than 1981. In addition, the survey found that chemical firms recycled more than 50 percent of the hazardous solid wastes they created. This figure compares very favorably with a recent EPA estimate that American industry as a whole recycles only about 4 percent of its hazardous wastes.

To my mind, this survey tells the story of an industry that recognized its vital role in hazardous waste management and that is trying to carry it out with vigor and ingenuity. The CMA principles I mentioned earlier endorse full cooperation with government agencies in dealing with past disposal problems. We are striving to make good on this pledge. For example, 3M Company began as early as 1980 to develop plans for correcting a landfill which was contaminating groundwater in Oakdale, Minnesota. Negotiations between itself and the government led to its committing 6 million dollars to clean up this site. Elsewhere in Minnesota, FMC Corp. will spend a similar amount to correct problems at a location that formerly had the dubious distinction of being No. 1 on EPA's list of potentially hazardous sites.

My own firm, the Monsanto Company, has for some time been taking inventory of our former waste sites and assessing their environmental effects. We have budgeted the money and assigned the project managers to make a concerted cleanup effort at sites in need of it. We are going after them with the same intensity that we apply to new construction projects.

All of these examples represent a start toward a more aggressive cleanup effort. Still, no meaningful progress can be made against the dumpsite problem without the full cooperation of industry, government, and the environmental groups. And it is meaningful progress that the public is demanding.

EPA thus far has put 546 hazardous waste sites on its list for priority cleanup under the Superfund law. This list eventually may include between 1,000 and 1,500 sites. To date, EPA has done emergency surface work at roughly 160 threatening waste sites. It has completely cleaned up only 5 of them. At this pace, we will be mired in cleanup problems well into the next century. By then, the public will have lost all confidence in the ability of this country's institutions to get an essential job done. That's a situation we can ill afford.

EPA Administrator William Ruckleshaus deserves high marks for recognizing the critical nature of the problem and taking some steps to accelerate the pace of cleanup. He has delegated additional decision-making authority to EPA's regional offices, and he has eliminated the requirement that state contributions be available before work can begin.

Also needed is a greater flexibility on EPA's part to accept cleanup shares from individual companies that correspond to their waste shares at a site. At present EPA continues to apply the concept of "joint and several liability" to cleanup actions. This means that once it has identified responsible parties, the agency will not work out a settlement with any of these parties, unless some or all of them will guarantee practically the entire cleanup cost. EPA used to talk in terms of 100 percent settlements only. Recently, it has suggested that 80 percent of total costs might be an acceptable figure. Unfortunately, even this threshold is much too high to encourage voluntary participation at most sites. The solution to the problem, in my opinion, would be for the government to allow willing firms to pay for cleanup shares that match their waste shares. Then the government should use federal Superfund money for whatever additional funds are needed to clean up the dump promptly. Finally, the EPA should take legal action against those parties who would not pay their fair share.

This strategy seems so logical that I continue to hope for further progress in this direction. But you should know that we are not waiting for an answer before pursuing other routes. For the past few months, under the auspices of the highly respected Conservation Foundation, key environmental leaders, chemical industry representatives, and other interested citizens have been discussing how we can work more closely together on the dumpsite problem. We have been searching for a mechanism that would allow us to assist EPA in accelerating the cleanup work. We don't know yet what form this mechanism may take. It may be a project to demonstrate, at a few sites, how a combined initiative could hasten corrective action. Or it may be a more permanent structure, such as a new mediation group to facilitate negotiations between the government and waste-generators, or perhaps a new, non-profit corporation, operating under EPA guidance, to actually manage the cleanup of sites.

We have kept key members of Congress and EPA officials fully informed on the progress of our talks. They have encouraged us to continue our efforts, while not bringing to a halt any of their own.

How the workings of our cooperative group would be meshed with those of EPA and how it would be funded are among the many questions still in need of answers. Our discussions are continuing, and we expect to make recommendations to EPA early next year.

Our chemical industry principles drive us toward helping on another key issue—that of determining whether hazardous wastes from old sites are causing widespread harm to people. There are those who are convinced that this is indeed the case. But they speak from anecdotal and often questionable evidence, not from a cool, scientific appraisal of the situation. In fact, anyone who has attempted such an objective look would have to conclude that, at present, the country is simply without the information to judge whether a serious human health risk is posed by abandoned waste sites, and whether changes in the legal system are needed to address it.

At the same time, those who believe that the chemical industry has closed its mind to the prospect of new approaches on public compensation are mistaken. We endorse the position that companies whose waste handling practices have injured another person would provide prompt and just compensation to that person. We contend just as vigorously that the public compensation terrain first must be accurately mapped before any marching orders can be given.

CMA is in the forefront of those gathering the data to create a reliable map. We, along with the Environmental Defense Fund, took legal action to get the government to compile information on health effects from hazardous wastes. In addition, CMA is taking part in discussions with public interest groups, sponsored by Colorado's Keystone Center, to identify areas of agreement on public compensation.

Further, CMA has contracted with a consortium of 15 universities for a one million dollar study to investigate the possible connection between waste and illness. Scientists at these schools are reviewing existing data for answers and will recommend certain follow-up epidemiologic studies. The respect accorded this effort in the scientific community is evidenced by a recent World Health Organization decision to collaborate on the study. Results of the consortium's investigation should be available for public scrutiny by mid-1984. At this point, Congress will have at least the beginning of a body of scientific information against which to measure the need for a new compensation law.

A rush to judgment on this issue could be a costly policy blunder. The chemical industry is prepared to carry its share of whatever the burden may be. But we ask that this be determined on the basis of good science rather than emotional appeals.

Another of our principles of conduct is a commitment to produce only those chemicals that can be manufactured safely. Our concern there is to protect our industry's more than one million workers— and our neighbors in the communities where our plants are located. These workers and residents increasingly demand more detailed information on chemical identities and toxicological properties. They say they have a right to know. And we say, indeed they do. The scientific facts about any chemical always should be provided to people who need this information for their well-being. The chemical industry acknowledges the right of its workers, and the public, to essential information about our materials.

We also seek their understanding of our right to protect certain trade-secret information that is our lifeblood in the marketplace. Situations occasionally will arise in which we cannot publicly disclose specific chemical formulas without jeopardizing our business and, hence, the interests of our employees and stockholders. But the responsibility for justifying this trade secret security is upon our shoulders and must not be abused.

I said at the outset of these remarks that dealing effectively with issues of the scope and complexity of those facing our industry will require the wholehearted cooperation of all elements of our society. I see heartening signs that such cooperation is beginning to take root. For example, last spring, environmentalists and the business community collaborated on an excellent handbook to inform citizens about the need for new, state-of-the-art hazardous waste facilities. Earlier this year, our own association and two environmental groups presented to EPA a mutually agreeable plan for curbing PCB chemicals incidentally created during the manufacture of other compounds. Just a few weeks ago, pesticide makers agreed with church and environmental organizations on pesticide advertising procedures to encourage safe use in less developed countries.

Whether we can expand this teamwork will depend upon how dedicated we are. Each group will have to discard old, combative ways of thinking and acting. We must recognize the legitimacy of the other person's viewpoint. We may have to sacrifice the more extreme items on our agendas, and, in the process, we may lose some of our ideologically rigid constituents. For the chemical industry, cooperation may mean a greater willingness to accept a costly new standard—even if scientific support for it is less than unanimous. And for public interest groups, cooperation may mean acknowledging that dollars and cents cannot be fully ignored in matters of health and pollution control.

The writer-diplomat Carlos Fuentes recalled recently that on a trip to rural Mexico, he stopped to ask a campesino how far it was to a particular village.

"If you had left at daybreak," the peasant farm worker replied, "you would be there now."

By the same token, if all of us involved with the environment had begun cooperating five or ten years ago, we could have been there now. But we didn't—so we've got to make up for lost time.

The chemical industry is anxious to get the journey underway. We have adopted forward-looking principles of environmental conduct to guide us. We are translating these into specific initiatives to serve as mileposts measuring our progress. But we need many companions on this journey to help all of us complete it successfully.

We need the combined energies and skills of environmentalists, government and all concerned citizens. The destination we seek is the same: an era of greater environmental renewal and harmony. It is a goal within our reach, but one that will elude our grasp unless we join hands together in its pursuit.

Business Beyond Profit

By Bruce Smart

Speaking in support of developing a sustainable society, this business leader makes a strong appeal for an ongoing dialogue between the business community and environmentalists.

The presumptions on which this article is based are: first, a sustainable future society is desirable, and second, a role for private industry in such a society is desirable. Neither presumption is proven. In fact, if present trends in population, economic growth, habitat destruction, and political expediency are extrapolated, neither is likely to materialize.

No legacy that any of us here can leave our children will be much use if their world isn't worth living in. No amount of money, no pride in ancestral rank or honors, no lands or castles, no fine education, nothing.

So it is pretty obvious that we all have a huge stake and an immediate task in making a sustainable society happen.

For society to be sustainable, world population must come to equilibrium within the carrying capacity of man's habitat—the ability of the earth to feed, shelter, clothe, care for, educate, amuse, and dispose of the wastes of its inhabitants. And that population must be sufficiently content with its lot to avoid triggering the destructive behavior typical of species living in excessively crowded conditions.

In the last 200 years world population has been growing rapidly, particularly as medical science greatly reduced the incidence of death before old age, and technology expanded man's ability to convert natural resources into the necessities of life.

Presently, the world contains 4-1/2 billion people, increasing at a rate of 1.6 percent per year. Most of this increase is now occurring in the less developed countries of the world. By the year 2000 the total will reach 6.2 billion.

Excerpted from remarks delivered at the Woodlands Conference on Sustainable Societies, the Woodlands, Texas, November 7, 1982. Reprinted with permission. Bruce Smart is chairman and chief executive officer of Continental Group.

New birth control technology, coupled with cultural and religious changes and reasonable economic progress, suggests that the established tendency of developed societies to have fewer children, and zero population growth, can in time become a worldwide phenomenon. If so, the view that world population will stabilize at about 10-12 billion in the 21st century seems rational.

If population does not stabilize, the alternative of ever-increasing numbers, leading to eventual reduction by world catastrophe hardly fits our definition of "sustainable."

The future world economy must provide its citizens with some acceptable modicum of goods and services. I believe it must also offer them satisfying employment, and an opportunity to improve their lot and that of their children—in short, personal hope for a better life based on improving quality of living. If not, a society possible in a physical sense will be unstable socially and politically.

An economically secure society will place great demands on the world's resources. A future scenario that assumes today's standard of living—with no increase—in the developed countries, and raises the standard of developing countries to America's current poverty level, would—for a total population of 12 billion people—require a 3-1/2-fold increase in world GNP, and potentially a similar rise in the output of pollutants and consumption of resources.

Present levels of consumption and methods of agriculture already are depleting the world's supply of farmland and ground water.

It has been estimated that man's current activities, if unchecked, will cause extinction of 20 percent of all varieties of plants and animals by the year 2000. With this irreversible loss of natural diversity will go substances of unknown—and untold—value to future generations.

So, to support projected levels of population, we will require a much higher degree of environmental understanding as a basis for more ecologically benign technologies and practices. If not, gradual destruction of the environment—man's habitat—will render our future society unsustainable. Assuming that the society of the future can become demographically, economically, and environmentally stable, how is it to be governed? Obviously, the time-horizons of its leaders—and its voters—must be lengthened.

Taking the United States social security system as an example, the political difficulty in confronting today's voters with tomorrow's problems is obvious, even when dealing with the social problems of a single affluent nation. Government's ability to moderate long-term environmental-economic tradeoffs is equally unproven.

The needs of unborn generations must rank equally with those now on earth. Yet the unborn do not vote, invest, or demonstrate. Someone must speak for them. If we do not, no one will. The next election and the next income statement cannot outrank the next generation.

In short, to reach a sustainable society major changes in social, economic, and political behavior must take place. There is ample evidence that awareness of the need for change is increasing. Twenty years ago Rachel Carson wrote *Silent Spring*. Twelve years ago "Earth Day" first called wide public attention to the problems of pollution and environmental degradation.

In the intervening years we have developed some answers—especially to the problems first highlighted—pollution of surface water and ambient air. But we have also come to realize that the ramifications of these and other problems—ground water, acid rain, toxic waste disposal—are more complex than we first imagined.

Yes, we can develop answers—but it will require a concentration of resources, including the input of many thinking people, to get on with the scientific inquiry and economic analysis necessary to reach consensus solutions.

Recently, my company, Continental Group, sponsored a study of the views of environmentalists, businessmen, and the public. It is quite encouraging. Three-quarters of the United States public now give high priority to protecting the environment, about the same number as give high ranking to the goal of maintaining a strong economy.

That there is potential conflict between these goals is recognized by the half who would accept slower growth in order to protect the environment, and the two-thirds who believe we should learn to accept a more basic standard of living.

Public environmental awareness has reached this level in 22 years, and is alive and well despite the current recession. In short, Americans and their environmental and business leaders are willing to consider the tradeoffs that are preconditions of the sustainable society.

The shape, benefits, and costs of this new society will be chosen by its citizens. To define these choices and measure their costs they must rely on their institutions—academia, environmental groups, the media, government, and industry, among others.

Since all segments must aid in developing the conditions for a sustainable society, there must be constructive dialogue between them, not uncommunicative hostility. This dialogue must develop facts, disseminate them, analyze them, draw scenarios, reach conclusions, plan and implement action.

This consensus-seeking process is home territory for the professional business executive. Normally, the management process is thought of as resolving the forces and competing claims of capital, technology, labor, and raw material supply to manufacture a market-preferred product at an affordable price. Now responsible businessmen are factoring in additional claims and costs—the claims of the future and the external social and environmental costs of their activities.

In 1972 the American Paper Institute participated in the drafting and supported passage of the Clean Water Act, even though that necessary legislation imposed a $2 billion investment cost on its members. The chemical industry has supported the creation of the "Superfund," by which today's companies are taxed to clean up wastes left—knowingly or unknowingly—by their predecessors.

My company is the leading producer of aluminum beverage cans, an energy-intensive product under frequent environmental attack as an article of litter and solid waste. In the last 10 years new manufacturing processes and new alloys have led to a reduction of 19 percent in the quantity of aluminum in each can.

Spurred by environmental pressures, we have also joined in setting up systems to recover used containers, so that now half of all aluminum cans are recycled. Using scrap in place of virgin ore saves 95 percent of the energy content of the can sheet.

As a result, your next six-pack will require about 60 percent less energy and virgin aluminum than 1972's. As these resources become scarcer and more costly, this market-driven system will automatically increase the percent of cans recovered.

Finally, business is recognizing and supporting the need for objective environmental data to replace the adversary research used by it and its opponents to defend preconceived parochial positions. Typical of research organizations strongly supported by business is The Conservation Foundation, which seeks to provide data and help to resolve conflicts polarized by concerns on the one hand for environmental protection and on the other hand for economic growth.

Private industry is the largest of the nation's institutions, commands the most resources, moves the most quickly and flexibly, is the least bound by traditional structure or ideology. It is the nation's engine of wealth creation, and the developer of most new technology. It has learned the rule of the marketplace—*change* or *die.*

The times call for massive change, and business knows how to manage change. One needed change is to improve the preservation and distribution of the world's food supply. Interestingly, food production has generally outpaced population growth in recent years, yet people are still starving. The reason: Spoilage and poor distribution. In the developing world, for example, a large percentage of food crops rot in the field, are consumed by vermin, or spoil on the way to market. One part of the answer—already commonplace in developed countries—is packaging, whose basic function is to preserve, protect, and facilitate distribution of perishable foods.

Lester Brown said in his recent book *Building a Sustainable Society* that "corporations can bring their impressive R&D capacity to bear on the transition" to a greater conservation orientation. In my opinion, they not only can but must, if they are to remain viable in the years ahead.

Thus, private industry and its executives can be valuable allies in the steps that must be taken to reach our goals. Given their numbers, skills, and influence, I believe it is unlikely that we can reach a sustainable society in the U.S. without their active participation and support.

Yet because private industry has been so associated with material progress, and because rapid material growth is seen by many to be in conflict with the sustainable society concept, business is frequently looked on publicly more as part of the problem than as part of the solution.

In the past, steel and paper mills, chemical plants, and automobiles have been convenient examples for making the valid point that uncontrolled industrial expansion threatens the environment. Often this finger pointing has been personalized by centering criticism not only on processes and products, but on individuals as well. No doubt some of this criticism was deserved by unresponsive executives whose view did not extend beyond the factory sewer outfall or the bottom line.

But some accusations have been grossly unfair. For example, Exxon's profits were called "obscene" when they reached a record

17 percent on capital in 1974. Their media critics then included the *Washington Post* and CBS, whose records two or three years later were 25 percent and 20 percent respectively. Over the last decade, Exxon and Mobil averaged 13.5 percent, the two media giants 16.5 percent.

Yet the impression that "big oil" is "ripping off" the public has been fixed by the media in the public's mind, stubbornly resistant to correction by anything the industry can say in its own behalf. Having been on the defensive so long, it is not surprising that some businessmen are paranoid about environmentalists, academics, and the press. Neither this paranoia nor the criticism that caused it serve any worthwhile current purpose.

It is time to lower our voices, to choke back the accusatory "bon mot" and the political cheap shot, in short to resist the urge to have a "last go at the bastards." Each of us is a responsible leader of society, chosen by it to be a steward of its future. We bring no greater personal merit or ethical position than the next person's to this debate, nor should we expect to gain wealth or power from it. Rather, the world's coming citizens count on us to work together, to see each other's viewpoints, to respect each other's objectives. We are *their* surrogates. It is *their* future.

Like other leadership groups, most businessmen recognize that a stable future is in their personal and professional best interest. Many recognize that business as usual must give way to environmental and social realities, and are already working to reach consensus on how to accommodate conflicting goals. Some are waiting for you and me to enlist them and put them to work. They often need encouragement more than conversion or coercion.

You who are not in business can be particularly helpful in this recruitment process if by your words and actions you show your understanding of the contribution my profession can make to the world's future. You do this best when you recognize that the principal role of business is the bringing together of resources for the purpose of creating wealth.

The sustainable society requires that this job be done—and done efficiently. Encourage—if necessary insist on—concern for the externalities of the process, but do not otherwise denigrate or impair this socially necessary and desirable function. Encourage businessmen to join in your deliberations. If you listen, so will they. Both will learn from it. Where appropriate, ask them to sit on your governing boards, and accept when they reciprocate. Seek out business as a source of ideas, not just money.

Protect the freedom of the marketplace, so that it can perform its function of allocating resources to the point of greatest need. When the market cannot cope with the externalities of industrial production, join with businessmen and government in seeking environmentally, socially, and economically sound regulation.

Support the concept of multinational corporations and free trade. International commerce is the best vehicle we have to spread technology, wealth, and environmental awareness to less developed countries. But insist that multinationals act in partnership with and with respect for host countries.

All of us must accept that there are few absolutes, and no corner on knowledge or wisdom. Our goals have more commonality than conflict. Businessmen do not hope to pillage the earth to satisfy their own greed, any more than environmentalists wish to freeze to death while starving in the dark. We must lower the critical voices. No one likes to be shouted at, or finds it easy to cooperate with someone he feels is treating him unfairly. Above all, we need to talk to each other.

Winning Through Mediation

By Jay D. Hair

The executive vice president of the National Wildlife Federation calls mediation a growth industry, and asserts that the move toward mediated settlements of environmental disputes is a move in the right direction.

Mark Twain once observed that "The art of prophesy is very difficult—especially with respect to the future." Nevertheless, I will give it a try. My prediction is that in ten years more environmental disputes will be mediated than litigated. The forces which are pushing environmental issues out of the courtroom and into negotiated settlements are building fast and show no signs of abating. In short, mediation is a growth industry.

Before I explain my prediction, I should clarify what I mean by "mediation." In its formal sense mediation means the use of a neutral party to develop non-binding options for settlement of disputes between contending parties. The use of a neutral mediator differentiates mediation from negotiation, which involves head-to-head bargaining between opposing parties, and its non-binding character differentiates it from formal arbitration, which usually does bind the parties. However, for simplicity, I use the term here to cover all structured mechanisms for dispute resolution that fall between the broad boundaries of, on the totally structured side, formal litigation and, on the totally unstructured side, cocktail parties and other such informal negotiating activities. The key word is "structure" and includes structured dialogue, negotiation, mediation, and even arbitration.

This move towards mediated settlements is a move in the right direction. In the past, mediation has been criticized as "what you do when you think you are going to lose," the implication being

---

Excerpted from a speech delivered at the National Conference on Environmental Dispute Resolution, January 25, 1983, sponsored by The Conservation Foundation. Reprinted by permission of the National Wildlife Federation. Jay D. Hair is executive vice president of the National Wildlife Federation.

that you will still lose, but you can cut your losses. Ten years ago—when the focus of environmental law was on the immediate need to block a highway through a park or keep an oil refinery out of a productive estuary—this was often true. When the choice is either "up" or "down," there is not much room to maneuver. But choices are no longer so restricted. As John Naisbett points out in his book, *Megatrends*, we are moving from a single-option to a multiple-option society. The choice is no longer between simply a Ford or a Chevy; there are now 752 different models of trucks and cars sold in the United States. As options proliferate, so does the ability to create solutions where both sides win. As we look to the future, it is clear that mediation is no longer a way to simply cut our losses, but to win.

The creation of multiple options allows both sides to "win" because it allows solutions to be tailored to the individual interests of the competing parties. An excellent example of this point is contained in Roger Fisher's book, *Getting to Yes*, where he describes two sisters quarreling over an orange. They settle the dispute by splitting the orange in two, whereupon the first sister eats the fruit and throws away the peel, while the second sister uses her peel in baking a cake and throws away the fruit.

This solution obviously involves waste due to the sisters' mutual failure to concentrate on underlying interests, not positions. But, in a multiple-option society, interests differ. The fundamental interest of the National Wildlife Federation is the maintenance of a high level of environmental quality so that we pass on to our children a world as biologically diverse and pollution-free as we found it. The fundamental interest of the private sector is to maintain open and free markets so we pass on to our children an economic system that produces and distributes goods and services at maximum efficiency. The legitimacy of these two interests is no longer subject to debate. The recent Harris Poll showing that the American people, by a margin of 15 to 1, believe the economy can be improved without sacrificing environmental protections simply shuts the door on those who doggedly attempt to portray environmental and economic interests as in fundamental conflict. As environmental dispute resolution moves away from "the environmental position" and "the business position" to concentrate on underlying interests, the demand for mediators to carve solutions where no piece of the orange is wasted and all needs are satisfied will increase.

This is not to say that environmental litigation will cease to be an important weapon in the arsenal of national environmental organizations. To the contrary, trying to mediate without the ability to litigate is like trying to clap with one hand: it produces no meaningful result. The relationship between mediation and litigation is symbiotic. Our ability at the National Wildlife Federation to take our concerns to court provides the leverage we need to convince business and government to sit down at the bargaining table. But it is mediation that will provide the affirmative solutions that courts alone cannot decree.

The forces that compel a move towards mediation and away from litigation appear obvious:

First, the courts simply can't handle the load. When Professor Joseph Sax suggested, in 1970, in his book *Defending the Environment*, that environmental disputes be settled in court, there was no Clean Air Act, no Clean Water Act, nor any of the other twenty-one environmental statutes spawned in the 1970s alone. In 1973, 47,000 cases were filed in Federal District Courts. In 1982 that figure rose to over 206,000. As more environmental "rights" are recognized, the potential for conflict increases. Courts simply do not have the time to be the exclusive arbiter of these rights. There are already signs that the courts are moving to restrict access to environmental plaintiffs through tougher "standing" requirements and greater deference to agency decision. This trend will probably continue.

Second, as recent books such as *Megatrends* and Alvin Toffler's *The Third Wave* document, the accelerating rate of technological innovation requires faster decisions. We at the National Wildlife Federation have for several years used computers to help us run our business activities more efficiently. But we are just beginning to understand how the rapid computerization of our entire society affects our environmental advocacy programs and shifts political power—through knowledge—to new political coalitions. Thirty years ago, Albert Einstein warned that "The world we have made as a result of the level of thinking we have done thus far creates problems that we cannot solve at the same level as the level we created them." This is most obviously true of the specific problem to which Einstein referred—the ability to wage nuclear war, the ultimate environmental disaster. But it applies equally to technologies with less drastic environmental implications such as disposal of the highly toxic byproducts generated by the production of silicon chips. Keeping pace with the accelerating rate of technological change is only possible through cooperation, not confrontation.

Third, environmental litigation is essentially injunctive in nature. Courts can say "no," but not "yes." Courts can legitimize rights, police procedures, and clarify obligations, but they cannot manage an agency or a business. Yet environmentalists, as proxies for the future, have a clear responsibility to "say yes," to come up with the management solutions needed to implement environmentally acceptable alternatives. Mancur Olson, in his new book, *The Rise and Decline of Nations*, pins the blame for the gradual economic dissipation of all great historical powers on the proliferation of special interest groups capable of paralyzing any movement away from the *status quo*. Even Lester Thurow, an MIT economist and hardly the pawn of any special interest group, charges any organization purporting to represent the public interest with the responsibility for finding ways to encourage tomorrow's economic winners and discard today's economic losers. Mediation can do this. Litigation cannot.

For example, in 1980, eighteen years after a group of lawyers filed suit challenging the licensing of a pumped-storage hydroelectric plant near Storm Highlands on the Hudson River, it was a mediator in the form of Russell Train who finally achieved a settlement. The agreement set new standards for the operation of hydroelectric facilities all along the Hudson River Valley, yet avoided the high cost of constructing closed-cycle cooling towers on all existing plants. The millions of dollars saved through this effort can now be used to ensure that the tomorrows we pass on to our children are *productive* as well as *nonpolluted*.

Fourth, and finally, the sad fact of the matter is that environmental organizations have insufficient legal resources to fight massive noncompliance with environmental statutes. Given the wholesale disregard for both the substance and spirit of our environmental laws, we must focus on those cases that have the largest programmatic impact. The Federation is presently a party to, or has chief litigation responsibility for, suits challenging (1) former Secretary Watt's National Coal Leasing Program, (2) the five-year outer continental shelf (OCS) leasing program, (3) the President's attempt to sell off federal lands to reduce the deficit, (4) the Department of the Army's attempt to issue nationwide dredge-and-fill permits affecting 70 percent of all the wetlands in the United States, (5) the attempt to gut the existing strip mining regulatory program, and (6) the attempt to open up 800,000 acres of wilderness study areas to oil and gas development. This doesn't even touch upon what is happening at EPA, nor does it begin to address the problem of agency non-compliance through budget cuts, staff reorganizations, and other measures that render agency environmental enforcement programs ineffective. If environmental organizations don't find new ways to broker the local and regional environmental disputes the national groups can no longer address, too many important issues will simply slip through the cracks.

These are some of the factors that make non-litigation options increasingly attractive mechanisms for environmental dispute resolution. At the National Wildlife Federation we are exploring several of these options. While we have not resorted to mediation in the formal sense, we are placing an increasing emphasis on solving problems before we get to the courthouse.

For example, we recently got into a scrap with the Bureau of Land Management when BLM issued permits for two major gas processing plants in the Wyoming overthrust belt without the benefit of an environmental impact statement. Fearful that these facilities would destroy important habitat for thousands of elk, mule deer, antelope, eagles, and other native wildlife, NWF, and its Wyoming affiliate, considered a lawsuit. However, we soon realized that all a lawsuit would get us was an EIS that would, at best, more fully analyze the threat to wildlife but would not prescribe any solution. We therefore used our litigation leverage to negotiate a solution where industry funded an $800,000 study of development impacts on wildlife, complete with citizen training workshops explaining what citizens could do to protect wildlife habitat during development. This effort, which will educate industry as well as citizens on wildlife values, should result in more habitat saved than would have occurred if we had simply made BLM jump through the right procedural loops.

Another example of on-going mediation resulted from an NWF shareholder petition filed against Weyerhauser Corporation regarding fish and wildlife management on Weyerhauser's extensive land holdings in Oklahoma and Arkansas. Rather than pursue the petition, NWF and Weyerhauser agreed to the creation of a "blue-ribbon" panel of experts—including wildlife scientists, silvaculturists, economists, and hydrologists—to investigate Weyerhauser's management practices and suggest solutions. The panel, after a year of investigation, recently filed its final report and steps are now being taken toward implementation of its recommendations.

But just as mediation has its benefits, it also has its limitations. From experience, here are what we have found are necessary ingredients to any strategy for winning through mediation.

First, there must be a problem of *timing* or *uncertainty*. These are the problems of "when" and "if." The private interest—let's say a developer—must have a real need to know if a development plan will be approved and, if so, when it can be implemented. It is our ability to bring certainty to the process within a specific time frame that gives us the leverage to negotiate a solution where both sides win. If there is no uncertainty, or if timing is not a problem, there is no motivation to mediate. This is why highway projects—especially interstate highway projects—are impossible to mediate. Since the statutory structure under which the Interstate Highway Program operates is predicated on 100-percent completion of the system, there is no motivation for highway interests to bargain. They can simply wait us out. In such a situation, mediation can only help citizens cut their losses. They cannot win.

Second, the environmental interests must be able to deliver on their agreements. This is especially difficult when an attempt is made to "mediate" public policy issues where no one group or coalition holds the proxy of the entire environmental community. A good example, I think, is the National Coal Policy Project. As I understand the result, the participants were able to agree among themselves but then were unable to obtain the agreement of their respective organizations for the consensus statements. The same problem occurred with the National Clean Air Commission, where the ink was not yet dry before all participants began to attack its conclusions. The fact of the matter is that *no one* speaks for *everyone* when value-judgments must be made on policy issues. Mediation, to be effective, must focus primarily on local resource disputes that can be brokered; not values, which cannot.

Third, the timing of mediation is very important. We have found that mediation is effective only in the pre-litigation stage. Once a suit has been filed, lines get drawn very fast. Since each side knows that any quarter given will be hailed as a "victory" by the other side, there is little room to maneuver without creating the appearance of a "win-lose" settlement. If mediation is to achieve "wins" for both sides—and that is its essential purpose—it must be applied before the die of litigation is cast.

Fourth, we have found that mediation, if it is initiated very early in the conflict resolution process, has the ability to achieve, not a "bargain" or a "deal," but true consensus. By looking at problems before they apply to a specific fact situation, opposing interests often find that they agree in philosophy more than they disagree. Americans, by their nature and history, have a deep—and I think healthy—suspicion of government. Yet, if government intervention is needed to save our fast-dwindling national inventory of wetlands—and it is—then the National Wildlife Federation is committed to such intervention. But we invite alternatives. Through the NWF Corporation Council, we are seeking to identify market-based alternatives for wetland protection. Of course, at some level of abstraction, mediation ceases to be dispute resolution at all, but simply dialogue. Yet this is where real progress can be made.

Finally, we have found that mediation with government agencies, under any circumstances, is extremely difficult. We must, therefore, carefully avoid overpromising on results when we engage in such efforts. This is not the fault of the government participants but of the nature of the effort. Government officials are charged with making decisions on behalf of the public and, as noted above, when any group purports to speak on behalf of the public without subjecting the result to public review and comment, trouble results. It is for this reason that NWF looks with great skepticism on OMB's draft proposal for negotiated rulemaking, where all the important decisions are made before the rulemaking goes public. Also, government officials often cannot deliver on their agreements any more than environmental groups can deliver on policy issues. Other agencies or Congress must ratify the agreement, which makes meaningful results problematical. For these reasons, we at the Federation view mediation with government officials with a healthy degree of skepticism.

These are some of the limitations we see on the use of non-litigative techniques in environmental dispute resolution. They are significant, but not prohibitive. They are obstacles to be overcome, not reasons for failing to try at all. I am confident that there are no experts in this new and exciting area of environmental mediation. We are all "groping in the dark." Nevertheless, we create our future each day as we struggle to find new ways to solve environmental disputes— ways that allow us to use the whole orange, the peel as well as the fruit. To the extent we succeed, we can rightfully defend the position to which we have laid claim as spokespersons for the future.

Dr. Kent Gilbreath has been a professor for the past eleven years in the Department of Economics and Finance at Baylor University where he specializes in Energy Economics. He is now serving as Associate Dean of the Hankamer School of Business at Baylor. He was selected "Most Outstanding Professor" at Baylor in 1982.

Dr. Gilbreath is currently serving in his third term as a member of the Board of Directors of the Federal Reserve Bank of Dallas. In this position he is involved in the supervision of financial institutions in the Southwest and in the formulation of monetary policy through the establishment of the Federal Reserve System's discount rate.

The University of Oklahoma has published a book by Dr. Gilbreath dealing with small business development. He has also published several articles dealing with such topics as world commodity markets, international finance, population projections for Texas, and tax reform in Texas.

Dr. Gilbreath attended Baylor University where he earned his B.A. degree in Economics *magna cum laude*. One year later he received his M.A. degree from Baylor, and then went on to earn his Ph.D. in Economics at the University of Florida.

46,342

DATE			
OCT 1 0 1990			
DEC 1 4 1992			
OCT 0 4 1999			
APR 2 4 2000			
APR 1 4 2001			